A HISTORY OF
MOTOR RACING

A HISTORY OF MOTOR RACING

Giovanni Lurani
Edited by David Hodges

HAMLYN

Published in Italy by l'Editrice dell'Automobile as
'Storia delle Macchine da Corsa'.
English-language edition © Arnoldo Mondadori Editore,
1972. Published in 1972 by
The Hamlyn Publishing Group Ltd.
London · New York · Sydney · Toronto
Hamlyn House, Feltham, Middlesex, England.

ISBN 600 34301 4

Printed in Italy by Arnoldo Mondadori Editore, Verona.

Contents

Introduction

Motor sport was inevitable as soon as a few horseless carriages were gathered together in one place, for man has always raced his principal means of transport – horses, horsedrawn vehicles, ships and boats, even trains – for personal satisfaction, for glory or for reward. The first organized motoring competition took place in France in 1894, almost before the horseless carriage was known in many prominent countries, and the first race as such, from Paris to Bordeaux and back, was run in the following year. From this point the complex sport which we know today has steadily evolved, although it only began to take its present shape after the 1903 Paris–Madrid race, the last of the primitive city-to-city events.

Races soon became distinguishable from trials of reliability, and racing classes began to emerge, the first being specified for the 1896 Paris–Marseilles–Paris race. These early classes were often within races, the first really notable distinct class race being the Coupe de l'Auto for voiturettes. During the late Edwardian years recognizable forerunners of sports car events took place, as trials, and in the 1920s the first major divisions came in road racing, when distinct sports car races were established, and the then much less significant touring car class, as such, came into being.

Since 1906, however, the premier class in road racing has been the Grand Prix class, and it is with Grand Prix racing above all that this book is concerned. But while it is logical to largely ignore sports car and saloon car racing – quite apart from the many other variations, from karts to stadium stock cars – it would be less than realistic to ignore other categories closely linked with the Grands Prix. Thus for want of better terms, this is the story of formula or 'open wheel car' racing, concentrating on the cars and races.

France was the pre-eminent nation in the early decades of the automobile industry, and of motor racing. Quite naturally, therefore, the sport was regulated in its early years by the Automobile Club de France, and international controlling bodies have had their headquarters in Paris. The first of these, the Association Internationale des Automobile Clubs Reconnus, formed its first distinct sporting sub committee in 1922; since 1947, when the AIACR was reconstituted as the Federation Internationale de l'Automobile (FIA), motor sport has been governed by Commission Sportive Internationale (CSI). This FIA body is responsible for all aspects of motor sport, and lays down its rules and regulations.

Since 1947 these rules as applied to the principal single-seater classes, with the exception of those of American track racing, have been known as 'formulae'. Thus, save for one exceptional period, the national Grands Prix which make up the World Championship series, have always been run to Formula 1, while the international subsidiary classes have usually been Formula 2 and Formula 3 (the exceptional Grand Prix period came when through coincidence there was every sign of one-make domination early in the 1950s).

The principal requirements of successive formulae are outlined in the appropriate chapters. For 35 years the Grand Prix regulations were not consistently sensible, or acceptable to constructors or race organizers – at times the AIACR seemed as bereft of a meaningful policy towards the Grands Prix as the CSI has sometimes been towards sports car racing in more recent years. The Grand Prix formulae, on the other hand, have invariably been successful, albeit outraged factions greeted the announcement of one with derision (in fact, there was proof of the soundness of even this in the racing it provided).

The basis for Grand Prix, and Formula 2 and 3 regulations, since the war has been engine capacity; this had been spasmodically used in earlier regulations,

Dieppe, 1907

usually to better effect than rules framed primarily around fuel consumption, weights or distances (the last two quantities have been incorporated in engine-size regulations, but only as secondary requirements aimed, for example, at prohibiting excessively flimsy cars).

In the subsidiary classes the limitations on engine size have been used principally as a means to restrict performances to levels considered appropriate. The voiturette classes were succeeded by formulae after the second world war, and at times the performance of Formula 2 cars has not lagged very far behind that achieved by Grand Prix machinery. As the performances of voiturettes were usually markedly inferior to cars in the premier class (although, as in

other aspects, there are exceptions to this generalization, most notably perhaps in the 1912 Coupe de *l'Auto* cars and the Alfa Romeo 158 Alfettas) this might seem surprising; in fact, it reflects the very rapid increase in the overall level of performances in motor racing.

After two earlier attempts to establish championships based on seasons' Grand Prix results had foundered, little noticed, the FIA inaugurated in 1950 the championships which have continued in unbroken use, for Grand Prix drivers and constructors. The drivers' championship, at least, has matched the general sporting pattern of the post-war era, when public and popular press attention has increasingly focused on personalities or 'aces'. To the regret of

some enthusiasts, this inevitably meant that the importance of the team as such declined, a process which was accelerated as soon as 'points sharing' between drivers who co-drove a car was discarded, and then as individual and team sponsorship grew rapidly in importance in the second half of the 1960s. With a few notable exceptions, Ferrari, BRM, and Matra, teams in the traditional sense have disappeared from the Grand Prix scene, and even those three names lack the ring of glory which attached to firms which once contested the races – Alfa Romeo, Mercedes, Fiat (then, however, the mirror of reminiscence may be distorting?). In the corresponding FIA sports car championship, the team has remained all-important, although here, too, some teams came to be identified

as much by their sponsors' names as by their constructors'.

Commercial sponsorship in formula racing really became obvious only in 1968, although a few discreet suppliers' decals had been used on cars earlier, when advertisements to cover a restricted area were permitted. Colin Chapman drove his Team Lotus through an enormous loophole in these restrictions in his agreement with Players tobacco company – Team Lotus became Gold Leaf Team Lotus and its cars, at that time in all three international formulae, were simply painted in the colours of Players' Gold Leaf brands. This of course signalled the end of national racing colours, which had been laid down in motor racing's first decade (in the 1960s regulations still required that cars be painted in the national colours of their entrants, but what race official would have ruled leading teams out of contention in a major race simply because this was infringed?). However, it did not lead to the rash of 'Grand Prix Specials' bearing sponsors' names, as in American track racing, which some purists feared. Indeed, two more seasons passed before other Grand Prix teams, notably BRM, adopted the house liveries of their sponsors.

In parallel with this fundamental change in the outward face of racing, drivers came to realize their own value as professionals and aspired to rewards matching those of top-flight performers in any other sport. This meant additional demands on teams – to the point where more than one manager admitted that mechanical development was not progressing as fast as it might because it had lower priority than securing the services of drivers – on the traditional suppliers, of whom retainers were expected, and on race organizers, who were faced with escalating starting money costs. During the 1960s the traditional image of the racing driver changed, too, probably more than in any other decade. Change of course has been continuous, in appearances, techniques and attitudes, but never have all Grand Prix drivers, and most in lesser formulae, been as thoroughly professional as they have become during the last decade. The drivers of the early years of racing indisputably were heroes – proud men who sat high on primitive machines, and whose exploits have become legendary. Some of them, notably Felice Nazzaro and Louis Wagner, raced on in the new age of the 1920s, when the roads were sometimes surprisingly little improved, but the cars were vastly different. The German machines of the 1930s paved the way for new techniques, and in keeping with the times the atmosphere changed – this was the period when front-line drivers appeared men apart, as they walked in immaculate overalls to their generously attended machines.

Monaco, 1933

This dubious quality was virtually lost after a second world war, when gradually a rather astonishing thing happened. Since racing began, the majority of leading drivers had been Latins, usually French or Italian; a few Germans reached the top, surprisingly few when the significant slices of racing history dominated by German constructors are recalled, and so did a very few British and American drivers. But from the end of the 1940s, English-speaking drivers appeared in increasing, and eventually dominant, numbers. This in fact fits into the overall pattern of racing history, yet it is still surprising to find that a time came in the 1960s when the mother tongue of all the front-rank Grand Prix drivers was English, almost as surprising as it is to find that for a period only one Grand Prix team was based outside England. This trend has only quite recently been reversed.

This period also saw the last of the playboy drivers in the Grands Prix, at least among the predictable and actual race leaders. It did not, however, see the last of the great drivers, as some prophets of doom implied it would as they predicted that all drivers would be reduced to a low common level by the 1·5 litre Grand Prix cars. In fact, driver mediocrity did not result any more than mechanical mediocrity, and for example the brilliance of Jim Clark and the honest craftmanship of Graham Hill and John Surtees came through. Then, of course, came a return to power under the 3-litre formula, and with it a splendid season for the first of a wave of driver-constructors, Jack Brabham.

The new status of racing drivers led to changes, as they voiced opinions, and pressed for action, on racing matters outside their cars. In itself, this was perhaps not new, but whereas in the past drivers' views had perhaps been made known disjointedly or spasmodically, and therefore usually to little effect, their approaches became increasingly unified, rather to the alarm of some of the old guard, who smelled trade unionism on every starting grid. Thus the short-lived Union des Pilotes Professionels Internationaux was somewhat unfortunately named; its successor, the Grand Prix Drivers' Association, which was formed in 1961 soon became a very real force in the world of racing.

Some changes would have come, inevitably, and some were very much in the traditional province of drivers in any case, the development of fire-resistant

clothing and the wide adoption of driver's safety harness, for example. Both of these developments were entirely logical, for modern drivers sit in glove-tight cockpits between and on fuel tanks, and the monocoque hulls of their cars are immensely resistant to distortion in accidents, so that in a crash a driver is much less likely to be injured if he is restrained within the hull rather than thrown out. Fire, of course, remained a great inherent hazard; despite increasing efforts to combat it, several drivers died in burning cars during the years of the 3-litre formula.

The biggest changes, however, were outward and very visible, on the circuits over which today's short races are run. As far as new circuits were concerned, this led to an apparently positive swing toward purely artificial road-racing autodromes, designed to be safe to the point of being clinical (a prime example being the Paul Ricard circuit in France). In parallel, and to the dismay of many enthusiasts, some of the great traditional road circuits fell into disfavour. However, this trend did not go as far as some feared it would, as for example the Nürburgring was transformed in 1971, and became acceptable to the GPDA.

On most circuits, miles of Armco barrier were erected to arrest errant cars, although there was no unanimity on the value of this safeguard, for Armco can be deadly to racing motorcyclists and the inflexibility of its supporting uprights may be held to have caused one or two potentially serious racing car accidents to become fatal accidents. On balance it has proved effective, as has the widespread removal of trees, walls, solid marshals' posts and so on, which for too many years were accepted as simply being part of the scenery.

The counter argument that such 'natural' hazards are part of the essence of real road racing hardly holds good, at least once other circuit 'improvements' are made in the interests of speed or spectacle, and the enormous increase in car performance is considered. (On the other hand, inherent hazards are accepted on an established hemmed-in and restricted circuit such as Monaco, where in 40 years there was only one fatal accident involving a Grand Prix car, and drivers race within the limitations imposed by the course). Fortunately, perhaps, it has been shown that the characteristics of true road circuits can be reproduced

Monaco, 1955

in artificial circuits, the Osterreichring and the extended Watkins Glen being notable examples.

The races which make up the World Championship series, and those for secondary classes, have always been contested on very varied courses, and although some classic circuits such as Rheims seem to have fallen into disuse, others have been radically modified, and some races have been run on new near-sterile autodrome circuits, the element of variety which over the series is essential to the spirit of single-seater road racing remains.

For many, spectators or participants, sports are more rewarding when there is an element of danger, but to others racing has always been open to criticism on this score. Queen Victoria once enquired of her ministers whether it might not be possible to ban the sport of Alpine mountaineering, and she has been echoed by critics of motor sport, especially in the recriminatory spasms which have followed some accidents. A universal ban of the sporting use of the

automobile would be no more feasible than a ban on the sporting use of mountains (although the Swiss banned all forms of motor racing on their soil in 1955, Swiss nationals still race), for apart from dubious tenets regarding the use of private land, it could simply lead to more competitive motoring on public roads.

Motor racing is dangerous – of course it is – but perspective is easily lost when there is a fatal racing accident, for inevitably this is well-publicized in the Press. From year to year however, more lives are lost in climbing accidents in the Alps than on all the circuits of the world. Danger can never be ruled out of motor sport, when drivers can walk away from high-speed accidents yet be seriously injured in apparently trivial incidents, but continuing efforts ensure that in fact it is being made much safer than to outward appearances it ever could be.

Invariably, many discussions on the value of racing have turned to its practical usefulness to the technical

Brands Hatch, 1971

evolution of cars. This is a complex theme, and a true evaluation is impossible. There is no question but that racing has been an invaluable spur, and a forcing ground, in the past, and it would be unwise to assume that technical developments of wide value will not appear in the future, in answer to the pressing requirement of gaining a fine edge in the fierce world of competition motoring. So although the real justification for racing nowadays is as a sport, and a spectacular one, its other values should not be blindly dismissed, as they once were by a famous critic in the French journal *L'Année Automobile*:

'It is the general opinion that this was the last motor race ever, at least in France, and I share this opinion, considering the point which the car has reached today.

Frankly ignoring the publicity angle sought by the manufacturers, is motor racing really indispensable to the progress of the motor industry?

It is said that light and at the same time powerful cars have been developed through racing; I agree, I recognize true progress, that materials have been perfected to give them greater wearing properties and make possible greater power outputs. But the speeds achieved are beyond practical needs, nobody can gainsay that.

There is no further need for races to test cars . . . I believe racing is finished . . .'

That had the same ring of authority about it as some of the mutterings of latter-day pundits. It was written in 1903, immediately after the tragic Paris–Madrid race, which was stopped at Bordeaux because of a series of accidents. These, incidentally, were due as much to the indiscipline of the public and the state of the roads as to faults in the cars.

So, in 1903 it was strongly and authoritatively argued that automotive progress had reached its zenith, and that racing could no longer serve a useful purpose. That article could have been written many times since 1903 – indeed, it has been, many times – with the same conviction. And the same lack of foresight . . .

However, in recent years motor racing at the highest level has become very much a mass entertainment sport, existing largely to that end alone, a fact which goes a long way towards undermining the premise that it is important to everyday production car development.

A major change came over racing when off-the-shelf engines became as widely available for road racing cars as they had been for two decades in American track circles. In retrospect, this phase probably began with the 500 cc Coopers, for other proprietary racing machines, from Bugattis to Cisitalias, had no long-term effect on racing in this respect.

The trend really accelerated during the period when most Grand Prix constructors came to use Coventry Climax engines. When later the Ford-sponsored Cosworth DFV was made generally available to constructors in 1969 the age of machines so aptly described by Robin Herd as 'British Standard Grand Prix cars' arrived. Quite simply, the DFV was a Grand Prix engine which was not only generally available, but an engine which had more potential than most others, even those built in very small numbers by constructors with long traditions of race engine development behind them.

This situation applied even more forcefully in the 1·6 litre Formula 2, where apart from an abortive effort by Ferrari and a long patient effort by BMW, every car was powered by a Ford-based engine, almost invariably the Cosworth FVA. This did not prevent the Formula becoming immensely popular among drivers and spectators, particularly in its last year, 1971, when even Ferrari and BMW had left the field, for the cars were very fast, capable of matching Grand Prix lap times of only a year or two earlier. But to claim that this racing was anything but an end in itself would be patent nonsense.

By 1970 the majority of Grand Prix cars were being designed for the Cosworth DFV; some designers followed what at times appeared to be almost a prescribed pattern, others endeavoured to gain advantages in chassis and running gear design. The most notable departures from the normal pattern were the Lotus 72 and March 711. Brilliant in conception though both of these cars may have been, advantages gained by their design have not in themselves been sufficient, however. They could be offset by variations in the power outputs of Cosworth engines and to a much greater degree by teams' tyre commitments.

Under the 3 litre Grand Prix formula, tyre development progressed at an unprecendented pace, as two giant American firms, Firestone and Goodyear, entered the field in earnest. The only European tyre company left in road racing was Dunlop, who had enjoyed a virtual monopoly during the year of the 1·5 litre Formula. At the end of 1970 Dunlop withdrew from major racing, although not from all motor sports involvements, simply because the expenditure required to keep pace became too great. Some spin-off benefits did accrue from their Grand Prix programme, but in the main it was to the end of publicity.

Nevertheless, it is in the field of ancillaries, in equipment such as tyre compounds and the ignition systems necessary to cope with multi-cylinder engines running at perhaps 12,000 rpm, that developments likely to be of value to the motor industry at large will be made on circuits. The actual racing car has become a purpose-built and highly specialized device, designed to carry one man and the fuel needed by its engine through a race, hopefully at a speed slightly higher than perhaps 20 other similar rival devices. Overall, therefore, the racing car has little to offer the everyday road car designer, although it may inspire a few exotic coachbuilders – even the rear, or mid, engine placing now inevitable in a racing car is no longer necessarily considered 'right' for a production model.

There is no denying, however, the benefits which in the past have found their way into production cars from the world of racing, or that the process continues, albeit nowadays in minutiea.

Motor racing, however, does not need extraneous justification. From the lowest to the highest level it is a sport, and at the highest is also a mass entertainment and a sophisticated medium for publicity and prestige – as indeed it often has been throughout its history. Nobody, for example, pretends that Mercedes-Benz re-entered Grand Prix racing in the thirties simply in order to gain knowledge and experience of advanced metallurgy, or that Ford entered the field three decades later for any reason other than a basic commercial one connected with prestige, as an aid to image-building. The commercial pressures upon everybody in racing are very strong but, as Graham Hill has remarked, once the flag drops racing becomes a sport, and it is just that for the millions of spectators who watch races all over the world, in growing numbers every year.

Grands Prix have been reduced to sprint-length races at least by comparison with the not-so-distant past – the 1971 Italian Grand Prix was run in 78 minutes. But the overall standards of competition are higher, and the only quality of the past which is no longer of prime importance is stamina; in all other respects the tests for men and machines which are Grand Prix races are no less severe than they ever have been.

THE FORMATIVE YEARS

Beginnings

The first motoring competition was a reliability trial from Paris to Rouen organized by the Paris newspaper *Le Petit Journal* in 1894. Before the end of the year, a committee of Paris-Rouen 'competitors' devised the first straightforward race, from Paris to Bordeaux and back again, over the enormous distance of 732 miles. The regulations were simple: manufacturers were permitted to enter any number of cars, but no two identical cars; only tools and spares carried on the cars could be used in repairs; drivers could be changed at will; the first car with more than two seats to finish would win.

Twenty-two vehicles set out from Paris on this ambitious race in June 1895; 15 were petrol engined and 6 were steam-powered, a Jeantaud electric car completing the field. Nine finished, headed by Emile Levassor in a single-cylinder 600 cc Panhard. He drove single-handed, day and night, to lead by three and a half hours at Bordeaux and five and three-quarter hours at the Paris finish. His time for the return journey was 48 hours 48 minutes, and his average speed 15 mph. Second was Peugeot driver Rigoulot, in turn five hours ahead of Koechlin, driving another Peugeot, which as the first car with more than two seats to finish was declared the official winner.

The success of this race opened the period of city-to-city racing, which culminated in the tragic Paris-Madrid of 1903, halted at Bordeaux by the French government following an appalling series of accidents. Some 35 races were organized on these lines between 1895 and 1903, the major events starting from Paris, and many returning to the French capital – Paris-Marseilles-Paris in 1896, Paris-Amsterdam-Paris in

1898, Paris-Bordeaux in 1899, Paris-Toulouse-Paris in 1900, Paris-Berlin in 1901 and Paris-Vienna in 1902.

The numbers of starters grew steadily, and speeds rose quickly as distinguishable racing cars began to appear. The total effective entry for the 1903 Paris-Madrid race was 275 vehicles, including 59 motorcycles, and over the 342 miles to Bordeaux, race leader Fernand Gabriel averaged 65·3 mph in an 11·2 litre Mors.

Few modern touring motorists would set themselves such a point to point target, and from this point of view one can begin to grasp the magnitude of Gabriel's drive. Roads at the beginning of the century were rough and narrow, thick with mud or dust – through the choking clouds left by other cars on the road to Bordeaux Gabriel passed 80 other drivers. Animals still unaccustomed to the horseless carriage were a constant hazard, as were crowds of uncontrolled and undisciplined spectators, still more familiar with the speeds of horsedrawn vehicles.

The easy way to speed was through brute power, through ever larger and more powerful engines. These were mounted in chassis which were usually anything but rigid, sometimes dangerously flimsy; frames of wood, or armoured wood, were the rule until 1901 when Mercedes introduced the pressed steel frame. Axles were rigid, shock absorbers as such virtually unknown, steering was heavy and until 1900 direct, without castor action. Wooden-spoked 'artillery' wheels were universal, and the pneumatic tyres first fitted to a Peugeot in the 1896 Paris-Marseilles were used on all racing cars by the end of the century. These were treadless and unreliable, and problems with them were aggravated by the state of the roads, including the presence of nails inevitable when road transport still depended largely on animal horse power. (For the first ten years punctured tyres had to be replaced with the wheel still on the car.)

Crews were seated high, exposed to rain, wind, dust

Left: end of an era. Fernand Gabriel at speed in a Mors in the last city-to-city race, the 1903 Paris-Madrid. But in an age when brute power was usually regarded as the simple recipe for racing success, light cars, especially Renaults, put up some remarkable performances. The brothers (above, Louis) drove their own cars in long-distance city-to-city races with considerable success.

and stones. Apart from simply keeping the car on the road by main force, the driver had to cope with the vagaries of quadrant gearboxes until the gate change was introduced in the early 1900s. The riding mechanic had to attend to such matters as drip-feed lubrication and keeping the tank pressurized, and warn the driver of hazards and overtaking cars – and, not least perhaps, stay on the vehicle, for which, taking into account the bumpy ride, little enough provision was usually made!

Racing began to change half way through this heroic first decade. The first circuit race was run in 1899 (although the first important circuit event was not organized until 1902), the first international series

Extremes are represented by the Gobron-Brillié (above) and the dainty voiturettes of the Renault team (below). The Gobron-Brillié boasted some features, in this photograph most notably the tubular frame, which were well in advance of contemporary heavy cars. The general shape of racing cars of the period is shown by the posed 3·75 litre Renault (opposite).

was launched in 1900, the first international regulation imposing a maximum weight, of 1000 kg (2204 lb), came into force in 1902.

The first international series of races, for the International Trophy, was devised by *New York Herald* proprietor James Gordon Bennett in 1899, and came to be known as the Gordon Bennett series. Rules were drawn up in consultation with the Auto-

mobile Club de France, which controlled the event, for France was the pre-eminent racing country. It was to be contested between national teams, each restricted to three cars, which had to be entirely constructed in the country entering them. These conditions eventually led to the abandonment of the Gordon Bennett, for they were to frustrate the flourishing French industry, which could have entered several teams, while other countries struggled to make up a representative team.

There were so few entries for the first Gordon Bennett races that they were run in conjunction with other events. The first, in 1900, attracted a full French team of three Panhards, a Belgian Bolide and an American Winton. The only finishers were two of the Panhards, Charron leading his team mate Girardot at the end of the 351 miles from Paris to Lyon (his average speed was 38·5 mph). Only the French team started in 1901, when Girardot was the sole finisher. The third Gordon Bennett saw the first British victory in an international race, S. F. Edge driving a 6·4 litre Napier to win at 34·3 mph. The race was run from Paris to Innsbruck, concurrently with the Paris-Vienna. In that Edge was the sole Gordon Bennett contestant to finish, and in the Paris-Vienna was effectively only 16th overall, his triumph was hollow.

But it was a sign that motor racing was no longer a French monopoly.

Just over a month after the Paris-Vienna Charles Jarrott drove a 13·8 litre Paris-Vienna Panhard to win the first important circuit race, the Circuit des Ardennes, in Belgium. Run over six laps of a 53-mile course, this attracted most of the leading drivers, and pointed surely to the future of racing. Roads could be closed with some security (although in the Ardennes race one driver did collide with a cow), a circuit race was easier to organize, entrants found it simpler, and spectators saw the cars more than once.

The accidents during the fateful Paris-Madrid in the following year were to prove to the ACF the impossibility of continuing with their traditional 'grand event' open road race; the Gordon Bennett remained basically unacceptable to the French because of its constricting entry conditions; so French thoughts naturally began to turn towards a new major annual event, for a Grand Prize, a 'Grand Prix'. The pattern of motor racing as we know it was beginning to take shape.

Meanwhile, Edge's Napier victory in the 1902 Gordon Bennett meant that 1903 saw the first international race to be held in Britain, where a special Act of Parliament had to be passed to make this

possible on public roads. Some little-used roads in Ireland were selected, where for the first time the Gordon Bennett was run as a circuit race (on two loops of roads centred on Ballyshannon). For the first time, too, the race assumed worthwhile proportions, as four teams of three cars were entered (three defending Napiers, three Mercedes representing Germany, two Panhards and a Mors from France, two Wintons and a Peerless from America). It was convincingly won by Camille Jenatzy, driving a 9·2 litre 60 hp Mercedes, basically a touring car hastily prepared for racing after the three 90 hp racing Mercedes had been destroyed in a factory fire. Saving Edge's fortuitous victory, this was the first real breach in the French manufacturers' domination of racing. The three French cars in fact finished in the next three places, none of the American cars completed the full race distance, and the only Napier to do so was disqualified. This Mercedes victory led in turn to the first major race to be run in Germany where in the 1904 Gordon Bennett there were 18 starters, representing Germany (Mercedes and Darracq), France (Richard-Brasier, Turcat Mery, and Mors), Britain (Wolseley and Napier), Belgium (Pipe), Austria (Mercedes) and Italy (FIAT). Elaborate arrangements were made around the 79·46-mile Taunus circuit (this incidentally was the net racing lap; neutralized sections through towns and villages brought the gross lap distance up to 87 miles), and the affair was accompanied by considerable pomp and ceremony. However, the Kaiser, his court and assorted German princelings did not witness another German triumph, the winner being Richard-Brasier driver Leon Théry, 'the Chronometer'.

Complications before the 1904 event were in the selection of representatives, for the British and French had to arrange eliminating competitions. Uniquely, in Britain it proved easier to arrange a

road race in 1904 than in France, as the legal complications attendant on the 1903 race were avoided by using an Isle of Man circuit, the Manx House of Keys having independent control over the island's roads. The French were on the point of organizing their race in Belgium, for after the Paris-Madrid their Prime Minister had publicly stated that there would be no more racing on the roads of France. At the last moment a motion was pushed through the Chamber of Deputies, enabling the ACF to hold their race in an isolated region near the Belgian frontier.

That event was the only important race to be run in France in 1904, while in other countries racing increased in stature. The Circuit des Ardennes reached its zenith, and was won by the Franco-American driver George Heath, driving a Panhard, while Vincenzo Florio's Coppa Florio, originated in 1900, attained international status. It was run over two laps of the very fast 115·6-mile Brescia-Cremona-Mantua-Brescia circuit, where the winner's average speed was 72 mph, by a considerable margin the fastest race speed achieved to that time. Moreover, the winner, Vincenzo Lancia, drove a FIAT, a marque born at the end of the 1890s, which had tentatively entered international racing in 1903 and was to remain prominent in the sport for two decades.

The last of the year's great races was run in America, and contested by some leading Europeans. This was the Vanderbilt Cup, sponsored by W. K. Vanderbilt Jr., a very close equivalent of Vincenzo Lancia, in that he was a millionaire, racing patron, and racing driver (he had driven a Mors to third place in the 1902 Circuit des Ardennes). The Vanderbilt regulations were in outline similar to those for the Gordon Bennett (for example allowing for it to be held in other countries – although it never was). Larger teams were admitted, however. It was organized by the AAA on a

22

Camille Jenatzy waiting to start in the 1903 Gordon Bennett
Trophy race, in a 60 hp Mercedes (far left). Although this was a
tuned touring model, hastily prepared for racing, it typifies
the competition car of the period. In 1905 Renault entered the
large-car class (left and above) using low-slung chassis and the
radiator-behind-engine arrangement, retained in their Grand Prix
cars and in some production Renaults until the 1930s.
Among the prominent men of the early years of racing posed
around this Mathis (below) in 1905 are Giovanni Agnelli (right),
Ettore Bugatti at the wheel, with Felice Nazzaro next to him, and
his brother Rembrandt between Vincenzo Lancia and Louis Wagner
on the rear seat.

triangular course on Long Island and, despite the rough roads, especially where railroads were crossed on the level, and negligible crowd control, it was a great success. A duel developed between Heath (Panhard) and Albert Clément (Clément-Bayard), who finished first and second 2½ minutes apart; two laps behind in third place was the first American car, Lyttle's Pope-Toledo.

The responsibility for organizing the 1905 Gordon Bennett passed with Théry's victory to the Automobile Club de France, to whom the French industry proposed that it be run concurrently with a new event, to

Grand Prix car that never was (above). This Gladiator was built in 1904 and is therefore not the Grand Prix car it is claimed to be; nevertheless it sums up the character of big racing cars on the eve of the first Grand Prix. Below: Otto Salzer posing proudly in a 1905 Mercedes.

be called the Grand Prix de l'Automobile Club de France. This was to be open to manufacturers' teams, with no national restrictions. The ACF accepted the proposal, but modified it to admit entries according to a French assessment of the strengths of national motor industries – France was to be permitted fifteen, Britain and Germany six each, Austria, Belgium, Italy, Switzerland and the USA three each.

An international wrangle was the inevitable consequence of this high-handed presumption, but at least out of the committee formed to thrash the matter out came a constructive result, the formation of the first international governing body of motor sport, the AIACR (Alliance Internationale des Automobile Clubs Reconnus), forerunner of the FIA. Eventually, the French backed down, abandoned their first Grand Prix proposals, and agreed to run the 1905 Gordon

Bennett to its original rules, the while stressing that it would be the last time they would have anything to do with it.

The Auvergne circuit centred on Clermont-Ferrand chosen for the race posed formidable problems, for its physical characteristics have been matched only by the Madonie circuit in Sicily, where the first Targa Florio was run in 1906. The 85 miles through the Auvergne mountains rose and fell with little relief, including gradients as steep as one in eight, and there were very few straight stretches (there were reputedly 145 corners, apart from minor bends). The Michelin tyre company, which had its headquarters at Clermont-Ferrand and had campaigned energetically for the selection of this circuit, was responsible for the facilities, including the team depots. Naturally, too, they arranged tyre supplies, and for the French team far and away the quickest changes seen before the detachable wheel rim came into use. As a car arrived, it was raised on lever jacks and each wheel was worked on by three-man teams; they unscrewed the wing nuts holding the cover to the rim, changed the cover, and while the nuts were being replaced inflated the tubes with compressed air. Thus four tyres could be changed in less than five minutes – and delays caused by tyre failures and tyre changes were absolutely crucial in races throughout the period.

Eighteen cars representing six countries started in the last Gordon Bennett, and as far as the lead was concerned the story was of a race between France and Italy. Vincenzo Lancia led for the first two of four laps, on his first setting the fastest lap; however, the radiator of his FIAT was holed, and his retirement left Théry's Richard-Brasier in an unassailable position. His winning speed was 48·4 mph, and he was followed by FIAT drivers Nazzaro and Cagno. The British starters finished eighth (Rolls' Wolseley), ninth

(Earp's Napier) and eleventh (Bianchi's Wolseley), while the sole American to complete the distance was Lyttle, twelfth in his Pope-Toledo at 35·9 mph. The Circuit des Ardennes was poorly supported, although interesting in that it was won by Hémery driving a Darracq designed for all-round balance rather than all-out power at the expense of every other quality. The Coppa Florio fell to Baggio's Itala, another marque new to racing.

Then the scene shifted across the Atlantic, to the American eliminating trials for the Vanderbilt Cup,

Grand Prix car that never was (below). Accessories such as horn and lights make this 'Grand Prix' Renault look most unconvincing, but in its basic shape it faithfully reproduces the lines of the first Grand Prix winner (it was probably one of a series of replicas, built up from stock parts for America). Above: very real – Vincenzo Lancia's FIAT at the pits during the 1906 Grand Prix.

and an abundance of technical novelty. Among the entries were six-cylinder engines (a Pope-Toledo and a Thomas), air-cooled eight-cylinder engines (a Franklin and a Premier, which proved to be grossly over-weight), one of Walter Christie's front-wheel drive cars, and a White Steamer (elsewhere, save for Serpollets in the French 1904 Gordon Bennett eliminating trials, the steam car had virtually vanished from front-line racing). The race, however, fell to two Gordon Bennett cars, a Pope-Toledo and a Locomobile.

The Vanderbilt Cup itself, over 283 miles of principally loose-surface roads, was again contested by leading European teams, and as in the Gordon Bennett, Lancia drove away from the field, gaining a 20-minute lead in seven laps. Then he collided with the Christie – which was on its third lap – and finally brought his damaged FIAT home fourth. Hémery (Darracq) went through to win, at 61·5 mph, from Heath (Panhard) and Tracy's Locomobile. No other drivers were able to complete the race, for the crowd invaded the circuit.

To declare the first era of racing closed after a convenient ten years and before the birth of the first Grand Prix is perhaps arbitrary. Much was to be carried over: cars, races and drivers.

The front-line cars of 1906 were to all intents and purposes those of 1905. Most of the races survived only to decline – the Circuit des Ardennes was run for the last time in 1907, while the Vanderbilt Cup lingered on reduced in status until 1916. The only race to survive from the first ten years of racing, albeit spasmodically and for widely varying types of

Above: a FIAT in the 1904 Coppa Florio trails a cloud of dust, one of the great hazards of early motor races. Below: Fabry's Itala before the 1906 Grand Prix. Opposite: the first large racing Renault was this 60 hp car built in 1904 to an American special order and raced by Maurice Bernin in the Vanderbilt Cup.

cars, is the RAC Tourist Trophy, which was first run for touring cars in the Isle of Man in 1905.

Once the pattern was set, the biggest feasible engine powering a car weighing 1007 kg, there was little real mechanical progress in the second half of the decade. Eight cylinder engines had been used in racing cars, by Clement Ader and Alexander Winton in 1903, when that exception to many rules, the Gobron Brillié, also appeared. This had a tubular chassis, opposed-piston engine, and even an essay into fuel injection for an alcohol-benzol fuel mix. A little later there had been an outburst of American inventiveness, to little apparent advantage in actual racing.

In general, originality and efficiency were to be found among the light cars, while the big cars conformed to a pattern, evolving slowly. This pattern was perhaps set by the rational simplicity and efficiency of Mercedes. The constant pre-occupation was 'added lightness', but advances in this aspect could by no means be consistently equated with progress.

Any parts which could be drilled, were drilled, extensively, and the large iron cylinders of engines were surrounded by copper sheeting, as thin as 1 mm, with cooling water circulating in the intervening space. Shaft drive slowly took over from chains, the racing world at last following the Renault example. The multi-plate clutch came into general use in place of the cone clutch, and gearboxes were mounted so as to be insulated from chassis flexing. One of the last armoured wood frames in major racing was used by de

Dietrich in 1904, for by that time the pressed steel chassis was almost universal.

Mors had experimented with friction shock absorbers and Bollée with independent front suspension, but neither was followed up immediately. 'Streamlined' bodies had also appeared, notably the Mors upturned boat bodies, and 'wind-cutting' noses, for example on Hotchkiss, Panhard and Napier. In some cases their overall value must have been dubious, for they were mounted above cumbersome running gear, and the torsos of crew members were left standing proud above them.

Tyres remained a constant problem – here the virtues of better balanced machines so clearly demonstrated in light car classes were largely ignored.

As far as engines were concerned, a stride forward came with the inclined valves introduced by Pipe and developed towards real efficiency in the 1905 FIAT. This 16 litre engine with 45 degree inlet and exhaust valves operated by push rods developed 120 bhp at a surprisingly low 1100 rpm. Tube radiators had given way to the honeycomb type early in the century.

Top line racing at the end of ten years still meant brutishly large and powerful, yet flimsy, cars being raced at extraordinarily high speeds. The drivers were unquestionably courageous, and they also had the qualities of ability, judgement and sympathy with machinery which would be regarded as essential in the top drivers of today. Several also showed an outstanding ability to adapt to the very different cars which were to emerge in the next decade.

The First
Grand Prix

The first great event of the next decade of motor racing was the first authentic 'Grand Prix', the French Grand Prix of 1906.

The French industry had quickly become frustrated by the Gordon Bennett series, and having failed to get the regulations revised, killed it. The Grand Prix de l'Automobile Club de France, which in effect took its place, was open to manufacturers' teams without the national restrictions which it was felt had weighed so unfairly against France in the Gordon Bennett races.

The regulations governing cars for this first Grand Prix were largely carried over, particularly the maximum weight stipulation of 1000 kg (2204 lb), plus a supplementary allowance of 7 kg for a magneto or dynamo. But whereas in the last Gordon Bennett races an unlimited number of mechanics had been permitted to work on cars, the Grand Prix regulations required that all work be undertaken by the driver and his riding mechanic, including tyre changes. This was a harsh ruling, for tyre failures were frequent and with conventional wheels a change required up to 15 minutes' Herculean labour. The one technical novelty of the first Grand Prix, the detachable rim with a replacement tyre mounted in it, therefore had

Left: Felice Nazzaro at speed in the winning FIAT in the 1907 French Grand Prix (above), and the famous Locomobile driven by Tracy and Roberston in Vanderbilt Cup races between 1905 and 1907. This is probably the least 'restored' of all historic racing cars, and still has its original paint. Above: the Itala which Alessandro Cagno drove to victory in the 1907 Coppa della Velocita at Brescia.

an importance which today seems out of all proportion, and was to be a decisive factor in the race. With these a tyre could be changed in little over four minutes. They were used by three teams in the 1906 Grand Prix, Renault, FIAT and Clément-Bayard.

Technically, none of the 32 starters would have looked out of place in earlier races. All save one had four-cylinder engines, most of them of more than 12 litres (the largest, Panhard, had a capacity of 18,279 cc). Most were 'L' head units, with valves and camshaft on one side (and consequently inefficient combustion chambers), but FIAT used their 'T' head engines developed in 1905, in which inlet and exhaust valves were inclined at 45 degrees and operated by pushrods from camshafts on either side of the block. Five manufacturers used chain drive, the other seven shaft drive. Most of the cars were fitted with artillery wheels – Darracq and Hotchkiss used wire-spoke wheels with metal rims – and all save one were high-built on massive frames. The exception was a Gobron-Brillié which had been built in 1903 and had a braced tubular frame to carry its equally unconventional opposed-piston engine.

The entry was predominantly French, with teams from Brasier, Clément-Bayard, Darracq, Hotchkiss, Panhard and Renault, and single cars from Gobron-Brillié and Grégoire. Foreign teams were FIAT and Itala from Italy, and Mercedes from Germany.

The circuit chosen was an immense 64-mile triangle of roads near Le Mans, which had to be lapped six times on each of two consecutive days. The long straights were well-surfaced by contemporary standards but two plank by-passes built to avoid town sections which would have been 'neutralized' in Gordon Bennett days were narrow and dangerous, while some of the corners were badly cut up. This was to be aggravated by drivers' cornering techniques, for with only rear-wheel brakes the practice was to skid the backs of these heavy cars through bends.

There were misgivings about the state of the roads, which filling, tar-sealing and rolling did little to allay, right up to the start, which as was usual for those days, was very early in the morning, at 6 am on Tuesday June 25th. Competitors started singly at 90-second intervals, and the first car ever to cross the start line in a Grand Prix was Vincenzo Lancia's FIAT, for the first driver to be flagged away, Fernand Gabriel, stalled the engine of his de Dietrich.

Lancia led at the end of the first lap, which he completed in 53 min 42·4 sec, and Brasier driver Baras at the end of the second. Then Francois Szisz took the lead in his flame-red Renault, and held it throughout the second day to win the 769-mile race at 62·88 mph. Second was Felice Nazzaro's FIAT, over half an hour behind and ahead of nine other finishers. The last of these, Mercedes driver Mariaux, straggled in over four hours behind Szisz. Baras, who finished only seventh in the race, put in the fastest lap over this immensely testing circuit in 52 min 25·4 sec, at 73·3 mph, from the standing start.

It was generally agreed that the race had been too long, and that too much had been expected of two-man crews – the unfortunate Rougier apparently just gave up after changing 14 wheels on his de Dietrich in 10 laps. At the next important race of the year,

Above: the early Vanderbilt Cup races achieved the stature of a major European event, and were contested by leading European drivers. In this crowded scene Vincenzo Lancia is waiting to start his FIAT in the 1906 event on Long Island. Left: the first British Grand Prix cars were the straight-eight Weigels raced in the 1907 and 1908 French Grands Prix.

the Circuit des Ardennes, there were again no restrictions on the number of people allowed to work on cars, and tyre specialists manned depots around the course – and all competitors used detachable rims. Arthur Duray won this race for de Dietrich, by the narrow margin of 92 seconds from Hanriot's Darracq.

Several of the outstanding European drivers again crossed the Atlantic to contest the Vanderbilt Cup, and overwhelmingly dominate it. This race was notable for its chaotic organization, and for the close on-the-road racing between Wagner (Darracq), Lancia (FIAT), Jenatzy (Mercedes) and Duray (de Dietrich). On time, Wagner led throughout, but second place constantly changed hands – indeed, Lancia and Duray were absolutely neck and neck at the end of seven

laps. Louis Wagner eventually won by 3 min 18 sec from Lancia, with Duray a mere 16 seconds behind in third place, while Jenatzy, fifth after a slow ninth lap, finished just over 2½ minutes behind Clément – close racing for those days.

Once again the American cars were interesting, especially in the eliminating trials, when the entry included three Frayer-Millers, which had centrifugal fans to force cooling air over their engines and drivers seated so low as to create the same impression as Chapman's semi-prone pilots more than fifty years later. Among the entries, although not the starters, was a Maxwell with a 12-cylinder engine.

The eliminating race was won by Tracy (Locomobile) at 54·1 mph over the same course and distance as the Cup itself, which compares with Wagner's Cup-winning speed of 61·4 mph to give a clear indication of the gap between European and American standards. Tracy was credited with the fastest lap in the Cup, although this is suspect as it was over five minutes faster than his second-fastest, and in the race he

finished a lowly 10th (best American car at the finish was a Thomas driven by le Blon, 8th overall).

In 1907 the Grand Prix became established, and other races attracted similar fields. First of these was the Targa Florio, which gained full international stature (the first Targa, in 1906, had been little more than an Italian national event, which proved the possibility of actually racing on the primitive Sicilian roads; it had been won by an Itala driven by Alessandra Cagno). French and German teams challenged the Italians, the Darracqs doing so most effectively until the last lap. At the end, however, Nazzaro won for FIAT with his team-mate Lancia second and Fabry's Itala third. This race was run to a formula which attempted to relate engine capacity to car weight, the bore of four-cylinder engines being restricted to 120–130 mm, and sixes to 75–90 mm; minimum weight was set at 1000 kg, with an extra 20 kg for every millimetre of bore above 120 for fours and 40 kg for every millimetre above the minimum 75 for sixes.

Early Grand Prix cars, a 1908 Austin and a 1908 Benz (above), and a 1907 FIAT (right). The 9·6 litre Austin was outclassed, although two were classified 18th and 19th in the 1908 Grand Prix. The 12·4 litre Benz finished 2nd and 3rd in that race, and were very successful in the USA, particularly in the hands of Victor Hémery. The FIAT – this example carries Nazzaro's 1907 French Grand Prix racing number – was the outstanding car of the year. This photograph shows the high seating position, chain final drive and bolt-on detachable wheel rims. Winning speed in the French GP over 478 miles was 70·61 mph.

Second of the year's great races was the Kaiserpreis, run on a 73-mile circuit in the Taunus mountains to a formula which for the first time limited engine capacity, to 8 litres, and with other restrictions was aimed at eliminating the pure racing car. This attracted 92 entries, so heats were arranged, almost unnecessarily as only 54 cars actually turned up. Lancia and Nazzaro won both preliminaries for FIAT, and the Kaiserpreis itself fell to Nazzaro, by just under five minutes from a Pipe driven by Hautvast and Jörns' Opel.

The French Grand Prix was run at Dieppe, over a shorter circuit of 47·8 miles, and to a fuel consumption formula. Each car was allowed 231 litres of fuel which in terms of miles per gallon set maximum consumption at 9·4 mpg. Individual allocations were carefully issued and tanks sealed on the day before the race, and cars and fuel supplies put under guard for the

night. On average, engines were smaller than in 1906, although one car had the largest power unit ever to be used in a Grand Prix, the 18,891 cc monster installed in Christie's front wheel drive car. The European Establishment did not approve of this device, while lesser men were highly amused as the racing number allocated by the organizers was applied to it – WC1. Less extraordinary, and hardly novel in that two of them had been raced before, were the first eight-cylinder Grand Prix engines, in the British Weigels, the French Porthos and the Swiss Dufaux-Marchand.

Outwardly, most cars appeared more compact than the 1906 contenders, and all used wheels with detachable rims – a hard lesson had been learned by those not using them at Le Mans. For this Grand Prix, all cars had to be painted in national racing colours: France, blue; Britain, green; Germany, white; Italy, red, and so on, as under the old Gordon Bennett

Contrasting conditions. The Isotta-Fraschini team cars prepared for the 1907 Targa Florio (above) and mechanics working on a Diatto Clément before the race (below). Opposite: Isotta-Fraschini voiturettes in more civilized surroundings at Dieppe in 1908, and an Aquila Italiana racing through the rugged countryside of Sicily during the 1907 Targa Florio.

regulations. The race turned out to be a battle between FIAT and Lorraine-Dietrich, and for much of the time the leading drivers, Lancia and Duray respectively, had each other in sight – a rare occurrence when cars were started at timed intervals (a minute apart at Dieppe in 1907). Towards the end the gearbox of the French car failed, and the engine of the FIAT started to misfire, so the 1906 winner and runner-up, Szisz and Nazzaro, went ahead. On the last lap their positions were reversed, Nazzaro scoring his third great triumph of the year for FIAT, when Szisz, perhaps worried about his fuel consumption, slowed.

Secondary events wound up the season. In the Circuit des Ardennes, Moore-Brabazon (later Lord Brabazon of Tara) won the 8 litre 'Kaiserpreis' class, appropriately driving a Belgian Minerva, and de Caters took the 'Grand Prix' class for Mercedes. At Brescia, Minoia won the 'Kaiserpreis' rules Coppa Florio for Isotta-Fraschini, while the separate Coppa della Velocita fell to Cagno's Itala.

These 1907 races had seen a general movement towards common racing rules, and at an international conference in the summer the 'Ostend Formula' to come into effect in 1908 had been devised. This imposed a minimum weight, of 1100 kg (2425 lb), and a maximum engine size, but restricted cylinder bores to 155 mm for four-cylinder engines, 127 mm for six-cylinder engines. The immediate result was that the engines in most entries for the Grand Prix were smaller, 12–13 litres; outrageously long-stroke engines did not result, at least immediately, and the 1908 'sixes' in fact had square engines.

In detail, power units still varied widely; Brasier and Renault still put their trust in side valves; Panhard, Germain, Austin, Porthos and the lone Thomas had 'T' heads; Benz, Lorraine-Dietrich, Fiat and Mors had pushrod-actuated inclined valves; Itala and Mercedes favoured the inlet over exhaust arrangement; the monobloc Clément-Bayard and Weigel engines

had hemispherical combustion chambers and 45 degree valves operated by overhead camshafts. Ten of the manufacturers who entered for the 1908 Dieppe race used chain drive, the other seven shaft drive.

The months before the race were noteworthy for one great controversy. The Automobile Club de France ruled the Rudge Whitworth detachable wheels, which were to be used on the Napier entries, out of order – when the rules were drawn up they just had not allowed for this development. Whereat the fiery S. F. Edge stirred up a furore, making enormous publicity capital out of the whole episode. This only persuaded the ACF to stand by their ruling, and the Napier entry was withdrawn (it appears quite possible that the cars would not have been ready for the race, anyway!).

The loss of one foreign team was of little real account for the entry was stronger than ever: 48 cars started at Dieppe in the third Grand Prix, 24 French, 9 German, 6 British, 6 Italian, 3 Belgian and the lone American Thomas. The Dieppe roads were in such poor condition that the organizers felt impelled formally to warn drivers of the need to protect their faces; however, plain-glass goggles ('safety' glass did not then exist), face masks and close-fitting helmets afforded little protection against flying stones, and many drivers were to be injured. Afterwards the roads were to bear an undue amount of the blame for a French debacle – 'foreign' cars led throughout the 477·5 mile race, Salzer for Mercedes, Nazzaro for FIAT, Hémery for Benz, finally and conclusively Christian Lautenschlager for Mercedes (at 69 mph).

French tyres, it was suggested, were inflated to lower pressure than those on German cars, and thus more likely to be cut by stones, and the new single-fixing detachable rims were too weak in the conditions. These were indeed bad – at the end of the first lap 11 cars stopped at the pits to change tyres – but they were of course the same for all competitors. In fact,

the Mercedes team ran out of spare tyres towards the end, and Lautenschlager had to drive his last two laps with this uncomfortable fact in mind – a heavy responsibility in his first ever race as a driver! A tyre failure was also responsible for the first fatal accident in the Grand Prix, Panhard driver Cissac and his riding mechanic Schaube being killed when he crashed after a front tyre blew, left its wheel and jammed the transmission chain. More than 20 of the starters were timed at over 100 mph, the fastest being Hautvast's Clément-Bayard at 105·1 mph. So there was an element of French misfortune, in that his team mate Rigal, whose fourth place prevented a complete German walk-over, had to stop 19 times for tyres. But the unpalatable fact for the French was that the finishing order was Mercedes, Benz, Benz, Clément-Bayard, Mercedes, Opel. This was a crushing blow to national pride. The immediate reaction was to look for revenge in 1909, but in fact the Grand Prix was to be abandoned until 1912.

The status of the Targa Florio had declined in 1908, when Trucco won for Isotta-Fraschini, and the German teams did not enter for the only other important European race of the year, the Coppa Florio at Bologna. Here Nazzaro resumed his winning ways for the FIAT, finishing ahead of Trucco's Lorraine-Dietrich and Cagno's Itala. Lancia had suffered yet another mechanical failure when in the lead after setting a staggering lap record of 82·3 mph.

The Vanderbilt Cup was revived, and won by Robertson's Locomobile 'Old 16'. But it was little more than a national event, overshadowed by the first Grand Prize of the Automobile Club of America. This was run over a 25 mile circuit at Savannah, where the visiting Europeans were impressed by the hospitality and, in marked contrast to the Vanderbilt races, by the organization and crowd control.

Once again, the American entry was outclassed, although in one technical respect again noteworthy – it included a Chadwick, which was the first car ever to race with a supercharged engine. The race turned out to be one of the most exciting run in the era which came to be known as the Age of Giants. Ralph de Palma (FIAT) led the first two laps, then fell out of the effective running, leaving Hanriot to lead the race for Benz for five laps. Louis Wagner (FIAT) led the next, Hémery (Benz) the 9th and 10th, Wagner the 11th. Then his FIAT team mate Nazzaro led until the 16th and last lap, when he fell from first to third as a tyre deflated, leaving Wagner to beat Hémery by a mere 56 seconds – for the first time a major race was won by less than a minute. Benz driver Erle and his mechanic were only slightly injured in a lurid accident, when a front tyre failed at around 100 mph; the flying tread knocked Erle unconscious, and the car careered on for another quarter of a mile before

rolling as it left the track, throwing out both men.

Little noticed, Haupt retired the Chadwick after four laps and the supercharger disappeared from racing until the twenties. And equally quietly the last Renault to race in a Grand Prix fell out, after Szisz had kept it among the leaders for six laps.

Opposite and above: the famous 21 litre 'Blitzen Benz' designed by Max Wagner and built in 1909, was raced by several famous drivers, including Victor Hémery, Barney Oldfield and Bob Burman. Below: the Lancia Alpha of 1908 was the first competition car built by Vincenzo Lancia, who later turned his back on motor sport.

Meanwhile, the majority of French manufacturers had been promoting an agreement to abstain from Grand Prix type racing. The high cost of constructing racing cars was cited, although the outside world, and posterity, concluded that a prime motivation was the plain distasteful fact that French cars were no longer superior – indeed, they had suffered all too many humiliating defeats. This suspicion was encouraged by the French industry's continuing support of secondary classes, where their cars still enjoyed their accustomed superiority.

Most of the leading firms were signatories to this agreement: Berliet, Bollée, Brasier, Clément-Bayard, Lorraine-Dietrich, Motobloc, Panhard and Renault for France, Germain, Pipe and Minerva from Belgium, Benz and Mercedes from Germany, Isotta-Fraschini from Italy. Mors emphasized their disagreement by entering for the abortive 1909 Grand Prix, while FIAT and Itala abstained more passively.

The lull in Grand Prix racing lasted for three years, but the complete break for only one. In 1910 the American Grand Prize was run again, over a new Savannah circuit, where it was fought out between Benz and FIAT. Hémery, Haupt and brilliant newcomer David Bruce-Brown led at times in the German cars, Wagner, Nazzaro and de Palma at times in the FIAT S61s. Bruce-Brown took his turn in front for the last two laps, and won by less than two seconds from Hémery, while the other top drivers were sidelined and Burman brought a Marquette-Buick home third. Last of the six finishers was Ray Harroun in a Marmon – a combination which became better known in 1911 for winning the first 500-mile race on a track in Indiana which had been opened in 1910.

Bruce-Brown's authoritarian mother, who had resorted to threats of legal action in an attempt to prevent him competing at Daytona beach in 1908, arrived at Savannah by special train to try to persuade him not to start, to the great joy of the gentlemen of the Press. Lore has it that when this formidable

Pit stops. Above: a typical Targa Florio scene in 1909, with an Isotta-Fraschini about to leave after refuelling. Left: Lautenschlager's winning Mercedes in the 1908 French Grand Prix. The driver is behind the cockpit, while his riding mechanic is preparing to change a front wheel rim, which is carrying a very badly worn tyre.

matron realized that her son was leading the race she belaboured other spectators with a parasol, for failing to spur her son on! Certainly she sprinted onto the track at the end, to embrace him before he could remove his goggles.

A Grand Prix, of a sort, was run in Europe in 1911, by the Automobile Club de l'Ouest at Le Mans, using a new 33¾-mile circuit. For this a very assorted field of 14 cars was assembled, ranging from a 1906 Grand Prix Lorraine-Dietrich to a 1·3 litre car of a new marque, Bugatti. The French Press poured scorn on the whole affair, naming it the Grand Prix des Vieux Tacots (usually translated as Old Crocks' Grand Prix). They were seriously worried about the fitness of the cars, apparently with reason, for Fournier was to be fatally injured in the race when he crashed after the front axle of his old Corre-la-Licorne broke.

However, it was a Grand Prix, and it did bring the name of Bugatti firmly into racing history, where he had so far been a shadowy figure. In the opening stages there was visibly racing. Fournier led until he crashed, and this left Duray to fight the old Lorraine against tyre troubles, heat and Hémery's Savannah FIAT, in effect a tuned touring car. When the Lorraine wilted, Hémery was left with no direct competition, only with the task of nursing his thoroughly sick FIAT through to the end. Second, but two whole laps down in the 12-lap race, was Ernest Fridrich's little Bugatti, and therein were the seeds of a David v Goliath legend which has somehow persisted. Third was a Rolland-Pilain, fourth a Côté light car.

Real racing continued on the other side of the Atlantic, where the principal Grand Prize contestants were again FIAT and Benz, with some opposition from a pair of privately-owned 1908 GP Mercedes. The early leaders were, Hémery (Benz), de Palma (Mercedes), Hearne (Benz) and then just before half-distance an American car, Patchke's Marmon. Hearne regained the lead for a substantial period, but towards the end Bruce-Brown forced his FIAT through to win (at 74·75 mph) from Hearne and de

One of the few early American racing cars to survive is this Buick 'Bug' of 1910, which is not representative but nevertheless of interest, as it shows an early preoccupation with aerodynamic efficiency.

Palma; Bragg (FIAT) was fourth and the first American car, Disbrow's Pope, fifth.

With this race the first golden era of American road racing ended. The Vanderbilt Cup and the Grand Prize were still run, but never again contested by leading Europeans. American racing increasingly focussed on Indianapolis, where for a while European road-racing machinery was to enjoy considerable success, but a quarter of a century was to pass before Grand Prix cars raced in a Grand Prix style event in the United States, and yet another decade before the true renaissance of American road racing got under way.

It is perhaps appropriate then, that the 1911 American Grand Prize was also the last race to be fought out exclusively between the giants of the first Grand Prix period. For although these cars were still to race, still to lead races, a new Grand Prix chapter was about to open.

Brooklands and Indianapolis

Track racing has always been a part of the motor sporting scene – the earliest races in some Continental countries were run on trotting tracks – and in 1907 the first permanent track in the world was opened at Brooklands. This was the brainchild of Hugh Locke King, who put up some £250,000 for its construction on his own land near Weybridge. His object was to provide both a racing venue on the British mainland, for the laws of the United Kingdom have always forbidden any form of motoring competition on public roads, and a development track for the motor industry.

The egg-shaped main track was completed in six months, too quickly perhaps, for it was built upon sand, on which the mass of concrete in its 20 feet high, 100 feet wide, bankings settled uneasily. These concave bankings were designed for speeds of 120 mph. The lap distance of the outer banked circuit was 2·67 miles, and within this first autodrome other circuits were to be devised.

For many years Brooklands was the Mecca of motor sport in Britain, and through the first half of its life was an invaluable asset to the sport. In the end it outlived its time, for it encouraged the construction of track-racing specials, which included some prime white elephants, and an attitude detached from the road-racing mainstream of Europe. Its shortcomings were soon recognized, but could never really be overcome within its confines.

Brooklands got off to a false start, admitting idiosyncracies like identification by drivers' 'jockey' smocks instead of car numbers, and persisting with

unhandicapped races between ill-matched cars. In 1908, however, racing was put on a proper footing, largely by the redoubtable 'Ebby', E. V. Ebblewhite. The first meeting to attract wide public attention, at Whitsun, featured the famous match race between two giants, the FIAT 'Mephistopheles' and the Napier 'Samson', both nominally 90 hp cars. Frank Newton led in Samson until its crankshaft broke, leaving Felice Nazzaro to win in the FIAT; officially, Nazzaro lapped at 121·64 mph, but the electric timing apparatus was deeply suspect, and the hand-timed 107·98 mph is more generally accepted.

Brooklands was of value as a test and development track in its early years, and as such the envy of Continental manufacturers, although when banked tracks were eventually built in Europe they were never fully utilized. The pre-war activities for which the track is best remembered were perhaps the record-breaking attempts, notably by a 21·5 litre Benz and Lambert's 4·5 litre 100-mile-in-the-hour Talbot (he actually covered 103 miles 1470 yards).

Track racing found its true home in the USA, most permanently of course at the Indiana state capital, which early in the century seemed to be developing as the centre of the American automobile industry. Four of its enterprising sons, Carl G. Fisher, James A. Allison, Arthur C. Newby and Frank H. Wheeler, joined together to build the Indianapolis Motor Speedway in 1909. A certain P. T. Andrews designed the 2½-mile oval (interestingly, his early designs incorporated an artificial road circuit). It was built just as quickly as Brooklands, and opened in August 1909. Main event of the three-day inaugural meeting was a 250-mile race, won by Bob Burman (Buick); a 300-mile event on the third day was declared 'no contest' at 235 miles because of fatal accidents.

Like Brooklands, the track was used before it had settled, and the surface disintegrated. Andrews was summoned and proposed a brick track. Crushed rock and sand was levelled over the old surface, and 3,200,000 bricks laid, the last being the famous 'golden brick'.

The early Indianapolis meetings were on Brooklands lines, with several short races, and odd feature events such as the 200-mile race in 1910 won by Ray Harroun, driving a Marmon Six. Then Fisher decided to concentrate on one great annual race at the Brickyard, and on Memorial Day in 1911 the first 500 was run.

This attracted 40 entries and, as much to the point, some 80,000 spectators. The winning car was the famous production-based Marmon Wasp single-seater, with the first rear-view mirror in racing history (an arrangement other drivers objected to – a mechanic to warn of overtaking cars was regarded as essential). The Marmon led for most of the way, although never by a great margin, driven through most of the race by Ray Harroun, even then referred to as a veteran driver and coming out of retirement for this one race (he was relieved for a spell by Cyrus Patschke, who was also co-driver of Dawson's Marmon, which finished fifth). Second was a Lozier driven by Ralph Mulford, third David Bruce-Brown's FIAT. The winning speed in the first '500' was 74·4 mph.

The 1912 event was also an American national race, notable for its dramatic final laps. Ralph de Palma set the pace throughout – his lead at 450 miles was 5 full laps – but with 2 laps, 5 miles, to go a piston failed in his Mercedes. This left Joe Dawson (relieved by Don Herr) to win in a National (at 78·72 mph) from Tetzlaff's FIAT and Hughes' Mercer.

Early Indianapolis cars to survive include the Marmon Wasp single-seater which Harroun drove to victory in 1911 (above) and the National which was placed second in 1912.

45

Light Car Racing

From the very early days racing had included classes defined by weight, the first event to have a separate voiturette class as such being the 1898 Paris-Marseilles (a weight of 200–400 kg was stipulated). In subsequent city-to-city races, competing cars were grouped in three classes, voiturettes (maximum weight 400 kg), voitures légères, or light cars (400–650 kg) and heavy cars (up to 1000 kg).

The handicaps built into the over-muscled large cars have already been mentioned, and the better-balanced and thus more efficient small cars benefited in terms of overall race placings. In the 1901 Paris-Bordeaux Giraud placed a Panhard light car sixth overall, while in the same year Renault claimed eighth place (out of 47 finishers) in the Paris-Berlin with a 1-litre Renault voiturette. Then in 1902 he won Paris-Vienna outright with a 3·7 litre Renault light car at 38·9 mph, and Edmond was third overall at 38·1 mph in a Darracq racing in the same class (Farman's "heavy" Panhard, which was second, averaged 38·4 mph). In the ill-fated Paris-Madrid of 1903, Louis Renault was second overall, driving a 6·3 litre

Renault in the light car class, at 62·3 mph compared with the 65·3 mph achieved by the outright leader Fernand Gabriel, driving a Mors in the heavy car class.

Thus the efficacy of the small car was early proved beyond dispute. The pace-setting Renaults were straightforward machines with L-head engines; more important, they were robust, their brakes were proportionately more efficient, and they were less demanding on tyres, so often a key factor in early races.

In racing's transitional stage after the Paris-Madrid there were few events for these cars, but in 1905 the proprietors of the French journal *l'Auto* (later to become *l'Equipe*) put up a trophy specifically for light cars. In that year it was little more than an extended trial, but in 1906 the Coupe des Voiturettes – which inevitably became known as the Coupe de *l'Auto* – was run as a race, the recognizable forerunner of all later secondary races. The regulations called for a *minimum* weight of 700 kg, and limited the bore of engines to 120 mm for single-cylinder units and 90 mm for twins.

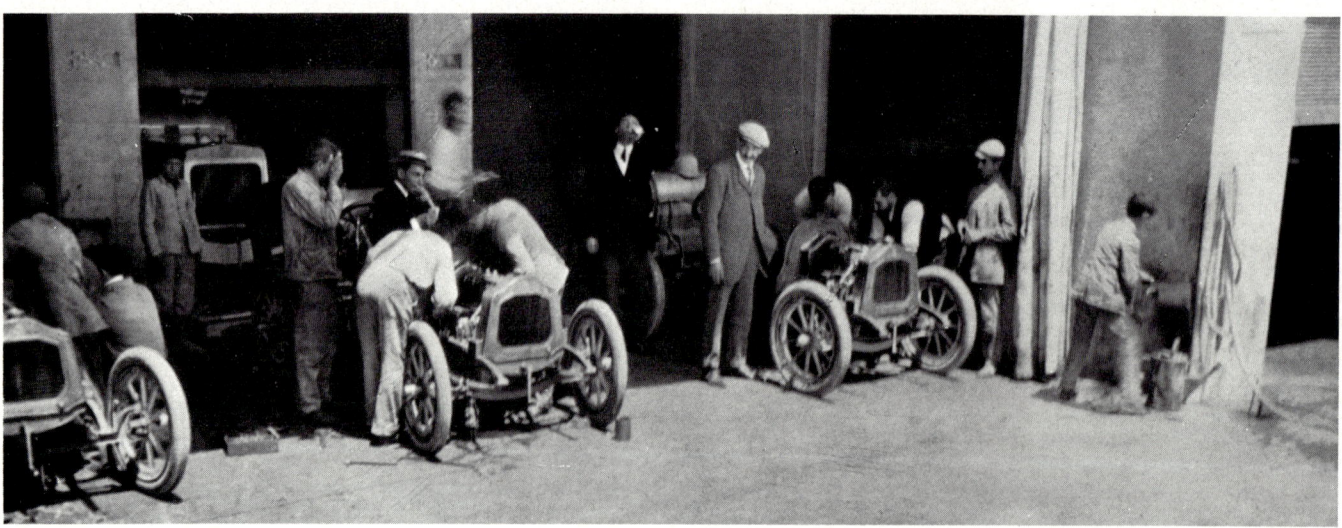

Lion Peugeots epitomized the second-generation voiturettes (above, left, at Mont Ventoux in 1909, and below, Giuppone winning at Boulogne in the same year). Opposite, below: a team of de Dion voiturettes being prepared for the 1907 Targa Florio. Above: an Isotta-Fraschini in another typically primitive racing situation.

As if to mark the establishment of this new category, the winning car was out of the ordinary; a Sizaire-Naudin, it had independent front suspension, by transverse leaf spring, and a square, 120 × 120 mm, single-cylinder engine, which produced some 18 bhp at 2000 rpm – in terms of bhp/litre this compares more than favourably with contemporary Grand Prix cars. Driven by Sizaire, it completed the 155-mile race at Rambouillet at 36·50 mph, ahead of a Delage and Lion-Peugeot.

In 1907 the rules were amended to reduce engine bores and introduce maximum weights. Naudin won in 1907 at 40·66 mph over 190 miles on the same circuit, having previously won the Sicilian Cup over the Madonie circuit, from his partner Sizaire, and Goux driving a Lion-Peugeot. A further change admitted engines with more than two cylinders in 1908 (bore restrictions 100 mm, 80 mm and 65 mm respectively for single, twin and four-cylinder engines, with appropriate maximum weights of 500 kg, 600 kg and 650 kg). This formula was not common to the class, the ACF varying it for their own Grand Prix des Voiturettes, for example. Of the important races, two Italian events fell to Lion-Peugeot driver Cesare Guippone, the ACF race to Albert Guyot, driving a Delage, and the Coupe itself at Compiegne to Naudin and Sizaire, of course driving Sizaire-Naudins, with Goux' Peugeot third. Both marques used single-cylinder engines with outrageously long strokes, and identical dimensions, 100 × 250 mm; power was around 40 bhp at 2400 rpm. These units were so tall that drivers had to look round rather than over them! Within the head of the 100 mm bore Lion-Peugeot cylinder were three inlet and three exhaust valves!

Following pages: an outstanding Coupe de l'Auto *car was the Coatalen-designed Sunbeam, three of which were placed third, fourth and fifth in the 1912 French Grand Prix.*

In the 1909 regulations there was a movement towards favouring four-cylinder units, although not far enough, as crankshaft and piston speeds were further limiting factors, where again the single-cylinder abnormalities of course had an advantage. Lion-Peugeot won the major races of 1909 (Goux in Sicily and Spain, Guippone the Coupe itself), while a significant new marque, Hispano-Suiza, appeared unobtrusively. Their Birkigt-designed cars had four-cylinder engines, and although they achieved little in their first year, save cause a sanitary new wind to blow through small racing car design, Paul Zuccarelli drove one to win the 1910 Coupe. Second was a V-twin Peugeot driven by Goux, third Chassagne with another Hispano, and fourth Boillot with a four-cylinder Lion-Peugeot.

Birkigt's T-head unit was enlarged to 65 × 200 mm (2650 cc) in 1910, in which form it developed just

Above: Felice Nazzaro in the cockpit of the 30-litre Fiat S.76.
Below: period piece. A Rolland-Pilain waiting to be sent off up the Mont Ventoux hill climb in 1909.

over 50 bhp at 2300 rpm. The dimensions of the Michaux-designed Peugeot V-twin were 80 × 280 mm (2803 cc), and the V-4 had an equally exaggerated long stroke, 65 × 260 mm to give a capacity of 3440 cc; the respective bore/stroke ratios were 1:3·5 and 1:4 – far removed from the early square Coupe engines!

In 1911 the Coupe regulations included a capacity limit, a step forward partly offset by the super-imposition of bore/stroke restrictions of between 1:1 and 1:2. However, in the 3 litre capacity limit was the basis of most subsequent racing regulations; together with the results of the previous year, it effectively ended the period of single- and twin-cylinder freaks. This time the Coupe was won by Bablot in a Delage, which had a four-cylinder in-line engine of 80 × 149 mm, compared with the 78 × 156 mm V-4 of the Lion-Peugeot Boillot drove into second place.

Across the English Channel, Sunbeam and Vauxhall built relatively short stroke engines, of 80 × 120 mm and 90 × 118 mm; neither made any impression on the Continent until the following year, when the Coupe was run concurrently with the Grand Prix, a race in which Sunbeam achieved a quite remarkable 3-4-5 in the overall placings. In 1910, a Vauxhall with Pomeroy's L-head engine had been the first 3-litre car to be timed at 100 mph, at Brooklands.

The 1912 Coupe victory was the last for a side-valve engine in front-line racing, and the race within a race was perhaps the high water mark in the history of the Coupe de *l'Auto*. In 1913 Boillot and Goux clearly defeated the Sunbeams, driving Peugeots with out-standingly efficient engines, refined versions of the 7·6 litre four which won the 1912 Grand Prix. A further version was built to meet the 2½ litre regulations for the 1914 Coupe de *l'Auto*; the race was never run, but the Peugeots survived the First World War, to win the first race to be run in Europe after its ending, the 1919 Targa Florio.

The Great Technical Advance

The modest success of the Grand Prix de France at Le Mans in 1911 persuaded the Automobile Club de France to revive their premier event in 1912. However, as entries materialized only slowly, the Club decided to combine the Grand Prix with the Coupe de l'Auto, for 3-litre cars. The only restriction applied to Grand Prix cars was almost irrelevant, a maximum width of 1·75 metres (69 in).

The prospect was for a fascinating race, for since the 1908 Grand Prix considerable technical progress had been made in the smaller racing class. But although at the end of the day the performance of the Coupe cars exceeded expectation, the Peugeot 7·6 litre Grand Prix engine which appeared overshadowed all else, for this represented a great leap forward in the motor racing story.

The inspiration for this engine came from a trio of driver-technicians, Georges Boillot, Jules Goux and Paul Zuccarelli, who were joined in its execution by the Swiss designer Ernest Henry. The precise part played

Top: last of the giants. David Bruce-Brown beside his 14·1 litre S74 Fiat before the start of the second day's racing in the 1912 French Grand Prix. At that stage he led the race, ahead of one of the 'new-generation' Peugeots. Above: first of the Alfas – Fracassi's ALFA in the 1914 Targa Florio.

by each has never been clearly defined, but Henry generally appears to receive too much credit, while Robert Peugeot, who backed the trio's proposals in the face of opposition from the executives of his company, generally receives none at all. He agreed to finance the construction of a series of engines, for the voiturette and Grand Prix classes, and made available small workshops near Paris, well away from the main Peugeot plant.

Here the unit which was to set the broad pattern for racing engines for decades ahead was built. It was a monobloc four-cylinder unit, with hemispherical combustion chambers, four valves per cylinder operated by twin overhead camshafts, driven by a central shaft at the front, and central plug location. Reciprocating masses were reduced, and the engine ran at an unusually high speed. In other respects it was a straightforward long-stroke unit (110 × 200 mm, 7603 cc, dimensions inherited from a proposed 1911 engine), with cast-iron block and head, one-piece five main bearing crankshaft and cooling circulation by centrifugal pump. The claimed power output was 175 bhp at 2200 rpm, which was perhaps a 25 per cent overestimate in response to the 200 bhp claimed for the 14 litre S74 Fiat engine which was to be matched against the Peugeot at Dieppe. On a power/capacity basis neither unit was outstandingly efficient, the Peugeot producing around 18 bhp/litre, the Fiat 10 bhp/litre. For the 3-litre Coupe Peugeot engine 90 bhp at 3000 rpm was claimed; more realistically the four-cylinder side-valve engines of the Coupe Sunbeams produced 75 bhp at 2800 rpm, or 25·1 bhp/litre.

The rest of the Peugeot did not match up to the engine in originality, for although rational enough, it reflected the passing Age of Giants in its lines – save for Rudge-Whitworth wheels – and was heavier than necessary, at 1400 kg (3080 lb) only 100 kg lighter than the Fiat.

In many ways the Fiat was a traditional, even antiquated, Grand Prix monster, to its chain final drive and artillery wheels with detachable rims (Rudge-Whitworths were tried on it, apparently to the considerable detriment of its handling qualities). Its engine (150 × 200 mm, 14137 cc) was in effect a pseudo bi-bloc, in that the cylinders were in two pairs, but with a common cylinder head, containing the Bugatti-type valvegear. This had already been raced successfully, at Savannah in 1911. The entries from the only other firm which had contested the first Grands Prix, Lorraine-Dietrich, were similarly old-fashioned 15·1 litre cars, although in common with the Fiats they did have ohc engines.

The Belgian Excelsior, with the only six-cylinder engine in the race, a 9·1 litre unit, had similar outward lines, and while the Rolland-Pilain entries looked less archaic they had chain drive, in common only with the Fiats and Lorraine-Dietrichs.

Thus four makes contributed a dozen cars in the Grand Prix class. The Coupe de l'Auto cars were a similarly fascinating mixture. The French entry was larger, as inhibiting misgivings about the agreement to abstain from Grand Prix racing did not apply, and the British challenge was substantial in potential as well as in numbers. Official practice periods, in which Boillot improved significantly on the Dieppe lap record, were an innovation at this Grand Prix. On the other hand, the ACF reverted to the tradition of a very long and testing race, requiring drivers to cover 956 miles on two consecutive days, and starting the first car at 5.30 am. First away was Rigal (Sunbeam), and he was followed at 30-second intervals by five other Coupe cars before the first Grand Prix contender, Hémery (Lorraine) was released.

Hémery led on the road at the end of the first lap, while on time Bruce-Brown (Fiat) led Boillot's Peugeot by 82 seconds and Hémery by 102 seconds. Honours were thus fairly even, and as the morning warmed up the old order appeared to be gaining the upper hand. Mishaps put the Peugeots of Goux and Zuccarelli out of the race, and at one stage Bruce-Brown and Wagner held first and second places for Fiat. At the end of the first day Bruce-Brown led Boillot by just over two minutes, but Wagner, third, had fallen well behind. Fourth and fifth were the Sunbeams of Resta and Rigal, while Hancock (Vauxhall) was sixth.

Rain on the second day handicapped the big-car drivers, particularly those of the short-wheelbase Fiats. Because Boillot stopped at the Peugeot pit immediately after the restart, Bruce-Brown initially extended his lead. Then the French driver began to reel in the American, and took a conclusive lead when the fuel tank of the Fiat was holed. Bruce-Brown took on fuel away from the pits, knowingly courting the

disqualification which inevitably followed. In his only major European race he had proved the brilliant reputation gained in America; later in the year he was killed in an accident during practice for the Milwaukee 200.

Georges Boillot kept the Peugeot securely in the lead, despite 20 minutes spent on the circuit with gearbox troubles, to win at 68·45 mph from Louis Wagner in the surviving Fiat. Two other Grand Prix cars finished, the Excelsior and a Rolland-Pilain, sixth and seventh, hopelessly far behind the intervening Coupe cars – if further evidence were needed, this really emphasized that the big-car era had passed. Those first three Coupe places were filled by British cars, Sunbeams driven by Rigal, Resta and Médinger – a brilliant triumph for Coatalen's cars which as a 1–2–3, let alone a British 1–2–3, was without precedent in a major road race. The times for the first six cars add perspective, particularly those for Wagner and Rigal:

1. Boillot (7·6 litre Peugeot), 13 hours 58 min 02·6 sec, 68·45 mph
2. Wagner (14·1 litre Fiat) 14:11:08·4
3. Rigal (3 litre Sunbeam) 14:38:36·0, 65·29 mph
4. Resta (3 litre Sunbeam) 14:39:51·8
5. Médinger (3 litre Sunbeam) 15:59:41·4
6. Christiaens (9·1 litre Excelsior) 16:23:38·8

The enfeebled Targa Florio, run as a 651-mile Giro di Sicilia is worth a passing mention, as for the first time it was won by a foreign driver, Cyril Snipe, who averaged 26·4 mph in a SCAT. At Le Mans a small-

beer GP de France cum Coupe de la Sarthe provided a walkover for Jules Goux' GP Peugeot at 73·01 mph. And that, effectively, was the 1912 European season.

The American Grand Prize, diminished in stature to an American national event, was run at Milwaukee and won by Caleb Bragg (FIAT) at 68·40 mph. Ralph de Palma had won the Vanderbilt Cup on the same circuit with a 1908 GP Mercedes (at 68·98 mph) – the Monsters were still alive in America.

In 1913 the French Grand Prix was in a 'twixt and 'tween stage. It was shorter (580 miles), and run over a shorter (19·65 mile) circuit at Amiens, which included one leg with a series of varyingly tight corners; it was run at a weekend, in rather belated recognition that spectators are important to a motor race (although the scheduled start time was 5 am!); retrogressively, fuel consumption and weight limitations were imposed, which allowed 20 litres of fuel per 100 km (approximating to 14·12 mpg) and admitted cars weighing between 800 kg (1763 lb) and 1100 kg (2425 lb). As if the outcome of the 1912 race had not been enough, this effectively ruled out the old-style GP cars. Intrinsically, it also produced some interestingly varied answers to the fuel consumption restrictions.

The only marque which had contested the first Grand Prix to enter in 1913 was Itala. Their designer plumped for lightly-stressed engines, with an rpm maximum of only 1400; these units were the largest in the race, at 7853 cc (125 × 160 mm), and had rotary

The 7·6 litre Grand Prix cars built by Peugeot in 1912 marked the watershed between the Edwardian monsters and the racing machines of the next two decades. This somewhat over-restored example is equally historic in specific detail, for it was driven to victory in the 1913 Indianapolis 500 by Jules Goux, the first European driver/car combination to win the American classic.

valves in their four cylinders. That the cars got to the race was something of an achievement – because of industrial troubles in Italy they were completed in England, and during unofficial trials at Dieppe, Bigio, an Itala director, and nominated race driver, was killed in an accident. Germany contributed two ineffectual cars, a 5 litre Opel and a 2·2 litre Mathis, Belgium two six-cylinder 6·1 litre Excelsiors, and Britain four Sunbeams, of which great things were expected after their 1912 performance. These were rather humdrum in make up, with six-cylinder versions of the 1912 side-valve engines (80 × 150 mm, 4523 cc) giving a claimed 110 bhp; these were the fastest-revving engines in the race, their maximum of 2600 rpm equating with 108 mph down the long straight leg of the circuit.

Peugeot returned to defend their 1912 title, with a trio of cars closely following the Dieppe cars in mechanical make up, with 5654 cc (100 × 180 mm) engines. A collision with a farm cart in Britanny cost Peugeot the life of Paul Zuccarelli; much of the inspiration behind the twin ohc engine had been his, and his death was an enormous blow to the team; all the subsequent products of Henry's drawing board were the poorer for the loss of Zuccarelli's testing and development skills.

Théodore Schneider, whose single 1912 Coupe de l'Auto entry had finished a creditable seventh overall in the Grand Prix, entered four V-nosed cars with four cylinder engines of similar capacity (96 × 190 mm), and Delage, long-time voiturette contenders, entered the Grand Prix lists with a pair of distinctively bull-nosed cars, with horizontal valve engines (105 × 180 mm, 6234 cc). Practice was largely concerned with the minutiae of fuel consumption tests, before the official ration was carefully issued. Fog – or thick early-morning mist – delayed the start for half an hour, then the cars were started away at minute intervals. Most got away rather anaemically, for the chill damp atmosphere coupled with economy-setting weak mixtures made for hesitant engines. Curiously, the first three at the end of the first lap were to be the first three at the end – Boillot and his Peugeot team mate Goux, followed by Jean Chassagne, mechanic to Rigal in the 1912 Grand Prix and now taking his place in a Sunbeam. An Itala and the third Peugeot were missing, and Moriondo rolled his Itala at the end of the lap; with the help of his riding mechanic, Giulio Foresti, another driver in the making, he righted the car and carried on.

Boillot slowed with minor troubles, Chassagne held second place for two laps, and by half-distance Albert Guyot led the race in a Delage. He lost the lead, perhaps the race, through one of those singular incidents which punctuate Grand Prix history. He ran over his own mechanic. As Guyot slowed to stop after a tyre failure that poor witling, one Semos, misjudged the speed of the car, jumped out and fell under a rear wheel. So Guyot had to change the wheel single-handed, get Semos back to the pits and start racing again, to finish fifth.

Extrovert Georges Boillot revelled in becoming the first man to win successive Grands Prix in Europe and the hero of France. His winning speed was 72·12 mph, and at the end he led Goux by two and a quarter minutes, third man Chassagne by twelve and a quarter minutes. Bablot put in the fastest lap in the second Delage (76·72 mph), and finished fourth. No Italas completed the distance, and the marque disappeared from Grand Prix history. For the first time, more than half the starters (11 of 20) finished a Grand Prix.

The Grand Prix de France at Le Mans might have been a return match, had the Peugeot entry not been withdrawn. In the main this left Delage to race against some of the Amiens also-rans, some relics (including a

Below: Dario Resta before the start of the 1916 Indianapolis 500, which he won at 84 mph. His 4·5 litre Peugeot bears the unmistakeable Henry stamp, although it is outwardly neater than its 1913 counterpart. Right: race fields appeared similar before and after the first world war, although in fact a great deal had changed. In this 1920 Indianapolis line-up were several cars with eight-cylinder engines, and for the first time since 1912 the race fell to an American car (Gaston Chevrolet's Monroe, Number 4 on the inside of the second row).

Richard-Brasier, reputedly the car which Théry drove to win the last Gordon Bennett) and the Pilette Mercedes. Théodore Pilette, Mercedes' Belgian agent, had attempted to enter for the Grand Prix itself, but was turned down by the ACF, abiding by its own rules, which admitted only direct entries by manufacturers. His quasi-works cars at Le Mans were an odd trio, and at least in part the object of the exercise seems to have been to race versions of the 75/80 aircraft engine introduced in the previous year. Two had 8·7 litre four-cylinder engines, the third a 12·5 litre 'six', which apparently shook the chassis to such an extent as to make steering difficult. All were sohc units, with paired cylinders enclosed by welded steel water jackets. Their chain drive was anachronistic (it was in fact the last appearance of chains in the transmission of GP cars), although not out of keeping with their chassis, which reputedly were of the 1908 GP type. A privately entered Mercedes chassis was undisputably of 1908 vintage, this having a Knight sleeve-valve engine. The Pilette cars gave the Delages quite a race, and at the end 15 minutes covered the first five cars: Bablot (Delage) at 76·5 mph, Guyot (Delage), Pilette (Mercedes), Salzer (Mercedes) and Duray (Delage).

The other major race of 1913 had been the Indianapolis 500 earlier in the year. Leading Europeans entered the 500 for the first time, notably Peugeot, with 1912 engines linered down within the 450 cu in capacity limit to 7·4 litres (for which 162 bhp at 2250 rpm was claimed, although Faroux reported that at Indianapolis Goux did not exceed 1700 rpm, equating this with 125 bhp). Pilette entered a Knight-engined Mercedes, and there was a private Brooklands Sunbeam for Guyot. Three Isottas reached Indianapolis only three days before the race, for their com-

pletion had been delayed by the same strikes which had afflicted the Itala Grand Prix team, and in the case of Isotta meant the use of hastily bought-out parts (including fuel tanks, of which two split in the race). Only one of the American entries was a European car, Mulford's Mercedes. The Peugeots started favourites, but Zuccarelli's fell out with failed engine bearings after only 18 laps, and Goux was headed in the early stages. A Mason held a tenuous early lead, then Goux got into his stride and was past. But not, as expected, away, for Bob Burman took the lead from him and tenaciously kept his Keeton in front for 80 miles. A carburetter fire cost him an hour, however, and left Gil Anderson to challenge for the lead in a Stutz, and twice get it in front.

The good Jules, however, was driving a well-paced race, fortified at his pit stops with champagne – from the prolific quotes which he scattered to the American Press on the virtues of this beverage, one almost gains the impression of an early false dawn to the age of outside sponsorship in racing. With 150 miles to go, he led by two-and-a-half laps, and he ran out the first single-handed winner of the 500, by 13 minutes and at 75·92 mph. A Mercer shared by Wishart and de Palma was second, Merz placed a Stutz third (covering the last lap with an underbonnet fire), Guyot finished fourth in the Sunbeam after an up-and-down-the-lap-chart race, while Pilette unobtrusively climbed through the second half of the race to finish fifth in the Mercedes-Knight.

Jules Goux was of course the first European to win the 500, Peugeot the first European manufacturer. America was surprised, politely complimentary, and patriotically gratified that American cars had made a fight of it. But this was only the beginning of the first European invasion of the Brickyard . . .

Edwardian Climax

Grand Prix racing crossed a watershed in 1914, in a Grand Prix de l'Automobile Club de France which was at once the climax to an age in motor racing and the prologue to a new era. In the sporting calendar this French Grand Prix followed the Indianapolis 500, but as the American event was to have a continuing story until 1916, chronological arrangement can conveniently be set aside.

For their Grand Prix the ACF imposed only two straightforward restrictions, on weight (1100 kg, 2425 lb, 'dry') and for the first time on engine capacity, which was limited to 4·5 litres. The circuit chosen proved to be one of the finest in Grand Prix history, made up of 23·38 miles of very varied roads near Lyon, calculated to test the qualities of men and machines to the full. It was hilly, had tortuous winding stretches and a galloping straight of some six miles – a circuit where road holding, brakes and engine flexibility were prerequisites.

The entry complemented the circuit, the 37 starters representing 13 manufacturers. Four three-car French teams were entered, Alda, Delage, Peugeot and Schneider; Germany was represented by Mercedes (five cars) and Opel (three cars), Italy by an Aquila-Italiana, three Fiats and three Nazzaros, Britain by three Sunbeams and three Vauxhalls, Belgium by a pair of Nagants and Switzerland by a pair of Piccard-Pictets. Four more Italian cars failed to come to the start, two Aquila-Italianas and two Caesars, while another interesting Italian machine, admittedly not a Lyon entry, was not completed at this time. This was the first ALFA Grand Prix car (its construction just predated Nicola Romeo's takeover, and the establishment of Alfa Romeo). Perhaps none of the Italians were too worried, as an Italian Grand Prix to the same regulations had been proposed for the Autumn of 1914 . . .

While the probable winner could be expected to come from one of four teams, the others were not at Lyon merely to fill the grid, as there were interesting technical aspects. All the engines save Mercedes were monobloc units, all save the sleeve-valve Piccard-Pictets had overhead camshafts, and Delage, Nagant, Peugeot, Sunbeam and Vauxhall had twin-ohc fours, all save the Aquila, the Fiats and the Pic-Pics had four valves per cylinder.

All the cars had shaft drive, and most used four-speed gearboxes. Chassis were generally slender, suspension on most was by four semi-elliptic leaf springs (Alda and Aquila had cantilever springs at the rear) and detachable wire wheels were universal. Quite new to Grand Prix racing, however, were front wheel brakes, used by Delage, Fiat, Peugeot and Piccard-Pictet. On the Italian cars the front and rear brakes operated in unison, whereas on the other three they worked independently.

Body styles varied. Most constructors were content to present square noses to the airstream, and most to square off at the other end with spare wheels traditionally across tails. However, Alda, Mercedes and Nazzaro had partly-streamlined noses, while Fiat and Peugeot had faired tails.

Approaches to the race also varied. The German teams were systematic and thorough, their cars were ready well in advance, and they reconnoitered the circuit metre by metre. Italian and British teams were ready last, particularly Nazzaro and Vauxhall. This was unfortunate as the Vauxhalls were potentially the fastest cars at Lyon, although their chassis did not match up to their high-revving engines. Delage and Peugeot were also curiously unready, apparently through over-confidence. Their star drivers, Guyot and Duray, Boillot and Goux, returned from Indianapolis only just in time to take part in the meagre practice periods grudgingly allowed at the last moment. Had the Peugeots been fully tested, shortcomings might have been found and corrected, notably the adverse effect on handling (and thus on tyre wear)

of the spare wheels carried 'fore and aft' in their tails. But was not the combination of Boillot and Peugeot invincible?

Felice Nazzaro, the first Grand Prix winner to build Grand Prix cars bearing his own name, got his cars to the scrutineers late, while Aquila-Italiana got only one of their three entries to the circuit. Fiat had a curious problem. As originally built their engines were marginally oversize, a fact spotted by the ACF representative who verified the cars in Turin. This gave rise to the legend that they were permitted to race only on the tacit understanding that if one should finish in the first three it would be disqualified! In fact

*Principal contenders in the 'Greatest Grand Prix', the 1914 Lyon race, Mercedes (opposite and below) and Peugeot (above) Paul Daimler's generally clean, but mechanically conservative, 4·5 litre 115 bhp Mercedes scored the first 1-2-3 victory in Grand Prix history (the car above has been repainted with the racing number of Christian Lautenschlager's winning car).
Georges Boillot drove a heroic race against the might of Mercedes; he led for much of the distance, but his Peugeot eventually succumbed to his merciless driving.*

due compensation was made for the slight offset of the crankshaft which was responsible for the slight excess in swept volume. The real contest in this 468-mile race was between Mercedes, Peugeot, Delage and Sunbeam, the order at the end of the first lap. The only other make to get a look in among the top half dozen runners for most of the race was a Fiat (Fagnano's) while right at the end his fall to last place let Dragutin Esser place a Nagant sixth in the final listings. Cars were started in pairs, and the ACF relaxed its masochism so far as to send the first off at a reasonably civilized hour, 8 am.

Sailer set the early pace in a Mercedes, starting two minutes after Boillot and passing him on the road during the third lap. This demonstrated the simple fact about the 1914 French Grand Prix which is usually lost behind a verbal smoke screen of theories about Machiavellian German tactics and so on – the Mercedes in the hands of an unknown was faster round the Lyon circuit than a Peugeot driven by the great Boillot.

Sailer's run ended after six laps, with engine failure. Boillot led again, but not comfortably as the 1908 winner, Lautenschlager, was harrying him in another Mercedes. At half-distance, Boillot still led, from Lautenschlager, Goux (Peugeot), Wagner (Mercedes), Salzer (Mercedes) and Sunbeam drivers Resta and Chassagne. The Vauxhalls had all retired, as had two of the Nazzaros, two Fiats and sundry also-rans.

Boillot flogged the Peugeot mercilessly, but was unable to shake off the Mercedes, with Wagner for a time ahead of Lautenschlager. However, through the last quarter of the race Lautenschlager piled on the pressure, and with two laps to go held a conclusive lead. On the last lap Boillot stopped on the circuit, primarily because of a valve failure in his engine, which apparently was in any case near to total seizure. To make defeat totally humiliating for France, in the late stages Goux fell back and Bablot and Guyot retired their Delages.

At the end of seven hours' gruelling racing, Mercedes scored the first 1–2–3 victory in Grand Prix history. Christian Lautenschlager won at 65·66 mph, by one and a half minutes from Wagner and five from Salzer. Goux finished his Peugeot fourth, Resta his Sunbeam fifth, 20 minutes behind the winner. The other finishers were completely outrun: Esser (Nagant), Rigal (Peugeot), Duray (Delage), Champoiseau (Schneider), Jörns (Opel) and Fagnano (Fiat) – 11 cars out of 37 starters.

This was the epic climax to the Edwardian era in racing. Mercedes' victory was not due to a grand strategic plan, but to meticulous preparation and the methodical application of experience. Yet, perhaps inevitably, recollections of the race centre on the human story of Georges Boillot's great virtuoso

drive, against mechanical odds which were too great. Tragically, he was to die in the war which broke out little more than a month after the 'Greatest Grand Prix'.

Racing in Europe abruptly stopped, but the contest between the principal European marques was continued on the other side of the Atlantic. The 1914 Indianapolis 500 was in some respects a carry-over from the 1913 European season, a triumph for France, and a crushing blow for America. Thirty cars started, thirteen ran the 500 miles; the finishing order read Delage, Peugeot, Delage, Peugeot, Stutz, Excelsior, Sunbeam, Beaver, Maxwell, Duesenberg – the first American car fifth, only four in the first ten, 'in the money'.

Christiaens led initially in an Excelsior, a car which had made little impression in Europe, before giving way to Goux, who in turn was passed by René Thomas. He held his Delage in the lead at the 100-mile mark, lost over a lap, and six places, changing tyres, but was back in the lead at 200 miles. Between 100 and

200 miles, Mercers driven by Wishart and Bragg briefly led, but this American showing was little more than illusory, as Guyot (Delage) and Duray (Peugeot) soon took matters in hand.

Thereafter Thomas dominated the race, running out the winner at the record speed of 82·47 mph. Guyot was third in the second of the 1913 Grand Prix Delages. Second was the 1913 Coupe de *l'Auto* Peugeot owned by Meunier and driven by Duray. This 3-litre car was by far the smallest in the race – contemporary reporters were hypnotised by the performance of the little 183 cu in machine, and rightly so, for Duray's 80·99 mph average would have been good enough to win any of the preceding 500s. The 1913 Grand Prix Peugeot drivers had a less happy race, continually troubled with tyre failures; Goux fought on to finish fourth, but Boillot was put out when a rear tyre burst. To patriotic applause, the flamboyant Barney Oldfield finished fifth in a Stutz at 78·14 mph.

Little noticed, a Bugatti appeared in a major race (the 1911 affair at Le Mans hardly qualifies for that description). This was a 5·6 litre 'Black Bess', driven by Friderich; he retired after 350 unobtrusive miles with transmission failure.

In 1915 the Mercedes-Peugeot duel was resumed at Indianapolis, under the 300 cu in capacity regulations. For the first time the race was postponed because of rain, for a week. Dario Resta (Peugeot) and Ralph de Palma (Mercedes) started as equal favourites, the former having convincingly won both the Vanderbilt and Grand Prize races earlier in the year, while de Palma put in the fastest Indianapolis qualifying lap at 98·6 mph.

The well-organized Stutz team made a three-cornered race of it, Wilcox and Anderson both leading in the early stages. This apart, the race was between de Palma and Resta, with luck playing a substantial

hand–a tyre failure cost Resta time, and towards the end the Peugeot's steering became increasingly erratic; de Palma limped the last lap with a failing engine. De Palma's winning margin was 3 minutes 32 seconds, and his speed of 89·84 mph improved substantially on the 1914 record. Anderson and Cooper took third and fourth places for Stutz, O'Donnell was fifth in a Duesenberg, and Burman sixth in a 1913 Grand Prix Peugeot.

Only one of the three Sunbeams finished, a 1914 Grand Prix car placed tenth despite pit stops costing an hour, by Noel van Raalte (incidentally, the first British driver to feature at the Brickyard). The Bugatti lasted only 21 laps in 1915; although it had the only 300 cu in engine in the race it was never in contention, appearing sadly deficient in power (the first two cars both had 274 cu in engines). The most original car was the 2-litre Cornelian driven by Louis Chevrolet; this had independent suspension all round and a sheet metal chassis–almost a forerunner of the monocoque! Its little engine swallowed a valve after 77 laps.

Most of the Peugeots built in the preceding years seemed to be racing in America in the years before that country entered the war, together with near replicas built by Premier. Other American companies, even Duesenberg and Stutz, turned to the European cars for more than inspiration (Stutz engines were almost Mercedes-Peugeot hybrids, and the origins of famous Duesenberg racing power units

can be traced back to the Peugeot Grand Prix engine).

In racing this was the period of proliferating tracks and board tracks. Dario Resta was the most successful driver, and as de Palma appeared only spasmodically with the Mercedes, his closest challengers drove Stutz and Sunbeams. The English company even produced some new cars for American racing, with twin-ohc six-cylinder 4·9 litre engines, while Fiat reworked their 1914 GP cars with an eye to competing in America in 1917.

The 1916 Indianapolis 500 was a lacklustre event, cut short at 300 miles, apparently by rain. Resta stroked his Peugeot to an easy win, at 84·05 mph, from d'Alene (Duesenberg), Mulford (Peugeot), Christiaens (Sunbeam) and Oldfield (Delage).

Racing ended in the twilight of the first American road racing era, with the Vanderbilt Cup and Grand Prize at Santa Monica in California. Resta won the first at 86·98 mph from Cooper (Stutz) and Wightman (Duesenberg), and a Peugeot driven by Wilcox and Aitken won the Grand Prize, at 85·89 mph over 400 miles. Save for isolated events in the twenties and thirties, those were the last ranking road races in the USA until the booming revival of the late forties, after a second world war.

BETWEEN THE WARS

Revival

The war ended in Autumn 1918, and motor racing began again in the following year.

The first major race to be run was the 1919 Indianapolis 500, resuming where it left off under the 300 cu in (4·9 litre) regulations. The list of leading finishers also suggests continuity with the 1916 race, but there was much that was new – the Chevrolets' Frontenacs, the Packard V-12, the Duesenberg and Ballot straight-eights.

These last were undoubtedly the most significant. Both owed something to Ettore Bugatti's war-time aircraft engine of this configuration and its 16-cylinder 'twin-eight' derivative – just how much tends to be a subject for polemics. However, the basic links are clear: through the Baras company in Paris, Duesenberg acquired the US manufacturing rights to Bugatti's aircraft engine (although apparently these were not exercised in the metal), and at the end of the war Baras' technical director, Ernest Henry of Peugeot fame, was invited by Ernest Ballot to design

racing cars for the house of Ballot (whose principal interest was in marine engines, hence the anchor motif in the Ballot car badge).

The Duesenberg engine was a 76 × 133 mm single ohc unit, the Ballot a 74 × 140 mm twin ohc unit. Claimed power outputs were 92 bhp at 3800 rpm and 140 bhp at 3000 rpm respectively, a difference which was surprisingly wide but probably not wildly inaccurate, for it was reflected in performances at Indianapolis. Both were mounted in conventional chassis, the Duesenberg's carrying handsome bodywork ending in a tapered tail. However, the whole Ballot closely resembled pre-war Peugeots. Apart from the common hand of Henry, this was hardly surprising, for Ernest Ballot conceived the idea of

Old and new lines. Above, the Mercedes which Max Sailer drove into second place in the 1921 Targa Florio shows clearly its pre-war origins, while the Fiat 801 Grand Prix car, at Brescia for the first Italian Grand Prix, with Pietro Bordino at the wheel, points very clearly to the new decade.

building a team of markedly superior racing cars on Christmas Eve 1918, and on April 26 1919 the four Ballots left Le Havre for Indianapolis. There was therefore scant time for departures in chassis design, Henry concentrating on his new power unit.

This famous 101 day miracle failed to bear full fruit, largely because at the Brickyard the rear axle ratio was found to be too high – in a neglect of detail perhaps hardly surprising in view of their extremely tight schedule, the team had no spare ratios. The smaller American wheels and tyres which they were therefore forced to use let them down, when the Ballots had been demonstrably proved the fastest cars on the track. Of their formidable quartet of drivers, Thomas, Guyot, Wagner and Bablot, only the first two finished, fourth (nearly fifteen minutes behind the winner) and tenth, forty minutes down.

Ironically, the winning car was one of Henry's 1914 Peugeots, albeit considerably revamped, which Howard Wilcox drove into the lead at 270 miles and kept there to the end (winning speed 87·95 mph). Second was Eddie Hearne, driving a Durant Special (in fact a Stutz, reputedly Anderson's 1915 car), third Goux in a 1914 Peugeot with 'Premier-Peugeot' engine.

The first half of the race had been dominated by de Palma in the Packard, challenged by Cooper's Stutz, Boyer's Frontenac and Bablot's Ballot. Of these, only de Palma finished 'in the money', sixth after long stops, for an exhaust valve and front wheel bearings to be replaced. Louis Chevrolet placed a Frontenac seventh, despite losing a wheel towards the end, and Gaston Chevrolet another ninth. Thomas set the fastest lap, 104·7 mph.

The only other classic race run in 1919 was the Targa Florio, at the end of November, when snow lay on the Madonie circuit. The first driver to start in this first

post-war race in Europe was one Enzo Ferrari, whose name was thereafter to run through the motor racing story, driving a CMN. Ernest Ballot was content to enter one Indianapolis car – assuming a duality of purpose unimaginable today! – for René Thomas. Fiat brought out a pair of their 1917-revised Lyon cars, with engines further reworked, for two rising stars, Antonio Ascari and Count Guilio Masetti. André Boillot, brother of the great Georges, drove one of the modified 1914 Coupe de l'Auto Peugeots entered. If the pairing of Boillot and Peugeot was largely evocative of the past, Giuseppe Campari and Alfa Romeo (specifically in the 1919 Targa a 1914 six-cylinder 40/60) foreshadowed a splendid future. Pre-war Grand Prix cars which started included an Aquila, and two Nazzaros from 1914 and two 1913 Italas.

New names. Enzo Ferrari at the wheel of his 1919 Targa Florio CMN (Costruzioni Meccaniche Nazionali) and, below, Jimmy Murphy winning the 1921 French Grand Prix in a Duesenberg.

This Targa proved to be André Boillot's one great race – he would otherwise have had to race on through the twenties forever in the shadow of his illustrious brother. He drove with inspired verve, set the fastest lap of the day from the start, crashed six times, and finished backwards, half way through a spin which ended against a grandstand. In nice final touches, Ernest Ballot advised him to drive back to the point where his spin had started as he over-braked to avoid spectators, to finish 'correctly'. Having done so, Boillot collapsed over the wheel, it is said with a cry of 'Pour la France!'.

Ballot's own entry was by then out of the race. Thomas had chased Boillot, perhaps not hard enough, until transmission failure put him out on the last lap. Boillot completed the 268 miles in 7 hours 51 minutes, at an average of 34·19 mph, finishing half an hour ahead of runner-up Moriondo in one of the Italas.

These two races poles apart in Indiana and Sicily were again the only major events in 1920, although two notable 'firsts' were recorded in secondary events– Giuseppe Campari won the Circuit of Mugello for Alfa Romeo at 37·7 mph, and Ernst Friderich scored

the first outright race victory for Bugatti, driving a Type 13 in the ACF Voiturette Grand Prix at Le Mans.

In 1920 the Indianapolis capacity limit was reduced to 183 cu in, 3 litres. Heading the European entry again were three Ballots, with in-line twin ohc eights of 65 × 112 mm, producing 107 bhp at 3800 rpm, and three Peugeots, the last front-line racing cars ever built by that famous old firm. Their 80 × 149 mm four-cylinder engines had *three* overhead camshafts, three inlet and two exhaust valves and two sparking plugs per cylinder, and produced 108 bhp at around 3800 rpm. A Grégoire team was of less consequence, for although 100 bhp was claimed for their 78 × 156 mm pushrod engines, their performance reflected the anti-quated outward appearance of the cars.

Front-line American cars ranged against them were the Duesenbergs, 'eights' closely following the 1919 machines, and the Chevrolet brothers' Van Ranst-designed Monroe-Frontenacs. The Ballots were again clearly the fastest cars on the track, again Ernest Ballot's perennial misfortune ('ma foisse') kept them out of the winner's circle. Joe Boyer led for most of the first 250 miles in a Frontenac, harried and occasionally

Ballot's famous 101-day miracle, the 1919 5 litre straight eight designed by Ernest Henry for the Indianapolis 500, where the car showed speed – Wagner raised the lap record to 104·7 mph – but was let down by a detail.

passed by Ralph de Palma and René Thomas, both driving Ballots. De Palma pulled out an apparently conclusive lead in the second part, but with only 50 miles to go one of the two magnetos of the Ballot failed, and he stuttered on to finish fifth. Neither of the other Ballot drivers were placed to challenge the ultimate leader, Gaston Chevrolet, for Thomas had been delayed at the pits, as had Jean Chassagne who had hit the wall when a Frontenac driver just ahead of him suffered the common Monroe-Frontenac complaint, steering failure.

So an American drove an American car to win the 500 for the first time since 1912, at 88·16 mph, by a convincing margin from Thomas. Tommy Milton and Eddie Murphy placed Duesenbergs third and fourth. This then was the beginning of the end of the first European era at Indianapolis; the next victory for a European car did not come until 1939, and the next for a European driver until 1965.

The Targa Florio, run in appalling weather, was won by G. Meregalli, who thus gained a classic race victory for the marque Nazzaro, from an Alfa Romeo driven by Enzo Ferrari.

In 1921 the French Grand Prix was revived, and a second European national Grand Prix was inaugurated, the Italian. Both were run to the 3-litre formula in common with Indianapolis 500, although a minimum weight of 800 kg (1763 lb) was also stipulated for the European races.

Most of the starters in the American classic had eight-cylinder engines, and the race proved to be the high water mark for the Chevrolet's Frontenacs. Almost as a matter of course, Ralph de Palma was the charger, but fated to finish with no better reward than the largest share of lap prizes. He broke his own half-distance record, then a connecting rod failed in his Ballot and Tommy Milton, driving a Frontenac in place of Gaston Chevrolet, who had been killed earlier racing in California, was left to win at an easier pace (89·62 mph, a little slower than de Palma in 1916). Second was Roscoe Sarles (Duesenberg), followed by Jule Ellingboe and Percy Ford (Frontenac), Jimmy Murphy (Duesenberg) and Ora Haibe in the only European car to finish, a Sunbeam.

For their Grand Prix, the Automobile Club de France returned to Le Mans, to the 10·726-mile

Circuit de la Sarthe, later to become familiar as the venue of the 24-hour race. The roads were supposedly resurfaced for the event, but in fact were atrociously cut up. The entry, too, appeared to be breaking up as the July date for the resumption of Grand Prix racing approached. The Fiat team was scratched, then the seven-car Sunbeam-Talbot-Darracq teams (three Talbot-Darracqs, two Talbots, two Sunbeams, all identical under their slightly varied bodies and different badges). However, Louis Coatalen and the STD directors relented under pressure, mainly from drivers, and re-entered the Talbot-Darracqs and Talbots, although they were far from raceworthy. The four Ballots were more or less raceworthy, although one of these eight-cylinder cars was damaged in a practice accident and a four-cylinder 2-litre car substituted. The only other European car was also a 'four', a 1·5 litre Mathis entered in no more than the hope that it would demonstrate its reliability, a faint hope at that, as it was barely completed in time.

The best-prepared team was a last-minute entry under the auspices of Albert Champion, an American of French origins whose name became famous for sparking plugs, and whose company's involvement in Grand Prix racing continues, and Earl Twining, manager of Champion (USA). Fred Duesenberg brought to Le Mans the first American team to contest a European classic at least on level terms with the Europeans. The car was a road racing version of the track Duesenbergs, with a single ohc engine giving 115 bhp at 4250 rpm, a three-speed gearbox and two novelties, one trivial, one important – it had left-hand drive, and it was the first Grand Prix car to have hydraulic brakes. In these the fluid, water and glycerine, was passed through the front axle to the front brakes.

The Rudge Whitworth wheels had detachable safety side pieces on the rims,

The only other technical departure in the race was the use of cast aluminium blocks in the STD cars, with steel liners, and alloy pistons. These Ballot-inspired units produced some 110 bhp at 4000 rpm.

Cars were started in pairs at half-minute intervals, and at the end of the first lap de Palma (Ballot) and Boyer (Duesenberg) were level on time. A logical order was established on the road during lap 2 – Murphy (Duesenberg), Boyer, Chassagne (Ballot), de Palma and then Boillot in the first STD car, a Talbot-Darracq.

However, the STD cars were also-rans, victims of ill-preparedness and tyre failures. The roads cut up so badly as to appear to consist simply of loose stones through some stretches (which led Joe Boyer to a much-quoted comment that the race was 'a damn' rock-hewing contest'). Segrave, who brought his Talbot home ninth and last, changed 14 wheels!

The race for the lead was between Duesenberg and Ballot, until just after half-distance when Jimmy Murphy began to build up a secure lead in his American car. His eventual victory was historic, the first for an American driver in a European Grand Prix, the only win for a wholly American car. His winning speed was 78·10 mph, and his winning margin over de Palma a decisive fifteen minutes. Goux placed the little four-cylinder Ballot third, and André Dubonnet, who had reputedly paid a stiff premium for his

The early 1920s were a golden age in the history of the Targa Florio. These 1921 photographs show Giuseppe Campari leaving the start in one of the big Alfa Romeos, still without the luxury of front-wheel brakes (below) and Giulio Masetti driving the winning Fiat, which was derived from the 1914 Grand Prix car (opposite).

Duesenberg seat after losing his STD ride, was fourth.

In September the first Italian Grand Prix was run over a 10·5 mile circuit on Montichiara Heath, outside Brescia. The entry comprised only six cars, Ballots for de Palma, Chassagne and Goux, and three 802 Fiats, for Wagner, Sivocci and Bordino, one-time mechanic to Lancia and de Palma. These Fornaca-designed cars outwardly followed their Fiat predecessor, being notably 'clean', while their engines were probably the most powerful of the 3-litre formula, giving some 120 bhp at 4600 rpm. Their eight cylinders (65 × 112 mm) were in two forged blocks of four, and followed the Mercedes example in having welded-on water jackets. Twin overhead camshafts operated two very large valves in each cylinder.

Pietro Bordino, later to become the idol of Italy, led the first 13 laps of the race, and set a lap record at 96·3 mph before retiring with a broken oil pipe. Wagner temporarily took over, but had to make repeated stops for tyres and finished only third behind the Ballots driven by Goux (89·94 mph) and Chassagne, to the displeasure of the partisan crowd.

The Grand Prix capacity limit was reduced to 2 litres for 1922, but two more 3-litre races were run in that year, in the Isle of Man and at Indianapolis. The Tourist Trophy was a small-beer affair, won by Chassagne (Sunbeam) at 55·78 mph. Although a similar 2 litre (122 cu in) capacity limit was to come into force at Indianapolis in 1923, European and US racing were going their separate road and track ways. Such European cars which ran at Indianapolis after 1922 were largely ineffectual – Mercedes eighth and eleventh and one Bugatti of five starters ninth in 1923, for example – while only occasionally were American cars raced in front-line European events.

At Indianapolis in 1922 Jimmy Murphy won in a 'Murphy Special', his 1921 Duesenberg with a Miller straight eight, at 94·48 mph, from Hartz' Duesenberg and Hearne's Ballot, while six of the next seven places were filled by Duesenbergs. Goux' Ballot and Wilcox' Peugeot fell out in the early stages, and a Bentley circulated slowly.

Meanwhile, the *formule libre* Targa Florio had seen the return of Germany to racing in 1921 (German entries were unacceptable for some time in several countries which had been at war with her). Germany, moreover, represented by Mercedes; Max Sailer pitted this car against a pair of works Fiats (Minoia and Bordino) and Alfa Romeos (Ascari, Campari, Ferrari and Sivocci), as well as 31 apparently lesser Italian fry. In fact, the winner came from among these, Masetti winning at 36·19 mph in a fairly aged 'GP-cum-Indianapolis' Fiat. Sailer finished only just over a minute behind Masetti, and the next three places were filled by Alfa Romeos driven by Campari, Sivocci and Ferrari, 3½ minutes covering the three.

Mercedes returned to Sicily in force in 1922, with six cars and an army of technicians, and marked their return in the grand manner with the re-introduction of forced induction to racing car engines. Two of their cars were substantially reworked 4·9 litre 'Lyon' cars, with four wheel brakes and engines with *inter alia* modified valves and magnesium alloy pistons, which revved to 5000 rpm (for Lautenschlager and Salzer); two were blown six-cylinder 28/95s (for Sailer and Werner) and two were 1·5 litre supercharged fours (for Minoia and Scheef). Against these were ranged four Fiats (a 3 litre eight for Bagio Nazzaro, nephew of the great Felice, two twin ohc 1·5 litre fours for Giaccone and Borghese, and fourth a normal 1·5 litre 10/15 for Lampiano), two 2-litre twin ohc Ballot fours (for Goux and Foresti) and amongst the Alfa Romeos, 4·5 litre cars for Ascari, Campari, Ferrari and Sivocci again. Interest was maintained in the lesser entry, Steyrs, Diattos, Ceiranos and an Austro-Daimler, driven by young Alfred Neubauer.

The finishing order, however, once again reflected the Madonie brilliance of Guilio Masetti, who drove his private 1914 GP Mercedes to win at 39·2 mph. It also reflected the almost customary bad luck of Ballot, for whom Jules Goux was a potential winner until the last lap, when he was forced to slow by worn brakes and tyres (he finished 1 min 47 sec behind Masetti, with team mate Foresti third). It also demonstrated that Mercedes might is not necessarily right, or that Mercedes come-backs are not always triumphant, for Sailer was the best-placed finisher in one of the works cars, sixth behind Ascari's big Alfa and Giaccone's small Fiat. Other Mercedes were 8th (Werner), 10th (Lautenschlager), 13th (Salzer) and 20th (Scheef), while the other Alfa *prominente* were 9th (Sivocci), 11th (Campari) and 16th (Ferrari). Otto Hieronymus, who had raced in the early city-to-city events, placed a Steyr 7th, and Neubauer finished 19th. The results illustrated yet again the motor racing truism, that on a difficult circuit driving skill and style can count for more than power, and science.

Golden Period

Under the 2-litre Formula Grand Prix racing entered a golden age, of technical development, of brilliant fields, of exciting racing – of change. Apart from the capacity limit, the rules simply required that cars be two-seaters, weighing not less than 650 kg (1433 lb).

Its first race was the 1922 French Grand Prix, run over a new circuit at Strasbourg. This was a simple 8·3 mile triangle of roads, with two long near-straight legs. Cars of six makes came to the circuit, and for what was to be their last Grand Prix only Ballot failed to produce a new design. Their four-cylinder cars were basically similar to those raced in the 1921 by Goux and in the 1922 Targa Florio, but with singularly unattractive 'barrel' bodies. For his first Grand Prix, Bugatti entered similarly-clothed cars, but with eight-cylinder (60 × 88 mm) single ohc three-valve engines, for which 86 bhp at 4000 rpm was claimed. This Type 30 featured a 'mixed' braking system, hydraulic at the front, mechanical at the rear, and the classic Bugatti reversed quarter elliptic rear suspension and wheelbase/track proportions of 2:1 (240 × 120 cm).

The third French team was Rolland-Pilain, returning to the Grand Prix after 10 years with theoretically advanced cars, which were unsuccessful in practice. Designer Grillot's monobloc engine was basically an aluminium casting, with bore and stroke of 59·2 × 90 mm. Grillot had made some progress with experimental desmodromic valvegear (i.e., mechanically, and thus positively, operated, valvegear) but the cars were raced with normal large valves operated by twin overhead camshafts. Drivers of these attractive

Classic. The Bugatti Type 35 and its derivatives – this is a supercharged example, some three years younger than the original T35 – are of the outstanding Grand Prix shape to come down from the 1920s. These cars had the definitive horseshoe radiator, and Bugatti's unique light alloy wheels, with flat spokes and integral brake drums.

modern cars were three veterans – Guyot, Hémery and Wagner (who never settled long with a team during his long career).

Britain contributed two teams, Sunbeam and Aston Martin. Designed by Ernest Henry, the Sunbeams had twin ohc 16-valve four cylinder engines (68 × 136 mm), which produced some 85 bhp at 4250 rpm, and apart from the distinctions of being Henry's last complete design and the last front-line GP cars with four-cylinder engines to appear for some time, were quite straightforward. The 1·5 litre Aston Martins were fours, too, and Henry had a hand in their design, for they owed much to the 1·5 litre Talbot-Darracq voiturettes of 1921 (and their existence owed much to the patronage of Zborowski, who was to drive one of the pair entered).

The only other team came from south of the Alps, to dominate the event from first practice to the end of the race. The Fiat 804 appeared a thoroughbred in every line, with a compact and handsome body. The Fiat design team, headed by Fornaca and Cavalli, and including Cappa, Becchia, Bertarione and Jano, had eschewed the contemporary eight-cylinder trend, and produced a 'six', which closely followed the 801 eight in mechanical detail. This 65 × 100 mm bibloc engine revved to 5000 rpm, at which speed it produced 112 bhp, although as raced at Strasbourg it gave 95 bhp at 4500 rpm – quite sufficient, it transpired. Fiat drivers were Felice Nazzaro, his nephew Biagio Nazzaro, standing in for the original nominee, Wagner, and Pietro Bordino.

This event introduced the mass start to Grand Prix

racing, and the luck of the ballot for places put Felice Nazzaro on the front row of the grid. The Indianapolis example was followed in a rolling start, at about 20 mph on a soaking wet track. Initially, Friderich kept his Bugatti in touch with the leaders, but the Fiats soon began to run away from the field and by the tenth lap (of sixty) were comfortably holding the first three places. At half-distance the fourth man, Ballot driver Foresti, was almost 10 minutes behind the leading driver, Felice Nazzaro, and five behind Biagio Nazzaro in third place. Most of the field behind them had retired, all the Rolland-Pilains, all the Sunbeams, both Aston Martins. Very soon both of the Ballots which had survived to half-distance also retired, leaving the Fiats and a pair of hopelessly outclassed Bugattis, straggling far behind.

The Italian team appeared to be heading for an overwhelming triumph, but in the closing stages tragedy struck. The rear axle of Biagio Nazzaro's 804 failed, it lost a wheel at maximum speed, and he was killed as the car turned over and over and hit a tree. With less than two laps to go to the end, Pietro Bordino's Fiat threw a wheel, and he retired. After the race it was found that the axle casings of all the Fiats were faulty; two fractured, one lasted the race distance, and the veteran Felice Nazzaro – surprisingly youthful in appearance – ran out the winner at 79·33 mph, 58 minutes ahead of runner-up de Vizcaya (Bugatti), and an hour and a half ahead of Marco's Bugatti, the only other car to complete the distance while yet another Bugatti was flagged off!

The Italian Grand Prix was run at the new Monza autodrome. Like Brooklands and Indianapolis, this was built remarkably quickly; unlike the British track it was sensibly conceived within the ethos of European motor racing, incorporating both a high-speed track and a road circuit. The ceremonial first spits were dug by Felice Nazzaro and Vincenzo Lancia in March 1922; spurred on by Antonio Mercanti and Milan Automobile Club president Silvio Crespi, the contractors completed the work for the Grand Prix to be run on September 10. The 150000 spectators at that first Monza meeting enjoyed a demonstration of Fiat superiority, but the anticipation of this denied them good motor racing, for the original entry for this Grand Prix simply melted away after the Strasbourg race.

The opposition to the three 804s came from a single Bugatti (three more were withdrawn because their gear ratios proved incorrect, and Bugatti could lay hands on only one set of spare wheels, borrowing them from Fiat!), two utterly outclassed German Heims, and a pair of Diattos. Through these the name Maserati enters the Grand Prix story, for although there was some Bugatti influence lurking in the background, the principal designer of the Diattos was Alfieri Maserati,

who also drove one in the race. Their twin ohc four-cylinder engines (79·7 × 100 mm) produced a modest 75 bhp at 4500 rpm, which was hopelessly inadequate in the face of the Fiats, now developed to produce their 112 bhp.

The race was the fiasco the field suggested it would be. Giaccone's Fiat clutch failed on the line, but the other two team cars galloped away. Maserati crashed, the other Diatto and the Heims retired, and the Bugatti was flagged off, still with over 50 miles to go to complete the race distance. Pietro Bordino won at 86·90 mph, two laps ahead of his team mate Nazzaro.

Major technical advances came in 1923, a supercharged Grand Prix engine and a rear-engined Grand Prix car. Generally, there was agreement on the format of engines, the classic twin ohc type, but a cuff-valve unit was tried (Rolland-Pilain gave up their desmodromic experiments, leaving it to Salmson to prove that theory in small-car racing), and a V-12 appeared with four camshafts. Odd essays in streamlined bodywork appeared, and even the forerunner of a monocoque chassis. Most of these were seen in the French Grand Prix, at Tours.

Here Fiat sprung their surprise, with a team of 805s which were driven over the Alps to the circuit. In this car Fornaca, Cavalli and Zerbi reverted to eight

cylinders (67 × 84 mm), and added a supercharger. At Tours this was a Wittig low-pressure vane-type device driven from the nose of the crankshaft, permanently engaged for racing, and passing its compressed air through the carburetter. Claimed power output was 130 bhp at 5500 rpm, which meant that Fiat had again stolen a considerable power advance on their opponents.

Lee Sherman Chadwick (whose parents' loyalties must have been divided between Confederacy and Union!) had produced supercharged engines in 1908, with some success although they were not immediately followed up. Sizaire and Birkigt both toyed with the idea of supercharged automotive engines, but the supercharger was really proved on aircraft engines in the first world war, and in a direct line of evolvement from these Mercedes re-introduced forced induction to motor racing, using Roots-type devices (which owed their name to Francis and Philander Roots of Indiana, who had taken out their first supercharger-cum-pump design patent in 1859; in one of those odd full circles of history, the first race apart from the Targa Florio where Roots-supercharged Mercedes ran was the 1923 '500', in Indiana).

First among Fiat's opponents at Tours – if only because of their relationship to Fiats and the result

The Ballot and Bugatti entries for the 1922 French Grand Prix at Strasbourg had very similar 'barrel' bodies, and both incorporated many production components. However, the Ballots (above, Goux' car during a pit stop) had four-cylinder engines, while the T30 Bugattis (below, Friderich's car being weighed in) had straight eights.

of the race, were the Sunbeams, the famous 'Fiats in green paint'. While these were not replicas of the 1922 Type 804, resemblances could not be denied – Coatalen had simply persuaded one of the design team responsible for that car, Vincent Bertarione, to design a new GP Sunbeam. The result was a competent car, with a 67 × 94 mm six-cylinder engine, producing just over 100 bhp at 5000 rpm.

Fiat and Sunbeam were the only foreign teams; France produced an interestingly varied assortment of cars. The Type 30 Bugattis are still recalled as 'tanks'; Bugatti used his 1922 straight eight engine, but clothed it in an all-enveloping body, and rounded the odd ensemble off by combining a wheelbase of 78 in with a track of 40 in, which did not make for good roadholding. Man of many parts, aircraft constructor turned motor manufacturer Gabriel Voisin entered a team of cars which outwardly appeared to make more aerodynamic sense, although the complete machines did not make a lot of sense in other Grand Prix respects. These were built almost in a fit of pique after a disagreement with the ACF about Voisin's entries for a touring car race, and incorporated many C-4 production model components – an odd way to enter Grand Prix racing in the face of the incumbent professionals. These cars had six-cylinder (62 × 100 mm) Knight-type sleeve-valve engines, semi-mono-coque bodies enveloping the rear wheels, and quaint track dimensions, 57 in front, 30 in rear.

There was little that was odd about the single Delage, although it was a novel and most advanced new machine. It was hardly ready to race at Tours, for Planchon completed his design work only four months before the race. His complex 60-degree twin ohc V-12 (51·4 × 80 mm, 1992 cc) was a very real Grand Prix departure, and in time was to be proved a sound one.

Finally, the Tours 'home team', Rolland-Pilain, produced two improved 1922 eights, and a car powered by a six-cylinder cuff-valve engine, designed by Dr Albert Schmid and developed by Ernest Henry, appearing for the last time in the Grand Prix story. This was reputed to run up to 6000 rpm, but its efficacy was not to be proved or disproved in this French Grand Prix as it expired during practice.

In the opening stages the Fiats dominated the race, Pietro Bordino leading and setting the fastest lap at 88·05 mph. Only Kenelm Lee Guinness (Sunbeam) and Albert Guyot interrupted the Fiat procession during the first few laps, but at the end of lap 8 the Englishman led – the first English driver, and the first English car, ever to lead a Grand Prix. Bordino crept in to retire, his supercharger ruined by road debris.

Guinness' lead did not last long, as his clutch began to slip; thus he was passed by the faster cars, although at half-distance he was keeping ahead of the surviving Bugatti and the Voisins. Giaccone had taken over the

lead for Fiat, until his unshielded supercharger began to fail, when Salamano went in front with the only Fiat running healthily at half-distance. His race ended, like the other Fiat drivers, with a failed carburetter.

The last race leader was, therefore, Henry Segrave, who scored a memorable victory for Sunbeam. His race speed for the difficult 496 miles was 75·30 mph, and Sunbeam team-mate Albert Divo was second despite a jammed fuel-filler cap, which meant that he had to refuel every lap.

In effect, the fastest cars at Tours were defeated by a trifling design fault, which Fiat corrected by substituting Roots-type superchargers in the 805. But this in no way detracts from Sunbeam's triumph, after years of persistence, and with cars which were fast and reliable. The only other finishers were a Bugatti, third, Guinness' Sunbeam, fourth after restarting with great difficulty on the last lap, and a Voisin, one and a quarter hours behind the winning Sunbeam.

Between the two major European races, two minor Spanish events were noteworthy for different reasons: the very short, steeply-banked, and short-lived Sitges track was opened near Barcelona, and among the drivers was one Tazio Nuvolari at the wheel of a Chiribiri, and Rolland-Pilains finished first and second in the first San Sebastian Grand Prix, Guyot averaging 58·1 mph for the 277 mile race.

Above: a Ballot, rather more portly and distinguishable by the anchor badge within the nose intake, and a Bugatti racing wheel to wheel past the mile-long grandstand erected at Strasbourg for just one race, the 1922 French GP. Neither marque was distinguished in this race, nor was Ernest Henry's Sunbeam Grand Prix car (below, wearing a splash board over the right front wheel to shield the driver from some of the road mud).

The Italian GP was the first Grand Prix de l'Europe, a grand but empty title devised to avoid a clash of dates, offered to the Italians provided they ran their race in September. Sunbeam did not contest the race, but of course Fiat entered, together with Rolland-Pilain and Voisin. The entry was made up with novelty and new names.

One of the oldest teams in motoring produced a team of cars at least a decade ahead of the rest of the field in conception. The Benz *tropfenrennwagenen*, 'tear drops' from their clean aerodynamic shape, had rear-mounted engines, gearbox behind the cockpit, and independent suspension all round, by swing axles at the rear, with inboard brakes. Their twin-ohc engines (65×100 mm) were not, however, supercharged. Like the Voisin, this completely new type of Grand Prix car was largely the work of an aeronautical engineer, Dr Rumpler; decades were to pass before the two sciences – some might prefer arts – of aircraft and racing car design and construction were to come so close again. Benz drivers at Monza were the veteran Minoia and two Germans, Walb, later to become racing director of Auto Union, and Horner.

First of the new names was Alfa Romeo, at last entering the Grand Prix lists, with the P1. Merosi's design was quite straightforward, with an unsupercharged twin ohc engine, which produced a modest 80 bhp at 4800 rpm.

Harry Miller is a racing name to conjure with, especially in the engine field. At Indianapolis, his straight eight had powered Murphy's winning Duesenberg in 1922, Milton's HCS Special in 1923, and most of the other leading American contenders in that first major race to be contested by a significant number of single-seaters. The three Millers which appeared at Monza were adapted for their new role only in the addition of front-wheel brakes, retaining their track-type three-speed gearboxes – not such a great handicap on the fast Monza circuit. The Miller straight-eights, twin-ohc 32-valve 58.7×88.9 mm units, with eight carburetters, were probably the most efficient engines at Monza, producing 120 bhp at 5500 rpm. Miller drivers were a mixed trio, Jimmy Murphy, Count Zborowski and the Argentinian Alzaga.

Tragedy struck both Italian teams in practice. Bordino crashed when a stub axle on his Fiat failed; Giaccone, riding with him in the mechanic's seat, was killed, and Bordino's arm injuries meant that he had to drive the Grand Prix with his mechanic changing gear for him. The Alfa Romeo team was withdrawn after Ugo Sivocci crashed fatally, and the P1 was never raced. Pietro Bordino led from the start, set the fastest lap at 99.8 mph, held the lead despite pit stops extended for attention to his arm, but retired exhausted after keeping his car on the track literally single-handed after a tyre failed. Felice Nazzaro,

standing in for Giaccone, took over the lead, but was delayed when an oil pipe broke, and lost the race to his team mate Salamano on the last lap. Salamano's winning speed was 91.08 mph, and his winning margin less than half a minute. Jimmy Murphy, the only other driver ever in the hunt, placed his Miller third; the other finishers were two of the Benz, Minioa and Horner, and Alzaga's Miller.

If 1923 was the season for novelties, 1924 was the high noon of the decade on the circuits. The season started as usual in Sicily, where the *formule libre* Targa Florio attracted a fascinatingly varied field. This was in contrast to the 1923 Targa, which had been devoid of interest. The first six drivers all improved on the 1923 winner's time, and the final placings show the variety of machinery engaged (although not the drama and incidents, such as Goux' and Boillot's off-road excursions, in 3-litre Ballot and Peugeot respectively, and Ascari's engine failure with the line in sight). In

this race, Werner gained the first post-war all-German victory in a leading event, driving a 2-litre supercharged 'Indianapolis' Mercedes, at 41·02 mph (team mates Lautenschlager and Neubauer were 10th and 15th); runner-up Masetti drove an Alfa Romeo RL 'Targa special', with 3·6 litre (80 × 120 mm) seven-bearing crankshaft 128 bhp engine; Bordino was third in a 1·5 litre supercharged Fiat, and passed out as he took the flag, so that for the additional Madonie lap which completed the concurrent Coppa Florio the car was driven by Nazzaro; then came Campari's 3-litre Alfa, Boillot's 3-litre Peugeot and a most unlikely Targa contender, Dubonnet's 4·5 litre Hispano-Suiza, which had an elegant but bulky tulip-wood body, and Rützler's Steyr.

Indianapolis was important as the 1924 500 was the first to be won by a supercharged car, and marked the return of Duesenberg. Their cars had duralumin chassis, and centrifugally supercharged straight eights.

These blowers ran at eight times engine speed, at over 40000 rpm, and more than any other single piece of mechanism widened the gap between track and road racing, for the effective engine rev range possible with this type of supercharger was very narrow, which meant that it was of real practical value only in track racing. Coram and Boyer duly won in a Duesenberg at 98·24 mph, narrowly beating Cooper's Studebaker.

A secondary event at Cremona was significant for the pre-French Grand Prix trial outing of the Alfa Romeo P2, the first racing car to come from the drawing board of Vittorio Jano, who had been induced to leave Fiat by Nicola Romeo and Enzo

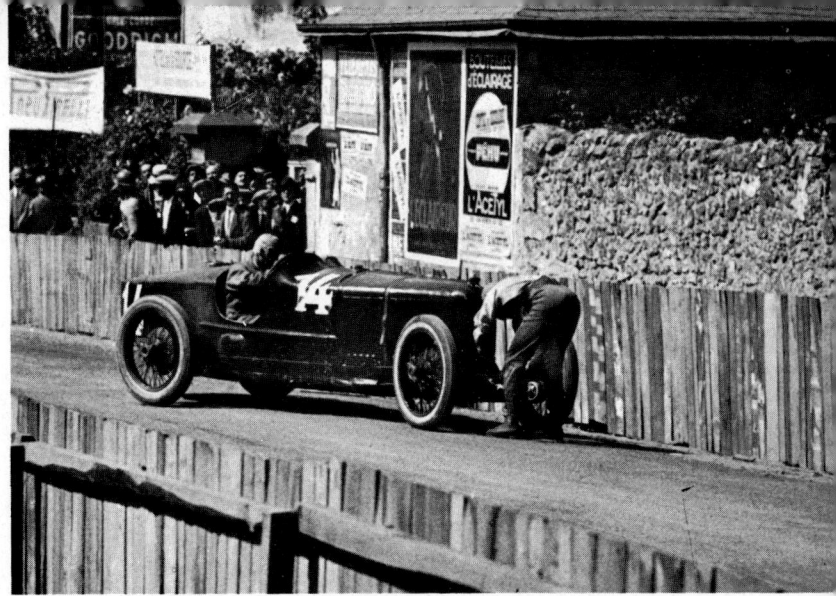

The 1923 French Grand Prix at Tours was contested by widely varying cars. On the facing page, top: three of the four Voisins drawn up before the start; far left, centre and bottom: two of the Sunbeams, Guinness' and Divo's during pit stops; left, centre: Giaccone's mechanic working on the engine of their Fiat, and, bottom, Friderich's T30 'tank' Bugatti. On this page, top: Salamano's mechanic attempting to restart the engine of their Fiat 804 on the circuit; centre, Giaccone standing by his retired car as Friderich races past; below, Guyot's Rolland-Pilain.

Ferrari. His P2, which replaced the P1, showed strong Fiat influences. He abandoned his work on super-charging the P1 six, for no more than 118 bhp at 5000 rpm could be extracted from it. The Roots-supercharged P2 straight-eight (61 × 85 mm) on the other hand produced 135 bhp at 5500 rpm for its first appearances at Cremona and Lyon. The car lacked the fine lines of some of its contemporaries, although its blunt nose and balloon type tyres were distinctive.

In its first race at Cremona, Ascari drove the new car to a convincing win, averaging 83·37 mph over the 117 miles, and lapping at 100·8 mph. Alfieri Maserati's Diatto was a poor second in this race.

The French Grand Prix was the finest race of the season, at least as deserving of the title the Greatest Grand Prix as the 1914 event. The race was run over part of the magnificent 1914 Lyon circuit, shortened to 14·38 miles by using a rather rough secondary road as a linking leg.

Following pages: Vauxhall built promising GP cars in 1914 and 1922, but the first were hopelessly inadequately developed for the 1914 Grand Prix, while the 1922 car was built to a formula which had expired in the previous year. Their racing was therefore confined to British events; in the late 1920s Raymond Mays and Amherst Villiers developed one of them into this potent Vauxhall-Villiers sprint special.

The final firm entry was 22 cars, half of them super-charged. Sunbeam returned to defend their 1923 honours with three cars, improved versions of the Tours sixes; these were supercharged, with Roots-type instruments for the first time on a Grand Prix car compressing mixture from the carburetter. In this form the engine produced 138 bhp at 5500 rpm. Drivers were Segrave, Guinness and Resta. The other supercharged cars came from Italy. The Fiat 805s had been improved in detail, and their engines now produced 145 bhp at 5500 rpm, and they were joined by the Alfa Romeo P2s, which were to be driven by Ascari, Campari, Wagner and Ferrari (who was however taken ill before the race, and returned to Italy).

In retrospect the P2 was perhaps the most important car at Lyon, as the first of a line of pace-setting Alfa Romeos. But less rationally, the race is usually recalled for the debut of the Bugatti Type 35, an outstandingly attractive Grand Prix car, but one which was seldom competitive so long as other front-line teams were in contention. However, a period was approaching when there would be no works teams in GP racing, and the T35 fully deserves its place in history simply for being an amenable Grand Prix car available to private owners.

This most elegant of GP cars had the Bugatti eight-cylinder sohc engine (in 2 litre form, 60 × 88 mm), producing an uncompetitive 105 bhp at 5200 rpm. Nothing if not a showman, Ettore Bugatti arrived at Lyon with an elaborate equipe, and five cars in exhibition trim for Chassagne, Costantini, de Vizcaya, Friderich and Garnier.

Albert Lory had taken over responsibility for the V-12 Delage, tried supercharging the engine but for the moment put this amendment on one side, to con-

centrate on making the basic unit raceworthy (success-fully, for the Delage team was the only one to finish the race intact). Two cars with Dr Schmid's cuff-valve engine appeared (Rolland-Pilains rebuilt and re-named Schmids), but only Goux' came to the start as

One of the meticulously built Millers which contested the European Grand Prix at Monza in 1923 (opposite, top, and below). The Alfa Romeo P1 (below left, with Antonio Ascari at the wheel), was withdrawn before the race, but Benz returned to the Grand Prix scene with the revolutionary Tropfenrennwagen *(above, Minioa being overhauled by two of the victorious Fiat 805s at Monza).*

Foresti damaged the other in a practice incident. Lastly, there was Zborowski's Miller, the first private entry ever to be accepted for the French Grand Prix.

From the rolling start, Segrave drew away from the field, Ascari, Guinness, Campari and the fiery Bordino following. Bordino fought his way through to second and then inherited the lead after three laps, when Segrave made the first of several pit stops. Altogether he was to lose 27 minutes at the pits, largely in changing plugs in attempts to cure misfiring, which was afterwards traced to faulty new magnetos installed just before the race. His team mate Guinness briefly led during the first half, and was second at half-distance, but retired when a main bearing failed. So Sunbeam were left with the poor consolation of a demonstration that when healthy their cars were competitive with the best French and Italian machines, and a fastest race lap of 76·25 mph, set by Segrave.

The half-distance leader was Campari, while of the other early leaders, Bordino was out with brake failure, and Ascari was fourth. In the second half the Alfas dominated, the lead switching between Campari and Ascari, with Divo and Benoist keeping their Delages never far behind. With a lap to go, the block of Ascari's engine failed, and the race inevitably fell to the burly Giuseppe Campari, at 70·97 mph. Divo

A mediocre car and a classic. Porsche's straight-eight Mercedes (above) made its debut in 1924, but gained few race victories and an accident-prone reputation. Jano's P2 on the other hand was one of the great cars of the decade, and firmly established Alfa Romeo as a leading Grand Prix marque.

finished only 65 seconds down, after 503 miles, and Benoist was third, ahead of Wagner's Alfa, Segrave's Sunbeam, Thomas' Delage and the Bugattis of Chassagne and Friderich.

As in the previous year there was no return round.

The San Sebastian Grand Prix, to all intents and purposes the Spanish Grand Prix, was contested by Sunbeam, Delage, Bugatti, Mercedes, Diatto and Schmid. Masetti led in one of the Mercedes, until he slid off the greasy road, leaving Segrave to win quite clearly for Sunbeam (at 64·12 mph), despite a stop beside Guinness' crashed car.

Fiat withdrew their Italian Grand Prix entry. The significance of this was not immediately recognized, but apart from an isolated effort in a secondary race in 1927, it meant that the Lyon race was the last major event to be contested by Fiat GP cars. Among the reasons for this, and the one most frequently publicized, was Agnelli's displeasure at seeing Fiat designer after Fiat designer lured away, to design racing cars which were clearly Fiat-inspired, which too often beat those produced by the old Piedmontese firm itself.

So Alfa Romeo became the pre-eminent Italian company in racing, a position which it was to maintain until 1951. To challenge the P2s at Monza, Mercedes entered four new cars, while two Schmids and two 1·5 litre Chiribiri made up the field. The Porsche-designed Mercedes had straight-eight engines (61·7 × 82·8 mm), with permanently engaged Roots super-chargers compressing the mixture from the car-buretter. These 160 bhp (at 6000 rpm) units were, however, inflexible, and mounted in inadequate chassis, which made for dubious road-holding. Caracciola later raced them effectively, by virtue of his skills, rather than any merit in the car.

The similar, but often overlooked, ability of Masetti meant that alone of Mercedes drivers he for a while was able to challenge the Alfa drivers at Monza. But when his team mate Count Louis Zborowski was killed in an accident at the Lesmo corner, the Mercedes were withdrawn and the Alfas raced on to a 1-2-3-4 victory, Ascari heading the procession at 98·76 mph.

In the last year of the 2-litre Formula, 1925, fields were smaller and no new Grand Prix cars appeared. The formula was amended, so that although two seaters were still raced (minimum body width 80 cm, $31\frac{1}{4}$ in), only the drivers' seats need be occupied, and cars in effect became offset single seaters. Existing cars were improved in detail, the Alfa P2 engines to give 170 bhp, the Sunbeam units 150 bhp, and the remarkable Delage V-12 with two Roots-type superchargers 190 bhp at 7000 rpm. Bugatti still eschewed super-charging, and his drivers could only hope that superior road-holding and braking would go some way toward

offsetting their considerable power handicap.

The next big event was at Indianapolis, where all the cars were supercharged, and Peter de Paolo, driving a Duesenberg, was the first 500 winner to exceed 100 mph (101·13 mph). A front-wheel drive Miller ('Junior 8 Special') driven by Lewis and Hill was second, and the Schafer/Morton Duesenberg placed third also averaged more than 100 mph. Millers gained five more places in the first ten, and tenth was a monoposto Fiat 805, shared by Bordino and Mourre.

A third Grand Prix was run in Europe in 1925, the Belgian race on the classic Spa circuit. The race was far from classic, Ascari leading from start to finish (winning speed 74·46 mph). The only other finisher was Campari; the third Alfa, driven by Brilli Peri, retired, as did all three cars of the only other team entered, Delage.

Bugatti and Sunbeam joined in at Montlhéry, where the French GP was run for the first time (the

Opposite: Fiat was the outstanding marque of the early twenties (above, Felice Nazzaro waiting to start in the 1922 Italian Grand Prix, the first to be run at the Monza autodrome). Successors to their crown were Delage and Alfa Romeo, represented on the front row of the grid for the 1925 Belgian Grand Prix by Robert Benoist's Delage V-12 and Giuseppe Campari's Alfa P2. By this time Peugeot's Grand Prix career was behind them, but their cars still competed to some effect in formule libre races, for example this car driven by Dauvergne in the 1925 Targa Florio.

This page: contrasts. The blunt-nosed 2-litre GP Mercedes and the aerodynamic 2-litre GP Benz (above), and (below) the Type 26 Maserati making its racing debut in the 1926 Targa Florio. The driver is Alfieri Maserati, his riding mechanic Guerino Bertocchi.

autodrome had been opened in 1924), over the longest distance of any GP since 1912, 621 miles. Once again Ascari and Campari ran away from the field, but at just over quarter distance Ascari crashed fatally in a long gentle left hand corner, when the left front hub of his P2 caught in the pale fencing lining the corner. The other Alfas were withdrawn as a mark of respect, leaving the race to a Delage shared by Divo and

French brilliance. Amilcars set high standards in voiturette racing with their supercharged 1100 cc 'sixes', which were far removed from the corresponding small-class cars raced in the early 1920s. Bugatti was the first constructor to produce Grand Prix cars for sale (and for use in several classes). This car (right) is the T37 'economy' derivative of the T35, with four-cylinder engine and conventional wire-spoke wheels.

Benoist, ahead of the Wagner/Torchy sister car, Masetti's Sunbeam and five Bugatti also-rans.

The Italian Grand Prix was the final event to count for the new manufacturers' World Championship (which was to last only two years). Once again Americans came to Europe to contest this race, Milton and Kreis with Duesenbergs with cockpits widened to comply with the regulations. As a third Duesenberg, for de Paolo, was not ready in time, he was offered and accepted the third Alfa Romeo entry. Guyot drove a sleeve-valve Guyot (for only a short distance in the race) while Materassi got a little further with a supercharged straight-eight Diatto, the immediate forerunner of the first Maserati. There were other runners on the track, mainly 1·5 litre (52 × 88 mm) Bugattis in the concurrent voiturette race.

Kreis led for three laps, then retired; Milton struggled on through most of the race with only top gear, in spite of this managing to close sufficiently on the Alfas to lead when they made their routine stops. Brilli Peri soon had a P2 back in front, where he kept it to the end (94·76 mph), finishing over 20 minutes ahead of Campari. Costantini actually placed one of the small Bugattis third, ahead of Milton and de Paolo, who lost a certain second when the exhaust fell off his P2 near the end.

The 2-litre Formula, which had seen so much brilliance, faded out with a lacklustre San Sebastian GP, where in the absence of real opposition once Masetti's Sunbeam had retired, Delage enjoyed an easy 1-2-3 (Divo, 76·40 mph, Benoist, Thomas), from a quartet of trailing Bugattis.

During the 2-litre period racing machinery had become remarkably sophisticated, especially racing engines. Power outputs in 1925 were roughly double those in 1922, engine speeds had increased considerably, 'exotic' fuels were in common use, the supercharger was almost universal, and in basic dimensions the long-stroke influence of Henry was receding. By comparison, chassis progress was slight. But racing had advanced enormously.

Secondary Racing in the Twenties

Throughout racing history progress in secondary classes has always exerted a considerable influence on the premier categories, on sporting policy and in the technical aspects. The original voiturette class as such had become a 3-litre class in 1912, and this in turn had become the second Grand Prix formula to be based on engine capacity, while in 1926 a 1·5 litre Grand Prix formula followed directly from the capacity regulations of voiturette racing in the first half of the twenties. Correspondingly, during the decade the concept of voiturettes changed, to the extent that it came to embrace engine capacities which in its first years would have been considered appropriate to cyclecars.

Economic conditions after the first world war had increased the European demand for small cars, and among these were many ultra-light and often rather questionable creations defined as 'cyclecars'. These usually spindly machines were not, of course, a post-war phenomenon, but they proliferated for a relatively

short period, in the rather peculiar conditions of the immediate post-war years until mass-produced 'real' small cars such as the Austin Seven became available. The cyclecar answer to the latent demand for cheap motoring had been essayed well before the war, when naturally cyclecar races had also been arranged.

These were often run at motorcycle meetings – the affinities between these two types of machine often being more obvious than those between cyclecars and cars. The usual cyclecar capacity limit was 1100 cc. Not all the machines in these early small car races were cyclecars, for small 'proper' cars such as Bébé Peugeots were run in them. But however flimsy the appearance of some of the devices, performances were not necessarily in proportion. In the 1910 Coupe

Extremes. The Frazer Nash cyclecar (above) in a British hill climb typifies the second-generation cyclecars raced after the first world war. The Sunbeam V-12 (below) was a remarkably adaptable and successful piece of heavyweight formule libre *and record-breaking machinery.*

Internationale des Cyclecars at Le Mans, Muraour averaged 46·3 mph over 170 miles in a Ronteix (which admittedly was one of the more substantial machines), while Bourbeau won the 160-mile 1913 Cyclecar Grand Prix at Amiens at 41·46 mph in a Bédélia, perhaps the best-recalled cyclecar of the period.

After the war two- and three-wheeled racing went its separate way, while cyclecars became part of the motoring scene, races for them often being run in conjunction with voiturette events. Very soon, too, a few of the most successful of these small machines, began to grow away from the cyclecar appearance. The dividing line between cyclecars and voiturettes was still at 1100 cc, although the 750 cc class was increasingly appropriate to the former.

Salmson was one of the cyclecar manufacturers to grow out of this class, where the company had started by building GNs under licence. The GN was the product of H. R. Godfrey and A. Frazer-Nash, with a V-twin 1087 cc engine; the GN company foundered in an attempt to move out of the cyclecar class, and Frazer-Nash later started a famous company under his own name. The Salmson company successfully made the transition, however, and their very light and advanced small cars became formidable contenders; among famous drivers who started their racing careers in Salmsons were Benoist, Biondetti, Borzacchini and Fagioli.

Small-car racing of consequence was resumed in Europe in 1920, most notably at Le Mans, where 21 machines started in the Coupe Internationale, run over a new circuit devised by Georges Durand in 1919, which was later to become famous as the venue of the 24-hour Race. The regulations stipulated a maximum capacity of 1400 cc, and weight limits were 350–500 kg. Seven cars finished, headed by Ernst Friderich, in a Bugatti T13, gaining the first race victory for that marque. The T13 had a single ohc 68 × 100 mm engine, which in 1921 gave 38 bhp at 3500 rpm. Friderich's winning speed at Le Mans was 57·6 mph over 257 miles, and the lap record was set by another T13 driver, Baccioli, at 65·87 mph. Bignans were second and third in the race, a Majola fourth.

A cyclecar grand prix run at the same meeting was actually the first car race run on this circuit. This was to the 1100 cc limit. The winner over 193 miles was two-stroke specialist Violet, who averaged 47·17 mph in a Major powered by one of his own twin-cylinder engines. Runner-up Lévêque drove a four-cylinder Ruby, a name more familiar for small engines, which were used by many light car manufacturers.

Bugatti produced the T22 derivative for 1921, with a single ohc 1453 cc engine for the new 1500 cc regulations. However, in that year it won only one front-rank victory, in the voiturette grand prix at Brescia (Friderich winning at 71·94 mph over 215 miles of that

The Grand Prix cars of the twenties were expected to be far more flexible than their one-purpose successors of later generations. One of the more successful cars of the decade was the V-12 Delage – above, Benoist at the pits during the 1926 Targa Florio. These cars were withdrawn from the race following Count Masetti's fatal crash.

very fast circuit, hence 'Brescia Bugatti') where the only real challengers were SBs (Silvani-Botta), as the side-valve OM was outclassed. The Bugattis in turn were outrun by the new Talbot-Darracqs, which were to enjoy two years of absolute supremacy, earning the sobriquet 'the Invincibles'. The four-cylinder engines of these cars had 65 × 112 mm dimensions, the same as Henry's STD Grand Prix eight, and were in effect half of that unit. Power output of this engine was 53 bhp at 4000 rpm. In 1923 Bertarione produced a successor, based on his Sunbeam GP engine, with two instead of four valves per cylinder, and dimensions 67 × 105 mm. This produced 70 bhp at 5000 rpm, and was then supercharged to give 100 bhp at the same engine speed. These STD cars scored 1-2-3 victories in the voiturette cup races at Le Mans in 1921 and 1922, and a 1-2 (there was no other finisher) in 1923. René Thomas won at 72·1 mph over 193 miles in 1921, while Guinness' winning average over 375 miles in 1922 was a tenth of a mile per hour faster. The Talbot-Darracqs also finished 1-2-3 in the first Junior Car Club 200 Miles at Brooklands in 1921 (Segrave winning at 88·82 mph), and won the race in 1922 and 1924-25.

The STD 'Invincibles' might have met their match in the Fiat 803, which also had a four-cylinder engine (to all intents and purposes half of their maker's 1921 GP eight). This initially gave 72 bhp at 5500 rpm, but in supercharged form in 1923 it at least matched the STD engine. In the voiturette race at the inaugural Monza meeting in 1922, the 803s scored a 1-2-3-4, Bordino winning the 373 mile event at 83·27 mph. But while the STD cars were fairly widely raced abroad, for example in the first 'ranking' Swiss race, the 1924

voiturette GP at Geneva (won by Guinness at 70 mph) and the Spanish Penya Rhin GP (which Guinness won at 65·3 mph in 1922), the Fiats were usually confined to Italy. When a pair were entered for the 1923 JCC 200, the STD cars were absent!

At least until Fiat retired from racing in 1924, there was little but the crumbs of minor placings for other teams when either of the two dominant marques was present. Alvis raced special versions of their 12/40 and 12/50 models, in 1923 using pushrod ohv engines (68 × 103 mm) which gave 53 bhp at 4400 rpm (C. M. Harvey drove an Alvis to victory in the 1923 JCC 200, at 93·29 mph). AC entered the class, using a single ohc 16-valve engine, which produced 55 bhp in unsupercharged form, but without significant success. The Aston Martin voiturettes have already been mentioned, as they contested the 1922 French GP; their Henry-influenced engines (with the familiar 65 × 112 mm engine dimensions!) developed 54 bhp at 4500 rpm, and were housed in bodies mildly old-fashioned even then; they were modestly successful.

There were numerous other British cars, which were hardly in the voiturette mainstream, although one or two appeared as Grand Prix cars under the 1·5 litre formula.

Apart from the Fiat 803, the only Italian voiturettes of note were built by Chiribiri, deep-bodied but shapely cars with twin ohc four cylinder engines (65 × 112 mm – again!), for which some 72 bhp at 5100 rpm was claimed in 1922. The appearance of these cars in Grands Prix has already been remarked, and in their class they were not without success (and, of course, were raced by the great Tazio Nuvolari early in his career).

In 1935 Bugatti produced a 1·5 litre (52 × 88 mm) T35 variant, but the story of Bugattis of this capacity is more properly part of the Grand Prix story from 1926. The 1·5 litre Mercedes were never raced in voiturette events, while the Austro-Daimler and Spanish Elizalde were not widely seen. Another Spanish car, the 1923 Ricart y Perez, with 16 valve four-cylinder twin camshaft engine giving 58 bhp

initially stripped sports cars or single seaters on the same chassis, with four-cylinder side-valve engines; this line culminated in the famous Jamieson-designed supercharged twin-ohc 'miniature Grand Prix cars' of 1936. French representatives in this class included the Ruby-engined Sénéchal, often driven by Robert Sénéchal himself, and the Sima-Violet two-strokes.

In effect, the 1100 cc class became the voiturette category when the 1·5 litre Grand Prix formula came into force in 1926. In 1100 cc racing French cars were outstanding, notably Amilcars and Salmsons. For 1926, Amilcar produced an extremely neat little car, powered by a supercharged twin ohc six cylinder engine (55 × 77 mm, 1097 cc). This machine eclipsed the Salmsons, and for some time dominated the class. The Salmson answer was a straight eight. This complex little jewel had its cylinders (50 × 70·8 mm) in two blocks of four, with a central gear train driving two Cozette superchargers, one on each side of the block. It also had the first effective desmodromic valvegear to be seen in racing. On the circuits, however, this Salmson was not outstandingly effective. Bugatti also produced three straight-eight 1100 cc cars, and overcame his reactionary instincts in supercharging their engines. Two of the cars had monoposto bodies, but they contested only one road race, the minor Alsace Grand Prix. Other French cars in the class included the Derby, with various proprietary engines, the BNC and the Lombard, an unusually low-built car with a Cozette-supercharged four-cylinder twin-ohc engine.

at 5600 rpm is of interest, as its designer was Wilfred Ricart, better known for his Alfa Romeos of the late thirties and his exotic Pegasos of the post-war period.

In parallel with the voiturette class, machines in the 750 cc and 1100 cc categories became more sophisticated, outgrowing their cyclecar origins. In the smaller class Austin Sevens were outstanding,

This Monza grid at the beginning of the thirties shows the variety of cars which contested the formule libre *events of the time, for it ranges from GP Talbots to a 7·1 litre Mercedes, and includes one of the early pace-setting cars of the decade, an Alfa Romeo 8C 'Monza'.*

The most complex of all 1100 cc cars was built by Itala, but never raced. This had a V-12 engine (45 × 55 mm), driving through the front wheels. Early in the 1930s the Maserati brothers built their first supercharged four-cylinder car, the first of a line which was to continue until 1951.

While the general popularity of motor racing continued to spread widely through the 1920s, the 1926–1927 1·5 litre Grand Prix formula was by no means universally popular, and in the remaining years of the decade there might as well not have been a formula. Consequently, there was a considerable increase in *formule libre* racing, which gave rise to some interesting cars. 'Specials' had always been part of the motor racing scene, especially at Brooklands, although many of these cars had been well outside the roadracing mainstream.

When the 1·5 litre formula lapsed at the end of 1927, a successor acceptable to even a minority of organizers and constructors could not be agreed, and many of the classics were run to *formule libre* rules, the French Grand Prix even for sports cars. In general this was

Bugatti's peak period and these cars, mainly T35 variants, are dealt with in chapter 10. Apart from the Bugattis, French cars included erstwhile Grand Prix Talbots and Delages, together with Delages dating from earlier in the decade, two 5-litre six-cylinder cars and the 10½ litre V-12, which briefly held the Land Speed Record in 1924, and had an outstanding track career. While Peugeot tended to concentrate on touring car racing after their withdrawal from the Grand Prix scene, their modified 4-litre cars had some success in 'free-for-all' racing.

The British counterpart of the Delage V-12 was the 4-litre V-12 Sunbeam (a pair were in fact built). This had a supercharged engine (67 × 94 mm, 3976 cc) giving almost 300 bhp at 5000 rpm, mounted in a chassis similar to those of the GP Sunbeams. They proved remarkably versatile machines, taking the Land Speed Record at 152·33 mph in 1926, racing competitively on the Continent (leading events as diverse as the Spanish GP and the Milan GP at Monza), and racing very successfully at Brooklands.

This track was a natural home for 'specials', such as the aero-engined Fiat (in a somewhat purer strain among the big Brooklands cars was Birkin's supercharged 4½ litre single-seater Bentley). Generally, hybrid cars on the lines of the big Fiat were hardly worthwhile in Italy, but two Italian cars which were fairly widely raced used power units derived from aircraft engines. These were an Itala special usually driven by its constructor, Emilio Materassi, which had a 4722 cc four-cylinder engine, in effect half of an Itala-built Hispano-Suiza engine, and an Isotta-Fraschini, powered by an Isotta-built Hispano engine, which was raced by Alfieri Maserati.

Apart from the big Alfa Romeos which ran in the Targa Florio, more obscure Italian cars in this very broad category included the 3-litre Ceirano CS4, the Diatto 20S, derived from a 2-litre production model, and four and eight cylinder twin ohc Bianchis, which were never fully developed.

Austro-Daimler's early post-war ambitions were frustrated for various reasons – their 1921 six-cylinder car (with 74 × 116 mm engine giving 109 bhp at 4500 rpm) was excluded for political reasons, while the 1922 90 bhp 2-litre cars were withdrawn after a fatal accident. Late in the decade, Austro-Daimler produced cars which were particularly coupled with the name of Hans Stuck in European hill-climbing; their 1928 overhead camshaft six produced 120 bhp, and was later enlarged to 3·6 litres to give some 200 bhp. These cars were also raced, but in this field were overshadowed by the big Mercedes Benz sports cars.

Several notable races were run to *formule libre* regulations during the two years of the 1·5 litre Grand Prix formula. The Targa Florio of course remained true to its great free for all tradition, and

The greatest rival to Amilcar in the 1100 cc class was Salmson, whose neat little cars became familiar throughout Europe, and beyond (the mechanic is securing the bonnet straps of Luigi Fagioli's Salmson on the old Tripoli circuit).

the 1926 field included works 12-cylinder 2 litre Delages and T35B Bugattis. The Delage team was however withdrawn after Count Giulio Masetti's fatal crash, which apparently resulted from a steering failure, leaving Costantini, Minioa and Goux to take the first three places for Bugatti. In 1927 Emilio Materassi won again from Bugatti (at 44·61 mph), from Conelli's Bugatti and Ernesto Maserati's Maserati.

Another classic was first run in 1926, the German Grand Prix at Avus, nominally for sports cars. It attracted a splendidly varied field of stripped sports cars, voiturettes (notably two 1925 Talbots), a 1·5 litre Grand Prix OM, and two of the notorious 1924 GP Mercedes. The race was run in heavy rain, and punctuated by accidents, to the Talbots driven by Chassagne and Urban-Emmerich, and to Rosenberger's Mercedes, which hit a timekeeper's hut and killed the three men on duty there (this accident naturally served to strengthen the 'killer' reputation of the 2-litre Mercedes). The Italian veteran Ferdinando Minoia led for a while in the Grand Prix OM, but at the end Rudolf Caracciola scored the first of his six German Grand Prix victories, at 83·95 mph in the second of the Mercedes.

In 1927 the race was run at the then-new Nürburgring, again nominally for sports cars, and dominated by the big 6·8 litre supercharged Mercedes-Benz. Otto Merz headed a 1-2-3 victory for these cars, at 63·38 mph over 316 miles, from Werner and Walb, while Mme Elizabeth Junek was fourth in a Bugatti.

The 1926 Spanish Grand Prix at San Sebastian was contested by 2·3 litre Bugattis, the erstwhile GP V-12 Delages and the Sunbeam V-12. Delages and the Sunbeam led, until mechanical troubles intervened, and Costantini brought a Bugatti through to win from Goux' Peugeot at 76·88 mph, which compares with the 70·53 mph achieved on the same circuit a week earlier by Goux in the 1·5 litre European Grand Prix.

There was a technical pause in Europe between 1927 and 1932, although engine development in particular continued for a while in the USA, where the 1·5 litre capacity limit was retained at Indianapolis until 1929, thus encouraging the development of superchargers. However in Europe racing continued to spread throughout the years of the Depression, although the machinery raced was often far from thoroughbred.

Towards a Decline

Concerned at the mounting speeds of 2-litre Grand Prix cars, the governing body of motor sport resorted to the easy 'corrective' for 1926 of further restricting the size of engines, to 1·5 litres, and increasing the minimum weight of cars to 700 kg (1322 lb). Most of the companies which had supported the 2-litre formula were expected to contest races under its successor, with the possible exceptions of Alfa Romeo and Fiat. Neither expectation was wholly fulfilled; although a sufficient number of cars were built, meagre fields were the rule; while Fiat did fleetingly appear, with an advanced car of apparently enormous potential. Generally, leadership in Grand Prix racing passed decisively from Italy to France. The years 1926–27 were crucial for motor racing. The number of races, and Grands Prix, increased, which meant that the status of the classic events was diminished, and the rewards for the successful firms were correspondingly reduced. So long as general motoring had been the privilege of the few, and there had been one great annual motor show and one or two great races a year, the manufacturers of cars which performed well in these events – not necessarily winning them – could be sure of an increase in sales. But the cost of constructing front-line cars continued to increase, and get increasingly out of proportion to the rewards. Prize money as such was still derisory, and starting money unheard of – on the contrary, entry fees were still the order of the day. The age of massive support from the component industries was still to come, as was the period of State backing for reasons of prestige.

So 1926 was a year of transformation. Alfa Romeo withdrew; the STD cars were Talbots and the Sunbeam designation was dropped (so therefore as far as the world was concerned was direct financing); Fiat experimented, and it was hoped that cars would actually materialize from the great Torinese firm; a string of other names were hopefully mentioned – Ballot, Mercedes, Rolland-Pilain; and so on. Rather

erratically, cars did appear, but as has often been remarked, no organizer managed to assemble on one grid all the leading cars. So Grand Prix racing entered a patchwork period, and the first race of the new formula was an absolute fiasco.

The Automobile Club de France neglected to include in their regulations for the 1926 French Grand Prix a routine clause to the effect that the race would not be run unless a certain number of entries was received. The symmetrical 5 km (2·1 mile) autodrome of Miramas was chosen as the venue, and three Bugattis appeared to contest the race!

Ettore Bugatti held several trump cards during this period, above all the relative simplicity and low cost of his Grand Prix cars. These were elegant, and the workmanship was of the highest order, even if the machinery was far from avant-garde. However, the 1·5 litre limit persuaded even Bugatti to turn to forced induction, using Roots-type Moglia superchargers on the 60 × 66 mm straight-eight of the T39, a derivative of the T35. One of these, driven by veteran Jules Goux, completed the 311-mile Miramas race at a modest 68·16 mph, quite unchallenged, for one of the other Bugattis failed to reach half-distance, while Costantini trundled his round very cautiously, to be flagged off after completing 85 of the 100 laps.

Although matters could hardly get worse, they were not much better at the next race, the European Grand Prix at San Sebastian. Here three Bugattis were joined by three of the new straight-eight Delages. These remarkable machines were the first evidence of technical progress under the new formula, and indeed,

The all-French combination of Robert Benoist and the straight-eight Delage won all four major Grands Prix in 1927 (above, in the French GP at Montlhéry). The late twenties were the peak years of the Bugatti, ranging from the 1·5 litre four-cylinder T37 (opposite, top) to the 2·3 litre supercharged T35B (right), which was the principal model used by the works team.

were the outstanding Grand Prix example (although, as will be seen later, much progress was made with Indianapolis cars to the parallel '91 inch' regulations). It was therefore the more unfortunate that in 1926 Lory's new cars were too frequently self-defeating, because of a minor fault in layout, rather than a flaw in their conception. The twin-ohc engine (55·8 × 76 mm) incorporated over 60 roller or ball bearings. In 1926 it produced some 160 bhp at 7500 rpm. It drove through a five-speed gearbox, and was installed in a chassis which had virtually no cross-bracing ahead of the cockpit and therefore flexed excessively. However, such road-holding deficiencies as resulted from this were not the principal fault of the 1926 edition of the car. The exhaust, on the right, passed too close to the cockpit, which led to serious overheating of cockpits and drivers.

At San Sebastian this problem was aggravated by the scorching sirocco conditions, and the cockpits of the Delages became unbearable after more than a few laps. So their race was punctuated by a series of pit stops for driver relief, and two of the cars were at one stage stationary for almost an hour! When running, they were demonstrably the fastest cars on the circuit, and despite all their troubles, one Delage, shared by Bourlier and Sénéchal, was classified second between the Bugattis of Goux and Costantini.

More cars appeared for the British Grand Prix, run over an artificial road circuit devised at Brooklands. The works Bugattis were not present (Campbell ran a private Bugatti), but the latest STD cars were. These were simply Talbots, designed by Bertarione and Becchia, and built in Paris. The supercharged twin-ohc eight-cylinder engine (56 × 75·5 mm) was a straight-forward Bertarione unit, which initially produced some 140 bhp at 6500 rpm. The whole car was really low, with the drive-line offset to the left and the driver

Sicilian scenes in 1926. Above: Albert Divo waiting to start his 2-litre ex-Grand Prix Delage in the Targa Florio, apparently surrendering to Vincenzo Florio, who created this classic event. Right: Emilio Materassi on his way to fourth place, driving a hybrid Itala.

sitting right down on the undertray. The chassis frame was very rigid, with single side members generously braced. Thus although the Talbots were at a power disadvantage compared with the Delage, there should have been compensation in the lower weight and frontal area, and in roadholding. In fact, these last STD Grand Prix cars were never developed to their full potential, and handling was certainly not all it should have been.

Also entered at Brooklands were three British cars, an Alvis, a Halford Special and an Aston Martin. The Alvis was an unconventional machine, with front-wheel drive and an eight-cylinder power unit ($55 \times 78 \cdot 75$ mm) in which the inlet and exhaust valves were horizontal, and operated by camshafts on either side of the engine. The British GP entry failed to come to the start, but later a pair started in the JCC 200 (both retired from this race). Frank Halford's car consisted of his own Roots-supercharged twin ohc six-cylinder engine (63 × 80 mm) and Aston Martin chassis and running gear.

In that first British Grand Prix, the Delage drivers suffered, took over from each other, and persevered, to be rewarded with first and third places (Sénéchal-Wagner, 71·61 mph, and Benoist-Dubonnet) sandwiching Campbell's Bugatti.

Intriguing Italian novelties had taken shape during the year, although nothing came of them on the circuits. First of these, in that a car was built (but not raced) was Guilio Cesare Cappa's front-wheel drive Itala. This was intended to use Roots-supercharged 60 degree V-12 engines in two sizes, 1100 cc (46 × 55 mm) for voiturette racing, and 1500 cc (50 × 55 mm) for the premier class, both designed to rev to 8000 rpm. The body had its monoposto cockpit on the centre-line, and the whole car was beautifully conceived and made, to the detail of aerofoil section suspension members. But for reasons unknown – company policy or poor performance on test are the obvious deductions – the V-12 Itala was never raced.

Meanwhile, Fiat had been experimenting with their futuristic Type 451 engine. This was the brainchild of Tranquilo Zerbi, and the design was executed by Scipione Treves and Giuseppe Sola. Basically, this was a supercharged two-stroke six, but it had 12 opposed pistons, each pair having a common combustion chamber, with inlet and exhaust ports opened and sealed by the pistons. Bench tests gave 152 bhp at 5200 rpm (Zerbi later claimed 170 bhp at 6000 rpm),

but overheating problems proved insurmountable, with metallurgical troubles beyond solution in the mid-twenties, and reliability could not be achieved.

Neither Delage nor Talbot contested the Italian Grand Prix, but a pair of the first true Maseratis made their Grand Prix debut (Type 26, simply because of the year in which they were built; in the first appearance of the marque Maserati, a Type 26 had won its class in the Targa Florio). The Type 26 was utterly conventional, with a straight eight (60 × 66 mm) developing a modest 120 bhp at 5300 rpm, in a rather heavy chassis. It was directly derived from Alfieri Maserati's Diatto designs, and was of course the first of a 'family' of Maserati eights.

At Monza, Ernesto Maserati and Emilio Materassi managed to challenge the Bugatti leaders for a while, but retired their Maseratis to leave Charavel and Costantini to enjoy another Bugatti benefit, the former winning at 85·88 mph.

During the winter of 1926–27 most of the leading cars were revised, the Talbots in detail (and their engines to give 150 bhp at 7000 rpm), while the Delages underwent major revisions. The exhaust and inlet valves of the engine were in effect swapped, so that the exhaust ran as far from the driver as possible, and the whole unit, together with transmission components, was offset to the left of the centre line. A single supercharger was substituted for the 1926 pair, and power output was up to 170 bhp at 8000 rpm. In this form the Delages dominated the 1927 season, yet they were not at the peak of their development life – in the mid-1930s Giulio Ramponi extracted 195 bhp from the engine, and with Dick Seaman driving, the nine-

year-old Delage became the car to beat in voiturette events. Alvis also revised their eight, transforming it into a conventional twin-ohc engine. Through the year, occasional new cars appeared.

Grand Prix cars ran in minor events early in the season, at Montlhéry, where Benoist won the GP de l'Ouverture in a Delage, and at Miramas, where Moriceau in a Talbot beat Benoist in a heat, and the main event was abandoned when the crowds invaded the track, frustrated by delays and the withdrawal of the principal contenders.

The once-great French Grand Prix was again poorly supported, with only ten entries. Seven cars actually started for Bugatti recognized that his T39s were not competitive, and withdrew his team on the morning of race day. The Delages duly won this race, as they were to win every other major event they entered in 1927 (Benoist winning at 77·24 mph, over the 362 miles, from team mates Bourlier and Morel). One of the Talbots was classified fourth, two retired – a miserable ending to the Grand Prix efforts of the STD combine, for the cars were never raced again by the works team. Louis Wagner, who retired one of the Talbots, was the last driver who had raced in the first Grand Prix, to drive in the ACF race, and as he never started in it again, another link was broken.

Materassi challenged the Delages in a Bugatti in the Spanish Grand Prix, and was actually leading when he crashed, leaving Benoist to win at 80·52 mph. Then came the much more interesting Monza meeting, where Indianapolis cars appeared again (two Millers and the 1927 500-winning Duesenberg), and where the Grand Prix OMs made their only appearance in a

formule race. A startling new Fiat also made its only appearance. Delage entered only one car for the 311-mile Italian Grand Prix, and Benoist kept it confidently in front of the field from start to finish. His winning speed on the wet track was 90·05 mph, and he was followed across the line by Morandi's OM and the front-wheel drive Miller (Cooper Special) shared by Cooper and Kreis.

The accompanying *formule libre* Milan Grand Prix, over a mere 31 miles, was won by a Grand Prix car which on paper and on its showing in this one sprint race was at least the equal of the Delage. This was the last Fiat Grand Prix car ever raced, the 806. The 806 was a remarkable machine which had a Roots-supercharged 12-cylinder engine (50 × 63 mm), with two vertical banks of six cylinders, two crankshafts geared together, and three overhead camshafts, the central one operating the inlet valves of both banks. This engine produced some 175 bhp at 7500 rpm at Monza, and over 185 bhp at 8500 rpm in bench tests – some 125 bhp per litre! It was installed slightly offset to the left in a low underslung chassis.

Unfortunately, after the Italian Grand Prix, Benoist decided that he was not fit to take his place on the Milan GP grid, so a direct race between Delage and Fiat was ruled out. On a track which was still wet, Bordino romped away in the 806, to win at 94·55 mph from Campari's P2 Alfa Romeo and Maggi's Bugatti. The Fiat 806 was never seen again . . .

There remained one last 1·5 litre Grand Prix, at Brooklands. The Fiat entry did not materialize in the metal, and the revised Alvis failed to come to the start, but Delage, Bugatti and the Thomas Specials

Opposite: The famous 1·5 litre 'Brescia' Bugatti, so named for Bugatti's triumph in the 1921 voiturette grand prix at Brescia, where these cars took the first four places. The Maserati 8C-2500 (above and left) of 1930 firmly established the small Bolognese firm in front-line racing.

did. These extremely low cars, 'Flatirons', were built by J. G. Parry Thomas around Roots-supercharged straight eights (52 × 88 mm), but were far from fully developed when he was killed in a land speed record attempt. Potentially competitive road racing cars, they wasted away in the backwater of British track racing.

In that 1927 British GP they were outrun by Delage and Bugatti. Materassi and Louis Chiron, who had made his Grand Prix debut when he took over Dubonnet's Bugatti in the Spanish GP, initially led in Bugattis, then Divo made the running in a Delage. In the later stages his team mates Benoist and Bourlier passed him, Benoist leading another Delage 1-2-3 to win at 85·59 mph, in the last British Grand Prix to be run until 1948. Louis Chiron, who would still be a front-line driver in that year, finished fourth at Brooklands in 1927.

Slightly ironically, that race at Brooklands was the last of an era of Grand Prix road racing, for during the rest of the twenties it lacked the cohesion of a common formula. Regulations were promulgated by the AIACR, forerunner of today's CSI, but were not generally acceptable – only the Italian Grand Prix was run to the ruling formula in 1928, when the French Grand Prix was a handicap event for sports cars. Meanwhile, the 1·5 litre (91·5 cu in) regulations, without the European restrictions on car weights and dimensions, were in force at Indianapolis from 1926 until 1929, a sufficient period for some continuity of development. As already remarked, this was concentrated on supercharged engines, Miller and Duesenberg both producing superb centrifugally supercharged straight eights, and both, like Fiat in Europe, being attracted into experiments by the theoretical advantages of the two-stroke.

Modified 1925 Miller engines were also raced from 1926, usually with special crankshafts to give a stroke of $2\frac{5}{8}$ instead of $3\frac{1}{2}$ in, to bring them within the capacity regulations, and both 'old' and 'new' engines were broadly similar. The 1926 unit (55·5 × 76·2 mm, $2\frac{3}{16}$ × 3 in) was a twin-ohc eight, with its rear-mounted supercharger driven from the crankshaft instead of the camshafts as in 1925. The supercharger turned at five times engine speed (the optimum was 7000 rpm, giving 155 bhp, although the unit would run to over 8000 rpm). The Duesenberg engine was also closely similar to its predecessor, with supercharger alongside the block.

The 1926 500 was a triumph for Miller, whose cars took eight of the first nine places, with only de Paolo's Duesenberg interrupting in fifth place. Rain cut the race short at 400 miles, when Frank Lockhart was declared the winner, at 94·63 mph, by almost three complete laps from Harry Hartz, who was followed home by Cliff Woodbury and Fred Commer. De Paolo's was the only new Duesenberg to finish – three others were entered but not ready in time – while the two-stroke Duesenberg was put out in an accident. European cars, Guyots and a Schmid (GP Rolland-Pilains, no less, with McCallum sleeve-valve engines) and the British Eldridge Specials (built in France, with Anzani four-cylinder engines) had singularly undistinguished races.

An unknown dirt track driver from the Midwest, George Souders, outlasted the acknowledged experts to win in a Duesenberg in 1927, at 97·54 mph (21 of the 33 starters retired). Millers took the next three places, Devore, Gulotta, and Wilbur Shaw, driving a Jynx Special Miller. The only new cars of note were two Duesenbergs with engines angled in their frames, and transmission running alongside their drivers; the front-wheel drive Detroit Special Miller driven by Durant had a two-stage centrifugal supercharger, another departure in racing engine development.

Millers, under a variety of names, dominated the final order again in 1928, when Lou Meyer won at 99·48 mph, the closest the 91 inch cars were to get to the magic three-figure average (for the first 300 miles the average was well above this, Duray covering the first 100 at 106·20 in a fwd Miller, Gleason 300 miles at 103·23 mph in a Duesenberg, while Gulotta in the Stutz Special which eventually finished tenth led at 100·99 mph at 400 miles, despite drizzle).

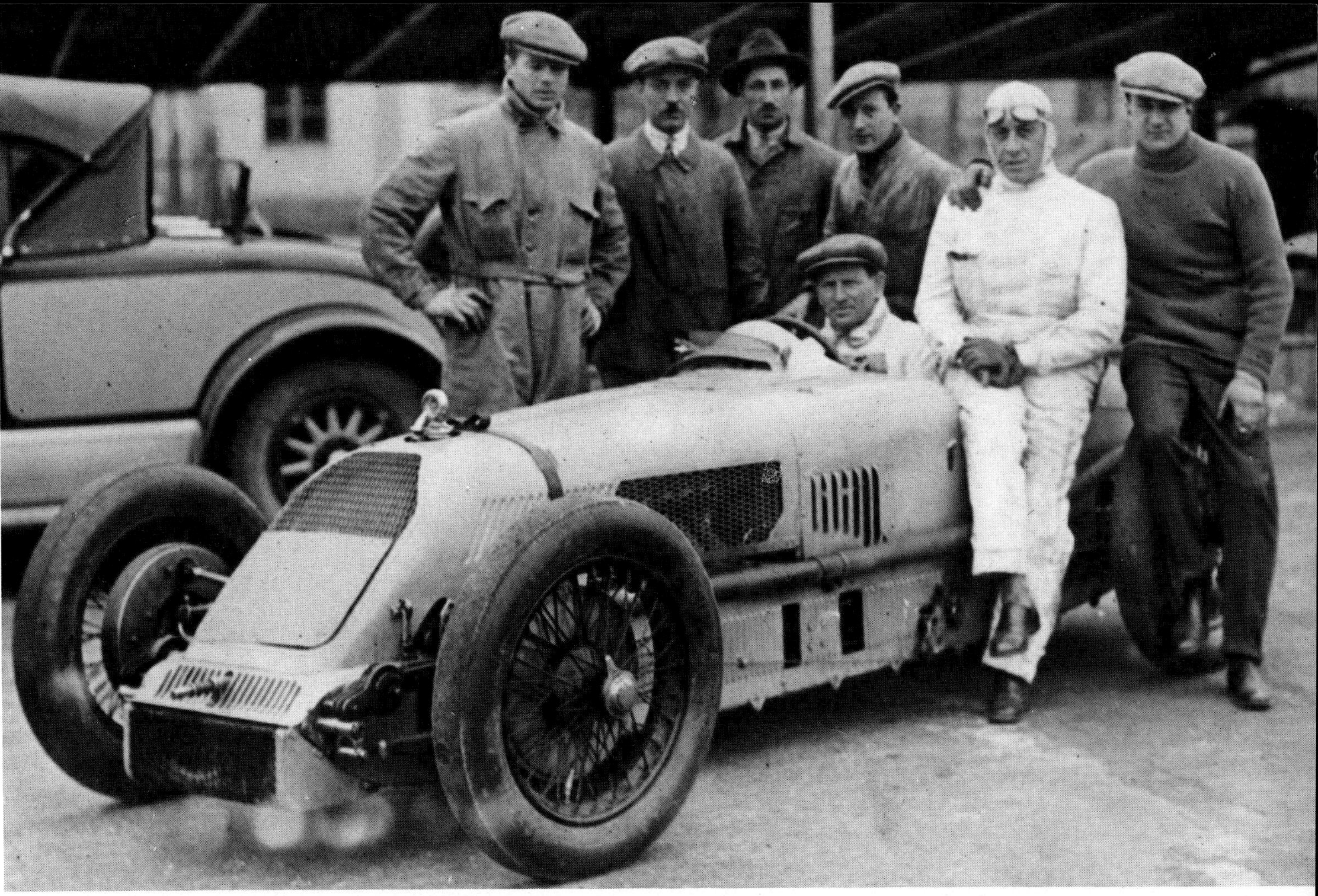

The 1931 Italian Grand Prix saw the triumphant debut of the 8C-2300 Alfa Romeo, which was dubbed 'Monza' Alfa for its success in that event. Left: the winning car waiting for the start, with representatives of the previous generation alongside and behind it, a Bugatti T35B and Ivanowksi's SSKL Mercedes Benz.

Above: Emilio Materassi built one of the first independent front-line teams around the 1926–27 1·5 litre Talbots (Materassi is in the cockpit in this Monza test shot, with his team mates Luigi Arcangeli and Antonio Brivio sitting on the car). Below: One of the adaptable T35B Bugattis, near Caltavuturo on the Targa Florio course.

Ray Keech won in 1929, at the slowest possible winning speed (in fact 97·59 mph), after holding back in the early stages but moving up the field as faster cars fell out, inheriting the lead at 150 laps and holding it to the end. Meyer took second place in another Miller, ahead of Gleason's Duesenberg. In seventh place was a European driver, in a European car, Louis Chiron, who drove a Delage to complete the distance at 87·73 mph.

In 1930 the 'Junk Formula' was introduced, and Indianapolis became irrelevant to mainstream racing until 1938.

With the withdrawal of manufacturers' teams from European racing after 1927, private teams and secondary races became increasingly important, technical progress was at a standstill, and the great sports car races gained in importance, particularly the Le Mans 24-hour Race, established in 1923, and the Mille Miglia, first run in 1927.

The first of the scuderias were set up by Nuvolari and Varzi, soon to become arch-rivals, and by Emilio Materassi, who invested to his last penny in the 1·5 litre Talbot Grand Prix cars. A little later the strongest of all independent equipes was formed, Scuderia Ferrari, which for a decade was to be firmly linked with Alfa Romeo.

Happily for the true independents, public interest in racing continued to grow, and organizers began to offer starting money, and component firms to increase their support for professional teams. Their cars were the redundant machinery of preceding years, Alfa Romeos, Delages, Talbots, or Bugattis or Maseratis, for apart from cars for the lesser classes and sports cars, only the autocrat of Molsheim and the artisan brothers of Bologna continued to build racing cars (which could and did wear wings and lights when appropriate).

The design pattern was established, the classic racing car having a straight eight supercharged engine in a fairly rigid frame, hard suspension by leaf springs, friction shock bearers, mechanical or cable compensated brakes and four-speed gearboxes.

The 1928 formula placed no restrictions on engine capacity, but imposed sliding weight limits, between 550 kg and 750 kg, and a minimum race distance of 600 km (375 miles). The only race run to it was the European Grand Prix at Monza, which was marked by tragedy when Materassi crashed among spectators on the 15th lap. He died in the accident, together with 23 spectators, the first members of the public to be killed in a Grand Prix accident.

The race was between 2·3 litre Bugattis, 1·7 litre Maseratis and the Alfa Romeo P2 shared by Varzi and Campari. At the end Bugatti driver Chiron won (at 99·36 mph), ahead of that formidable pair and Nuvolari, driving another Bugatti.

The 1929 formula was no more realistic, although the French and Spanish Grands Prix were run to it. The principal limitation was on fuel and oil consumption: 85 kg of these fluids were allowed, 14 kg per 100 km (assuming oil consumption to be modest, around 14-15 mpg). Both races fell to Bugatti drivers, to Williams from Boillot's aged Peugeot at Le Mans, and to Chiron, Philippe and Bouriat, and Lehoux in a 1-2-3 sweep at San Sebastian. The result of the 1930 Belgian Grand Prix at Spa, the only race to be run to the slightly modified fuel consumption formula in 1930, was similar – Chiron, Bouriat and Divo, all Bugatti-mounted, filled the first three places.

The other classics were run for sports cars, or as formule libre events. The Targa Florio fell to Divo, driving Bugattis in 1928 (when no fewer than 19 Bugattis started, and Elizabeth Junek led the male aces for two laps) and in 1929. Achille Varzi drove an epic Sicilian race in 1930, surviving mishaps which included a fire, to gain the last major success for the P2 Alfa Romeo, albeit this car was in a much-modified form.

In the previous year he had driven this car to victory in the Monza Grand Prix, at 116·65 mph on the banked track, a much higher speed than had then been achieved at Indianapolis. Nuvolari placed a Talbot second, Momberger a big Mercedes-Benz third. This race was also notable for the demonstrated potential of the front-wheel drive Millers ('Packard Cable Specials'), brought over to Europe by Leon Duray. Financially embarrassed after the race, he disposed of both cars to Ettore Bugatti, in exchange for three 2·3 litre Bugattis and the transatlantic fare. Bugatti thus gained possession of advanced twin-ohc racing engines; in 1931 he introduced his own first twin ohc engine, in the Type 51, which bore more than a passing resemblance to the Miller eight in its head and valve-gear . . .

Earlier in 1929, the most exotic of all Grands Prix was run for the first time, in the Principality of Monaco. This was conceived at least in part to back up the Automobile Club de Monaco claims to be a national club, for in order to achieve recognition it was felt necessary that an international event should be run within the boundaries of the Principality. So Antony Noghès and Louis Chiron came to devise the first circuit completely within a town, the setting for the first 'round-the-houses' race, and the only one to survive for more than a few years. Moreover, the Monaco Grand Prix is now the only classic established before the second world war to be run on a circuit unchanged since its inception, and remains a most exacting test for men and machines.

The 1929 race attracted 16 starters, an excellent field at that time. It seemed tailor-made for the Bugattis which made up half the field, and Williams

American classic. Harry Miller's centrifugally supercharged eight-cylinder engine was outstanding in its 91 cu in (1500 cc) form, powering his very successful front wheel drive cars, of which this Packard Cable Special is a beautifully preserved example. The detail (left) shows how the front wheel drive was accommodated with a beam front axle, this being swept back at each end to the steering ball joints.

(the expatriate English driver, Grover Williams) duly won in a T35B, at 49·83 mph, from Bouriano in another Bugatti. But the leader at half-distance, and third at the end of 100 laps, was Rudolf Caracciola in a 7·1 litre SSK Mercedes-Benz. His was the first of many heroic drives at Monaco, in a car totally unsuited to the sinuous circuit.

Thus, admittedly slightly out of sequence, the story of racing in the 1920s ends on a high note, for this audacious idea of racing through the streets of a town was proved wholly successful, and racing was given a new exotic dimension.

Grand Prix Recovery

In some ways it is unrealistic to open a new chapter at a convenient calendar date, yet while 1930 was almost an extension of the 1928-29 doldrums in technical respects, racing in general began to move forward again, towards the final flowering of the old order which preceded the very rude awakening in 1934.

The one really new car of 1930 pointed the way. This was the Maserati 8C-2500, which in most respects was a new design, owing little to the 1929 8C-1100. The straightforward 65 × 94 mm eight-cylinder engine produced adequate rather than astonishing power, some 175 bhp at 6000 rpm, and apart from the detail of electron castings in some components, there was little new about the chassis, transmission or running gear. But the engine had good torque characteristics, the 8C at least had better road-holding qualities than earlier Maseratis, and the whole machine looked clean and efficient. This it unquestionably was, proving to be sufficiently far ahead of other cars on the circuits to help persuade other manufacturers to get on with new cars for 1931.

Meanwhile, in 1930 its principal opposition comprised a pair of substantially revamped Alfa Romeo P2s, numerous Bugattis, and sundry stripped sports cars. The formidable *Sedici Cilindri* V4 Maserati also appeared in racing, after briefly showing its speed potential in 1929. This was the first of several 'twin-engined' cars which were to be built, as constructors attempted to take advantage of the freedom from engine capacity restrictions without going to the lengths of building completely new power units. The 16-cylinder engine of the V4 was made up of two twin ohc eights mounted side by side on a common crankcase, to produce a 3958 cc engine, and some 350 bhp at 5200 rpm. However, the V4 was not a car for every circuit, and apart from an international class record in 1929, its only real success came in the 1930 Tripoli Grand Prix, which Borzacchini won at 91·05 mph. Other constructors were to take up the 'twin' theme,

and Maserati returned to it with their rather more successful V5 in 1932.

That Tripoli race opened the season, and it was followed by the second Monaco Grand Prix, in which a dozen Bugattis (three of them works T35Cs) were joined by seven curiously assorted machines, including an SSK Mercedes, an Austro Daimler, one of the Materassi Talbots and a pair of Maserati 26Bs. There was nothing in that lot to challenge the Bugattis, and indeed none of them survived to half-distance, leaving Dreyfus, Chiron and Bouriat to head the only one-marque final order ever achieved at Monaco.

Apparently there was little to stand in the way of a similar rout in Sicily, but in fact Achille Varzi triumphed over the combination of the Madonie circuit and a P2 to win the Targa Florio at the record average of 48·48 mph. Then the new Maserati made its debut in the Rome GP, where Arcangeli drove one of the new cars to win the 160-mile race at 83·43 mph, and the pendulum of racing fortunes swung firmly in favour of the trident.

Where the new cars were not run, matters continued much as they had for two years, with Bugattis generally holding sway (for example in that sole 1930 formula race, the Belgian Grand Prix), while the elderly Alfas occasionally challenged in Italian races (although the last race for a P2 was in the Czech Masaryk GP in 1930 where Nuvolari placed one third).

The 2·5 litre Maseratis were back in action at Montenero, where Fagioli drove one to win the Coppa Ciano at 54·47 mph from Campari's Alfa, and at Pescara, where Varzi (75·37 mph) and Ernesto Maserati placed them first and second. Then the Monza GP saw a Maserati 1-2-3, Varzi winning the final at 93·48 mph from Arcangeli and Ernesto Maserati.

Maserati and Alfa Romeo revived Italian fortunes in 1931. Above: a Maserati in the Targa Florio, and right, Nuvolari refuelling the Monza Alfa which he co-drove with Campari (in cockpit) in the 1931 Italian Grand Prix.

Varzi rounded off his season by taking the Spanish Grand Prix for Maserati.

None of the Italians appeared for the *formule libre* French Grand Prix at Pau, postponed from its mid-season date when the ACF despaired of running it as a formula race, and contested largely by French entries and Birkin's stripped 4½ litre 'Blower' Bentley. The Englishman drove a splendid race, placing his big car second only 2½ minutes behind Etancelin's winning Bugatti, a car which barely finished.

The complex weight and capacity regulations proposed for 1931-1933 were abandoned in favour of the simple requirements that cars have two-seater bodies (but carry only a driver) and that national races be of a minimum duration of 10 hours (which normally meant two drivers for each car). There was also to be a drivers' championship, carrying cash prizes. On the face of it, this could have led simply to an extension of the racing situation of the preceding years; in fact, Alfa Romeo and Bugatti built new cars, and three works teams were in the field, so that a measure of the old glory returned to the Grands Prix.

The mainstream Alfa Romeo was Jano's 8C, with a 2·3 litre (65 × 88 mm) straight eight derived from the very successful six-cylinder 1750 sports car unit. It was in two blocks of four cylinders, with a central gear train to drive twin overhead camshafts, the Roots-type supercharger and pumps; at its debut it gave a dependable 165 bhp at 5500 rpm. The 8C first ran as a sports car, and in that guise was to gain many successes, notably at Le Mans. However, its 'Monza' title was owed to its 1931 Italian GP victory. Alfa Romeo was also attracted by the 'twin' idea, and built the Type A for high-speed circuits. This had two 1750 sixes (65 × 88 mm) installed side by side, each with its own clutch and gearbox (these were of course interconnected to making driving feasible!). The 3504 cc engine produced some 230 bhp at 5200 rpm. Apart from the 1100 cc Bugatti and sundry British specials, the Type A was the first European monoposto with a central cockpit and steering column.

Bugatti meanwhile had introduced the Type 51, which was very similar to the T35, outwardly and in the chassis and running gear. However, it had a twin-ohc engine, derived from the 4·9 litre T50 sports car unit and with assumed indebtedness to Harry Miller. The T51 engine was a 2270 cc (60 × 100 mm) eight, giving some 160 bhp at 5500 rpm. Bugatti, too,

Vittorio Jano's masterpiece, the Alfa Romeo Type B, or P3 monoposto, which set new standards when it appeared in 1932. Its classically simple lines marked the end of a period in racing car design.

produced a 'twin', uniting two T39 engines on a common crankcase; he did not go very far with this, recognizing that a better method of achieving a large-capacity engine for fast circuits was to develop a full racing version of the 4·9 litre T50 unit. In the T54 which appeared later in 1931, this 4972 cc engine produced some 300 bhp at 4500 rpm – power which was not an end-all, for although fast, the T54 was difficult to drive.

The T51 made its debut in the Tunis Grand Prix, where Varzi drove it to a convincing victory at 86·15 mph. The scene then shifted to Europe, to Monaco, where the 10-hour minimum duration ruling was ignored and the race run over 100 laps (this was to remain one of the consistent features of the Monaco GP until the late sixties). Here Monégasque driver Louis Chiron gained his only Monaco victory, in a works T51 (this occupied him for 3 hours 39 minutes, which equals 54·09 mph, quite long enough for that circuit!). He was followed by Fagioli's short-chassis Maserati 8C and fellow T51 driver Varzi. Then Nuvolari and Borzacchini gave the new Alfa its first victory, ahead of Varzi's Bugatti in the Targa Florio.

The first full 10-hour Grand Prix was run at Monza, largely between Alfa Romeo and Bugatti as the Maserati team was licking Sicilian wounds. The Alfa 8Cs took the first two places (Campari/Nuvolari and Minioa/Borzacchini), obedient to political instructions – Alfa Romeo proposed to withdraw their entries after Luigi Arcangeli had been killed practising with the Type A, but Mussolini apparently felt that the prestige benefits accruing from an Italian victory essential, and ordered the team to race.

Positions were reversed at Montlhéry, where Chiron and Varzi won the French Grand Prix at 78·66 mph in the only works T51 Bugatti to run for 10 hours, ahead of an Alfa Romeo and two Maseratis, the second driven by Birkin and Eyston. Bugatti won again in Belgium, Williams and Conelli (82·01 mph) heading two of the Alfas in this final 10-hour Grand Prix. Minioa, co-drove the Alfa placed third, and thus gained the championship, by virtue of three good subsidiary placings in the three races.

Although this first, largely ignored, championship was settled, the season was by no means over. Rudolf Caracciola drove another of his inspired wet-weather races to win the German GP from Chiron, who then finished second to Nuvolari's Alfa Romeo in the next race, the Coppa Ciano. However, he won at Brno over the fearsome 18-mile Masarykring, after three of his principal rivals, Fagioli, Varzi and Nuvolari (leading in that order) were eliminated when Varzi felled a temporary bridge across the circuit!

Before the Czech race, the season reached its annual climax at Monza, in the Monza Grand Prix. The heat for cars of up to 3 litres went convincingly to Maseratis with engines enlarged to 2·8 litres, and the unlimited capacity heat to Varzi's T54 Bugatti, making its debut. The final was between Nuvolari's Type A Alfa, which had engine failure, two T54 Bugattis, which threw tyre treads, two 2·8 litre Maseratis, of which Dreyfus' retired and Varzi's won at 96·60 mph, and two 8C Alfas, of which Borzacchini's finished second.

The 1932 season opened on a little changed scene, although practice for the Monaco race fleetingly saw a great novelty, the T53 four-wheel drive Bugatti making its only circuit appearance before it was banished to hill climbs. Monza Alfas, with engines bored out to 2·6 litres, won this race (Nuvolari, 55·81 mph), and the Eifelrennen at the Nürburgring (Caracciola, 70·70 mph), while Fagioli won the Rome GP with the V5 Maserati, and Nuvolari held off fierce pressure from Chiron and Varzi to win the Targa Florio for Alfa Romeo.

As well as cutting the minimum duration of races to five hours in their 1932 regulations, the AIACR had waived their 'two-seater' rule, and in June the first definitive monoposto Grand Prix car appeared. Much more than this, Jano's new Alfa Romeo was the peak design of the classic racing car line. Designated Type B – popularly P3 – it had a 2·65 litre engine derived from the 'Monza' eight, with the same 65 mm bore, but stroke increased to 100 mm. This gave some 180 bhp at 5400 rpm, modest enough in terms of specific output, but in 1932 sufficient for a car weighing just over 15 cwt. The engine was mounted in a narrow frame, and drove through twin propeller shafts, splayed at 30 degrees from a universal joint behind the gearbox, to twin bevel final drives.

Nuvolari drove the P3 to a first-time-out victory in the Italian Grand Prix, at 104·09 mph, from the 16-cylinder Maserati shared by Fagioli and Ernesto Maserati, which was far and away the fastest car on the circuit (Fagioli lapped at 112·22 mph), but which was handicapped by abysmally slow pit work. A month later Nuvolari, Borzacchini and Caracciola placed the P3s 1-2-3 in the first French Grand Prix to be run at Rheims, where the suddenly outpaced Bugattis filled the next three places. The German Grand Prix saw another Alfa Romeo 1-2-3, this time in the appropriate order Caracciola, Nuvolari, Borzacchini – once Nuvolari's fiery ambitions to upset the ordained finishing order had been dampened with a long-drawn-out pit stop. Nuvolari went on to take the Coppas Ciano and Acerbo with the P3.

The Monza Grand Prix heats went to Caracciola, Fagioli and Campari, and in the final Fagioli with the 16-cylinder Maserati was the only combination able to challenge the Alfa Romeos in terms of speed. However, he was slowed with plug troubles, finishing second to Caracciola (110·8 mph) and ahead of Nuvolari, whose P3 had a malfunctioning carburetter.

Line-up for the unlimited heat of the 1930 Monza Grand Prix, with Alfieri Maserati's Sedici Cilindri *Maserati nearest the camera, then Babe Stapp's Duesenberg, Rudolf Caracciola's SSKL Mercedes-Benz, Fritz Calflisch's SS Mercedes-Benz and an old four-cylinder Itala. The Monza scene on the right is of greater significance, for it shows one of Nuvolari's two pit stops with the brand-new P3 in the 1932 Italian GP. The maestro is snatching a drink before driving on to give the car a first-time-out victory.*

On the other side of the coin, the two P3s which started in the Czechoslovak Grand Prix had troubled runs, Borzacchini retiring his with a broken rear axle, while Nuvolari had to stop for a magneto to be replaced in his, so that the race fell to Chiron (Bugatti T51), from Fagioli (Maserati) and Nuvolari. In the very minor Marseilles Grand Prix at Miramas, a lapse in the Alfa pits let Raymond Sommer cross the line in his Monza ahead of Nuvolari in a P3.

These were the only races in which the P3 was beaten in 1932, and at the end of the year Alfa Romeo withdrew from direct competition, entrusting their 1933 affairs to the Scuderia Ferrari. The P3s were withdrawn, too, leaving Ferrari to campaign Monzas with engines bored out to 2·55 litres, to give 180 bhp (as the Monza weighed some 200 kg more than the P3, it obviously had not the same potential performance, despite the on-paper power parity). Maserati did some work on a front-wheel drive version of their proven eight, but settled for a conventional monoposto development of that car. Their engine was enlarged to 2992 cc (69 × 100 mm) in this 8C-3000, to initially produce 200 bhp at 5500 rpm and a little later 220 bhp at the same engine speed. The chassis and running gear remained largely unaltered, save that hydraulic brakes were fitted to all four wheels – 12 years after that Duesenberg French GP victory, a European manufacturer at last followed the Americans' example.

For most of the season the new Bugatti remained a promise, the works team carrying on with the T51, independents increasingly turning to Alfa Romeo or Maserati for cars.

The first major race of 1933 fell to Bugatti fair and square, after a most intense duel around the streets and quais of Monaco. Here for the first time in Grand Prix history, grid positions were determined by practice times, not by the luck of the draw, and another competitive element was introduced into motor racing. Achille Varzi therefore became the first Grand Prix driver to gain a pole position by his own toil, and immediately behind him on row 2 was his great rival Tazio Nuvolari. By the end of the first lap, Nuvolari had his Ferrari Alfa close behind Varzi's works Bugatti, and thereafter the two were locked in lead-swopping conflict, almost to the chequered flag. Nuvolari led at the end of 66 of the 100 laps, Varzi at the end of 34, including the last vital lap, when both drivers over-revved their engines; the Bugatti eight held up under abuse, an oil pipe split on the Alfa, so that Nuvolari did not even finish the last lap . . .

Varzi won the next race, too, but perhaps less than fairly, for it was the famous rigged Tripoli Grand Prix. This was run for the first time on the very fast new

Start of the 1933 Italian Grand Prix, with a field largely made up of P3 and Monza Alfa Romeos, Bugatti T51s and 8C Maseratis. Below: the 8CM-3000 Maserati monoposto raced by Nuvolari.

112

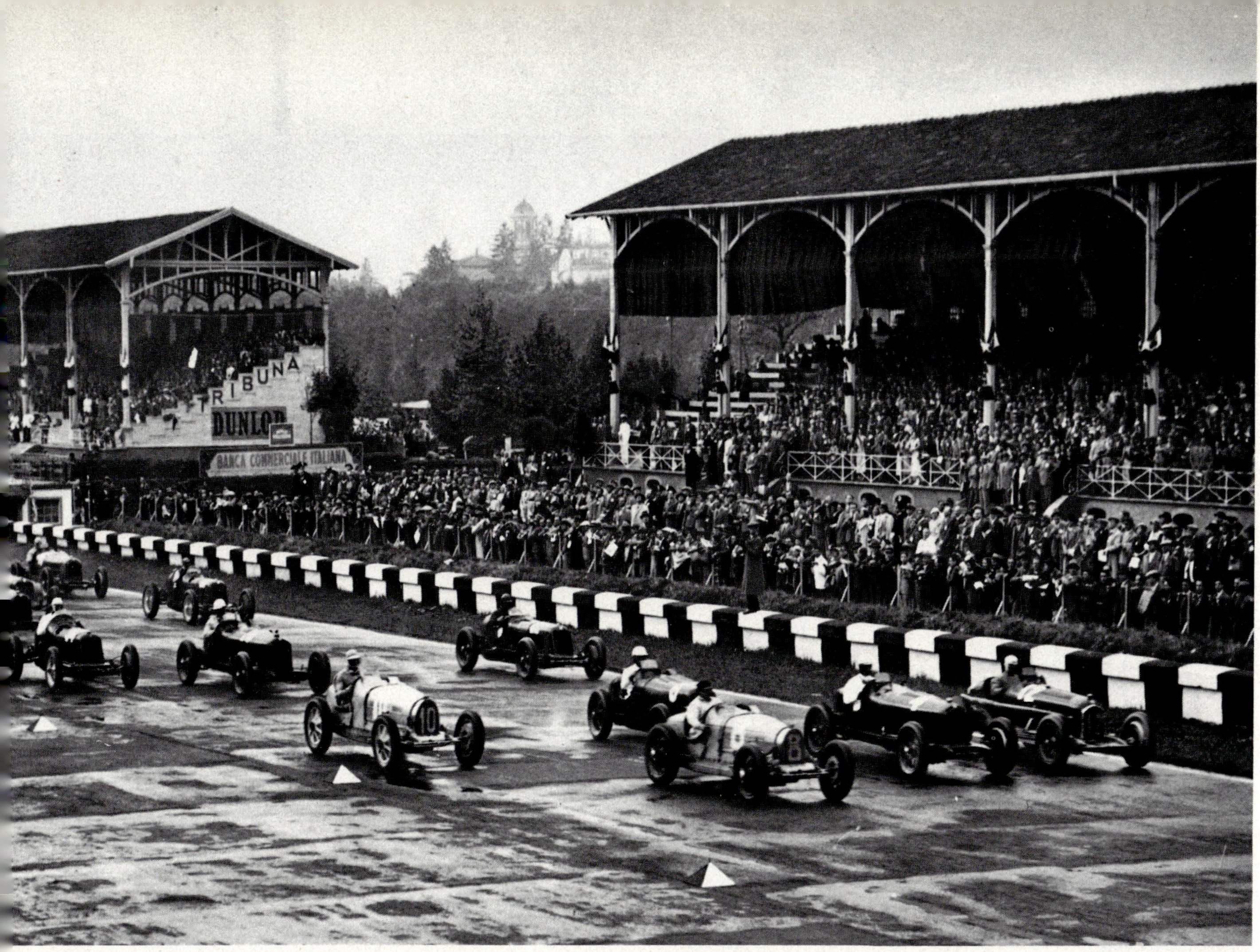
TRIBUNA
DUNLOP
BANCA COMMERCIALE ITALIANA
10

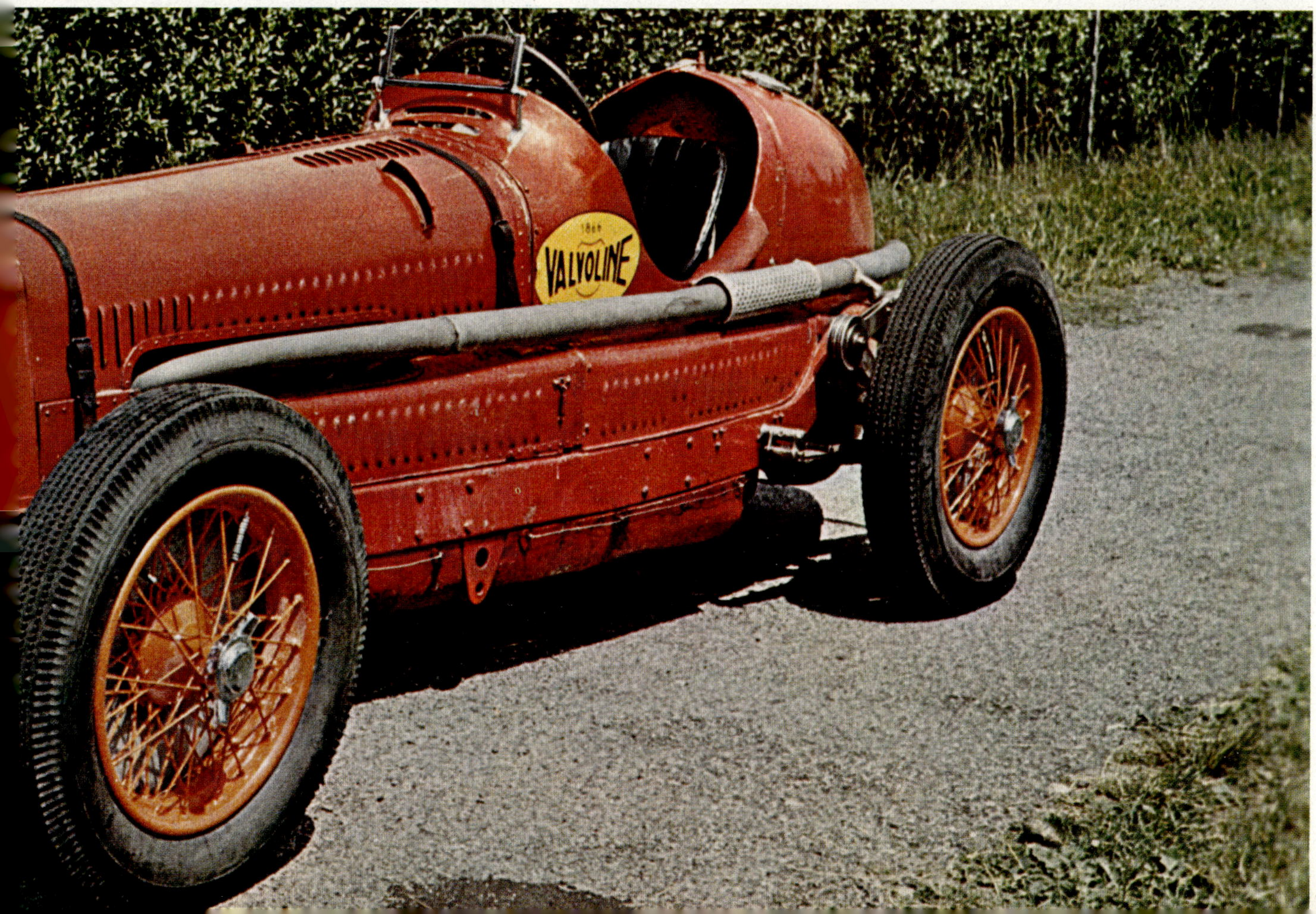
VALVOLINE

Mellaha circuit, and for the first time in conjunction with a huge lottery, in which tickets drawn were coupled with drivers' names. Varzi, Campari, Nuvolari and Borzacchini and their respective ticket holders came to an arrangement which was hardly orthodox... their plans were threatened by Sir Henry Birkin, who led the race for five laps, but the final order was Varzi, Nuvolari and Birkin (tragically, he burned an arm on the exhaust of his Maserati during a pit stop, and from this innocuous injury contracted septicaemia, which proved fatal). Varzi's winning speed was 104·76 mph, some aggrieved drivers, not party to 'the arrangement', blew the gaff; in 1934 the lottery system was changed!

The next race, the Avusrennen, was even faster, Varzi driving a 4·9 litre Bugatti to victory at 128·48 mph, from Czaikowski (also driving a T54) and Nuvolari and Borzacchini, who tied for third place (Varzi's speed was a considerable improvement over the 120·7 mph achieved by von Brauchitsch in 1932, driving a 7·1 litre Mercedes-Benz fitted with a fully aerodynamic single-seater body).

So to Montlhéry, to a French Grand Prix which had an oversubscribed entry list – times were indeed changing – from which 13 Alfa Romeos, 13 Bugattis and 2 Maseratis were selected. Only 19 of these materialized. Bugatti, protesting that his new T59 was not ready (after promising up to the eve of race day that it would be) and his T51s not overhauled since the Monaco GP (run 49 days earlier!), scratched his cars. Caracciola had been seriously injured in a Monaco practice accident, and Birkin in Tripoli, while Bouriat and Louis Trintignant had been fatally injured in the minor Picardy Grand Prix. No drivers got within seconds of Nuvolari's practice times, but he burst the engine of his own Alfa after a few meteoric practice laps, the transmission of Borzacchini's Alfa in which he started the race, and the transmission of Taruffi's Alfa which he took over at half-distance. And in the next major race, the great but temperamental little man appeared in the cockpit of a Maserati . . .

The fight for the French Grand Prix lead was between Etancelin (Alfa Romeo) and Campari (Maserati), and the race fell into the burly Italian's lap as Etancelin stopped on the last lap, then crept to the line with his transmission failing. Sadly, this was Giuseppe Campari's last victory.

The Belgian Grand Prix at Spa saw the return of the Bugatti team, still with T51s, and Nuvolari in a

Maserati cockpit; far from satisfied with its road-holding, he had the flexible chassis modified at the Imperia works between practice and race. This he won without difficulty, once Chiron had retired his Alfa, at 89·23 mph from Bugatti drivers Varzi and Dreyfus. Together with Nuvolari's wins in the next two races, the Nice GP and the Coppa Acerbo, this persuaded Alfa Romeo to dust down the P3s, and hand them over to Scuderia Ferrari to retrieve a degenerating situation. This Fagioli did for them in the Coppa Acerbo, in part through the defaults of Campari's crash and Nuvolari's long pit stop; he followed up the good work in the Comminges GP, and Chiron then took the Marseilles GP for the Scuderia.

So to the Monza climax. The Italian GP turned on a battle between Nuvolari and the P3 drivers, Fagioli, Chiron and Taruffi, and on pit stops. All four drivers led, and victory passed from Nuvolari to Fagioli two laps from the end, when a rear tyre failed on the Maserati. Fagioli's winning speed was 108·58 mph, Nuvolari and Zehender placed Maseratis second and third.

The Monza Grand Prix, which was run on the afternoon of the same day, proved to be a tragic race. Czaikowski won the first heat in a 4·9 litre Bugatti, but the Ferrari Duesenberg, which was driven by Trossi, lost its oil in the South Curve. This was not properly cleared when the second heat started, and on the first lap both Campari and Borzacchini crashed at the South Curve, and were killed. Incredibly, and despite long delays, there was still oil in the corner when the final started, and on the eighth lap Count Czaikowski also crashed on it, and was killed. The tragic race went on, to be won by Lehoux.

There remained the Czech GP, which Chiron won for the third time, driving a P3, and the Spanish GP, where the T59 Bugatti at last appeared. One is tempted to add 'almost too late', for in its final full season it was to be overtaken by machines which must have been beyond the comprehension of Bugatti. As it was, the T59 was to all intents and purposes the last Grand Prix car on classic lines, lacking such refinements as independent suspension. Fittingly, therefore, it was a most handsome car. Its supercharged straight eight initially had a capacity of 2·8 litres, soon to be enlarged to 3257 cc (68 × 100 mm), to produce 240 bhp at 5400 rpm. This was mounted low in a typical Bugatti chassis, which was born on unique wire wheels, in which the spokes were little more than reinforcement. In Spain they finished fourth and sixth, behind the Alfa Romeos of Chiron and Fagioli, and Lehoux' T51, and split by Wimille's Alfa.

There the season ended, with Grand Prix racing apparently at one of its periodic peaks. It was a peak, and the last complete season of a period, for a new era was to open under a new formula in 1934.

Top: An Alfa Romeo P3 during a Monza test session; Luigi Bazzi (wearing a cap) and Giulio Ramponi are standing behind the bonnet, while Luigi Fagioli looks almost uncharacteristically happy in the cockpit. Centre: line-up for the 1933 Tripoli GP, with one of the 1·5 litre Talbots converted to a single-seater by Gigi Platé in the foreground, with a Monza Alfa and a T51 Bugatti alongside it. Bottom: an American car, a Scuderia Ferrari Duesenberg with 'Didi' Trossi in the cockpit.

Revolution

After years of evolution in racing, 1934 was a year of revolution. There were not in fact a great many things that were absolutely radical in themselves, but the sum of the parts certainly was. When the new formula was announced in the Autumn of 1932 there appeared to be nothing in it to hint at anything startling to come. However, during the Spring of 1933 two German companies looked at it with open minds, and came up with answers which were very different, yet were to achieve similar results. The established French and Italian companies looked at the new formula, and decided that their existing cars would serve, with slight modifications to conform to its rules.

Basically, the sporting committee of the AIACR was concerned to pull racing together after the vagaries around the turn of the decade, and to restrain racing speeds at roughly the level attained in 1932. Thus a maximum dry weight, without tyres as well as liquids, of 750 kg (1653 lb) was prescribed, together with minimum body dimensions at the cockpit of 85 cm wide, 25 cm high, and a minimum race distance of 500 km (312 miles). To introduce some stability, the formula was to run for three years.

The Bugatti T59 was completed in knowledge of the forthcoming formula, and complied with it. Alfa Romeo, by this time under the wing of the Institute of Industrial Reconstruction, and thus to a degree under national control, had no financial worries, and were expected to uphold the prestige of Italy (Mussolini was well aware of the propaganda importance of major race successes). And Alfa Romeo had the P3, which needed only body modifications to comply, although for good measure the cylinder bore of its engine was increased to 69 mm, to give a capacity of 2·9 litres.

Lacking Government backing, Maserati proposed to achieve results without means, and the Bolognese firm had more problems in adapting their cars, principally to meet the weight requirement (the narrow chassis of their 1933 car had to be widened by 50 per cent).

So much for the old order. The formula seemed to block a race towards larger engines, greater power and higher speeds. But the three-year term was to be extended by a year, and by 1937 the most powerful Grand Prix cars ever raced were built to it, with engines producing over 600 bhp, and capable of speeds approaching 200 mph.

Adolf Hitler was also well aware of the prestige to be gained in international sport, and motor sport offered opportunities to demonstrate national technical superiority as well. Thus German companies were offered a straight prize, as well as more subtle subsidies and contracts, as inducements to compete. Two took up the challenge, the ancient and honourable house of Daimler-Benz, and a consortium of lesser manufacturers, Audi, DKW, Horch and Wanderer, who established a new marque, Auto Union.

Auto Union's car appeared first, the revolutionary P-Wagen designed by Dr Ferdinand Porsche. This had its engine between cockpit and rear axle, in a rigid chassis frame of two large tubular side members and tubular cross members. All four wheels were independently sprung, by trailing arms and torsion bars at the front and a swing axle and transverse spring at the rear. The five-speed gearbox was mounted behind the rear axle, the drive being carried from the crankshaft under the differential, and then forward again. The fuel tank was placed immediately behind the cockpit, in order that weight distribution would remain unaltered as fuel was consumed.

Porsche's engine was also novel. It was a 45 degree

Spurred on by Government backing in the intensely nationalistic atmosphere of the thirties, Mercedes-Benz returned to Grand Prix racing in 1934 with the W25. Although W25s won only four races in that year, two grandes épreuves *and two secondary events, they were beaten only four times in 1935, when Caracciola won six events and Fagioli three.*

116

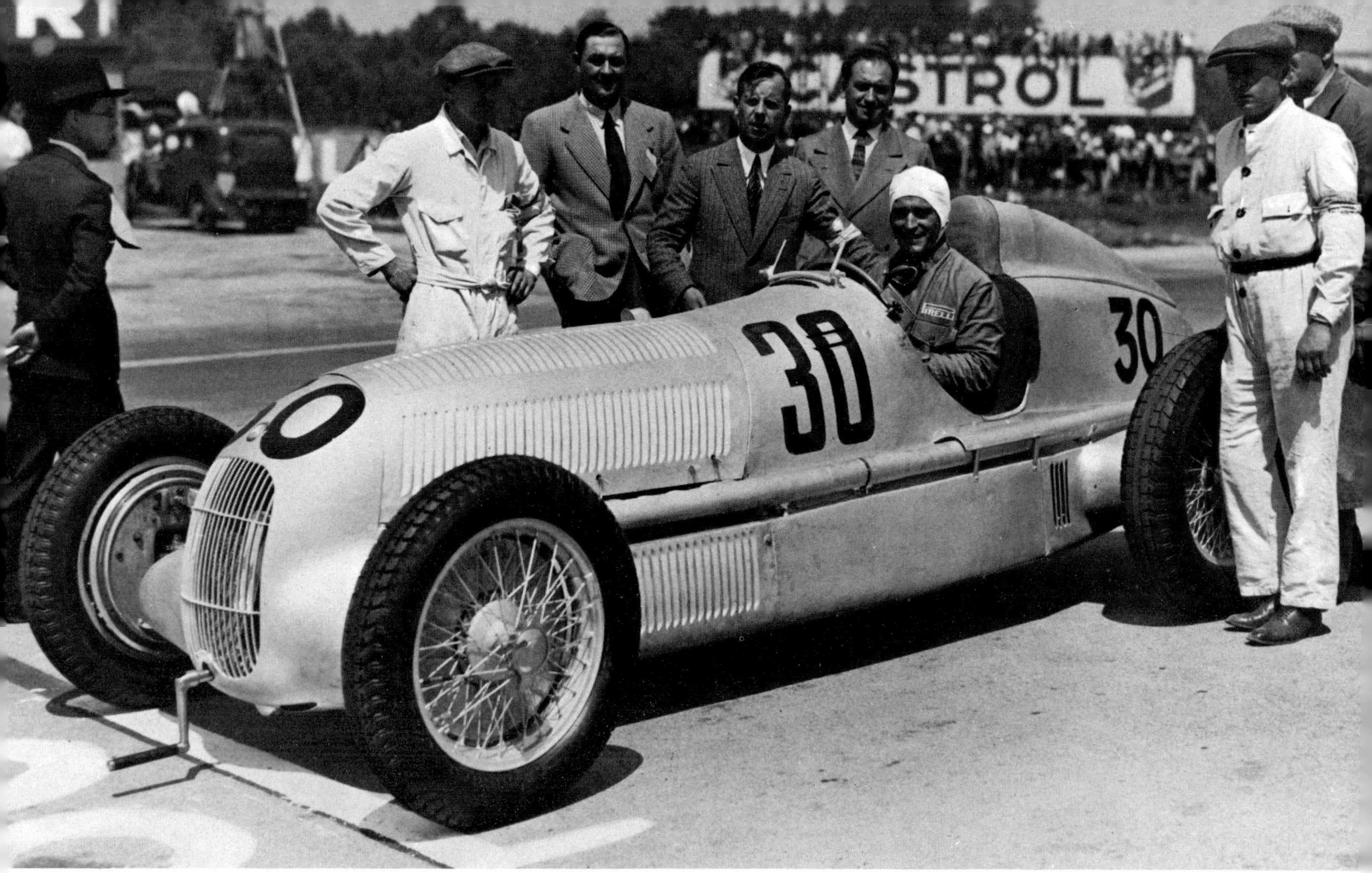
CASTROL
30
30

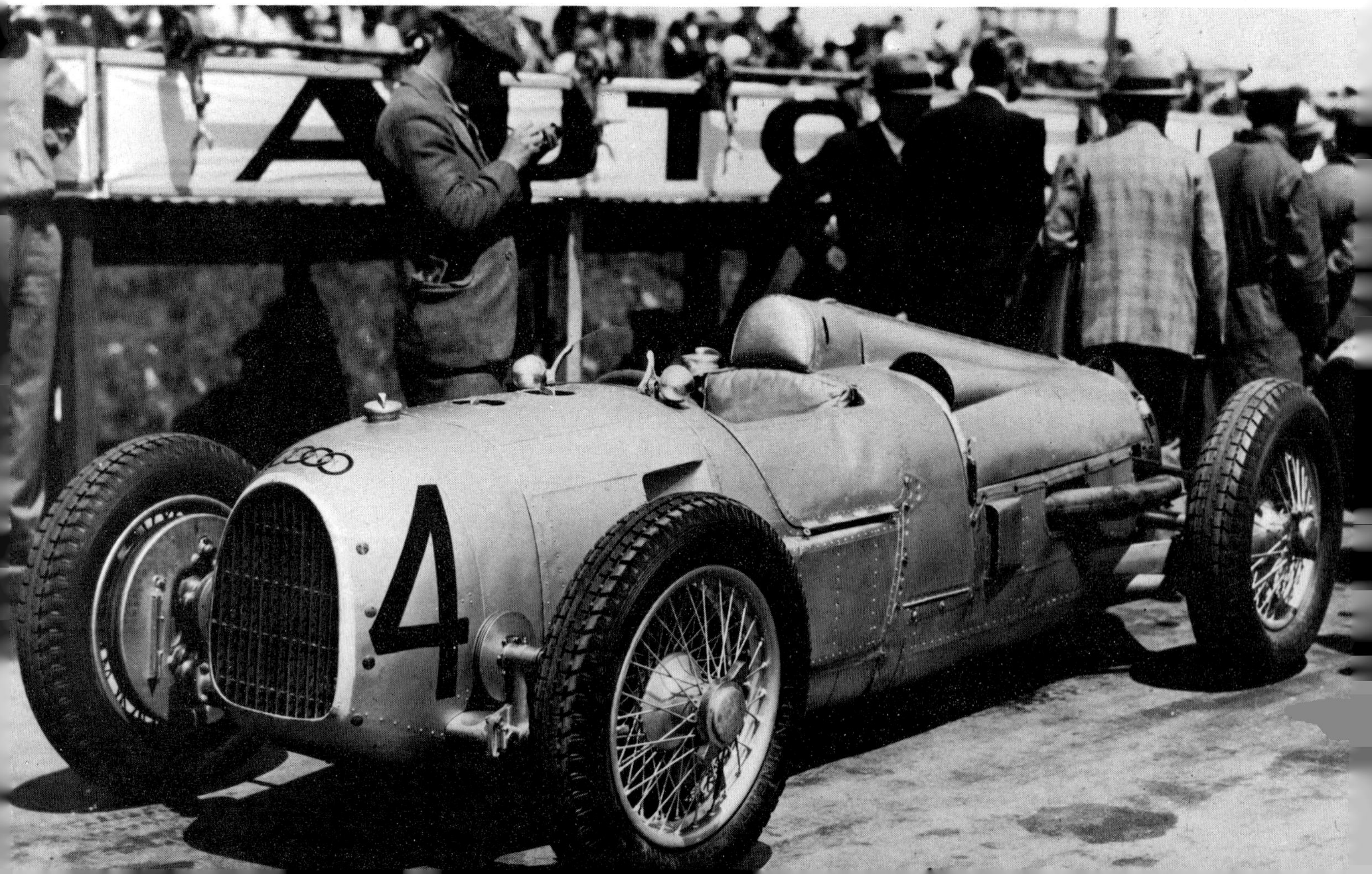
4

V-16, with a single overhead camshaft between the banks to operate all 32 valves. With a capacity of 4360 cc (68 × 75 mm) it was the largest GP engine of 1934, and developed its maximum 295 bhp at a relatively leisurely 4500 rpm. The driver sat low in a cockpit ahead of the engine, and this posed problems, for developed 'seat of the pants' senses had to be unlearned.

The Mercedes-Benz W25 was not so radical (although the two cars had much in common, not least the background of Mercedes and Benz past experience, to which Porsche had been as privy as W25 designers Nibel and Wagner). For the first time in a front-engined car, Mercedes brought together in the W25 all-independent suspension (by wishbones and coil springs at the front, swing axle and transverse quarter elliptics at the rear), hydraulic brakes and a gearbox/differential unit attached to the frame, and therefore sprung weight. The M25 engine followed orthodox Mercedes practice in having individually-cast cylinders with a welded steel water jacket. A Roots-supercharged twin ohc straight eight, 78 × 88 mm (3360 cc), it gave just over 350 bhp at 5800 rpm in its first tests, and by the end of 1934 this had been increased to 390 bhp. The car appeared very sleek beside its Italian contemporaries, and to save weight the thin-gauge alloy bodies were left unpainted, hence the 'silver arrows' beloved of the popular press.

The German teams did not contest the opening

The new and the old orders at Montlhéry for the 1934 French Grand Prix. Left: Mercedes W25 and Auto Union P-Wagen. Above: Louis Chiron in the Alfa Romeo P3 which he drove to win the race, and below, Tazio Nuvolari in the Bugatti T59 which he drove for only eight laps, before letting Wimille take over.

races, at Tripoli, where Varzi (115·67 mph) headed an Alfa Romeo 1-2-3 once Taruffi had crashed in the 5-litre Maserati, and at Monaco, where Guy Moll won from his Scuderia Ferrari team mate Chiron, who led comfortably with two laps to go, then spent time extricating his car from the station hairpin straw bales, where he had overshot.

At Avus the Auto Unions appeared to race for the first time, and showed their paces. Stuck drew away from the field at the start, but the team had yet to achieve reliability and efficient pit work, so that Moll came through to win in an Alfa Romeo which had an aerodynamic body designed by Pallavicino of the Breda aircraft company. His speed on the wet track was 127·5 mph, and he was followed across the line by Varzi in another Alfa and Momberger in the surviving Auto Union.

The Mercedes team appeared for the Eifelrennen at the Nürburgring, where Fagioli and Brauchitsch took their W25s into an immediate lead. The Italian fell out,

while the German won at 76·12 mph, from Stuck (Auto Union) and Chiron (Alfa Romeo).

Thus the stage was set for the French Grand Prix, which returned to its old greatness, with only manufacturers' teams admitted, and turned out to be a race charged with drama. Alfa Romeo, Auto Union, Mercedes-Benz, Bugatti and Maserati entered, the last two in supporting roles. Caracciola returned to racing to lead the Mercedes team, and Nuvolari was back after a crash in the Bordino GP, but in the cockpit of an outclassed T59.

Louis Chiron once again made capital of his ability to fractionally anticipate the starter's flag, and led the first two laps. By then Stuck had got into his stride, and he took the lead. But on lap 10 Chiron was back in front, as Stuck made the first of a series of pit stops, and Fagioli took up the pursuit in a Mercedes. Four laps later he retired, with a brake pipe fractured after being misled into running out of road by Chiron.

Brauchitsch was already out, and a Mercedes debacle was complete as Caracciola stopped on the circuit. At half-distance Stuck's Auto Union was the

only German car left in the race, and that was being driven gently, in an attempt to get it to the finish. As the Maseratis and Nuvolari's Bugatti had already gone, and Benoist was making only hesitant progress in the other T59, the Alfa Romeos were left to run on to the chequered flag in first, second and third places. More than a decade was to pass before that happened again in a front-rank race, but for the moment the old order had triumphed. Above all, it was a triumph for Chiron, who had fought and held the new cars in a P3. He won at 85·06 mph, half a lap ahead of team mates Varzi and Moll, who had taken over from Trossi when the Count tired of racing with only three gears.

One more inspired victory was to be gained by a P3 driver, but that Montlhéry race saw the end of its front-line winning career in its original form. Between June 1932 and July 1934, the P3s had started 62 times in 26 major races; 57 had finished, winning 22 races and taking the first three places in seven. Now the turning point had been reached, and although the Alfa Romeo was to be revamped, it was to be outclassed, along with the Bugattis and Maseratis. Both of these companies looked to larger engines for immediate solutions, Bugatti using 3257 cc (72 × 100 mm) eights in his Montlhéry cars, Maserati introducing a revised version of the Type 34 'six' (84 × 100 mm, 3325 cc) giving 260 bhp, installed in the 8C chassis.

None of these was more than a hopeful stop gap. The Germans won their home Grand Prix at the Nürburgring (Stuck taking the flag at a 76·39 mph average, ahead of Fagioli's Mercedes and Chiron's Alfa), and then carried the challenge to Italy. The Coppa Acerbo was tragic for Ferrari, as Moll was killed when he crashed. Chiron's Alfa was burned out, and Varzi broke two in his efforts to hold the German cars. Caracciola also crashed, when leading, and at the end Fagioli was left to win comfortably for Mercedes at 80·26 mph. Auto Union had a field day in the first Swiss Grand Prix, run at Berne's Bremgarten circuit, where Stuck and Momberger placed the rear-engined cars first (at 87·21 mph) and second, ahead of Dreyfus' Bugatti and the demoralized Ferrari team. None of this augured well for the Italians at Monza, where chicanes were introduced for the Italian GP, presumably to slow the German cars to level terms. Despite this, Mercedes led Auto Union past the flag, Caracciola sharing the winning drive with Fagioli, who retired his own W25. They were chased by Stuck, who had taken over Leiningen's P-Wagen, then by the Alfa shared by Comotti and Trossi, and then Nuvolari, who had driven his new Maserati almost brakeless through the race, as hydraulic fluid emptied to get the car down to the weight limit had not been replaced!

The last two ranking events of 1934 fell to the

Opposite: the very unconventional Trossi-Monaco, designed by Augusto Monaco for Count Trossi for the 750 kg formula. It had a Zoller-supercharged radial two-stroke engine of 3926 cc, which produced 250 bhp and drove through the front wheels. It was abandoned after initial trials.

The ERA voiturettes were built on the same classic monoposto lines as the Alfa Romeo P3 (below), using straightforward Roots-supercharged six-cylinder engines of three capacities, 1500 cc, 1100 cc (shorter stroke) and 2 litres (increased bore and stroke). In these classes they built up a superb racing record during the second half of the 1930s.

German teams. The Spanish GP saw a Mercedes 1-2, Fagioli leading Caracciola, after an almost insolent early Bugatti challenge by Wimille and Dreyfus. Stuck won the Czechoslovak GP at 79·21 mph from Fagioli, while Nuvolari placed a Maserati third.

The superiority of German technology had indeed been demonstrated, for although the retirement rate achieved by both teams had been extraordinarily high, the Mercedes and Auto Unions which lasted usually finished in front. Both used larger engines in 1935, Mercedes the 3·99 litre (88 × 94·5 mm) 430 bhp M25B, and Auto Union a 375 bhp 4·95 litre V-12 in the B-type. Other changes were minor, Porsche replacing his transverse rear spring with torsion bars, Wagner adding a ZF limited-slip differential to the W125.

Bugatti did little, the established Italians perhaps essayed too much, and really achieved little, and two oddities were at least completed in the metal. These were Count Trossi's Monaco-designed front wheel drive car, which had its air-cooled radial two-stroke

engine ahead of its front wheels, and never appeared in a race, and the stodgy French SEFAC, with a 2·8 litre eight-cylinder engine comprising two side-by-side blocks of four cylinders, which for years haunted entry lists but seldom completed a racing lap.

South of the Alps, Ferrari sought an immediate solution in a further revamped P3, enlarging the engine to 3165 cc and the 3822 cc, to give 330 bhp, and adopting Dubonnet independent front suspension, which in turn meant hydraulic brakes.

Alfa meanwhile made slow progress with a V-12 successor, and the Scuderia put together a pair of 'specials' for fast *formule libre* races, at Tripoli and Avus. This famous Bazzi and Rosselli *Bimotore* used P3 parts, notably two engines in each chassis, one ahead of the cockpit, one behind it. Both drove through a central three-speed gearbox to the rear wheels, through which something like 540 bhp was to be put on the road, and was, so long as tyres lasted, which was not very long. At least Nuvolari was able to take the flying mile record at 200·73 mph in a *bimotore*; in the races for which they were intended they finished second (Chiron at Avus) and fourth and fifth (Nuvolari and Chiron at Tripoli).

In 1935 the Mercedes-Benz team dominated racing with a revised version of the W25, here seen in front of the Tripoli pits.

Maserati enlarged their six to 3729 cc, to be rewarded with no more than flashes of promise, and introduced the V8RI, with light alloy frame, independent front suspension, and a Roots-supercharged sohc V-8 of 4785 cc (84 × 108 mm) which produced 320 bhp at 5300 rpm (and won only at Pau in 1936).

The supreme confidence of the Germans was shaken only once, ironically in their home Grand Prix. Fagioli led from flag to flag at 58·17 mph in the opening race at Monaco, although his team mate von Brauchitsch lasted only one lap and Caracciola was hounded to burst his engine by Etancelin in a Scuderia Subalpina Maserati. Achille Varzi, newly-recruited to the Auto Union team, enjoyed an untroubled victory in the Tunis GP, but failed to gain his third successive Tripoli win when he had tyre trouble in the closing stages and finished second between the Mercedes of Caracciola (122·98 mph) and Fagioli. Mercedes took a 1-2 in the Penya Rhin GP and the scene shifted to extremes in Germany, to the Avus near-track event and the Eifelrennen on the sinuous Ring.

The Avusrennen final went to Fagioli at 148·83 mph, while Stuck set the lap record at 161·88 mph. Bernd Rosemeyer made his debut on four wheels in that event, and in the Eifelrennen actually led the established stars, at the end placing his Auto Union second behind Caracciola's Mercedes.

At Montlhéry three strategic chicanes enabled Nuvolari and Chiron to battle with Mercedes rather than trail them, but their Alfas wilted, leaving Mercedes to cruise to victory. Mercedes team discipline was ruffled at Spa, where Fagioli duelled with Caracciola, the eventual winner, for the Belgian GP lead, then walked off in a huff during a pit stop (Brauchitsch was hastily put in his cockpit). Then the world was turned topsy-turvy in the German Grand Prix, where Mercedes fielded five cars and Auto Union four – and at the end of 10 laps Nuvolari led in an Alfa Romeo. A broken fuel pump handle cost him 134 seconds at the pits, and five places, but back in the race he flogged the P3 through into second at the start of the last lap. The leader was Brauchitsch, always hungrily ambitious but never kind to machinery, so that it was almost justice that a rear tyre on his Mercedes failed . . . But Nuvolari's victory owed nothing to others' misfortunes, everything to his own virtuosity.

Matters returned to normal in the Coppa Acerbo, where Varzi and Rosemeyer placed Auto Unions first and second in spite of the iniquitous chicanes, and German cars swamped the Swiss GP (Mercedes 1-2-6, Auto Unions 3-4).

All the Mercedes retired in the Italian GP, Stuck won, and Nuvolari fiercely challenged in his own Alfa until the engine failed, when he took over Dreyfus' and placed it second. There remained a Mercedes 1-2-3 in the Spanish GP, and the Czech race, which

Mercedes did not contest and where fast-rising Auto Union star Rosemeyer gained his first victory.

Mercedes built a new short wheelbase car for 1936, with the 4·74 M25E engine developing 494 bhp at 5800 rpm, while Auto Union produced the C-type, which had its engine enlarged to 6 litres (75 × 85 mm) to give 520 bhp at 5000 rpm. Alone of the other constructors, Alfa Romeo persevered, using the 4 litre V-12 and 3·8 litre eight in chassis with all-independent suspension. Maserati efforts became spasmodic, as the firm increasingly turned to the voiturette class. Bugatti was eclipsed, although a new 'experimental' car appeared in the Swiss GP; experiment was confined to fitting a 4·7 litre T50 engine in a T59 chassis, and clothing it in a rather inelegant streamlined body (this was the first *monoplace* GP Bugatti); experiment, however, did not extend to independent front suspension!

The opening races at Monaco and Tunis fell to Mercedes, Caracciola winning both. But after that the best placing of the season for the three-pointed star was a second, in the Penya Rhin GP behind Nuvolari's Alfa Romeo. After an excellent start, the new Mercedes-Benz was unreliable and difficult to handle.

So 1936 became Rosemeyer's year, for he rose to the important occasions, and won the Eifelrennen, German Grand Prix, Coppa Acerbo, Swiss Grand Prix and Italian Grand Prix for Auto Union. Alfa Romeo enjoyed a brief resurgence, Nuvolari taking the Hungarian Grand Prix, Circuit of Milan, Coppa Ciano and Vanderbilt Cup. This race, run on the Roosevelt Field 'Mickey Mouse' circuit was a false dawn to the American road racing revival, for although it was repeated in 1937 America was not very appreciative and another decade was to pass before road racing returned to popularity in the New World.

This was the last pre-war season in which the Italians were able to mount an effective challenge to the Germans, who were to enjoy a season of climactic power supremacy in 1937, under the 750 kg formula extended for a year. In 1936 the Auto Unions had still been at a disadvantage on twisting circuits – certainly when Nuvolari was present in a healthy Alfa Romeo – while quite apart from Mercedes' mechanical troubles, this team was a little ragged at the edges, as clashes of personality developed. Above all, it was Rosemeyer's year, for the only other Auto Union driver to win a race was Varzi, on his Tripoli happy hunting ground. Only four races were run over more than 500 kilometres, all falling to Auto Union, three to Rosemeyer. In the Swiss Grand Prix he set the lap record at 105·42 mph, and this still stands although the Bremgarten circuit was a regular Grand Prix venue until 1954. In this race, Auto Union also gained a 1-2-3, the objective of every major team in those days of full racing teams.

German Supremacy

The original three-year span of the 750 kg formula, under which racing speeds had risen as never before, ended in 1936, but a new formula was not promulgated until the early Autumn of that year, and so by general agreement the 750 kg regulations were extended for 1937.

For this one season Auto Union made few changes to their 6 litre C-type, and increasingly relied on the brilliance of Bernd Rosemeyer, whose skill compensated for the considerable horsepower deficiencies which his car had in relation to Mercedes. Alfa Romeo could call on drivers of equal calibre, but could not provide them with competitive machinery – the 12 cylinder 4495 cc engine produced 430 bhp at 5800 rpm, which in isolation was a notable advance by the standards of 1933, but in comparison with the output of the German engines of 1937 meant that their drivers had to start races with insurmountable power handicaps. For Mercedes there was only one course; the 1936 car was abandoned, and its place taken by the formidable W125.

Fortuitously, Max Wagner and Rudolf Uhlenhaut had started work on a long-chassis car for the anticipated new formula, and into this an enlarged version of the M25 engine could be dropped. The chassis was built around two large and extremely rigid tubular side members. A twin wishbone and coil spring ifs system was used, and a de Dion axle at the rear, for the first time in a Grand Prix car, with fore and aft location looked after by radius arms. This suspension was much softer than any previously seen in racing cars, but made for greater stability and better general handling (the power of the engine meant that oversteer, 'built into' the W25 suspension, could now be induced at will).

The engine, M125, was the ultimate development of the M25, bored out to 94 mm, which with the 1936 M25E stroke of 102 mm gave a capacity of 5660 cc. Initially, the Roots-type supercharger blew air into the carburetter, but during 1937 Mercedes at last conformed to normal practice, installing it between the triple-bodied Mercedes carburetter and the engine, so that mixture was compressed (and the Mercedes 'blower' scream became a sound of the past). Up to 560 bhp was obtained in early tests, race drivers later had some 640 bhp available, while in bench tests 646 bhp was achieved.

Drivers were seldom able to make full use of this power, and indeed few drivers could handle the German cars of 1937 (against their inclinations in this nationalistic period, both teams continued to employ 'foreigners'). The W125 in particular was the most powerful Grand Prix car ever built, and in this aspect has been surpassed only by recent CanAm sports-

Top: the simple and rational chassis of the Auto Union, and (above), the equal simplicity of the W125 Mercedes cockpit; the steering wheel was detachable to allow the driver to get in and out. Right: the W125 Mercedes of 1937 was the most powerful Grand Prix car ever raced.

Above: start of the 1936 Swiss Grand Prix, with Caracciola in a Mercedes leading away from the Auto Unions driven by Rosemeyer and Varzi. Below left: a Grand Prix Mercedes with an all-enveloping streamlined body for the very fast Avus circuit. Above right: final drive and de Dion rear suspension of the 1937 Mercedes W125. Below right: a 12-cylinder Alfa Romeo before the start of the 1937 Italian Grand Prix.

racing cars. With the W125 Mercedes re-established their superiority in 1937, when the team won seven races, to Auto Union's five, and all other teams were eclipsed – in the 12 major events, only one third place fell to another marque, Rex Mays finishing third in the Vanderbilt Cup in an eight-cylinder Alfa Romeo.

Hermann Lang, the up and coming driver of the Mercedes team, whose rise from the oily-fingered ranks was not viewed very favourably by his colleagues, took the first two races at Tripoli and Avus, from pairs of Auto Unions and at the astonishing speeds of 134·25 mph and 162·61 mph. The Auto Union team came back in the next three events, Rosemeyer winning the Eifelrennen and Vanderbilt Cup, and while the team effort was split between Europe and America, his team mates Hasse and Stuck took the first two places in the Belgian GP.

Mercedes took the next two Grands Prix, Caracciola and Brauchitsch finishing first and second in the German event, Brauchitsch and Caracciola first and second at Monaco, after racing between themselves and against team orders. The Coppa Acerbo fell to Rosemeyer but in the Swiss GP Caracciola headed a

Mercedes 1-2-3. He also won the next two races, the Italian and Czech Grands Prix, and the season ended in England, on the sinuous Donington Park circuit, where spectators more accustomed to the third-rate at Brooklands were astounded by racing of a ferocity they had known only by report. Here Rosemeyer headed the Mercedes pair, Brauchitsch and Caracciola (at 82·26 mph) to round off the season, satisfactorily for Auto Union in view of Mercedes' absolute power superiority.

The formula which came into force in 1938 attempted to equate unsupercharged and supercharged engines, stipulating respective maximum capacities of 4·5 and 3 litres, coupled with a sliding scale of minimum weights, e.g. for cars with engines of the upper capacity limits, 850 kg (1874 lb). These regulations were altogether more realistic, although the advantage was still with the supercharged cars – the capacity ratio of 4·5:3 was not wide enough to give equality of power output, and the compensatory advantage of the vastly better fuel consumption of the normally-aspirated engines was not enough to bridge the gap and enable them to race on equal terms.

The weight regulations gave constructors no trouble. The ruling German teams produced more efficient machines, which despite the enforced loss of power potential were no slower round circuits than their 1937 counterparts, by virtue of better road holding. French constructors were tempted back to the Grands Prix, while the Automobile Club de France

decided to run their premier race for Grand Prix cars again, for they had thrown in the towel and arranged sports cars substitutes in 1936 and 1937. And the Italians essayed a return.

Mercedes' car was the W154, using a 2962 cc (67 × 70 mm) 60-degree V-12 in the W125 chassis. In 1938 this engine produced some 425 bhp at 7800 rpm, which was increased to 485 at 8000 rpm in 1939, when the car had a much sleeker body and was redesignated W163. Porsche's successors at Auto Union, Werner, von Eberhorst and Feuereisen, produced a new car, although early in the season the future of the team was in doubt, as Bernd Rose-meyer's life had been sacrificed in a singularly stupid

record attempt. But the decision was, go ahead. The car used a new, shorter, 60 degree V-12, with three camshafts, the central one operating the inlet valves of both banks. Its output in 1938 was 420 bhp at 7000 rpm; in 1939, with two-stage Roots supercharging, it produced 485 bhp at 7000 rpm.

Revived French interest largely centred on un-supercharged engines, although the SEFAC fleetingly appeared again, and Bugatti brought out the 1936 *monoplace* with a 3-litre engine (a twin ohc straight eight giving a modest 285 bhp at 6000 rpm). Bugatti still refused obstinately to admit independent suspen-sion, and the philosophy behind this was about as obsolete as the whole machine – had this been the

128

general standard of supercharged Grand Prix cars in 1938, the French constructors who tried the unsupercharged alternative would have enjoyed a good season!

Those firms were Delahaye and Talbot, both starting from the basis of tuned sports cars, and gradually evolving pure racing cars. The Delahaye had some advanced features, notably a de Dion rear axle located by twin radius rods, but its 4490 cc (75 × 84·7 mm)

During the late 1930s, Italian constructors increasingly turned to the voiturette classes, and Maserati produced a series of neat four- and six-cylinder cars, of which this is a 1938 example (above). French constructors, on the other hand, returned to the Grands Prix with unsupercharged cars, such as this 12-cylinder Delahaye (driven by Dreyfus at Leghorn in 1938).

V-12 engine produced only 250 bhp at 6000 rpm. In spite of this it was to achieve a moment of glory. Anthony Lago was able to persevere longer with the Talbots, which at the beginning of their Grand Prix career were simply stripped sports cars, progressed to proper single-seaters in 1939, and were further developed after the second world war. The engine was a long-stroke single ohc 4485 cc straight six, which was at least lightly stressed, economical and reliable. Its 245 bhp was transmitted through a Wilson pre-selector gearbox.

Alfa Romeo built three cars to the formula, using chassis evolved from their earlier cars, and three engines. Helpfully designated, these were the 308, a 3-litre eight (69 × 100 mm) which could be directly traced back to the B-type unit and gave a modest 295 bhp; the 312, a 63 × 73 mm V-12 which gave 320 bhp,

and the 316, a 58 × 70 mm V-16 which produced 350 bhp. None of these figures matched those obtained from German units in 1938, although optimum engine speeds, 6000 rpm in each case, were as high. The V-16 incidentally, was in effect a 'doubled' version of the 158 'Alfetta' eight which was destined to have such an illustrious career (confusingly, the 316 first appeared in a race before the 158 to which it owed its origin).

Above: Mercedes W154s lined up for the start of the 1938 Tripoli GP, which was dominated by these cars. In front of them are their portable electric starters. Below left and opposite: even the great Tazio Nuvolari drove German cars, Auto Unions, in the last pre-war seasons, here at speed and during a refuelling stop in the 1939 German GP. Italian cars were raced only spasmodically in the Grands Prix, usually by independent drivers, such as Raymond Sommer in this Alfa Romeo 8C308 in the 1939 French GP (below).

Maserati also supported the new formula, unfortunately less than wholeheartedly as their 8CTF more than once matched the German cars in speed, although not in reliability. A typical Maserati live rear axle chassis was used, with an eight-cylinder 'square' (78 × 78 mm) 32-valve engine, in effect a doubled in-line version of the 1·5 litre 4CL voiturette unit. It gave some 355 bhp at 6500 rpm. Although in specification almost obsolescent in Europe, the 8CTF was advanced by American standards and rudely upset the established order at Indianapolis.

The 1938 European season opened with a rude shock, too, when in a minor round-the-houses race run partly in a snow-storm at Pau, Rene Dreyfus drove a Delahaye to beat a Mercedes W154 shared by Caracciola and Lang. After abandoning a burning Alfa 308 in practice, Nuvolari swore never again to race a car of that marque; later in the year he joined Auto Union, a welcome addition to their otherwise merely competent driving strength.

However, until he got used to the rear-engined cars, Mercedes had matters their own way. A 1-2-3 in the Tripoli Grand Prix (Lang winning at 127·45 mph) was followed by a 1-2-3 in the French Grand Prix – more than adequate compensation for the fall from grace at Pau. At Rheims Brauchistch won at 101·13 mph from Caracciola and Lang, and only one other car was classified, Carrière's Talbot, 10 laps behind. The German Grand Prix saw Nuvolari race an Auto Union for the first time, and a victory for an English driver,

Left and above: the most efficient Grand Prix car built before the second world war, the Mercedes W163. Below: a most inefficient attempt to match German power superiority was the Bimotore Alfa Romeo, built earlier in the thirties. The best race placing for one of these twin-engined cars was a second, although in the autostrada record attempt illustrated Nuvolari was successful.

133

Richard Seaman in a Mercedes-Benz (at 80·75 mph from the W154 shared by Caracciola and Lang, and Stuck's Auto Union). The results of the Coppas Ciano and Acerbo brought refreshing changes in the top placings, for although Mercedes won both races (Lang and Caracciola respectively), Giuseppe Farina placed a 316 Alfa second in both, and older Alfas took the third places. The Swiss Grand Prix saw another Mercedes 1-2-3, *regenmeister* Rudolf Caracciola being absolute master of the Bremgarten circuit in the rain, while Seaman was second.

Two major races remained, to be won by Nuvolari. He took the Italian Grand Prix at 96·7 mph by a full lap from Farina (Alfa Romeo) and the Mercedes shared by Brauchitsch and Caracciola. At Donington Nuvolari drove one of his virtuoso races, to win the last Grand Prix to be contested on a British circuit for a decade. His speed over the 250 miles was 80·94 mph, and he was followed across the line by Mercedes drivers Lang and Seaman.

Mercedes was again the dominant marque in 1939, and Hermann Lang now the top driver. He won four of the year's principal races for Mercedes, the Pau, Belgian and Swiss Grands Prix and the Eifelrennen (as well as the Tripoli GP, which had been 'downgraded' to 1·5 litre status, which led Mercedes to build their

Above: the aggressive nose of the W163 Mercedes and, below, its V-12 engine, mounted in the chassis at an angle to the centre line and canted down towards the rear (left). Right: the voiturette alternative – four and six cylinder Maseratis lined up in Palermo's Favorita Park before the start of the 1938 Targa Florio.

The Grand Prix power and glory of the 1930s is summed up in this Mercedes-Benz W125.

one-race W165 voiturette). The Belgian Grand Prix was a tragic race, for Britain's greatest driver of the era, Richard Seaman, was killed in an accident. Rudolf Caracciola gained his last great victory in the German Grand Prix, which he won for the sixth time. Two races fell to Auto Union, the French Grand Prix after a Mercedes debacle, and the Yugoslav Grand Prix, which Tazio Nuvolari won a few hours after the outbreak of the second world war. In these races, Mercedes took four second places, Auto Union four.

In the third placings, other marques got a look in, Talbot at Pau (where there were only two Mercedes, and no Auto Unions) and in the French Grand Prix, while a Maserati was third in the German Grand Prix. This last was something of an anti-climax to a remarkable drive by Paul Pietsch, who actually led the race for a short while in an 8CTF. Equally remarkably, Giuseppe Farina held second place for seven laps on the Bremgarten circuit in a 1·5 litre Alfa Romeo 158, among the 3 litre Grand Prix cars.

At this time, Alfa Romeo were building a new car, a wholly new car, which was to challenge the Germans in 1940. This 162 had a 135 degree 'square' (62 × 62 mm) V-16 with two low-pressure superchargers, and produced some 490 bhp at 7800 rpm. Only one of six laid down was completed, a low stubby car with a de

Dion rear axle. On paper it looked promising, but the opportunity to prove promise never came. The Auto Unions never raced again, and the next time Mercedes raced their W163 conditions were very different, and could hardly have been foreseen in 1939 (in South America *formule libre* events in 1951, when they were beaten by a 2 litre Ferrari).

The second world war closed a six-year period of supreme racing and cars, which abruptly ended the life of the 'classic' racing car, passed through a phase of brute power, and ended with the approach becoming increasingly scientific. This in fact pointed to the future, although it was not truly picked up again until one of the German firms, Mercedes-Benz, returned to Grand Prix racing in 1954.

Indianapolis Vicissitudes

The upsurge in Grand Prix racing was generally reflected in other classes through the 1930s, in the sports car classics and, particularly, in secondary racing car events. Track racing remained largely a world apart, though the shortcomings of Brooklands were increasingly recognized and attempts, vain or valiant depending on individual standpoints, were made to simulate road racing conditions within the Surrey autodrome.

The Indianapolis Motor Speedway Association deliberately went its own way in 1930, with the 'Junk

Formula'. This was intended to cut the cost of racing, and encourage major manufacturers to return to the Brickyard with modified production engines. To these ends the capacity limit was raised from $91\frac{1}{2}$ cu in to 366 cu in (approximately 6 litres), and the use of pure racing engines was inhibited by detail mechanical

In 1939 Wilbur Shaw drove this 8CTF 'Boyle Special' Maserati (above) to victory at Indianapolis, thus upsetting a routine pattern which was becoming established around cars such as the Miller-based machine below.

137

restrictions; more constructively and well ahead of Europe, dual braking systems were called for; quite retrogressively, provision had to be made for riding mechanics.

Inevitably, this led to very mixed fields, which almost as inevitably were led by pure racing cars with engines well below the capacity limit – Millers with engines less than half the permitted 366 cu in won in 1930–33. Two 16-cylinder cars ran in 1930, Meyer placing the Sampson Special Miller fourth, Borzacchini completing only seven laps in a Maserati. Duesenbergs featured among the leaders at the end of the 500 for the last time in 1932, when Frame and Gleason placed them second and sixth (and a Cummins with a 360 cu in diesel engine ran the distance without a single stop, placing 13th at 86·17 mph; this car later appeared at Brooklands).

In 1932 Fred Frame at last broke de Paolo's 1925 record, winning at 104·14 mph in a front-wheel drive Hartz-Miller. Among the retirements in this race were a pair of four-wheel drive Millers, and a Miller with a 45-degree V-16 engine, made up of two eight-cylinder blocks.

Limitations on fuel tank capacity, to 15 gallons, and oil consumption, to 6 gallons for the 500 miles, were imposed in 1933. These changes were made with safety in mind, and it was cruelly ironic that in the race two drivers and a riding mechanic should be killed in accidents. Louis Meyer's winning average in 1933 was 104·16 mph, and speeds continued to slowly rise until 1937, the last year of the formula, when Wilbur Shaw won in a Gilmore Special at 113·58 mph.

This car was notable as the first Indianapolis winner to be powered by an Offenhauser 'four', an engine based on a marine power unit designed by Harry Miller back in 1926. It was to have a long and glorious career at Indianapolis, while Miller dabbled in other varied and more exotic designs, from the handsome and unsuccessful Ford V-8 engined front wheel drive cars of 1935 to the Gulf-backed failures of 1939, rear-engined, four-wheel drive, disc-braked cars.

In 1938, the Indianapolis and Grand Prix regulations were once again identical in the principal matter of engine capacity, and European cars once again became a force in the 500 (they had not been entirely absent in preceding years – a Bugatti was not qualified in 1936, while Mays and Stapp retired an Alfa Romeo and a Maserati respectively in 1937). The Alfa and Maserati entries made no impression again in 1938, when Floyd Roberts won in a four-cylinder Miller engined car at 117·20 mph, but in 1939 Wilbur Shaw brought the Boyle Special Maserati 8CTF to the Brickyard, and won quite clearly at 115·035 mph, while Babe Stapp placed an Alfa Romeo 308 fifth.

This Maserati victory was the first for a European car at Indianapolis since 1919, and in the following

year Shaw repeated his victory in the same car, at 114·82 mph in a race slowed by rain. Trying for a hat trick in 1941 Shaw crashed when in the lead; he never raced again, but the Boyle Special 8CTF was raced in the 500 for several years after the second world war, Ted Horn placing it third in 1946 and 1947, and fourth in 1948.

The last Indianapolis 500 run before America entered the second world war was won by Floyd Davis and Mauri Rose, in a Noc Out Hose Clamp Special, an Offy four, at 115·117 mph. Mays and Horn were second and third in 1941, when Ralph Hepburn finished fourth in a car powered by a centrifugally-supercharged eight-cylinder engine, the first Novi.

Second-level racing took on a new impetus in 1938, when the Alfa Romeo 158s (opposite, top, numbers 14 and 26) made their debut at Leghorn. Below: attempts were made to simulate road courses at Brooklands, but as this late-1930s shot shows, the atmosphere of the autodrome remained wholly artificial.

Secondary Racing in the Thirties

During the 1930s the voiturettes flourished, playing a secondary role which became increasingly important and more closely equivalent to the modern Formula 2. As the decade opened, Bugattis were numerically dominant, usually the four cylinder T37 or its blown alternative the T37A, while some privileged drivers had 1·5 litre Bugatti eights, in single ohc (T39) or twin ohc (T51A) form. Gradually, Maserati built up a challenging reputation for their small cars, particularly those deriving from the 4CTR-1100 of 1932. In 1936 Maserati produced the 6CM, with a twin ohc six-cylinder engine which developed 155 bhp at 6200 rpm, compared with the maximum of 130 bhp at 5600 rpm achieved by their fours. This was installed in a very rigid chassis, with torsion bar independent front suspension and semi-elliptic rear suspension – in these respects it was a replica of contemporary larger Maseratis.

Outstanding among Maserati's voiturette competitors was a British car, the first to challenge Continental 'pure' racing cars on road circuits for a decade. The ERA was in effect derived from Raymond

Mays' famous White Riley of 1933, and owed inspiration to the Continental monopostos. It was conceived by Mays and Peter Berthon, and the English Racing Automobiles company was backed by Humphrey Cook. The engine was a straightforward pushrod ohv six, basically 1500 cc (57·5 × 95·2 mm), with short stroke 1100 cc and increased bore and stroke 2 litre alternatives, all with Jamieson Roots-type superchargers. The 1500 cc engine developed 150 bhp at 6500 rpm. Reid Railton's chassis was on classic monoposto lines, with a rigid front axle and semi-elliptic sprung live rear axle. A novelty on a racing car was a Wilson pre-selector gearbox. These cars were competitive with the best of Continental machinery, and gained many successes on the circuits of Europe.

Their opposition was not, however, confined to contemporary cars, for in the mid-1930s the old 1·5 litre GP Delage of 1926–27 emerged as a formidable voiturette contender. In particular, Richard Seaman

Above: very mixed field! Richard Seaman's MG Magnette and a Maserati leading the eight-car voiturette Grand Prix away at Pescara in 1934. Below: Promise unfulfilled. One of the ten Ford-engined front-wheel drive Millers built for Indianapolis. Right: beyond expectations. The ERA was the pre-eminent British racing car of the 1930s, and most of those built are still active in historic car racing today.

acquired Lord Howe's car, on the advice of Giulio Ramponi, who meticulously rebuilt it, to perform better than it had in its Grand Prix heyday. With this remarkable old car, Seaman consistently beat the best of modern machinery, before moving on to drive Grand Prix Mercedes.

In 1937 the Italians were increasingly turning to the voiturette class, Bugatti was a fading force, the ERAs were still competitive, although lack of development was soon to begin to tell, and Geoffrey Taylor's Alta was beginning to make its mark in British races, although it suffered from a lack of resources (rather than ideas). Throughout Europe there were some

twenty-five front rank races for the 1·5 litre voiturettes during the year, on circuits ranging from Avus, where Charles Martin won in an ERA at 119·68 mph, to the Crystal Palace, where Pat Fairfield won the first major race on this little London circuit at 53·77 mph. Even the Targa Florio was run for voiturettes, from 1937 to 1940, and debased further by a shift of venue to Palermo.

Indications were that the Italians would run more of their important races for 1·5 litre cars, and this was underlined when the leading Italian company, Alfa Romeo, entered the class seriously. Their car, the 158, was laid down at the Scuderia Ferrari plant at Monza,

Above: the ERAs of Seaman, Mays and Fairfield monopolizing the front row of the grid for the 1934 Dieppe GP, with Lord Howe's Delage on the second row. Below: greater variety at Pescara for the 1936 Coppa Acerbo; Seaman is again in pole position, this time with his famous Delage, with Trossi's Maserati and an ERA alongside him. Opposite, top: Seaman on his way to victory at Pescara in the black Delage. Below: ERAs, Maseratis and a Bugatti preparing for the start of a race on Berlin's Avus track.

whence designer Gioacchino Colombo was detached to work. The 158–1500 cc, eight cylinders – power unit departed from Jano's Alfa practice of having a central gear train between two blocks of four cylinders, Colombo placing the drive to camshafts and ancillaries at the front of the engine. This 58 × 70 mm Roots-supercharged eight gave 180 bhp at 6500 rpm when first bench tested, and by the time the car was first raced, some six months later, this had been increased to 195 bhp at 7000 rpm. The 158 had a chassis built up around two near-rectangular tubes, which was to prove adequately rigid over a period of twelve years – a long time in racing – and independent suspension all round, by trailing arms and transverse leaf spring at the front swing axle and transverse leaf spring at the rear.

The 158 'Alfetta' won first time out, in the 1938 Coppa Ciano, and during the year also won the Prix de Milan; in two other events weaknesses showed up, but potential was resoundingly demonstrated.

Maserati's answer to the 158 in 1938 was the 4CM, with a four-cylinder twin ohc engine in the 6CM chassis, and in 1939, the brothers introduced their 4CL. In effect, this used half of the 8CTF 'square' engine, giving some 220 bhp at 8000 rpm in its original form; this proved less than sufficient to compete with the

Following pages: the 750 cc Austin was one of the most sophisticated of all small-capacity racing cars, with a phenomenal performance potential which was never fully realized. It had classic – although foreshortened – Grand Prix car lines.

Brute power and sophistication. Above: John Cobb in the 24-litre Napier Railton with which he established the all-time Brooklands record at 143·44 mph, leaping from one of the track's notorious bumps. Below: the Mercedes-Benz W165, built in response to a last-minute change in the regulations for the 1939 Tripoli GP, which these cars dominated.

Alfetta in 1939. The basic design was of course to be continued after the war as the 4CLT Grand Prix car.

English Racing Automobiles changed hands, and in 1939 introduced the E-type, with a tubular frame, torsion bar independent front suspension and de Dion rear axle. However, this car proved disappointing, before and after the war, while the older cars, some modified with Tecnauto independent front suspension and the D-type with Zoller supercharger, continued to race on, although their race successes in 1939 were largely confined to British events.

The great surprise of 1939 was sprung by Mercedes. Among the races to be run for 1·5 litre cars in that year was the Tripoli Grand Prix, far and away the richest race on the European calendar, and one to which considerable prestige attached. Both Auto Union and

form produced 260 bhp at 8500 rpm. It was later developed with two-stage supercharging to give 278 bhp.

At Tripoli the two Mercedes shared the front row of the grid with Villoresi's aerodynamic Maserati, and in the race blew off the Italians in no uncertain fashion – the works Maseratis did not last through the opening phase, and although Farina held a brief lead in one of the four Alfa Romeo 158s which started, these cars overheated and only one finished, in a distant third place. Lang, in the higher-geared of the two Mercedes, won at 122·91 mph from team mate Caracciola, and put in the fastest lap of the race at 133·5 mph. The Mercedes W165 never raced again – one of the fascinating might-have-beens of motor racing was the never-fulfilled rumours that they would be brought out again to face the Alfa Romeo 158s in Grands Prix after the second world war . . .

Alfa's Tripoli lapse was soon corrected by a revised cooling system, and the 158s were not beaten again in 1939 or 1940. Although in 1940 a direct revenge match was not possible, Alfa Romeo scored a 1-2-3 with the 158s in the Tripoli Grand Prix, and winner Farina averaged 128·22 mph, significantly faster than Lang in 1939, and indeed faster than Lang's winning speed in a 3-litre Mercedes in 1938. In the many voiturette races where the Alfa Romeos were not run, Maseratis generally reigned. The immediate day of the ERA was over, although they were to race again after the war, when despite their antiquated appearance they proved to be more than mere grid-fillers in Grands Prix. Most of those built are still actively raced today, in historic car events.

Mercedes Benz had read the clear writing on the wall and proposed 1·5 litre cars; the Auto Union V-16 was never raced, but to the consternation of the Italians, Mercedes got two W165s to the Tripoli grid. This car was perhaps the most efficient piece of racing machinery built by either of the German firms during the 1930s; it resembled a scaled-down W163, and was built in less than six months. The chassis, running gear and transmission were identical to that of the Grand Prix car, the engine was a compact supercharged over-square (65 × 58 mm) 90-degree V-8, which in Tripoli

Above: the E-type ERA. Unlike its predecessors, this car was unsuccessful in racing. Below: Earlier ERAs in their prime. One of the most famous finishes at Brooklands came in the 1936 JCC International Trophy race, when Bira took the lead from Mays on the last lap.

In parallel with these principal voiturettes, smaller capacity racing classes also gained ground. Maseratis were consistently in the forefront of 1100 cc racing throughout the decade, but at least during the first half the MG Magnette K3 was a considerable force. This was basically a sports car, and as such is probably best remembered, above all for its Mille Miglia and TT performances. But like others of its kind, it could be 'stripped' to run under racing car regulations. Despite weight and somewhat archaic appearance apparently telling against it, the K3 proved very competitive. It had a very simple chassis frame, with semi-elliptic leaf spring suspension front and rear, a single ohc six-cylinder engine (57 × 71 mm) and a Wilson pre-selector gearbox. Odd cars were converted to single-seaters, notably Raffaele Cecchini's, with which he took the Italian 1100 cc Championship in 1934.

In two consecutive years, 1933 and 1934, the voiturette race on the great Pescara circuit (Coppa Acerbo

Maserati came back into the forefront of racing with the 3 litre 8CTF, which showed promise in Europe and as the Boyle Special (above) won at Indianapolis, and with the closely-related 1·5 litre 4CL (below).

Junior) fell to K3s, to Whitney Straight at 75·48 mph in 1933 and to Hamilton at 73·42 mph in 1934 (this K3 was clocked through the flying kilometre at 122·25 mph). These were the most notable K3 performances on the Continent, where until the arrival of the ERA these MGs were the only British cars to make a consistent showing in racing car events.

Outstanding in the 750 cc capacity class were the last of a long line of Austin racing cars, which stemmed originally from the famous Seven. The positive link with these was finally broken in 1936, when the side-valve engine was abandoned in favour of a supercharged twin-ohc four cylinder unit of 744 cc (60 × 65 mm), which gave just under 100 bhp at 7800 rpm, but was never developed to its full potential (116 bhp was obtained from the engine in sprint form, and it was designed ultimately to peak at 12000 rpm). In terms of bhp per litre, therefore, this little racing engine compared more than favourably with most contemporary Grand Prix power units.

Apart from their actual racing career, these 'miniature Grand Prix car' Austins are of incidental interest as the last monoposto racing cars to be built and raced as a team by a major British manufacturer.

During the 1930s, second level racing broadly took on the form which it has today, although the intention was not so deliberately to 'step' racing car classes towards the premier Grand Prix class. In retrospect, the cars appeared much more varied than they do today, reflecting their constructors' lines rather than conforming to a general overall pattern. There were, of course, fewer cars, and races were more often organized for mixed classes. This exaggerated the appearance of wide performance variations, which would hardly be acceptable to modern race crowds accustomed to closely matched fields.

The pattern which we know today was well and truly laid before the second world war, and was to be picked up again surprisingly quickly after it.

THE LAST CLASSIC ERA

The Second Revival

The second world war resulted in far wider devastation than the first, and left deeper scars, yet motor sport recovered more quickly, and the recovery was more cohesive and constructive. It was a sport very much in tune with the times and proved to be one of the leading growth sports in Britain and the United States. At first, the old habits and traditions were resumed, but together with the carried-over, and sometimes impromptu, organizations, they were soon to be transformed.

Appropriately, the first post-war race meeting was organized in France, in the Bois de Boulogne in Paris on September 9, 1945 – three months after the 'end of hostilities' in Europe. The principal race resulted in the last victory for a single-seat Bugatti to be recorded in this book, a 4·7 litre car driven by Jean-Pierre Wimille (at 70·10 mph); he was followed across the line by Sommer and Chaboud (Talbots).

The true revival got under way in 1946, when the races were contested by drivers of the pre-war era – albeit there were some sad gaps in their ranks. Most notable absence was that of Robert Benoist, who had lost his life in a German concentration camp. The cars were necessarily a somewhat aged and mixed collection, but during the year the first works team of stature appeared, the Alfa Corse 158s. There were of course no German teams – the Auto Union headquarters and equipment was in any case in East Germany, and although the marque name was to be revived in 1950, the link with the past racing combine was tenuous; the Mercedes were scattered, and before the parent factory could start collecting them again, a 'liberated' W163 was taken to America and run at Indianapolis (where its complexity baffled its American crew, and it was later ruined with a native mill), while on the other hand strenuous efforts to extricate a pair of

Above: new era. The start of an F2 race at Florence in 1948, and, left, Raymond Sommer bringing in the winning car, a 12 cylinder Ferrari 125. Below: the old order. Jean-Pierre Wimille on his way to victory at the first post-war race meeting, in the Bois de Boulogne, driving a monoplace Bugatti, and, right, a visually incongruous pairing of an archaic ERA and a San Remo Maserati.

W165s from a Swiss garage failed.

The first 1946 race of real consequence was the Coupe René Lebègue, or St Cloud Grand Prix, run over a sinuous little circuit in the Paris suburb. Here two Alfa Romeo 158s appeared, from their interment behind the wall in a dairy produce factory (whence they had been spirited when the German army took over control of Monza in 1943). From this point, the 158 was to undergo five years of almost continuous development, to uprate its performance out of all recognition as Alfa Romeo's last Grand Prix car. The company abandoned their 512 project, a some-

what cumbersome rear-engined car designed by Ricart, with a 54 × 54·2 mm two-stage supercharged V-12, which gave some 335 bhp at 8600 rpm.

At St Cloud both Alfa Romeo drivers, Farina and Wimille, retired with transmission troubles – a complete team failure which was to be unique in the postwar career of the 158. The 112-mile race fell to Raymond Sommer in a 308 Alfa, at 67·99 mph from Louis Chiron, returning to full-time racing after an accident in a short-chassis Mercedes W25 in the 1936 German Grand Prix.

Before the next major race came an event at Albi which revived all the atmosphere of the once-numerous 'regional' Grands Prix, which were still to thrive for a few years. The nostalgia was enhanced when it was won by Tazio Nuvolari, driving a Maserati.

A fuller return to pre-war standards was seen at Geneva, where after their tentative trial outing at

St Cloud, Alfa Corse ran a full team of 158s, which were placed 1-2-3 in the Grand Prix des Nations by Farina (64·10 mph), Trossi and Wimille. Here the first step in the uprating process was seen, for two of the cars had engines with two-stage superchargers, which increased power to over 250 bhp, at 7500 rpm. These 158/46Bs were seen again in two other races in 1946, where they demonstrated what would happen under the first post-war Grand Prix formula which was to influence racing in 1947, although it did not officially come into force until 1948. Five were started in the Turin Grand Prix, and the first past the flag was driven by Achille Varzi, completely rehabilitated after a period of drug-induced degeneracy; his winning speed was 64·62 mph, and sulkily obedient to team

orders, Wimille followed him in another Alfa 158.

The Milan Grand Prix heats fell to Varzi and works test driver Sanesi, who was allowed one of his occasional race outings and made up for Farina's out-of-sorts mood (after this race Farina parted company with Alfa Romeo until 1950). In the final, Trossi, Varzi and Sanesi placed their 158s first, second and third, then the cars were put away until 1947, when they emerged as one of the most formidable forces in the history of Grand Prix racing (from that Geneva race, five full years were to pass before the Alfa Romeo team suffered a race defeat).

These 1946 races had been run to *formule libre* rules, and the same type of event now stimulated a resurgence of circuit racing in South America. In

One of Lou Moore's famous Blue Crown Specials, which took first and second places in the 1947 and 1948 Indianapolis 500-mile races.

Brazil there had been a period of European-type circuit racing during the second half of the thirties – in 1937 Pintacuda achieved a fairly rare distinction, by driving an Alfa Romeo to victory over the Auto Union sent out to contest the Rio de Janeiro Grand Prix – but the general South American background was of wild open-road races, often over enormous distances. These *turismo carretera* races were usually contested by tuned American sedans, and reached a peak in the immediate post-war years, when the outstanding drivers were the Galvez brothers and one Juan Manuel Fangio. During this same period, a

surprising number of obsolescent European racing cars found their way to Argentina, and some European drivers took others down during the northern hemisphere off-season to campaign in the increasingly important local circuit races. The trail was blazed by Achille Varzi with an Alfa Romeo 308 and Luigi Villoresi with a 1·5 litre Maserati in 1947; they ran in five races, between them scoring four wins and three second placings.

Varzi and Villoresi were joined by Farina and Wimille, as well as several lesser Europeans, in 1948, and the Argentine Automobile Club purchased a pair of up-to-date cars, 4CL Maseratis, for Fangio and Oscar Galvez, although the latter preferred his Alfa Romeo 308.

The results of the 1948 races illustrated the fascinating variety of the fields. Villoresi won two races at Buenos Aires in a 4CL Maserati, the first from Chico Landi's Alfa 308, the second from Galvez' 308. In the Mar del Plata Grand Prix Farina scored the second of only two road race victories ever to fall to a Maserati 8CTF (the first was in a heat at Buenos Aires two weeks earlier), while Varzi was second in a V-12 Alfa 312. Wimille and Galvez placed Alfas third and fourth and were followed by Fangio, appearing for the first time in a race results list coupled with Maserati.

In the Rosario Grand Prix, Fangio actually duelled for the lead with Wimille. Both were driving 1220 cc Gordinis, which were much better suited to the sinuous circuit than the big cars, as was shown by Fangio's fastest race lap of 58·53 mph, in very exalted company. At just over half-distance Fangio blew his engine, leaving Wimille to win from Landi and Villoresi, but the point was not lost to visiting Europeans. This led to Fangio's first visit to Europe, with Oscar Galvez, and to his inauspicious first appearance in a formula race, at Rheims.

The South American series continued on a *formule libre* basis for several years, increasingly contested by current European cars, while the older cars run by

The improvised street circuits which were created out of necessity were often completely innocent of the safety trappings considered essential today. Below: the grid for the 1946 Milan GP, with representatives of the leading Italian marques, Alfa Romeo, Maserati, and Ferrari on the front row, and, left, Achille Varzi swinging an Alfa 158 round an unprotected lamp post in the race. Right: start of the 1947 Lausanne GP, with Alberto Ascari leading in a 4CL Maserati, from Villoresi in another Maserati and Wimille (Simca Gordini).

locals were correspondingly outclassed. In the 1949 Mar del Plata Grand Prix, Fangio scored his first victory in a European formula car, a Maserati; later that year he raced a fairly full European season, and his story becomes part of the mainstream Grand Prix story. The Argentine temporada saw an odd flashback in 1951, when Mercedes dusted down three 1939 Grand Prix W163s and ran them in the Peron Cup and Eva Peron Cup races at Buenos Aires, where one was driven by Hermann Lang, and the others by Karl Kling and Juan Manuel Fangio. The cars were never quite *au point* and past glories were not recaptured, for in both races the W163s were beaten by a 2 litre Ferrari, driven by Froilan Gonzalez.

Ferrari was one of the new marque names to come into existence in that first full post-war year, out of Enzo Ferrari's Auto Avio Costruzioni company, which he had established at Modena when he severed his long-standing association with Alfa Romeo in

1939. BRM also had its beginnings in 1946, created around the nominal company Automobile Racing Developments Ltd by Raymond Mays and Peter Berthon, who had of course been largely responsible for the ERA. In Italy Cisitalia SpA was established, while in France Amédée Gordini began to emerge as more than a gifted Simca tuner, and work began on the CTA-Arsenal project. None of these was to affect racing in 1946 – indeed, some were to prove lost causes – but the first steps had been taken towards developing a new generation of cars. Nobody, however, could have read any significance into the competition debut of an odd little special at a Prescott hill climb in July 1946; this was the first rear-engined Cooper, the first of a line which little more than ten years later was to turn the Grand Prix world upside down.

Would-be British race organizers faced a curious problem – on the British mainland there were no circuits on which to run races. Brooklands and Donington Park had been ruined during the war, and the Crystal Palace circuit was not to reopen until 1955. The first post-war British race meeting was held at Ballyclare in 1946, when B. Bira drove an ERA to win the Ulster Trophy, while on the mainland the potential of the runways and perimeter tracks of redundant military airfields was being investigated. The first of these to be used as a race circuit was Gransden Lodge, where a meeting was organized in July 1946; two years later the Goodwood and Silverstone circuits were opened. Amenities at these were primitive, but imitation road circuits were created which were at least adequate, and where the new enthusiasm for motor racing could flourish.

In the same year road racing was reborn in America, on a circuit of very genuine roads at Watkins Glen. Within its 6·6 mile lap were town streets and a railroad crossing. The first Watkins Glen Grand Prix was run for a very free formula field in October 1948, and won by Alfa Romeo driver Frank Grimwold. The original Watkins Glen circuit was abandoned after an accident involving spectators, and an artificial road circuit opened in 1956. By that time, road racing was very firmly re-established in the United States.

Meanwhile track racing had of course been resumed. The Indianapolis track had been allowed to deteriorate badly during the war years – Speedway president Eddie Rickenbacker apparently lost interest in it – and it was left largely to Wilbur Shaw and local industrialist Tony Hulman to regenerate interest and revive the 500. In this they succeeded, and in 1946 the race was run again, like the European events apparently picking up again where it had left off, and under the same 3 litre supercharged/4·5 litre unsupercharged regulations (which were to remain in force until 1956).

The 1946 500 attracted European entries, first and

The superb centrifugally-supercharged Novi (above) was far and away the fastest car at Indianapolis in the immediate post-war period, but never had the stamina to lead for 500 miles. So year after year the race fell to Offenhauser-engined 'roadsters', of which Lee Wallard's 1951 winning Belanger Special (left) is representative.

foremost an Italian team with three Maseratis, a new 8CL with the familiar 78 × 78 mm 'double four' straight eight, for which 420 bhp at 7000 rpm was hopefully claimed, for Villoresi, and two 1·5 litre cars for Varzi and an American driver, Duke Nalon. Rudolf Caracciola, by then a Swiss citizen, tried hard to get one of his W165 Mercedes to Indianapolis for the race, failed, and went as a spectator. Once there, he accepted Joel Thorne's invitation to race a Thorne Special, but during the ritual qualifying trials he

crashed, hitting his head on the track as he was thrown out of the car; two years were to pass before he fully recovered from the after-effects of concussion. Somewhat ironically, the 1946 500 was won by George Robson, driving the other Thorne Special, at 114·82 mph, from Jackson and Horn, in an unblown Offenhauser and the supercharged Boyle Special Maserati respectively. Luigi Villoresi placed the 8CL seventh, in the best Indianapolis showing for a European driver for many years, past or to come.

So, in a remarkably short time racing was re-established, and even expanding. In Europe at least this was in the face of severe shortages, which extended beyond mere components such as tyres and plugs, to the general fuel supply situation. This meant that organizers using some of the traditional circuits away from large towns lost money because of poor spectator attendances, and that round-the-houses town racing enjoyed a brief period of enhanced popularity. This phase passed, and the great circuits such as Rhiems and Spa soon came back into favour, for racing closer and faster than any that had gone before.

Italian Domination

Although the first Grand Prix regulations to be distinguished by the now-familiar term Formula did not come into effect until 1948, they were anticipated and applied to the principal races run in 1947. In their main stipulation, these were more realistic than those applied immediately before the war, equating 1·5 litre supercharged engines with 4·5 litre unsupercharged units, and in five years did lead to parity in performance. Thus the one-time 1·5 litre voiturettes were brought into direct competition with unsupercharged cars derived from the unsupercharged Grand Prix machines of 1939. Voiturette continuity was preserved in a new Formula 2 in 1948, for cars with unsupercharged engines of 2 litres, or supercharged 500 cc engines, and a little later the first Formula 3 was created around the unsupercharged half-litre cars which by 1950 had gained enormous popularity, especially in Britain.

Until the World Championship was inaugurated in 1950, the major teams did not feel obliged to contest all the major races, simply in order to gain points. Hence, in the 1947 *grandes épreuves*, Alfa Romeo ran a team in only three, the Swiss, Belgian and Italian events, entering four, but in fact ignoring the revived French race (although two cars were run in a secondary event at Bari).

Where the Alfas were raced in 1947, they won, for there was little real opposition (a comment in no way intended to belittle the gallant efforts of some other drivers, notably Raymond Sommer, with outclassed machinery). The 158s were little modified, for with minor improvements the power output of the two-stage engine was 275 bhp, which was quite adequate. The 158/47 engine which was developed and ready was not needed (in this form, with an enlarged low-pressure blower, it gave 310 bhp, still at 7500 rpm).

Maseratis were the only other supercharged cars to be really successful on the circuits, winning eight of the principal secondary races. Most of those raced in

1947 were 4CLs, but the new 4CLT appeared, to show promise, especially in the hands of Alberto Ascari and Luigi Villoresi, driving for the quasi-works Scuderia Ambrosiana team. The 4CLT was the first product of the new Maserati company, for the three surviving brothers, Bindo, Ernesto and Ettore, had sold their original firm to the Orsi family in 1947, and returned to Bologna to set up Osca. In the 4CLT a tubular frame was substituted for the original box-section chassis, and during the year work was started on a more comprehensive revised version for 1948.

The E-type ERA appeared spasmodically, and progressed erratically – the older, and in appearance archaic, ERAs achieved better overall results during the year. Geoffrey Taylor revived his Alta, now using a tubular chassis and independent suspension all round (by wishbones and rubber in compression), and eventually progressing to a two-stage supercharged version of his four-cylinder engine (which gave some 230 bhp at 7000 rpm). This achieved no great successes in Formula 1, but the engine was to become the basis of competitive Formula 2 cars.

Another supercharged car appeared once, for its only race. This was the French CTA-Arsenal (built at a government arsenal by the Centre d'Etudes Tech-

Above left: coming man, coming marque – Alberto Ascari (Ferrari) in the 1949 Swiss GP. Right: a pair of Maseratis leading an assortment of cars – Lago-Talbot, Ferrari, ERA, Simca-Gordini and Alta – around the sand dunes of Zandvoort in the 1949 Dutch GP. Below: classic revived – the start of the 1948 Monaco GP, with eventual winner Farina, Wimille and Villoresi leading away, and (left) Giraud-Cabantous' Talbot racing along a Monaco quai.

niques de l'Automobile et du Cycle, hence its name). The engine, designed by Lory of Delage fame, was a 90-degree V-8 (60 × 65·5 mm) with two-stage super-charging. In early bench tests this gave a very respectable 266 bhp at 7500 rpm, and was estimated to have a potential of at least 300 bhp. However, Lory was not responsible for the rest of the car, the rather dated box-section chassis, torsion bar independent suspension, or the transmission. The car appeared in practice for the 1947 and 1948 French Grands Prix, but got to a grid only once, in 1947. Sommer qualified it for the fifth row of the 1947 grid; at the start the clutch first jammed, then freed and went in suddenly; a half-shaft broke, and that was the end of the one and only race

appearance of that exemplary white elephant.

A pre-war machine of the same breed also lingered on – the elusive SEFAC, which with its engine stripped of superchargers and enlarged to 3·6 litres, was re-named Dommartin. True to its former self it featured in entry lists, but never actually came to a starting grid.

Meanwhile, work had started on the elaborate Cisitalia Grand Prix car, the Type 360. Piero Dusio, who had founded Cisitalia in 1946, in effect commissioned a design through the Austrians Carlo Abarth and Rudolf Hruscka, to the Porsche Büro. In concept, Ferry Porsche's design would have been advanced at any time in the next 20 years, and was thoroughly approved by his illustrious father, Dr Ferdinand

Porsche (who was released by the French in the summer of 1947, and was to live to see the company bearing his name well and truly established). Unfortunately, Dusio's ambition outran his resources, and his Grand Prix Cisitalia never appeared on a Grand Prix circuit.

The Type 360 had a simple but rigid tubular space frame, Porsche-type torsion bar suspension, independent front and rear, its engine mounted behind the driver, an all-syncromesh five-speed gearbox, and two- or four-wheel drive, which could be selected by the driver. The engine was a flat-12 (56 × 51 mm), each bank having two overhead camshafts and its own vane-type supercharger. With two single-stage superchargers it produced 296 bhp at 8500 rpm; the target with two-stage supercharging, which was never in fact fitted, was 550 bhp at 12000 rpm! When Cisitalia went into liquidation in 1950 the only complete car was taken to Agentina by Dusio, where it made one fleeting circuit appearance. Two cars now exist, one built up from parts; both are in museums.

There remained the unsupercharged French cars. Some Delahayes lingered on, undeveloped; the Lago-Talbots were steadily improved, although never to the point of completely losing their sports car origins. In 1947 the single inclined overhead camshaft operated by pushrods was retained, while a version of the engine using two similar camshafts was developed.

White elephants. Above: Raymond Sommer in the CTA-Arsenal during practice for the 1947 French Grand Prix, and (left) Tazio Nuvolari posing in the cockpit of the Cisitalia 360.

Ferraris dominated the first Formula 2, as they do the front of this Monza grid.

Although these Talbots were considerably heavier than their 'pure' racing contemporaries, and their engines at least 60 bhp less powerful than that of the dominant Alfa 158, the Talbot was much more economical and so could complete a regulation 500 km *grande épreuve* with at most one stop for fuel against the two or three required by the blown 1·5 litre cars. Hare and tortoise tactics thus allowed drivers of the outclassed Talbots to cause even Alfa drivers to over-stress their engines on occasions. Above all, the Talbots were usually completely reliable.

Four of the *grandes épreuves* – which roughly means the European national Grands Prix, of the status which later qualified as World Championship events – were run in 1947. The first of these was the Swiss Grand Prix at Berne in June. Here the heats fell to Alfa 158 drivers Varzi and Wimille, while the final saw an almost inevitable Alfa 1-2-3, Wimille winning at 95·42 mph from Varzi and Trossi; fourth was Raymond Sommer in a Maserati 4CLT, ahead of Alfa fourth string Sanesi. The Belgian Grand Prix saw the same three Alfa drivers in the first three places, Wimille's winning speed being 95·28 mph.

The Italian Grand Prix was run at Milan. Wimille was absent from the Alfa Romeo team, apparently after an undisciplined display at Spa where he needlessly duelled with Varzi. So it became Trossi's turn to win, from Varzi, Sanesi and – such was the insolent superiority of the Alfa team – mechanic Gaboardi in fourth place, ahead of acknowledged ace Sommer (who admittedly was delayed by one of the frailties

apparently built into 4CLT Maseratis). The 'Ecurie Wimille' Alfa 158 entries did not appear for the French Grand Prix, presumably for the reason that after Spa J-P was in disgrace in Milan! So this race round an odd makeshift circuit at Lyon was more open. Here poor Raymond Sommer suffered the indignity of the CTA-Arsenal clutch failure, and Louis Chiron fully justified one of his nicknames, the Wily Fox. The opening phase was dominated by 4CL and 4CLT Maseratis, but then Chiron calmly drove an Ecurie France Talbot into the lead, and stayed there, in the late stages cruising past the pits to disguise the fact that the cylinder head gasket of his engine had failed. The opposition was neatly deluded into thinking that Chiron considered he had the race sewn up, and did not urge their drivers to press him. So he won by a comfortable margin from Maserati driver Louveau, three more Talbots and a Delahaye, while Peter Whitehead brought home his aged R10B ERA into seventh place.

Through the year there were numerous secondary events, of which several were out of the ordinary for various reasons. Alfa Corse ran a pair of 158s in the Bari GP, where Varzi and Sanesi placed them first and second. The name Ascari appeared again in race programmes, and at Modena at the end of September at the head of the results list, for Alberto was following in the footsteps of his father Antonio (like so many other drivers, Alberto had started his racing career on motorcycles, in 1936; in 1940 he had driven his first car race, in an '815', a Ferrari in all but name, in the Mille Miglia, and had then placed a 6CM Maserati ninth in the 1940 Tripoli GP).

Then at Turin the first race victory for a 'true' Ferrari was gained by Raymond Sommer, at the wheel of a 125. This car was the basis of several sports, sports-racing and racing Ferraris, including the first Grand Prix car of that marque, in 1948. These were built around Gioacchino Colombo's 60 degree V-12, which was to be the basis of so many Ferrari engines. In 1·5 litre Formula 1 guise, it was oversquare (55 × 52·5 mm), and in 1948 was raced only in single ohc form, with a single stage Roots supercharger. In this form it produced some 225 bhp at 7500 rpm. It was installed in a simple tubular chassis, light and very short (the short wheelbase made for tricky handling, and was extended for the following year). Suspension was independent, by wishbones and transverse leaf spring at the front; initially torsion bars were used at the rear, but were soon replaced by a swing axle and transverse leaf spring arrangement. The transmission, through a five-speed box and limited slip differential, was another weak point of this first GP Ferrari.

Also new in 1948 was the 4CLT/48 Maserati, which had a neater tubular frame, and hence lower body,

coil spring suspension, and two-stage supercharging to its substantially redesigned engine, which now gave over 240 bhp at 7500 rpm. From its first race victory at San Remo in June, this model gained its 'San Remo' popular name (perhaps of greater import, it was driven to that victory by Alberto Ascari, who thus gained his first formula race win).

These cars apart there was little mechanical novelty on the circuits in 1948. Alfa Corse raced the 158 and 158/47, or 158A, in only four events, and their presence again set these apart. The Alfas first came out for the Swiss Grand Prix, for a tragic Bremgarten meeting. In practice on a soaking circuit Achille Varzi made a rare error, and was caught out by the acceleration of the 158/47; he was killed as the car overturned. Later in practice Italian motorcycle champion turned voiturette driver Omobono Tenni was killed, and the opening laps of the race Kautz, de Graffenried and Fagioli were involved in a multiple accident, in which Christian Kautz was killed. The Grand Prix fell to Trossi – this was to be his last race victory – from his Alfa team mate Wimille, and Villoresi (Maserati 4CLT/48).

The French Grand Prix returned to Rheims, where Alberto Ascari drove his only race for Alfa Romeo, his father's team, where one J. M. Fangio first appeared

Left: primitive beginnings – the first Grand Prix at Silverstone, on a section which apart from the addition of safety banks and a bridge has not changed since. The winning Maseratis of Villoresi and Ascari are starting from the back of the grid. Above: sponsorship in 1950? Alberto Ascari applying opposite lock in a 4·5 litre Ferrari embazoned with the name of a medical compound and, right, cornering a Maserati with absolute precision during the 1949 Argentine Temporada. Bottom: characteristic Phi Phi – Etancelin with his cap back to front, driving a Talbot in the 1949 GP de Paris.

in a *grande épreuve*, where Tazio Nuvolari raced in a *grande épreuve* for the last time, and where the CTA-Arsenal made its second appearance, before disappearing to gather museum dust.

Wimille won the race at 102·96 mph, from Sanesi and Ascari in the inevitable Alfa 1-2-3. Fangio retired, little noticed. Nuvolari drove a few laps in Villoresi's Maserati 4CLT/48, the only car of the marque to run through the race (finishing seventh); Nuvolari never raced a Grand Prix again, and died quietly in his bed in 1953. The CTA-Arsenal did not even get to the start, and French honour was upheld by the Talbots which finished 4-5-6 behind the Alfa Romeos.

The next race contested by the Alfa team was the Italian Grand Prix, in Turin's Valentino Park. Here Wimille won in a 158/47, and the two 158s which started failed to last the distance. So Villoresi placed a 4CLT/48 second, and Sommer a Ferrari third. Then the opening of the Monza autodrome was celebrated with a full-length Grand Prix, which proved to be an Alfa Romeo benefit; 158/47s filled the first three places, Wimille (109·98 mph), Trossi and Sanesi, while that racing jack of all trades, Piero Taruffi was fourth in a 158, ahead of Ascari's Maserati and Chaboud's Talbot.

Above: the clean but generally outclassed Alfa, and below, the cluttered but within its limits effective Cisitalia (Bonetto in the cockpit at Florence in 1948). Opposite: Maserati in the rain at *Buenos Aires, and an E-type ERA in the sunshine, in the Isle of Man during the 1949 British Empire Trophy.*

But these 'Alfa' races were far from the whole story of the 1948 season. The Monaco Grand Prix was revived in June, and over its traditional 100 laps Farina won in a 4CLT Maserati at 59·74 mph, from a motley field (at the end from Chiron's Talbot, de Graffenried's 4CL, and Maurice Trintignant's 1·4 litre supercharged Simca-Gordini).

Then the new Zandvoort circuit was opened in Holland, with a race organized by the British Racing Drivers Club and won by Bira, driving a Maserati 4CL at 73·25 mph. The Pedralbes circuit in Spain saw racing again, with Villoresi and Parnell in Maserati 4CLT/48s winning the Penya Rhin GP from Chiron's Talbot. Villoresi also won at Albi, Pau and Comminges, while Farina took the Grand Prix des Nations at Geneva for Maserati, from Swiss driver de Graffenried (Maserati) and Sommer (Ferrari).

At the first Goodwood meeting, in September, the principal race was won by Parnell, driving a 4CLT/48, from a field of miscellaneous Maseratis and ERAs. In the following month the first of the post-war series of British Grands Prix was run, at Silverstone. It was dominated by Villoresi and Ascari, in Maserati 4CLT/48s, who arrived too late for official practice, started from the back of the grid and led after three racing laps. Villoresi won, at 72·28 mph, from Ascari and Bob Gerard's old ERA, of which more was to be heard . . .

Alfa Romeo withdrew from racing in 1949; their experimental department was pre-occupied with work on the production 1900, there was a shortage of funds, and three great Alfa drivers had died, Achille Varzi at Berne, Count Trossi of cancer, and Jean-Pierre Wimille while practising with a Simca-Gordini at Buenos Aires early in 1949. The absence of Alfa Romeo made for a very open season, with no single marque gaining dominance.

Among the year's non-events, the BRM too slowly took shape, while its French counterpart, the CTA-Arsenal, was quietly abandoned and its rival in complexity, the Cisitalia 360, was completed only as the Cisitalia company collapsed.

This left Maserati, Ferrari and Talbot. Maserati were not left in command, for attempts to extract more power from the engine, mainly by raising supercharger pressures, drastically reduced reliability; 4CLT/48 retirements, often with drivers oil-soaked, became ever more common. Ferrari became more prominent, and in the late summer introduced a new GP car; this had a longer wheelbase, lowered chassis, and a twin ohc V-12, which with two-stage supercharging had a power output approaching 300 bhp at 7500 rpm. A little more power was squeezed from the Talbot 'six', which coupled with the frailty of the supercharged engines, made the French cars a little more competitive (meanwhile, Lago began to lay plans for a supercharged 1·5 litre V-16).

The early-season races in Europe were remarkable for the performances of Fangio in a Maserati, at San Remo, Pau and Perpignan, and in a Simca at Marseilles. His other European victory of the year came at Albi, in high summer.

The first national Grand Prix was the British event, again at Silverstone but on the 'perimeter track' circuit which has been used ever since (although in 1949 a straw bale chicane was arranged, to improvise a slow corner). Italian participation was limited to Villoresi of the front-rank drivers; he retired after

165

which was run for sports cars in 1949 – at Rheims ended in victory for Louis Chiron, driving a Talbot. But only after Peter Whitehead had pulled out an apparently conclusive lead, only to lose it in the closing laps as his Ferrari stuck in fourth gear.

The Zandvoort Grand Prix heats were won by Villoresi and Parnell, and the 104 mile final by Villoresi at 77·12 mph from de Graffenried, Bira and Farina, all Maserati-mounted. The International Trophy at Silverstone attracted a better entry than the British GP, and after Bira and Villoresi had taken the heats, Ascari won the final for Ferrari, at 89·58 mph from Farina (Maserati), Villoresi (Ferrari), de Graffenried (Maserati) and Peter Walker, for whom an E-type ERA performed reasonably well (he put in third-fastest race lap in this usually temperamental machine). Two major races were left, both to be won by Ferraris. The new twin-ohc cars appeared for the Grand Prix of Italy and Europe at Monza, and one of these was driven to victory by Ascari, a lap clear of Etancelin's Talbot in second place. Ascari's winning speed was 105·04 mph, compared with the 109·98 mph achieved by Wimille in a 158/47 Alfa Romeo over the same distance in 1948 (but then Ascari was not hurried in the second half of the race, as most of his frontline opponents had retired – only nine of the 23 starters finished). Quite remarkably, Cuth Harrison placed his venerable ERA sixth, at Monza!

The last race of the season saw a victory for an English driver, Peter Whitehead, the first since Seaman won the 1938 German Grand Prix. This was the revived Czechoslovak Grand Prix, run over a short-

leading in the early stages, leaving the race to three other Maserati drivers, Bira, Parnell and de Graffenried, of whom the Swiss survived to the end, winning at 77·31 mph from Gerard's 12-year-old ERA ahead of the first of the Talbots, Rosier's. The British GP was hardly established as a classic in 1949, and the first event of that stature, the Belgian GP, fell to Louis Rosier, who kept his Talbot rumbling steadily round to cover the 314 miles at 96·95 mph and cross the line ahead of three Ferrari drivers, Villoresi, Ascari and Whitehead. However, the Ferraris, lead-ballasted for stability, were on top again in the Swiss Grand Prix, Ascari winning from Villoresi at 90·76 mph.

A Grand Prix de France – not a French Grand Prix,

Opposite, top: happy warrior. Bob Gerard with the ERA he campaigned remarkably effectively after the war, amid the straw bales which distinguished the sometimes vague 'road' edges on the concrete wastes of airfields. Left: start of the Rome GP, among more real trackside markers, and with the inevitable Ferraris in front. Above: a relaxed Count Trossi accelerating an Alfa 158 out of a corner.

ened Masaryk circuit of 11 miles. The race was marred by accidents, to Farina, Parnell and Bira among the leaders. Whitehead drove his Ferrari into the lead during the second half of the race, and finished just over half a minute ahead of the Talbot driven by Etancelin.

Racing was at low ebb in 1949. The full-length Grands Prix tended to be processional, and all too often the star drivers were let down by their cars very early in races. Further, the cars which did race were obviously inferior to the Type 158 Alfa Romeo, which was not raced, so that the season was overshadowed by a ghost.

The year ended on a note of optimism, with change in the air. Aurelio Lampredi had joined Ferrari during

1949, to start work on unsupercharged large-capacity engines, for the futility of attempting to match Alfa's years of development work on supercharged power units had been realized, and rumour had it that the Maserati brothers were contemplating building an Osca on similar lines. It was already apparent that Dusio's Cisitalia ambition was beyond realization, but at the end of the year the BRM at last appeared in the metal. It was gently demonstrated to the Press on the bleak airfield at Folkingham, where BRM had a test circuit, to a printed reception which varied from the mildly jingoistic to an honest admiration of its conception mingled with doubts about its complexity.

And it was known that the Alfa Romeo 158 engine had been further developed . . .

The Last Supercharger

In 1950 the World Championship of Drivers was introduced, and Alfa Romeo returned to the Grand Prix circuits, to face a new supercharged challenge, and a growing unsupercharged threat. Effectively, there were six world championship races (the Indianapolis 500 was a seventh, anomalous, point scoring round); the new supercharged GP car proved to be quite ineffectual, but the new unsupercharged cars proved to be a very real force. In many ways, events of the 1951 season, which was to be the last when supercharged cars were of any account in road racing, were foreshadowed in 1950.

The Alfa Romeo decision to race the 158s again was quietly made known in the early spring. The cars were little changed, but work on the engine induction system had realized another increase in power, to 350 bhp at 8600 rpm. Regular team drivers were to be the 'three Fs' – the perfectionist Giuseppe Farina, back in favour, the grizzled Luigi Fagioli, less temperamental than of old and accepting his number two role, and Juan Manuel Fangio, whose selection was by no means wholly palatable in Italy.

The Maserati 4CLT/48 could no longer be considered a front-line Grand Prix car, although development of the Maserati-Milan variant continued under Mario Speluzzi. This car had a new tubular chassis and suspension, and a high-boost two-stage supercharged engine, for which 335 bhp was claimed; in performance it failed to live up to its paper promise, and proved hopelessly unreliable into the bargain. Supercharged Ferraris were also in the field, but after the opening races only in a secondary role as the Scuderia increasingly turned to the unsupercharged alternative offered by the formula.

Amédée Gordini's petit cars emerged as full Grand Prix machines, with Wade-supercharged pushrod ohv engines, which invariably were overstressed and unreliable to a degree.

Of the supercharged cars, there remained the BRM. In retrospect, the Type 15 BRM was misconceived – the project was too advanced, too complex, for the original BRM team to turn into practical reality, particularly during a time of economic shortages. The enormous potential of the car was never in doubt; unfortunately it could not be made raceworthy before the formula to which it was designed was abandoned...

Heart of the first BRM was its 135 degree V-16 engine, 49·5 × 48·2 mm; basically this was orthodox in layout and of course in perfect balance. The blocks were in groups of fours, and a half-speed drive was taken from the centre of the crankshaft to the clutch; ancillaries were also driven from the centre, notably the forward-mounted two-stage centrifugal super-charger. In itself, this functioned as intended, but it was not matched by engine breathing (the valve gear was largely at fault). The original estimated power of the BRM V-16 was 600 bhp at 12000 rpm, but the maximum achieved in practice was 485 bhp at 10000 rpm, a specific output of some 320 bhp/litre.

This engine was mounted in a simple but stiff frame, constructed of superimposed main longitudinal tubes with welded-on sheet steel spacers, and generous cross-members. Transmission was through a rear-mounted five-speed gearbox. The de Dion rear suspension followed that of pre-war Mercedes GP cars, save that it incorporated oleo-pneumatic struts instead of torsion bars. At the front a Porsche-type trailing arm suspension, again with 'air' struts, was used; the arms were insufficiently rigid, and consequent deflections did not make for good roadholding. As already remarked, the car was shown to the Press at the end of 1949. From that point, development progressed frustratingly slowly, so that the enterprise was carried through its first hesitant racing season more on hope than achievement.

Meanwhile, the unsupercharged challenge was

Supreme Grand Prix car of the first post-war period, the 1·5 litre Alfa Romeo 158, which changed little in outline during its front-line career between 1938 and 1951. One of the most successful Grand Prix cars ever built, the 158/159 gained 31 victories in 35 race starts between 1947 and 1951.

gathering momentum. Anthony Lago abandoned his supercharged V-16 ideas, and produced an improved version of his faithful old 'six', with two plugs per cylinder and three horizontal, instead of down-draught, carburetters. Around 275 bhp at 5000 rpm was thus achieved, together with a tendency to over-heating, which spoiled the grand old Talbots' reliability record. But in any case, they were left well behind by other developments.

In 1949 Aurelio Lampredi joined Ferrari, and started work on an unsupercharged V-12, a 60-degree single ohc unit which was steadily developed through 1950. It owed much to Colombo's V-12, and like it was oversquare. Lampredi's engine first appeared in 3·3 litre (72 × 68 mm) form, and was first raced in a sports car in the Mille Miglia. This was followed by an interim 4·1 litre version, and at the end of the 1950 European season by a full 4·5 litre (80 × 74·5 mm) engine. These were mounted in a light chassis developed from the preceding cars, with wishbone and transverse leaf ifs and de Dion axle and radius arms rear suspension. The whole machine was some 150 lb lighter than the Alfa Romeo 158, which helped to offset a gross power deficiency in the unsupercharged engine.

A single Alfa was entrusted to Fangio for the early-season San Remo Grand Prix, and he duly won the 187-mile race at 59·65 mph from Villoresi (supercharged Ferrari) and a flock of Maseratis.

The first front-line event in the 1950 calendar was the British Grand Prix at Silverstone. Alfa Romeo entered four cars, the fourth for 'guest' driver Reg Parnell, and these led the race more or less as they pleased, 1-2-3-4 until Fangio retired with engine failure. This left Farina to win at 90·95 mph from Fagioli and Parnell. Two laps down came fourth and fifth drivers, Giraud-Cabantous and Rosier in Talbots, and then a further lap in arrears Gerard's evergreen ERA. Two much more modern E-type ERAs started, and retired; the BRM was displayed in

a tent, which hardly encouraged its supporters.

The Monaco Grand Prix was revived after a lapse of a year. Here Ferrari again entered long-chassis supercharged cars against the Alfas, Gordinis appeared for the first time in Formula 1 guise, the redoubtable

Above: start of the 1950 Pescara GP, with Fangio just out-accelerating his Alfa Romeo team mate Fagioli. Left: growing force – the unsupercharged Formula 1 Ferrari, here in 4·2 litre form. Below: Reg Parnell, Maserati-mounted, and giving the V-16 BRM a successful race debut at Goodwood in 1950.

Froilan Gonzalez got a Scuderia Achille Varzi Maserati onto the front row of the grid, and Harry Schell was allowed onto the back of the grid with a Cooper (a 1·1 litre JAP-engined car, and no more than a curiosity – then). The race became a non-event on the first lap, when Farina 'lost' his Alfa 158 on the spray-wet Tabac corner, and car after car piled up in a chain reaction. The field was reduced to ten cars, and then nine when Gonzalez abandoned his burning Maserati at the next corner. All this left Fangio to cruise to victory, a lap clear of Ascari's Ferrari (while Gerard was sixth in his ERA).

Both Ferraris, one the ultimate 1·5 litre supercharged Ferrari, with two-stage supercharged twin ohc engine and de Dion rear axle, retired early in the Swiss GP. The Alfa Romeo procession was spoiled when Fangio's engine swallowed a valve, leaving Farina (92·76 mph) and Fagioli to win by a lap from Rosier's Talbot, Bira's Maserati and Bonetto's Maserati-Milan, showing unusual stamina.

Two weeks later, the Belgian Grand Prix was an event of much greater significance, for the first un-supercharged Ferrari appeared. During the spring, the Spa circuit had been very considerably modified, to make for much higher lap speeds (which 20 years later were to be the cause of its near-abandonment). With the hairpin by-passed, there was only one slow corner within its 8·76 mile lap, the rest being a succession of long straights, very fast sweeping curves and fast corners. Hence in 1951 GP practice the fastest lap, by Farina and Fangio, was 114·03 mph, compared with the 1939 record of 109·12 mph (21 years later the record was to be set at 162·08 mph, by Siffert in a sports-racing car).

Ascari, driving the new Ferrari, could not match the 158s in practice or race, nor could Villoresi in the latest supercharged Ferrari. But in the race Raymond

171

Sommer did, in a Talbot, actually taking the lead when the Alfas made their first refuelling stops, and holding it for four laps. He was running third, with the Alfas still to make their second stop, when his engine blew up. Rosier placed another Talbot third at the end, for Farina slowed with low oil pressure, while Fangio won from Fagioli at 110·05 mph. Ascari was fifth, a lap down, in the new Ferrari.

Alfa Romeo were again dominant in the French Grand Prix at Rheims, where in practice Fangio was timed at over 180 mph in the team's spare car, which reputedly had an engine developed to produce 370 bhp (the potential maximum of the normal 158, geared for Rheims and at 7500 engine rpm, was 170 mph). The single Ferrari was withdrawn. Once again Farina fell back with a minor component failure, and Fangio led Fagioli past the flag (at 104·84 mph). Perhaps more to the point, they were three laps ahead of the next driver, Whitehead in his private Ferrari. Manzon's Gordini was a rather flattering fourth; none of the six Maseratis which started were racing at the end, and only two of the seven Talbots.

For the Grand Prix des Nations at Geneva, Ferrari produced a 4·1 litre car, for Ascari, who held it in second place for 62 of the 68 laps, before retiring with a wrecked engine. Fangio drove a commanding race,

slowly easing away from Ascari, and was leading by 40 seconds when the Ferrari engine failed. Villoresi crashed on oil in the 3·3 litre Ferrari, and Farina deliberately crashed to avoid hitting the wreck; the other two Alfa drivers, de Graffenried and Taruffi, filled second and third places; fourth man Giraud-Cabantous was five laps down in the 68-lap race!

Notice had been served that the Alfa Romeo 158 was no longer invincible. The team drivers could no longer race with revs in hand, nor to the same end of reliability could cars be sent to the grids with 'easy' final drive ratios. Supercharger pressure was again increased, to squeeze out another 20 bhp, and stress the engines a little more; together with other detail improvements, for example to the brakes, this was considered sufficient justification for redesignating the cars Type 159.

In August the International Trophy was run at Silverstone, where a BRM appeared on a grid for the first time. However, as Sommer let in the clutch, a drive shaft failed, so that only in the finest sense could this be rated a first race start (this incident was extra-

ordinarily reminiscent of Sommer's only race start in the CTA-Arsenal!). The two Alfa Romeos present duly won, Farina averaging 90·16 mph to head Fagioli in team order, with Whitehead third and on the same lap, and then a pair of aged ERAs.

The climax to the season came at Monza, where the two great Italian teams met for the last time in 1950. Alfa Romeo entered five cars, two of them 159s for Farina and Fangio, in a show of strength unequalled since the war. Ferrari entered two 375FIs, with 4493 cc engines giving some 330 bhp at 7000 rpm, for Ascari and Serafini, standing in for the injured Villoresi. The Ferrari challenge was obvious from the start of practice, and emphatic at its end: Fangio took pole position from Ascari by a fifth of a second. However, Farina led from the start, followed by Ascari and Fangio. Ascari took the lead for two laps, then fell back, to hound Farina until his engine failed on the 22nd lap. One Alfa, Sanesi's was already out, and soon Fangio's gearbox failed; he took over Taruffi's car, and retired again. Meanwhile, Ascari had taken over the Ferrari which Serafini had kept in the picture, and despite the loss of a gear started to attack the surviving Alfas. When Fagioli made his second routine fuel stop, Ascari slipped through into second place. His Ferrari lacked the all-out speed to catch Farina's Alfa, although close enough to take advantage of any slip by the driver, or mechanical failing in the car. Farina, in fact, eased a little, and won by 77 seconds, at 109·67

Ferrari versus Alfa Romeo in 1951 – a pair of cars of each marque on the front row of the German Grand Prix grid. Opposite: deluge at Silverstone – a pair of Talbot drivers groping through the monsoon conditions, which caused the abandonment of the International Trophy.

mph. Fagioli finished third, and then at a very respectful distance – five laps, or nearly twenty miles – came a pair of Talbots. This result on a fast circuit showed beyond question that the unsupercharged challenge was at last real.

The two teams did not meet again in 1950, Alfa Romeo discreetly withdrawing their entry from the non-Championship Penya Rhin GP at Barcelona. However, this race did see the Continental debut of the BRM. The team were encouraged to enter a pair of cars by Reg Parnell's fairly comfortable victories in short Goodwood sprint races, which were at least nominally international. In Spain the BRMs faced three Ferraris, two 4·5 litre cars and one with a 4·1 litre engine, and proved to be much faster in a straight line, although so much slower through and out of corners that their speed advantage was more than offset. Both BRMs made poor starts, although Parnell made spectacular amends by climbing from 19th to 4th on the first lap; then his supercharger drive sheared. Walker worked his car up to 4th, but retired after 33 of the 50 racing laps. Meanwhile, the Ferraris had marched away, Taruffi recovered third place after a spin, and they finished 1-2-3, Ascari and Serafini leading in the 4·5 litre cars.

That race rounded off the mainstream season. Alfa Romeo were still on top, the 158 still unbeaten since 1946. Giuseppe Farina was the first World Champion, his team mates Fangio and Fagioli were runners-up. On a more sombre note, Raymond Sommer drove his last Grand Prix at Monza, for later in September he died at the wheel of a little Cooper in an obscure French national race at Cadours.

Effectively, the scene was set for 1951. Ferrari did

remarkably little work on the V-12 during the off-season, revising it in detail, for example in the ignition system, to increase output to 380 bhp at 7500 rpm. Alfa Romeo did much more work on the 159, to less effective end. More power was extracted from the engine, which was run for long test periods at over 9500 rpm; quoted maximum power was up again, to 425 bhp at 9300 rpm, although in racing drivers were instructed to limit engine revs to 8500–9000 rpm. The supercharger drive absorbed more power, fuel consumption increased (eventually to about 1·6 mpg) so extra tankage was provided (in normal cars to 66 gallons), so weight increased, and handling suffered. To combat this, the swing axle rear suspension was replaced with a de Dion arrangement on some cars. Little more could be done with a design which was basically 13 years old, but as Alfa Romeo were not inclined to commit resources to a new car, the 158/159 had to serve for one more season.

Ferrari and Alfa Romeo were the only real contenders for outright honours. The effective racing lives of the Talbots and first-generation Orsi Maseratis were at an end, that of the BRM had not yet begun. Gordini could not keep pace in the power race, and the Maserati brothers lacked the resources to properly develop the 4·5 litre V-12 Osca.

So these cars were to play supporting roles – in some cases, bit parts – while two Italian teams fought out the seven Championship races (Monaco was dropped from the list, and the German and Spanish Grands Prix were added to it). Ferrari and Alfa Romeo were so well matched that it was at least obvious that the days of Alfa Romeo processions were over. Driving strengths were fairly equal; Alfa Corse depended largely on Farina and Fangio, with Sanesi and Bonetto, and 'national' drivers de Graffenried and Pietsch occasionally on the strength, and Fagioli in reserve. Ferrari had the services of Ascari and Villoresi, Piero Taruffi, and the fiery Argentinian 'Pepe' Gonzalez, who had made a great impression in beating the Mercedes W163 team on his home ground during the European off season.

Alfa Romeo contested the pre-Championship International Trophy at Silverstone, where their only challenger was Parnell in Vandervell's 4·5 litre Ferrari 'Thin Wall Special'. Parnell finished second in the first heat, between Fangio and Bonetto, while Farina and Sanesi confidently saw off Bira's Osca in the second heat. The final started in a deluge and was abandoned after six laps, when Parnell was leading.

The first *grande épreuve*, the Swiss GP, was also run on a wet circuit, and led and won quite clearly by Fangio. But Taruffi gave the other three Alfa drivers a real race, and finished 36 seconds ahead of third man Farina.

However, Farina was on top at Spa, leading for most of the distance in the Belgian GP, and winning at 114·26 mph from Ferrari drivers Ascari and Villoresi. Then the French GP saw a similar Alfa-Ferrari-Ferrari result, save that at Rheims the winning car was driven by Fagioli and Fangio (who took over when his own car developed ignition trouble) at 110·97 mph over the 377 miles; Ascari was again second, having taken over Gonzalez' car and led the race until forced to stop for attention to its brakes, while Villoresi was third ahead of Parnell.

The turning point came in the British Grand Prix at Silverstone, a contrived and in many ways inadequate

circuit, but now the setting for an historic Grand Prix. Moreover, the BRMs at last appeared to contest a *grande épreuve*. At Silverstone, drivers of the supercharged cars would not exploit the maximum speed potential of their cars; on the other hand the torque characteristics of the slower-running Ferrari V-12 were admirably suited to the circuit, and Gonzalez rose to the occasion. He was fastest in practice, sharing the front row of the grid with Fangio and Farina and his Ferrari team mate Ascari. The BRMs were at the back, for they had not been prepared in time for official practice.

Surprisingly, Bonetto led initially, then Gonzalez took over, then Fangio, who was then hounded by Gonzalez. Both drew away from Farina and Ascari, battling equally closely for third place. Fangio's fuel stop inevitably cost him the lead, and he never regained it; Ascari and Farina drove their cars, or each other's, to retirement, so that Villoresi finished third, with Bonetto fourth. Reg Parnell courageously suffered the infernal heat of his BRM cockpit to place it fifth, ahead of Sanesi's Alfa Romeo and Walker's BRM (these were to be the only places ever gained by V-16 BRMs in a *grande épreuve*). Gonzalez' winning speed was 96·11 mph. So Ferrari at last vanquished Alfa Romeo, Enzo Ferrari in effect beat his old team, the cars which he had conceived in a very different era.

In 1951 the German GP regained full status, and at the 'Ring the tide ran more strongly against Alfa Romeo, for whom Fangio fought alone, as Bonetto, Farina and Pietsch retired early (the latter backwards into a bank). Ascari won, at 83·76 mph, while Fangio was second, ahead of four more Ferraris.

Alfa Romeo ignored the Pescara GP, which fell to Gonzalez, but surprisingly – and in the outcome gratifyingly – contested the Bari GP, where Fangio beat Gonzalez, while Ascari and Farina retired. Thus the Alfa team was encouraged for the Italian GP, where four cars, revised and redesignated 159M, were entered. The Ferraris were also revised, with increased fuel tankage in longer tails. The BRMs showed promise in practice, but were withdrawn in conditions which smacked of fiasco (their nominated drivers were Parnell and Richardson, BRM chief mechanic, who practised the car but was denied a race by the ultra-conservative RAC; Stuck was a last-minute replacement, but on race-day morning mechanical gremlins struck, and the cars were withdrawn).

Fastest laps in practice were put in by Fangio and Farina, then the four Ferrari drivers, Ascari, Gonzalez, Villoresi and Taruffi. Ascari gained an early lead, lost it to Fangio until a tyre failed on the Alfa, then held it conclusively from lap 14 to the chequered flag on lap 80. Farina, driving Bonetto's car once the engine of his own Alfa had blown, fought the Ferraris gallantly, but hopelessly once a split petrol tank

The outstanding unsupercharged cars of the first post-war formula were the Ferrari (above, an Indianapolis car, and therefore a 'Ferrari Special'), and the Lago-Talbot (below).

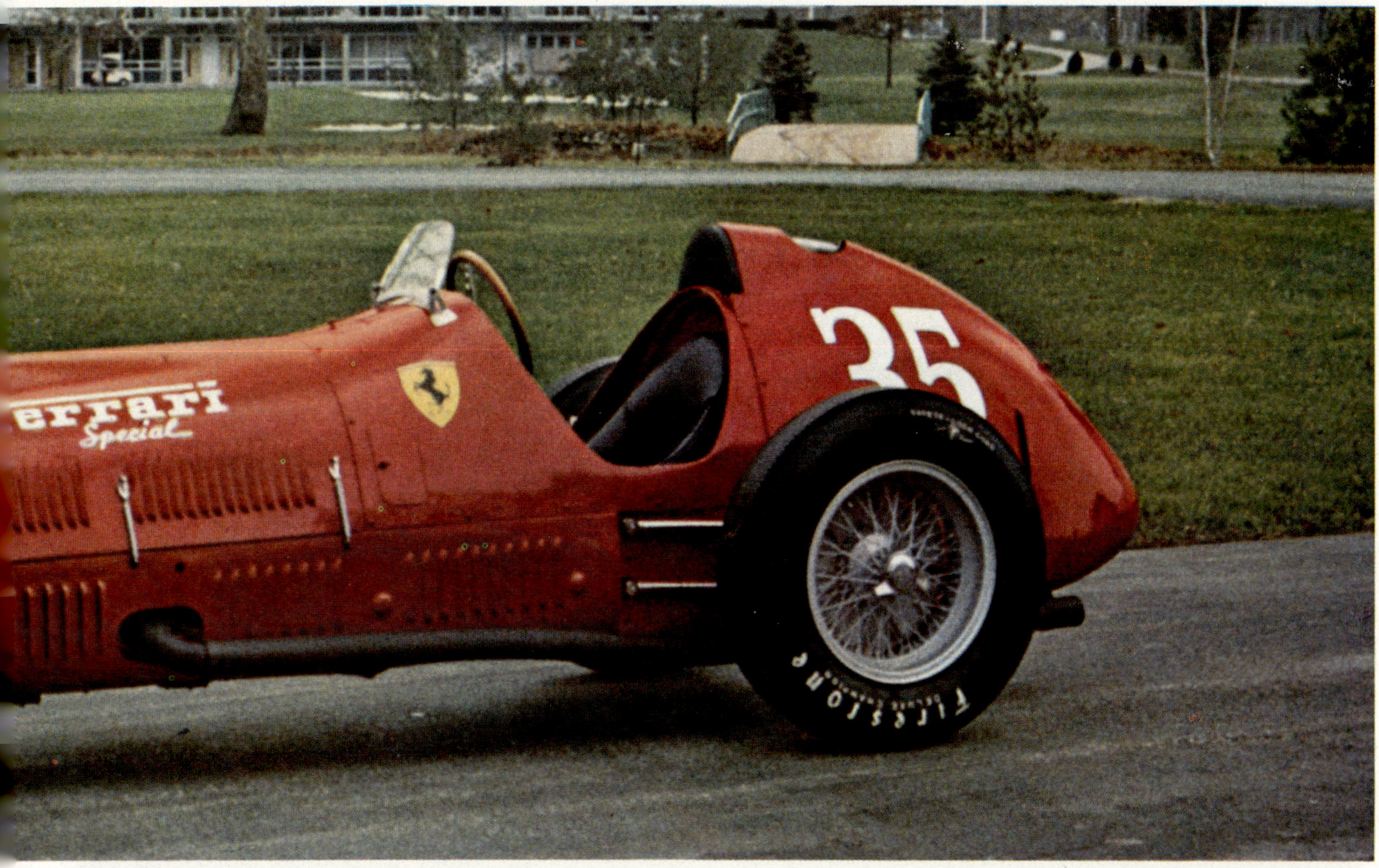
errari
Special
35
Firestone

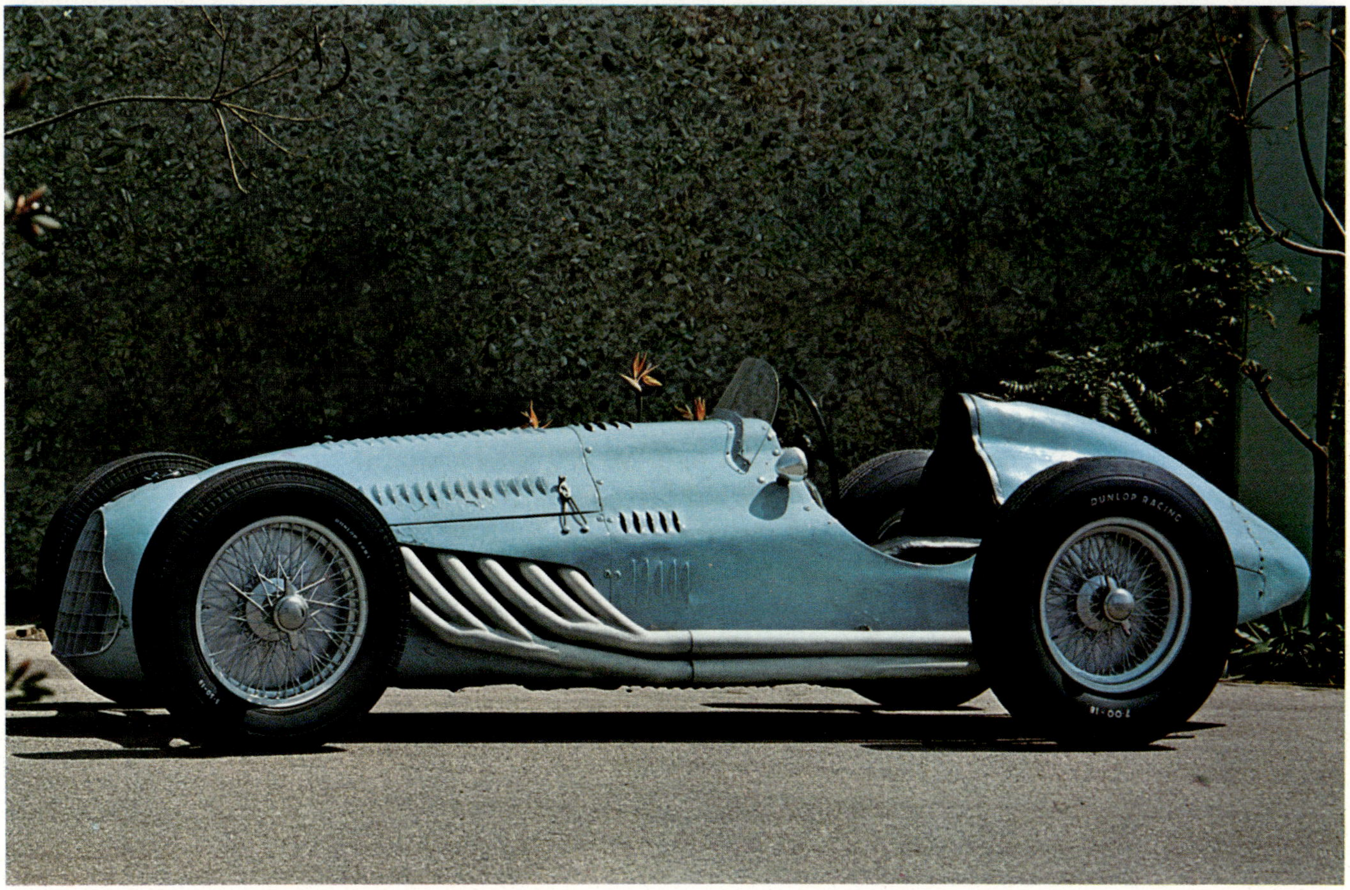
DUNLOP RACING

had enforced an additional pit stop, and he could only finish third, two Ferraris (Ascari, 115·53 mph, and Gonzalez) ahead of him, two behind him (Villoresi and Taruffi).

Thus as far as major races were concerned, honours were even as the teams gathered at Barcelona for the last Grand Prix of the season. Each took four cars, for a race which seemed increasingly open as practice went on – on the grid Ferrari and Alfa Romeo occupied alternate places in the first eight. But the Ferrari team lost the race before the start, loading their cars with enough fuel to run the 275 miles non-stop, and thus overloading the tyres on 16-inch diameter rear wheels, smaller than those used in preceding races. The consequence was a series of thrown treads, and a victory for Alfa Romeo, Fangio winning at 98·76 mph from Gonzalez (Ferrari), Farina (Alfa Romeo) and Ascari (Ferrari). And Juan Manuel Fangio gained his first World Championship.

This Spanish Grand Prix marked the end of an era. It was Alfa Romeo's last Grand Prix, it saw the last Grand Prix victory for a supercharged car, it was the last race of any consequence under the first Formula 1 regulations.

Alfa Romeo withdrew from racing, apparently leaving the field open to Ferrari, for BRM assurances that their team would contest the 1952 Championship events were received with considerable scepticism. Increasingly, therefore, race organizers abandoned Formula 1 in favour of the 2-litre Formula 2, and when the BRM entry for the early-season Turin GP was withdrawn, Formula 1 to all intents and purposes collapsed, and the FIA agreed that the World Championship series would be for Formula 2 races (ironically, this led to an unbroken succession of Ferrari victories).

Odd Formula 1 races were run, and the BRMs did race again outside Britain, notably at Albi. In 1952, when the Ferrari team was pre-occupied at Indiana-polis (where only Ascari qualified to start, and retired when a wheel failed in the race), the BRMs driven by Fangio and Gonzalez led, but retired with engine failures, leaving the race to the private 4·5 litre Ferraris of Rosier and Landi. In 1953 BRMs faced true works opposition for the last time, in the form of Ascari's 4·5 litre Ferrari. This retired early in the Formula 1 heat, and when Farina retired the Thin Wall Ferrari, the BRMs were left to cruise to victory, Fangio (110·48 mph) heading Wharton. But in the final the BRMs threw tyre treads, and only Gonzalez' car lasted to the end of the race, finishing second behind Rosier's Ferrari.

Apart from these races, and an expedition to New Zealand in 1954, which netted a second and a third place, the V-16 BRMs were confined to *formule libre* races in Britain, where they were usually matched against Vandervell's Thin Wall, which was the only other Formula 1 car developed in 1953.

BRM Limited had been taken over by the Owen Organization at the end of 1952, and during 1953 work started on a new 2·5 litre car for the formula which was to come into effect in 1954. Yet in 1954 two Mk 2 V-16 BRMs appeared, shorter, lighter, with tubular space frames and modified suspension. The engine gave 485 bhp, with reasonable reliability, but apparently still within a narrow rev range, which handicapped drivers. At least the continuing duel with the Thin Wall attracted crowds, until a V-16 BRM raced for the last time, at Castle Combe in October 1955. By that time it was a long way removed from the Grand Prix arena, and the glories of the 1·5 litre supercharged/4·5 litre unsupercharged formula were four years in the past, together with the supreme Alfa Romeo which the BRM had been conceived to defeat, and met only once.

The Half Litre Formula

After both world wars small-engined racing classes flourished, perhaps reflecting periods of general austerity. The pre-1914 cyclecar theme was taken up enthusiastically in the early twenties, and then gradually waned; its post-1945 equivalent, the 500 cc class, proved to be of more lasting significance. Other attempts to pick up the voiturette line in classes below the level of the 2-litre Formula 2 which was to come into effect in 1948 made little impression on the international scene. Quite outside the mainstream, and therefore usually overlooked, midget racing on loose- or hard-surfaced ovals flourished again, notably in North America; this rough and tough nursery produced many top American drivers, and it is not entirely irrelevant to road racing, as at about this time a future triple World Champion was cutting his racing teeth on midgets in Australia – Jack Brabham, who was four times Australian midget car champion.

Although really outside the scope of this book, midgets are worthy of passing mention, for in the immediate post-war era at least, this type of racing accounted for a surprisingly large slice of the overall single-seater racing cake. Above all, midget racing has always been an American sport, and the cars were midgets only by American standards. A compensated formula was applied to engines: up to 140 cu in (2294 cc) for side-valve units, up to 125 cu in (2048 cc) for engines having overhead valve parallel to the cylinder axis, up to 105 cu in (1720 cc) for inclined valve engines, and up to 61 cu in (1000 cc) for two-strokes.

The best-known and most popular midget engines were four-cylinder Offenhausers. Chassis were in effect scaled-down Indianapolis roadsters, in view of the tight tracks with very severe limits on wheelbase dimensions, and 12-inch wheels were universal wear.

Formula 3 mainstream – Coopers at Aintree (above). National sidestream – an Italian 750 cc formula Giaur at Brindisi (below).

A typical midget. Racing in this class was usually tight – as suggested by the quintet below – but served no more than an immediate thrills and spills end.

They raced on short tracks of asphalt, cement or cinders, invariably in an anticlockwise direction. There was little interest in midgets outside the USA, although spasmodic attempts to promote them were made in Europe. Interestingly, supplementary Swedish regulations for them anticipated road racing requirements for driver protection by many years, for example in stipulating roll-over hoops, and driver cages were used on midgets long before they appeared on circuit cars.

The first quartet of 500 cc cars appeared in 1946. Only the Cooper had a professional air about it, and the success of the early Cooper 500s meant that half-litre competition gained full international status, when it might so easily have mouldered as a national amateur class. From these simple devices sprang a line of Cooper cars which in little more than a decade was to transform racing. For the Cooper 500 played a quite disproportionate role in bringing about the fundamental changes in road racing in the fifties: these cars proved the mid-engined layout more conclusively than any Continental fore-runners, however illustrious, and at least in part the emergence of Britain as a predominant racing country can be traced back to

them. Formula 3 racing became a forcing ground for a new generation of drivers, and in this respect, too, the balance of power was to shift across the Channel.

None of this can have crossed Charles Cooper's mind when with his son John and Eric Brandon he built his first 500 in the summer of 1946. Practicability with limited resources and a feeling for what was 'right' rather than theory and calculation determined the make-up. The front suspension assemblies from two Fiat 500s were used, joined by a simple box-section and tubular frame. A single-cylinder J.A.P. motorcycle engine was mounted behind the cockpit, driving through a Triumph motorcycle gearbox and chain.

These simple specials set the pace in races fostered by the Five Hundred Club, and in 1950 their national class became an International Formula, the first Formula 3. By that time the little Coopers were in large-scale production – the first proper batch, of 12 cars, had been laid down for 1948, although it soon became obvious that the demand had been hopelessly under-estimated. The cars began to grow up, a first outward and visible sign being the adoption of cast Elektron racing wheels in place of the Fiat discs in 1948. Progressively such refinements as rack and pinion steering, all-tubular chassis and, on the Mk IX of 1955, rear disc brakes were adopted.

The push-rod J.A.P. engine remained standard for some time; other power units, BSA, Matchless, Vincent, were tried but by 1951 these were generally supplanted by the twin-ohc Norton single-cylinder engine – the famous double-knocker. This was powerful – and expensive. Norton would sell only complete motorcycles, and car constructors often had to buy these for the sake of their engines. At best the Norton engine produced around 48 bhp, which perhaps seems unimpressive until it is translated into a power/weight ratio of over 150 bhp/ton. Hence by 1956 the Silverstone F1 and F3 lap records were 102·3 mph and 91·6 mph respectively, while on more sinuous circuits

Giovanni Savonuzzi in the cockpit of one of the famous 1100 cc Cisitalias. Below: the 'Home of 500 cc Racing', Brands Hatch. Typical F3 fields on the first 1-mile 'anti-clockwise' circuit, and in 1954 on the newly-opened Druids Hairpin extension.

the pro rata performances of the nimble 500s were even more startling (for example, the 1956 Crystal Palace F1 and F3 records respectively were 79·94 mph and 75·82 mph).

Throughout the Cooper reigned supreme, although not unchallenged. The Kieft, with its rubber-in-torsion swing axle rear suspension was perhaps the most advanced F3 car, but it was really successful only in the hands of the youthful Stirling Moss. Paul Emery tried the front-wheel drive approach with some success in his Emeryson. None of the other British cars – Arnott, Revis, Leston, Martin, Staride and so on – made any real impression.

In France DBs using the Dyna Panhard air-cooled

opposed twin driving the front wheels were built in some numbers. Italian interest was limited, and until Formula 3 was adopted internationally Italian constructors preferred to concentrate on their own national 750 cc class, and their 500 cc cars tended to be adaptations of 750 cars, which made little impact despite the availability of excellent motorcycle racing engines. A few NDs (Nardi-Danese) cars were built, with single-cylinder Carru and four-cylinder Gilera motorcycle engines, Taraschi's Giaur used a linered-down Fiat engine, and had classic front-engined racing car lines – attractive, but hopelessly out of touch with reality.

The Effyh, best described as a Scandinavian car as it was designed by Swedes and built in Copenhagen, appeared in some numbers, and on its home ground was raced on dirt tracks against American-type midgets as well as on circuits. Although a surprising number of 500s were built in other European countries, Belgium, Germany, Holland and Switzerland, few progressed beyond the one-off special stage, and only a handful of cars were built outside Europe, in South Africa and Australia.

Increasingly through the fifties, Formula 3 racing became one-make racing, and thus lost much of its appeal. The general racing scene was becoming increasingly sophisticated, too, and the 500s increasingly out-of-step with it – their performance remained surprising, but in their principal characteristics they seemed increasingly removed from 'proper' racing cars. Towards the end of the decade Formula 3 declined rapidly.

In 1948 the first post war racing formulae came

into force, and appeared to leave a gap which the 500s would not fill, and so on the Continent the 1100 cc voiturette class was revived.

French and Italian constructors had in fact started to develop these little cars immediately after the war, usually around engines derived from the popular Fiat 1100 cc push-rod ohv unit.

In France Amédée Gordini was prominent. 'The Sorcerer' already had a formidable reputation for his ability to squeeze power from Simca production engines (in effect the Fiat four), and in 1947 he built his first single-seaters around Simca-Fiat parts, engine, transmission and suspension. His chassis were simple and light, and went some way to compensate for the relatively modest output of the 1100 Gordini engine.

The best-known Italian constructors in this class were Piero Dusio and Vittorio Stanguellini. Dusio, industrialist and racing driver, formed the Cisitalia firm in Turin in 1946 and brought into it some notable collaborators, Dante Giacosa, later technical director of Fiat, Giovanni Savonuzzi, later Chrysler's director of engineering research, and Piero Taruffi, who was to become development driver and racing manager.

The 1100 Cisitalia was an attractive car on scaled-down traditional lines, with a tubular space frame which was advanced by contemporary standards, modified Fiat suspension components and a Cisitalia pre-selector gearbox. Later versions were fitted with 1300 cc engines and occasionally appeared in Grands Prix, driven by Taruffi and even the great Nuvolari. Perhaps appropriately, Dusio gained the first Cisitalia victory, in the 1946 Coppa Brezzi at Turin (a race

perhaps better recalled for its contribution of a detail to the Nuvolari legend – the Maestro drove two laps waving the rim of his steering wheel, and steering with the remaining spoke!).

Dusio's original intention was that these cars, of which about 30 were built, should be used in marque feature races. Well-known drivers were to draw their cars from a pool immediately before the start of each race; predictably, the scheme did not get off the ground, and only one Cisitalia circus race was run, in Cairo. (On similar lines, René Bonnet launched his Monomill scheme for young drivers, using 850 cc front-wheel drive DBs, in France in the mid-fifties; this was a little more successful within its more modest limits, but the one-make circus class has never attracted a wide following). By 1949 the ambitious Cisitalia Grand Prix project, described in Chapter 17, and Dusio's attempts to expand the company, had bankrupted it, but as long as interest in 1100 cc racing lasted, the little Cisitalias continued to race, under the wing of Carlo Abarth.

Stanguellini was less ambitious, and his company more permanent. It sprang from a typical Italian speed shop – where his work on Fiat engines had earned him the nickname 'Wizard' – and its first cars were built to the 750 cc Italian Formula 3. His 1100 cc cars were not widely seen, or prominent in races, but they were in effect forerunners of the pacesetting Stanguellinis of the first year of Formula Junior racing.

Late in the day the Maserati brothers returned to 1100 cc single-seater racing – they had supported the corresponding class in the thirties – with a version of their 1100 cc Osca sports car. These were relatively

183

sophisticated machines, with twin-ohc racing engines, and at the end of this 1100 cc period showed clean tails to all the other contenders in two voiturette grands prix at Monza, in 1950 and 1951.

Generally, British interest at this capacity was confined to sports cars, but odd Coopers were fitted with 996 or 1097 cc J.A.P. V-twins. These Coopers were very effective sprint machines, but their extraordinary power to weight ratio (over 200 bhp/ton with the 1097 cc engine giving around 95 bhp) led to considerable road-holding problems, and over-worked the chassis, so that the cars lacked stamina in racing. There was, however, a notable exception in one race . . .

Although Dusio's original circus schemes never came to fruition, many top drivers were happy to race these responsive 1100s, in the class or with enlarged engines. This above all made the class interesting. Ascari, Biondetti, Bonetto, Chiron, Farina, Nuvolari, Stuck and Taruffi raced Cisitalias in their heyday, while Bira, Sommer and Trintignant campaigned Simca-Gordinis. Jean-Pierre Wimille drove these little French cars with enormous verve, but tragically was killed when practising in a 1430 cc version at Buenos Aires (another great French champion,

Formula 3 vignettes. Left: Stirling Moss racing a Kieft, centre, the light and simple front suspension of this car and, below, a very young Stirling Moss in a Cooper, talking to his father Alfred. Top: John Cooper acknowledging a chequered flag at Rouen, in a Cooper of course! Right: Spike Rhiando racing an earlier Cooper at Silverstone.

Raymond Sommer, died at the wheel of a Cooper which he was driving 'for fun' in a minor French race).

The racing was often close, if not particularly fast. But on suitable circuits the 1100s could live with superior company, as for example when Trintignant beat a motley collection of Formula 2 cars at Angoulême in 1949. Then there was that virtuoso performance by Stirling Moss in his first Continental race, when he placed his 998 cc Cooper third behind the Formula 2 Ferraris of Villoresi and Tadini in the 1949 Circuit of Garda, losing only just over three minutes to the winner in a race lasting an hour and a half.

This of course was a slow circuit, and the 1100s were not too impressive in their big Monza set pieces, as for example when Bonetto won the 1950 race in an Osca at 93·77 mph from a strung-out field.

However, none of these 'scaled-down "proper"' racing cars made a lasting impression on the wider racing scene, nor did the Continental national classes play a significant driver-training role. Formula 3 was important in both respects. Out of the Coopers grew Formula 2 and then Grand Prix cars, in a direct line of evolvement, and future Grand Prix winners cut their single-seater teeth in the class.

Furthermore, the success of Formula 3 gave an enormous impetus to the still immature British racing car industry. In time the centre of road racing, and road racing car manufacture, was to shift across the English Channel–a possibility hardly imaginable in the first post-war years.

The First Formula 2

As soon as racing revived in 1946, the voiturettes of the 1930s were brought out to race again, as Grand Prix cars. Hence another second-level class was created, the first Formula 2 as such, to come into effect in 1948. This was for cars with engines of 2 litres, or 500 cc if supercharged. This formula was to remain in force until 1953, but its history falls into two distinct parts–until the end of 1951 it was the second racing class, for its last two years it was the Grand Prix class.

Many of the first Formula 2 cars were simply modified sports machines, but as racing settled down purpose-designed cars appeared and the general standard of design and, pro rata, performances kept pace with the premier class.

Ferrari supported the 2 litre Formula 2 throughout its run, generally set the pace, and gained the major share of victories. The first F2 Ferrari was a version of the V-12 125 sports car, and its Italian challengers were six-cylinder A6G Maseratis and sports Oscas, and Cisitalias with enlarged engines. The principal French contender was Gordini, while the first British entries in the class were Oscar Moore's BMW 328-based OBM and the first Alta-engined car built by John Heath and George Abecassis, based on an Alta sports car and the forerunner of the HWMs. The BMW 328 was also the basis of the first post-war

Ferrari set the pace in the first Formula 2, with supercharged V-12 engined cars, above, and behind Bira's Simca-Gordini, below, on a grid at Florence.

A varied and tightly-packed grid for the 1948 Circuit of Florence, with two Cisitalias nearest the camera (Bonetto, 38, and Taruffi, 12).

German racing cars, built by Ernst Loof (a one-time BMW experimental engineer), and known variously as Veritas, or Meteor outside Germany.

Ferrari won the first races of the Formula, at Bari, where Landi beat the Cisitalias driven by Bonetto and Varzi, and at Florence, where Sommer won. Then the Nuvolari Cup at Mantua saw a Cisitalia 1-2-3, Bonetto, Cortese and Varzi, while Villoresi won for Osca at Naples. Three races fell to Simca-Gordinis, at Perpignan, Angoulême and Skarpnack, near Stockholm.

Ferrari took the formula more seriously in 1949, when selected Ferrari drivers had a genuine single-seater chassis, that of the Grand Prix car with the V-12, in this unsupercharged form giving 140 bhp at 7000 rpm–a power output which was to remain a target for most constructors until the last season of the formula! The Maseratis faded, as did Cisitalia, but Gordini extracted more power from his four-cylinder 1443 cc engines, although never quite enough to seriously challenge the Ferraris.

Of the ten principal races in the season, Ferrari won eight (Villoresi at Brussels, Luxembourg, Rome and Garda, Ascari at Bari and Rheims, Fangio at Monza and Vallone at Naples). Gordini drivers Trintignant and Sommer won at Angoulême and Lausanne. Other marques did feature in the leading placings, Meteor/Veritas second and third at Brussels for example, Maserati fourth and fifth at Rome, Moss' 998 cc JAP-engined Cooper a remarkable third at Garda, Stuck's AFM (another BMW 328 derivative) fourth at Lausanne, and Heath's Alta fifth at Rheims.

Ferrari superiority was maintained in 1950, works drivers Ascari and Villoresi having cars with long-wheelbase chassis and de Dion rear suspension; the V-12 engine was restrained well within its potential, to give some 160 bhp at 7000 rpm, and thus its excellent reliability record was maintained. Independent Ferrari owners had to make do with the superseded rigid or

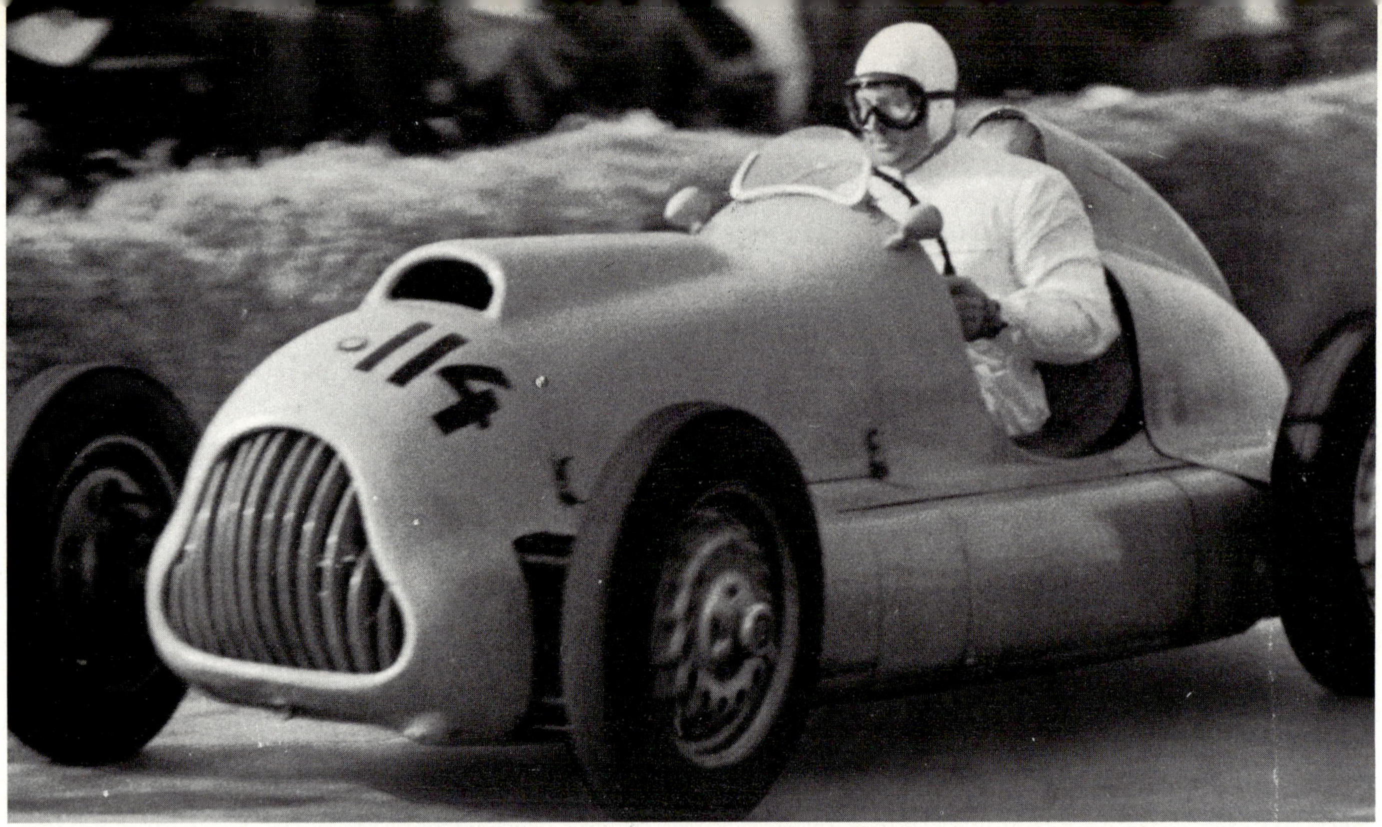
114

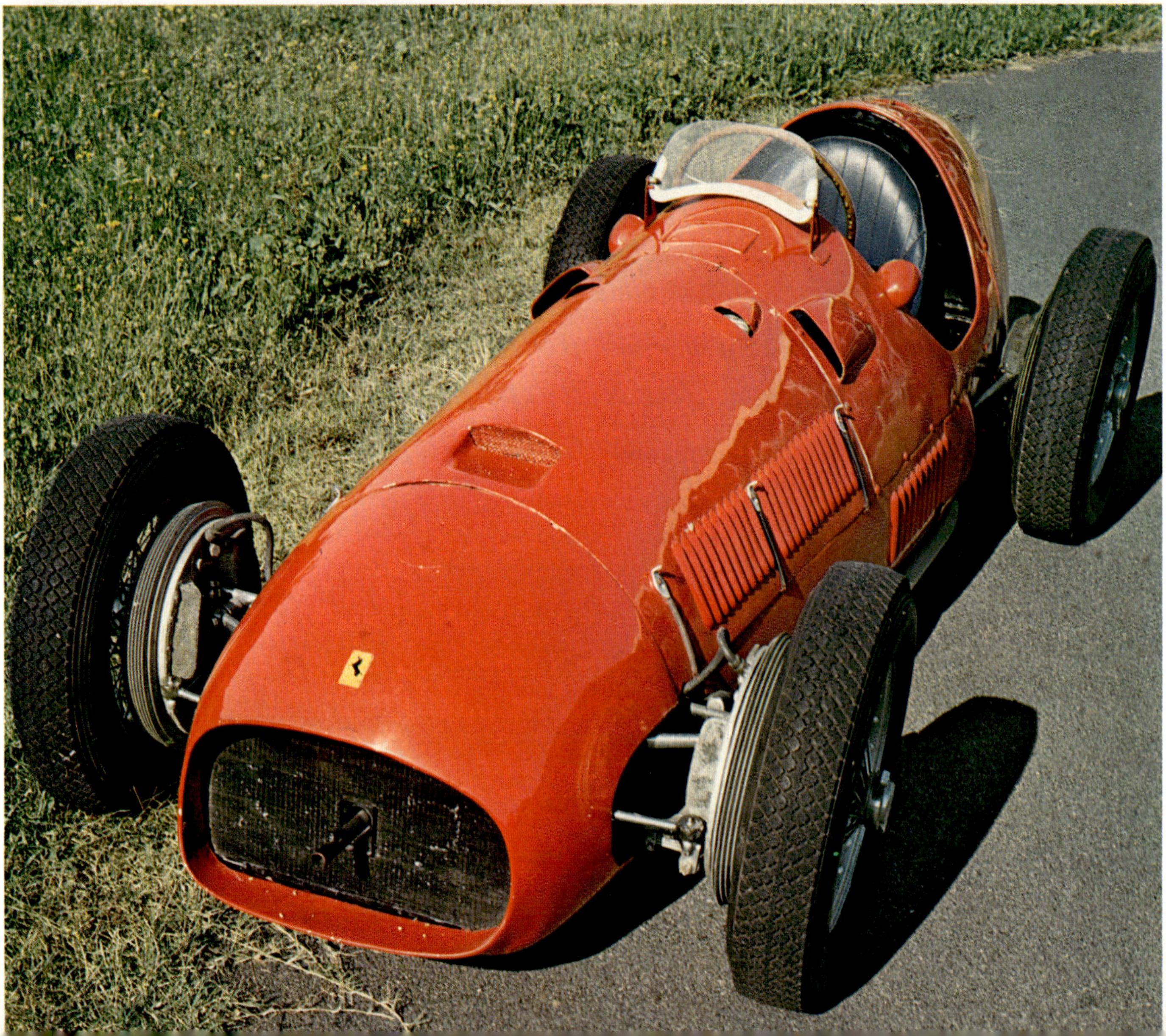

German constructors returned to front-line single-seater racing with Formula 2 cars built around BMW components; the Veritas was the best-known of these (opposite top, Kling at Cologne in 1949). Ferrari's domination of the formula was almost complete, with the T500 and Alberto Ascari (on the right of the photograph above).

swing axle rear suspension arrangements—not such a great handicap as might appear, for their power advantage over all other cars but the works Ferraris was still considerable. (Little more than 100 bhp was claimed for the engines of Gordini's cars, which in terms of race successes were distant runners-up to Ferrari over the whole season.)

Next in order of achievement came the first team of British cars to race on the Continent after the second world war, the HWMs. These succeeded the HW-Alta

of 1949, and still used the 83·5 × 90 mm four-cylinder Alta engine, which in 1950 produced some 120 bhp at 5300 rpm. At this stage, the HWMs had light tubular frames, but carried rather heavy two-seater bodies, so that they could double as sports cars (although they were not so used), and had independent suspension by wishbone and transverse leaf front and rear.

Maseratis were overshadowed, although Fangio gained one victory for the marque at Angoulême, as were Veritas, which despite Loof's new single ohc 'square' (75 × 75 mm) engine, had little success outside German national events. A new AFM with a twin ohc V-8, designed by Kuchen, proved very fast in the hands of Stuck, but also very unreliable; before it was developed to raceworthiness Alex von Falkenhausen closed down the AFM operation. The original one-off

Connaught, with a modified 1·75 litre Lea Francis engine, also made its first appearance.

In the 18 principal F2 races, Ferraris scored 13 firsts – four 1-2-3s – and Simca-Gordinis three victories; HWM and Maserati each scored single victories. For Ferrari Ascari won six times, Villoresi three, Sommer three and Cortese one. Gordini's victories were gained by Robert Manzon and Maurice Trintignant, HWM's in the Frontières GP at Chimay by Claes, and Maserati's by Fangio at Angoulême. Perhaps the most notable single event of the year was the German GP, for it marked the revival of full international single-seater racing at the Nürburgring. Over 277 miles Ascari won at 77·67 mph, quite clearly from the Gordinis driven by Simon and Trintignant and the first German car, Ulmen's Veritas.

The 1951 story was very similar. Throughout the season Ferrari raced the same engine, although a revised 180 bhp twin ohc V-12 was prepared and held in reserve, and a new Lampredi-designed twin ohc four (90 × 78 mm) was raced once. Save in the adoption of twin overhead camshafts for the engine, Gordini's cars were little changed, and his fortunes did not change. HWM still fielded the only British works team, in 1951 with new cars. These were tubular-framed single seaters, with coil spring and wishbone front suspension and de Dion rear axles (which were to prove a weak point). Connaughts were expected to appear, but the programme was allowed to get too far behind. Veritas slowly slipped out of the picture.

Ferrari won 10 of the 12 major races, Gordini the other two. Ascari gained only three of the Ferrari victories, at Modena with the new four-cylinder car, and Villoresi only two, other victories for the marque going to independent drivers Fischer, Marzotto, Rafaeli and Whitehead. Gordini's victories came at Chimay, where Claes won again, and Mettet, where Manzon, Simon and Trintignant scored a 1-2-3. In these races HWM scored three second places and five thirds, driven by Macklin, Schell and Moss.

In all save the dominance of Ferrari, Formula 2 changed considerably in 1952. It achieved new status with the virtual collapse of Formula 1, and the decision to run the *grandes épreuves* to the 2 litre regulations. Reflecting the upsurge of interest in racing in Britain, no fewer than seven British makes contested the class – albeit some were only one-offs, which appeared spasmodically – and proprietary engines began to feature in Grand Prix cars, for that is what the F2 cars became by virtue of the race organizers' abandonment of Formula 1.

The immediate promise of closer Grand Prix racing, at least on the slower circuits, was not fulfilled, simply because race after race became a procession of unchallenged and unstressed Ferraris. The Maranello team now raced their four-cylinder Type 500 as a

In makes if not in race-winners there was wide variety in F2 racing. Above: Stirling Moss in an HWM in 1951 and below, a Veritas. Opposite, top: the distinctive figure of Mike Hawthorn in the Cooper with which he leapt to fame (number 11) getting away at Silverstone, together with two HWMs, a Gordini and a Connaught. Below: Louis Chiron racing an Osca in 1953.

matter of course. Lampredi's engine produced some 180 bhp at 7000 rpm, had excellent torque characteristics, and reliability at least the equal of the V-12. A low alcohol-content (approximately 20 per cent) fuel was used, to give the car Grand Prix range without resort to enormous tanks. Handling was good, with a straightforward wishbone and transverse leaf spring ifs and de Dion, transverse leaf and radius rod rear suspension, and a well-proportioned wheelbase.

Cornering powers were of course now of increased importance, for Grand Prix drivers no longer had an excess of power and fast laps depended more upon speed through corners than outright speed.

Maserati interest revived, although the new A6GCM did not make its debut until mid-season, and was not *au point* before its end. This car was designed by Colombo and Massimino around a square (75 × 75 mm) six-cylinder twin ohc engine. This was mounted in a tubular frame, with coil spring and wishbone front suspension, and a one-piece rear axle sprung on quarter-elliptics and located by radius rods. Meanwhile Enrico Platé regularly campaigned converted 4CLT/48 Maserati-Platés in Formula 2.

The Maserati brothers also essayed a Formula 2 car, which like other racing Oscas suffered from a lack of development resources. Its 76 × 73 'six'

followed classic Maserati lines, and 155 bhp was claimed for it; the only novelty in the rest of the car was the inboard mounting of its rear brakes.

Gordini had now severed his last connections with Simca, and built cars with entirely new 2 litre engines, twin ohc 75 × 75 mm units theoretically capable of at least 180 bhp (although in fact Gordini depended on the light weight of his cars to make up for a lack of sheer engine power, and some inflexibility in the unit). Gordini also used a live rear axle and torsion bar rear suspension, which did little to cut the high rate of transmission failures. Nevertheless, despite frailties of engine, transmission and suspension, these Gordinis

offered the only serious challenge to Ferrari throughout most of 1952.

Also in France, work started, and was almost finished, on a car which owed allegiances to the design philosophy behind the ill-fated Grand Prix Cisitalia, and like that car held the same paper promise of upsetting established practice by revolution (rather than through the evolutionary process which was to come to fulfilment later in the decade). This was the Sacha-Gordine, designed by Cesare Vigna, a disciple of the great Dr Porsche. Vigna mounted his twin ohc V-8 engine behind the driver, with the gearbox behind it, in a tubular chassis with torsion bar independent suspension front and rear. The result was a car which would not have looked out of place in 1962, but which never ran in 1952, the year in which it was almost completed.

Mechanically, the numerous British cars proved to be outclassed, although the ability of some of their drivers was beyond question. This is a far-reaching qualification, for it signalled a turning point when the average British drivers could no longer be dismissed as amiable amateurs.

HWM were still in the forefront, with cars modified in detail at the rear, with transverse leaf spring replaced with torsion bars, and brakes mounted inboard – a notable departure in detail. The HWM was powered by the Alta four-cylinder engine which was also used – obviously – in the Alta, which had a chassis and running gear closely similar to Taylor's earlier supercharged Grand Prix Alta.

The name Cooper was firmly introduced to the Grands Prix in 1952 (Schell's 1950 essay at Monaco hardly being representative). The T20 was the first racing Cooper to have its engine mounted ahead of the cockpit, in a tubular chassis which followed the lines of those used on F3 Coopers, while the transverse leaf spring and wishbone suspension front and rear was identical. The engine was the six-cylinder pushrod ohc Bristol unit, 66 × 96 mm, which derived from the pre-war BMW 328 and was developed for Bristol by BMW designer Fiedler. Power output at this stage was a modest 127 bhp, but the car was light and handled well – in all, an ideal independent's machine. However, it became prominent not because examples were driven in a gentlemanly manner among the back markers, but because of the very forceful driving of Mike Hawthorn.

The Connaughts did not achieve the results expected of them, for their Lea-Francis-based pushrod ohv engines simply lacked power (140 bhp at 6000 rpm was claimed for them), although the cars were competitive in other respects such as road-holding. Torsion bar suspension was used all round, with wishbones at the front, and a de Dion axle at the rear. Pre-selector gearboxes were fitted.

Maserati's mixed F2 fortunes are summed up in this photograph (above) of Fangio walking away from his car at Zandvoort. Below: Pre-war star Hans Stuck at the wheel of an AFM. Opposite: Mixed field at Avus in 1953, with streamlined German cars naturally much in evidence.

Lesser British machines included a Frazer-Nash using many production parts (including a rigid back axle) and the Bristol engine, and a pair of the ingenious Aston-Butterworths, which had Butterworth opposed-piston four-cylinder air-cooled engines, in tubular frames with independent suspension by transverse leaf springs (these cars were abandoned after their unsuccessful 1952 season). Then there was the last of the ERAs, the G-type, which was powered by a Bristol engine. Its offset single-seater body was built up on a light-alloy frame based on deep-section tubes. Unsuccessful in racing, it was later used by Bristol, virtually as a sports car prototype.

In the seven World Championship Grands Prix of 1952 Ferrari ruled, absolutely. Ascari won the Belgian, French, British, Dutch, German and Italian Grands Prix and, of course, the World Championship. His team-mate Piero Taruffi won the Swiss Grand Prix, and finished third in the Championship (the other member of the Ferrari team, Farina, was second). Speeds generally were down, particularly on the high-speed circuits, and only in the Italian Grand Prix did the Ferrari team have to fight, against Gonzalez. He led the race until he had to stop for fuel, fought back from fifth and at the end placed his Maserati second. Ascari's winning speed at Monza was 109·8 mph, compared with the 115·53 mph he had achieved with a 4·5 litre Ferrari in 1951; his 1951 and 1952 speeds at the sinuous Nürburgring were 84·4 mph and 82·2 mph.

The second-rank series of eight Grands Prix de France, of which the Rouen event ranked as the French Grand Prix, almost went the same way. Ascari won at la Baule, Comminges, Marseilles, Pau and of course Rouen, Taruffi at Montlhéry and Villoresi at les Sables d'Olonne. These were all fairly short, slow circuits, which suited the Type 500 Ferrari admirably. The eighth, Rheims, race was an exception, the more so since the right angle in the village of Gueux had been by-passed, and provided an exceptional result. Jean Behra, French motorcycle champion and for some time to come the leading French racing driver, led the race from flag to flag in a Gordini to win at 105·33 mph, with Farina out of sight in second place. This moment of triumph had to last French supporters for a very long time, for the next victory for a French car in a top-flight race did not come until 1968, when a Ford-engined Matra run by a British team won the Dutch Grand Prix. . . .

In the rest of the GPs de France series, Gordinis gained a second and three thirds, HWM a second (Collins at Sables d'Olonne) and Maserati-Platé a third.

This left a dozen other secondary F2 events, of which Ferrari won half, and did not contest half. Maserati received a setback when their team was at last ready to race, in the Monza GP. Fangio drove overnight to this event from the Formula 1 Ulster Trophy, run the previous day, crashed in the opening laps and was put out of racing for the rest of the season; Gonzalez' engine blew, and he did not really challenge again until late in the season.

Although in the absence of the Ferrari team, HWM achieved some good results, notably Frère's victory

in the GP des Frontières, and Macklin's in the Silverstone International Trophy, the best British results were achieved by Mike Hawthorn in the *grandes épreuves*. He placed his Cooper third in the British GP, and fourth in the Dutch and Belgian GPs. Apart from this, Wharton placed the Frazer-Nash fourth in the Swiss GP, Frère an HWM fifth in the Belgian GP, Poore and Thompson Connaughts fourth and fifth in the British Grand Prix.

The situation at the end of 1952 was very similar to that at the end of 1950, except that instead of Ferrari threatening Alfa Romeo dominance, Maserati was poised to challenge Ferrari. During the off season Ferrari did little to the Type 500, which during the year was to be raced with 190–195 bhp available to its drivers, and of course had the advantage of being thoroughly race-proved. The A6SSG Maserati 'six' was reworked by Colombo, and gave some 195 bhp at 7100 rpm, later 208 bhp at 7800 rpm on the bench. Maserati roadholding and brakes had been improved, with the rear suspension quarter-elliptics supplemented by additional radius arms and new brake drums, while larger fuel tanks were fitted to give the cars full-race duration. In driving strength the teams were very evenly matched, Ferrari lining up Ascari, Villoresi, Farina and Hawthorn, Maserati Fangio, Gonzalez, Marimon and Bonetto.

The neat little Osca twin ohc six reappeared, now with outboard brakes, and a second example was built, for Chiron (he gained two second places in non-Championship events with this Osca, while Elie Bayol continued with the first car, and although a pure amateur, won at Aix-les-Bains with it). Gordini carried on with his shoestring team, but lacked the

Above: Hans Stuck racing a German AFM. Climax to the Formula came in the 1953 Italian GP, when Fangio (Maserati) Farina and Ascari (Ferraris) and Marimon (Maserati) raced wheel to wheel for the entire race distance. Here they lap Chiron (Osca) and Bira (Maserati).

year (fruitlessly in both cases, it was to transpire).

While the British cars were improved, they too fell back in relation to the Ferraris and Maseratis, and none could be considered competitive. Cooper introduced the Mk 2, or T23, with a new space frame and detail refinements. Three of these were run with Alta engines in place of the Bristol unit; two performed creditably in minor events; the third, Stirling Moss', was developed with an SU fuel-injected engine, to give over 180 bhp by the end of the season. This, coupled with Moss' driving, was enough for it to be able to at least challenge some of the Italian works cars. It succeeded Moss' first Cooper-Alta, which during the first half of the season was so modified by Moss, Ray Martin and Alf Francis as to become a Moss-Martin-Francis-Alta special, with little left of the original but the space frame (with, incidentally, disc brakes at the front, drums at the rear). However, it was never free of teething troubles, and re-modifications, and was abandoned at mid-season.

The HWMs were re-engined with slightly more powerful, but never adequately powerful, engines and their bodies were revised. But the team had a poor season, in part because the need to race whenever and wherever possible in order to balance the budget meant that there was often too little time for proper overhauls between races. Connaught also extracted more power from their engine, and essayed Hilborn

resources to develop his cars during the off-season, and so relatively lost ground. Like Ferrari, Gordini also raced a 2·5 litre car in *formule libre* events in 1953, in preparation for the Grand Prix formula which was to come into effect at the beginning of the following

fuel injection on their works cars. Altogether, ten of these Type A Connaughts were built, and in 1953 they gave good accounts of themselves in British national events; at a higher level they were as outclassed as most British F2 cars.

To all intents and purposes, the season opened in Argentina, for although the temporada events were still run to *formule libre* rules, they were now very much part of the main racing scene. The Ferrari team simply slipped 2·5 litre engines into their cars, and these dominated both races, Ascari winning the first at 78·32 mph from Villoresi and Gonzalez, Farina the second at 72·47 mph from Villoresi and Hawthorn.

The first of the front line races to be run in Europe was the Pau GP–the Syracuse GP in March was ignored by works teams, leaving de Graffenried to drive his Maserati to a clear three-lap victory over Chiron. Scuderia Ferrari made no mistakes at Pau, where Ascari and Hawthorn finished three laps ahead of Schell (Gordini). At Bordeaux Ascari and Villoresi again headed a Gordini, which although it was driven by Fangio lost four laps in the 123 lap race. Then Ferrari split forces, sending Hawthorn to beat Salvadori and Rolt in Connaughts in the Silverstone International Trophy, and Farina to beat Fangio and Gonzalez in Maseratis in the Naples Grand Prix.

The Championship season opened at Zandvoort, where Ascari led from start to finish, to win from Farina. At Spa, Ascari made a poor start, and did not take the lead until Gonzalez and Fangio retired their Maseratis–indeed, until that development, the Argentinians had been pulling away from the Ferrari drivers on this fast circuit. Ascari's speed was 112·47 mph.

The scene changed to the fast open Rheims circuit, and to one of the two outstanding races of the formula. Practice showed the two principal teams to be nicely balanced, and Gonzalez started his Maserati with half-full tanks, to set a cracking pace and perhaps pull out a lead sufficient to allow for his inevitable pit stop; in this he failed, and his stop cost him five places. It left Fangio fighting for the lead with Hawthorn. With two laps to go, they crossed the line wheel to wheel; on the last lap, Hawthorn beat Fangio on acceleration out of the last corner, and to the chequered flag. This was the first victory for an English driver in a race of this stature since Richard Seaman's in the 1938 German GP. Hawthorn's winning speed was 113·65 mph, and his winning margin exactly a second; Fangio just held off Gonzalez, who finished a mere two-fifths of a second behind him, third.

The Ferrari drivers held the Maserati challenge at bay in the next three races, Ascari winning the British GP at 92·97 mph from Fangio, Farina, Gonzalez and Hawthorn; Farina winning the German GP at 83·89 mph from Fangio and Hawthorn; and Ascari heading a Ferrari 1-2-3 at 97·17 mph in the Swiss GP.

Swaters in a Ferrari T500 leading round the notorious Avus banking.

For the Italian GP, Ferrari entered a six-car team, including two revised models with new, 93·5 × 73·5 mm, engines (these proved less stable than the tried cars in practice, and so were raced by 'juniors' Maglioli and Carini). The race was a fight between a quartet, two Maseratis, two Ferraris, Fangio and Marimon, Ascari and Farina. These were equally matched in speed, Ferrari drivers had the edge braking into corners, Maserati drivers accelerating out of them. Marimon dropped out of the battle after 46 laps, but played a part when the race was decided on the last corner: Ascari led into it, only to find his line occupied by Fairman's Connaught; he tried to change it, but his Ferrari was on the limit of adhesion and slid broadside, to be rammed by Marimon's lapped Maserati. Farina took to the grass to avoid the melee, while Fangio slipped through to win, and at last break the Ferrari stranglehold. His speed was 110·69 mph, his winning margin over Farina 1·4 seconds–as big a lead as any driver had held during the 80 laps race. Villoresi and Hawthorn followed, both a lap down.

Minor races followed, but this event was the climax to the season–which saw Ascari win his second World Championship–and of the enormously successful 2-litre Formula 2. By this time, the regulations for another Grand Prix formula which was to be equally successful had been based on it.

Return of Mercedes

In 1954 a Grand Prix formula which was to run for seven years was introduced, with very simple requirements; it admitted cars with engines of 2·5 litres, or 750 cc if supercharged. There were no restrictions concerning weight or fuel, although after four seasons the type of fuel to be used was closely defined, and the minimum distance of *grandes épreuves* remained at 186 miles, or 3 hours. Such attempts as there were to build supercharged cars were of no significance – the one example which actually raced performed dismally – and the mechanical pattern at least appeared to have been clearly laid down in the preceding years of Formula 2 Grands Prix.

This, however, was misleading. The established order of things, Italian superiority, was rudely upset in the opening two years of the formula; in the middle period, British cars became a powerful force; in the closing years, the whole Grand Prix scene underwent fundamental changes, and the whole concept of the Grand Prix car changed.

As the first season opened, the incumbent Italian pace-setters seemed to be well-placed to maintain their positions. Scuderia Ferrari had run prototypes of their 2·5 litre cars in 1953, and the 625 was a very straightforward development of the 500 (1953 Type 500s, with 2·5 litre engines, were also raced in 1954). The 625 had an oval-tube frame, coil spring front suspension and a de Dion rear end with the gearbox mounted behind the axle line. The normal engine in these cars was a 94 × 90 mm four, giving 230–250 bhp at 7500 rpm, in two versions with differing valve-gear; Ferrari also raced a 100 × 79·5 mm four during the year. Later in 1954 another Ferrari appeared, the Lampredi-designed Type 553 'Squalo'. This was a short-chassis car, with front suspension by wishbones and leaf springs (later to be replaced with a coil spring layout), and a de Dion rear end. Fuel was carried in tanks on either side of the frame, in the interests of keeping this variable weight mass within the wheel-

base. This required a change of technique on the part of drivers – as did the contemporary Lancia D50 – and at least in part the reputation which this car gained for tricky handling was due to drivers' reluctance to change, and their preference for the known qualities of the 625.

The new Maserati was to be the only car competitive throughout the first phases of the 2·5 litre formula, until the fuel regulations were changed, and the 250F has become one of the classic Grand Prix cars. It had a new space frame of small-diameter tubes, with the wishbone and coil spring front suspension of preceding Maseratis, but a de Dion rear end. The engine was a logical development of the 2 litre F2 unit, 84 × 75 mm, which in 1954 had a power output of some 240 bhp at 7400 rpm (this was also used in some early races of the formula in A6GCS chassis).

Gordini's cars were virtually identical to his F2 cars, with six-cylinder 84 × 80 mm engines. These Gordinis and the A6GCS Maseratis were the only GP cars raced in 1954 with live rear axles.

HWM attempted to continue in Grand Prix racing

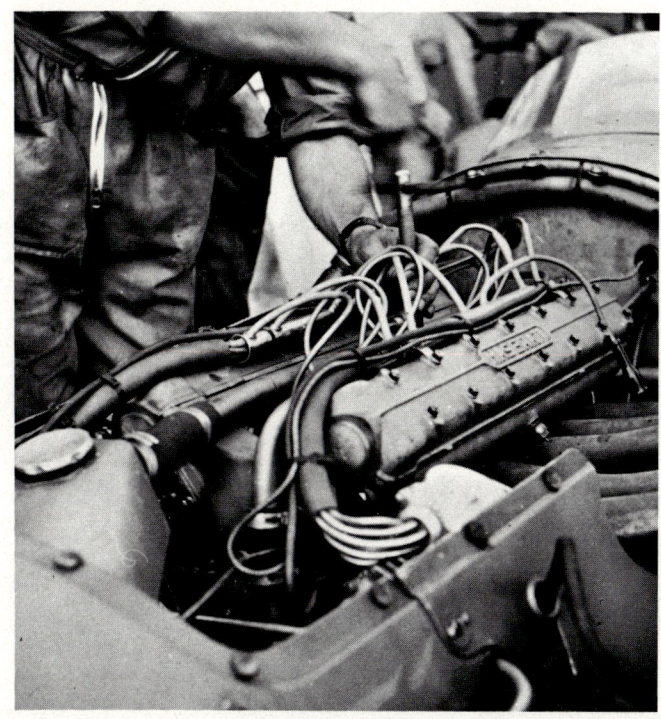

Prelude to a new era – the Mercedes team lined up in front of the Rheims pits before the 1954 French Grand Prix (left: the canted straight-eight engine and inboard front brakes of the W196).

with enlarged F2 engines, but this proved futile, and was soon abandoned. Of the other British cars in preparation for the 2·5 litre formula, the four-cylinder Vanwall Special was raced in its opening season. This had been intended for the 2 litre Grands Prix, which had run their course before the first car was completed, and thus it was handicapped with a 2 litre engine when it first raced; later in 1954 it ran with 2·3 litre, then 2·5 litre engines. These were four-cylinder units, owing much to Norton motorcycle practice, consisting of four separate cylinder barrels spigoted to a light-alloy crankcase and cylinder head. An unusual feature of the early Vanwall Special was an external surface radiator, atop the nose, but this was later replaced with a conventional radiator. While in 1954 the car was of no more than incidental interest, it was the progenitor of a successful Vanwall line.

Connaught also built cars to the new formula, using Alta engines developed by themselves and Weslake, and enlarged to 93·5 × 90 mm; initially, Connaught essayed a streamlined body with distinctive tail fin. Like the Vanwall, the Type B Connaught was of no significance in 1954. Work on the 2·5 litre BRM progressed characteristically slowly. . . .

The great might-have-been of the year was the T160 Alfa Romeo. An Alfa design team under Orazio Satta proposed a very original machine, built around a large tubular backbone which was to carry all the mechanical components. However, the only part of the car which took shape in the metal was the 12 cylinder 'boxer' engine (68 × 57 mm), for which the target output was 300 bhp. The possibility of adapting the car for four-wheel drive was envisaged, brakes were inboard front and rear, and it was proposed that the cockpit should be behind the rear axle line (in October 1952 an adapted 158 was tested by Sanesi to prove this extraordinary possibility, which appears almost to have been an over-reaction to problems encountered with the forward cockpit of the rear-engined 512). Production car realities forced the abandonment of the 160 project.

Two other very significant cars were built, although neither was ready for the opening races of 1954. Mercedes-Benz returned to the Grands Prix with the W196, a car bristling with novelty and generously backed, technically and financially. The straight-eight engine (76 × 68·8 mm) had two notable features, fuel injection and desmodromic valve gear. Tradi-

The Super Squalo was one of the least successful of all GP Ferraris, while the 250F (below) was the most famous of all GP Maseratis (Ascari in a 250F cockpit in front of the Rheims pits, Gianni Lancia watching).

Vittorio Jano's Lancia D50 turned out to be the least conventional Grand Prix car of the period, and showed enormous promise (right, Ascari in the cockpit during early tests).

tionally, the cylinders were in two blocks, with central power take-off and ancillary power drives, with integral heads and welded-on water jackets.

The engine was laid almost flat in a space frame of main tubular members and triangulated small-diameter tubes. The ifs was conventional, by double wishbones and torsion bars, while at the rear a swing axle arrangement was used, with an exceptionally low roll centre (the swinging arms carrying the hubs were centrally pivoted, only six inches above ground level). Drum brakes were inboard front and rear. A fully streamlined body enclosing the wheels was used when the W196 was first raced, but save for ultra high-speed circuits (Avus and Monza) was soon abandoned.

The Lancia D50, the first Grand Prix car built by that old-established company, and carried through by Gianni Lancia in the face of his father's known wishes, did not appear until the closing races of 1954. Designed by the old master, Vittorio Jano, it had an ultra-light chassis built up of small diameter cross-braced tubes, and the front suspension was mounted directly to the engine, which thus played a load-bearing role. Front suspension was by double wishbones, the lower ones being connected by a transverse leaf spring, while a de Dion arrangement was used at the rear, again with a transverse spring, and radius rods. Fuel and oil was carried in outrigged sponsons between the wheels, so that as in the Ferrari Squalo their varying weight was within the wheel base. Alternative engines were tried, 76 × 68·5 mm (2490 cc) and 73·6 × 73·1 mm (2487 cc); the latter version was used in racing, initially giving 260 bhp at 8000

rpm (thus almost matching the Mercedes engine).

The first races of the new formula, run in South America, saw a resumption of the familiar Ferrari-Maserati duel, with Gordini playing a supporting role. The Argentine Grand Prix fell to Fangio, driving a Maserati while he waited for the Mercedes to which he was committed to be ready. His winning speed was 70·2 mph, and he finished over a minute ahead of the Ferraris driven by Farina and his erstwhile team mate Gonzalez. The non-Championship Buenos Aires GP fell to Trintignant, now a Ferrari driver, from Mieres in a Maserati (this race was marred by tragedy, when Enrico Platé was killed as he stood in front of the pits).

Back in Europe, the first *grande épreuve* was the low-key Belgian Grand Prix, in which only 14 cars started, to be led past the flag by Fangio, at 115·08 mph; Trintignant placed his Ferrari second and Moss his private Maserati third.

The French Grand Prix at Rheims was much more portentous, for Mercedes-Benz chose this race for the debut of their new Grand Prix cars, forty years after Mercedes triumphantly returned to Grand Prix racing at Lyons, twenty years after they first ventured outside Germany with their new Grand Prix team in the thirties. The streamlined W196 was eminently suited to the fast Rheims circuit, and even the prospect of its performance there caused some consternation in the Italian ranks. These therefore closed, in that Ascari and Villoresi, contracted to Lancia, were temporarily released to drive for Ferrari and Maserati.

Fangio was the only star driver in the German team, and during the season was to prove to the full his value to it, but such was the superiority of the W196 at Rheims that it hardly mattered that the other two drivers were not of front-rank calibre – indeed, Karl Kling placed his W196 on the front row of the grid, alongside Fangio's. In the race Fangio and Kling ran away from the field, and crossed the line in team order, a tenth of a second apart, Fangio winning at 115·67 mph. Behind them the field was shattered; Manzon brought a Ferrari home third, lapped by the two flying Mercedes, and only seven of the 21 starters were classified.

This was a devastating result, but the next race showed that this generation of Mercedes was not necessarily going to be all-conquering. Fortunes were reversed on a gusty day of showers at Silverstone, when the drivers of the W196 found that road-holding was a little uncertain, and their task was complicated as with enclosed front wheels it was difficult to place their cars precisely through corners marked by drums. Here Gonzalez took the lead in a 625 Ferrari, and held it to the end. Fangio desperately clung to second place for 50 laps, but was passed by both Moss and Hawthorn. The former retired with only 10 laps to go, leaving Gonzalez (89·69 mph) and Hawthorn to score a 1-2 for Ferrari, from Marimon's Maserati and Fangio. Seven drivers shared the fastest lap!

The European Grand Prix at the Nürburgring was of course of prime importance to Mercedes, who had the first open-wheel W196 completed for Fangio. He again took pole position, while Hawthorn and Moss put cars of the leading Italian marques onto the front row of the grid alongside him. At the start, however, Gonzalez took the lead, although he had been demoralized by the fatal practice accident to his compatriot Onofre Marimon. Retirements left Gonzalez fighting alone against four Mercedes – veteran Her-

Early British 2·5 litre GP cars showed little more promise than their predecessors, and the BRM Type 25 (top, being tested by Moss) did not become a Championship race winner until 1959. The early Vanwall Special (left) had an unusual external radiator. Gordini largely depended on his six-cylinder engine (centre).

mann Lang had been brought into the team for this race – but after 17 laps he handed his car over to Hawthorn. The English driver restarted third – two of the Mercedes had retired – and when Kling slowed in the third W196 he moved into second place. Although Hawthorn narrowed the gap in the closing stages, Fangio was well in command, and won at 82·77 mph.

Although it could not be foreseen at the time, the Swiss Grand Prix at the end of August was to be the last run on the Bremgarten circuit, and the last Grand Prix ever to be run on Swiss soil (this meeting also saw the last race appearance of another great driver, Rudolf Caracciola, who crashed in a Mercedes during practice for a sports car race, and once again suffered complicated thigh fractures). The three principal

Widely differing racing scenes in England. Above, Parnell (Ferrari) leading a mixed field (Cooper F3, Cooper F2, Connaught and HWM); below, the fiery Froilan Gonzalez leading the 1954 British GP.

marques were again represented on the front row of the grid for the Grand Prix – Gonzalez (Ferrari), Fangio (Mercedes) and Moss (Maserati). Once again Fangio led from the flag, from Moss until the Maserati again failed, from Hawthorn until his Ferrari had fuel system troubles, then from Gonzalez to the end. Fangio's average speed for the last Swiss GP was 99·17 mph, his fastest lap on a damp circuit 101·9 mph.

The Italian teams put their maximum efforts into the Italian Grand Prix, and surprisingly the stream-lined Mercedes proved to have little or no speed

advantage at Monza, for fastest practice laps produced the start line-up Mercedes (Fangio – of course), Ferrari (Ascari), Maserati (Moss – now virtually a works entry), Mercedes, Ferrari, Maserati, Ferrari, Mercedes, Maserati, while the 13th fastest of the 17 starters was the 2·5 litre Vanwall, driven by Peter Collins.

Practice accurately foreshadowed the pattern of the race. In the opening stages the lead lay between Ascari and Fangio, with Moss, Villoresi and Gonzalez in close attendance. At half-distance, 40 laps, Villoresi moved into second place, only to retire, so that Moss took second, then the lead as Ascari slowed. Fangio responded briefly, then Moss began to draw steadily away from him. But the Maserati was losing oil, and Moss had to stop; after a call at his pit he started to regain ground lost to Fangio, but his engine had been starved of oil, and failed completely. So Fangio gained a very lucky victory for Mercedes, at 111·99 mph, by a lap from Hawthorn, and by another lap from the Ferrari shared by Maglioli and Gonzalez. The other surviving Mercedes was fourth, a further lap behind, and at three-quarter distance behind the Vanwall then placed sixth (Collins then had to stop for an oil pipe to be fixed, and finished seventh).

There remained the Spanish Grand Prix, revived on the Pedralbes circuit, where the Lancia D50s at last appeared. However, Villoresi retired his after only one lap of the race, and Ascari his after leading with apparent ease after nine laps. Then Harry Schell led in a Maserati, until he spun, and his place was taken by Trintignant, until his Ferrari expired. This left Hawthorn to gain a rare victory for a Squalo Ferrari, at 97·93 mph from Maserati driver Luigi Musso, and Fangio, who struggled grimly with a rattling Mercedes. Fangio had undoubtedly saved the season for Mercedes, and in doing so had gained his second World Championship, by a substantial points margin from Gonzalez and Hawthorn.

Meanwhile, the secondary Formula 1 races once so common on the European calendar had been run, some of them for the last time, for in 1955 a freak accident in a sports car race was to have far-reaching consequences.

Slowly, Britain's place in the European scene was becoming more important, too – in little more than a decade it was to become the only country where non-Championship races were run for Grand Prix cars. These were run in 1954 at two meetings at the new Aintree circuit, created round the famous horse-racing course in the suburbs of Liverpool. Moss won three events in his Maserati, two *formule libre* races, and a Formula 1 race from Hawthorn. The Silverstone International Trophy saw a victory for Gonzalez

The streamlined Mercedes W196 was by no means wholly successful, and the German team soon evolved open-wheel versions (above, Moss on his way to victory in the 1955 British GP).

(Ferrari). Moss won the Oulton Park Gold Cup and lesser events at Goodwood and Snetterton fell to Parnell (Ferrari) and Moss.

In Italy, Ferraris won at Bari (Gonzalez) and Syracuse (Farina), while Maseratis won at Pescara (Musso) and Rome (Marimon). In France, Gordini victories came at Cadours and Pau (Behra), Ferrari victories at Caen and Rouen (Trintignant) and Bordeaux (Gonzalez). In Germany, Grand Prix cars raced again at Avus, for the first time since the war, largely to give Mercedes a demonstration run in front of a home crowd – the issue was never in doubt, for the opposition was slight, and Kling duly won from Fangio and Herrmann, at 132·58 mph.

The 1955 season opened on a note of great promise. All the teams had improved their cars and three, Lancia, Maserati and Mercedes-Benz, appeared to be evenly matched. Ferrari, despite their record in 1954, were not in such a competitive position, for their four-cylinder engines were outclassed by the sixes and eights, and not for the first time there was dissension within the Scuderia, which led to Lampredi's departure.

Mercedes sought to consolidate the superiority marginally gained in 1954 with refined versions of the W196, of which short and long wheelbase variants were built. The former perforce had outboard front brakes; in the latter the engine was set well forward, and this, with minor suspension changes, transformed the hitherto somewhat dubious handling characteristics of the car. Its engine was rated at 282 bhp at 8500 rpm at the beginning of the season, 290 bhp for the final races.

Lancia did little to the D50, apart from modifying the oil circulation system; handling remained hyper-sensitive by the standards of the time, and the car's rapid attitude changes were to catch out the greatest of drivers. Maserati sensibly made few changes in the 250F, standardizing five-speed gearboxes by mid-season and experimenting with, but not racing, fuel-injected engines. Ferrari had greater problems, and tended to ring the changes of combinations of 555 and 625, invariably to end up with deficiencies in power and roadholding.

Perhaps the greatest changes in these teams were in driver line-ups. Increasingly the Italian teams employed non-Italian drivers, for only Castellotti and Musso came forward to take the place of a disappearing generation – during the season Ascari was to lose his life in a training accident, while Farina and Villoresi went into semi-retirement. Jean Behra led the Maserati team, and after early-season disappointments with the Vanwall, Hawthorn returned to Ferrari. In the Mercedes team, Fangio gained the sorely-needed backing of another top-line driver when Moss signed for the German team.

In France, Gordini struggled on without front-rank drivers, and for most of the year with the outdated 'six'. Only at the end of 1955 was the Gordini straight eight (75 × 70 mm) introduced, in a new tubular chassis with all-independent suspension. The only car built to the 750 cc supercharged alternative permitted by the formula also made a fleeting, and desperately uncompetitive, appearance during 1955, in the Pau GP. This was an adapted front-wheel drive DB Monomill, with its twin-cylinder engine Roots-supercharged (interestingly, Mercedes-Benz had flirted with the idea of a supercharged engine for their Grand Prix return in 1954, but soon abandoned the project).

The Vanwall operation became more significant (and the 'Special' appellation was discarded). The engine now had Bosch fuel injection, gaining power at some cost in reliability. Vandervell's intention was to contest the *grandes épreuves*, but in fact the cars proved to need more race development work before they were battle worthy for these. Team drivers at the beginning of the season were Ken Wharton and Mike Hawthorn, whose place was later taken by the exuberant Franco-American Harry Schell.

Rodney Clarke and Mike Oliver continued development of the Type B Connaught, which was handicapped by an engine giving only 240 bhp at 7000 rpm. The heavy and vulnerable streamlined body was abandoned. Like the Vanwall, the Connaught used disc brakes. Finally, the 2·5 litre BRM appeared in secondary events at the end of the season, but the story of this car is more properly part of that of the next phase in the 2·5 formula.

Until June the season progressed normally. Fangio was one of the few drivers unaffected by the intense heat in which the Argentine Grand Prix was run, and duly won the race for Mercedes, from Farina in a Ferrari. Before the main season opened in Europe, the customary non-Championship F1 races were run, Ascari winning for Lancia at Naples and Turin, Maserati drivers taking the other events, Behra at

The second version of the Vanwall, driven by Mike Hawthorn (opposite). Eugenio Castellotti (Lancia) leading Nino Farina (Ferrari) through the station hairpin at Monaco in 1955 (above).

Bordeaux and Pau, Simon at Albi, Collins at Silverstone, Salvadori at Goodwood.

In May the Monaco Grand Prix was revived again, to start its longest unbroken period. The race saw astonishing changes of fortune. Fangio and Moss led, but both effectively retired (as did Simon in the third W196). As Moss stopped, Ascari appeared set to take the lead, but in fact he went straight on at the chicane – and into the harbour! So while he swam, Maurice Trintignant took the lead in an old Ferrari 625, and gained a surprise victory at 65·63 mph, from Castellotti (Lancia), Behra and Perdisa (sharing a Maserati) and three veterans, Farina (Ferrari), Villoresi (Lancia) and Chiron (Lancia).

Now the season started to go sour. Alberto Ascari was killed in a sports Ferrari on a test day at Monza; after this the Lancia effort virtually collapsed, and a D50 appeared as a Lancia only once more, in the Belgian Grand Prix (where Castellotti retired it with a burst engine). Fangio and Moss placed Mercedes first and second in this race, and in the Dutch Grand Prix, followed respectively by Farina (Ferrari) and Musso (Maserati).

Before the next Grand Prix, 'Pierre Levegh' (Bouillon) crashed into the crowd at Le Mans, and this appalling accident triggered off a wave of anti-racing sentiment throughout the world. The Grands Prix of France, Germany, Spain and Switzerland were cancelled; all forms of racing were banned in Switzerland, and have been ever since; no races were run in France for the rest of the year, and several of the French provincial Grands Prix were never run again; the American Automobile Association completely revoked its control of the sport in America.

Only two Championship Grands Prix were left, the British event, run for the first time at Aintree, and the Italian classic, run for the first time over the new combined circuit at the Monza autodrome, which incorporated the high-speed banked track. At Aintree Mercedes took the first four places, Stirling Moss becoming the first British driver to win the event (at 86·47 mph). A possibly diplomatic and courteous Fangio was a fifth of a second behind him at the flag, then came Kling and Taruffi, ahead of Musso (Maserati) and the Ferrari shared by Hawthorn and Castellotti. Schell and Wharton placed a Vanwall ninth, after losing 15 laps at the pits with a broken oil pipe. Little noticed among the back markers was a Cooper special, built up around a sports car chassis, with a 2 litre Bristol engine and an all-enveloping body. Its

The near-invincible Mercedes pair Fangio and Moss leading Hawthorn (Ferrari) in the 1955 Dutch Grand Prix.

builder and driver was an Australian, one Jack Brabham. . . .

The Italian Grand Prix should have seen the first race of the Lancia D50s bearing the prancing horse emblem of Ferrari, to whom they had been entrusted, together with an annual Fiat subsidy of 50 million lire for five years (and the services of Jano and Massimino as consultants). However, the D50s threw tyre treads in practice, so for the race the Scuderia relied on Super Squalos. Once again Fangio won for Mercedes, at 128·5 mph, from Taruffi (Mercedes), Castellotti (Ferrari) and Behra (Maserati). Fangio and Behra drove streamlined cars, and for its debut the eight-cylinder Gordini, driven by Lucas, also wore streamlined bodywork, and was noticeably slow until it retired.

The truncated Championship was won by Fangio, from Moss and Castellotti. Mercedes-Benz, having won nine of the twelve Grands Prix which they contested in two years retired from racing, and the Grand Prix world looked to further change.

Some indications of this came on British circuits in the Autumn. The new four-cylinder BRM first appeared at an Aintree meeting, and was first raced by Peter Collins in the Oulton Park Gold Cup, where it showed speed, but retired (with what proved to be a faulty gauge!). At Aintree, Salvadori won in a Maserati, at Oulton Park Moss in a Maserati, ahead of

Hawthorn in a Lancia and Titterington in a Vanwall. The two Vanwalls had already finished first and second in a minor event at Snetterton, and in October Schell gained two victories at Castle Combe, in an F1 race and a *formule libre* event, over a 1·5 litre V-16 BRM, being raced for the last time.

The last race of the 1955 season was historic, the first Grand Prix to be won by a British driver in a British car since Seaman won in Spain in 1924.

Surprisingly, Connaught decided to contest the Syracuse Grand Prix, entering newcomer Tony Brooks and Les Leston, who faced nine Maseratis, some of them front-line cars, and two Ferraris. For eight laps Brooks held third place, for the next 46 laps he ran second, for the last 16 laps he led, to win by 48·3 seconds from Maserati drivers Musso and Villoresi, at 99·05 mph. The world of racing was astounded.

Fading Tradition

A new phase in Grand Prix racing opened in 1956 with a season-long duel between Ferrari and Maserati, while after several false dawns British Grand Prix cars at last grew to competitive maturity. The disappearance of Mercedes-Benz did not lead to falling standards – indeed, speeds increased and competition became fiercer.

Having inherited the Lancia D50, Ferrari threw away the rather outlandish plans for the '116' twin cylinder engine and an 82·4 × 78 mm 'six' (the twin was to have dimensions of 118 × 114 mm, and expected to produce modest gross bhp but exceptional torque, and was thus to be used on a 'horses for courses' basis). Through the winter, Ferrari work was concentrated on the erstwhile Lancias, which were slowly to be transformed out of all recognition, and inevitably become known as Lancia-Ferraris. Immediately, the output of the engine was increased to 280 bhp, suspension was improved in detail, and the fuel tank transferred from the sponsons to the tail,

where its weight improved stability. The Super Squalos were run again in South America at the beginning of 1956, and through the season Ferrari hybrid derivatives appeared, for example the D50-engined Super Squalo.

Maserati refined the 250F in detail, extracting a little more power from the engine (generally, however, this car was slower in a straight line than the Ferraris). This year the fuel-injected engine was raced, although still on an experimental basis, a streamlined car was essayed for fast circuits, and Maserati cautiously experimented with Dunlop disc brakes.

The power of the Vanwall engine had already been demonstrated, and in 1956, the car took on a startling new outward appearance, with a large, high-tailed and smooth body designed by aero-

Above: Ken Wharton driving a Vanwall at Aintree. Below: Fangio drifting a Maserati 250F with absolute mastery during the 1957 French Grand Prix, followed by Musso (Ferrari).

dynamics expert Frank Costin. Functionally, this proved very efficient, and additional scoops or holes to let unallowed-for air in or out were never needed. Under this unconventional skin was a revised suspension and a new space frame of small-diameter tubes, the work of a promising young designer, one Colin Chapman. Disc brakes were of course retained, and mounted inboard at the rear.

The new B-type Connaughts were officially dubbed 'Syracuse'; the team found a little more power for their engine, but inadequate support for any other development, or indeed for more than a shoestring racing programme, concentrated in Britain.

The BRM which had appeared at the end of 1955 was an uncomplicated, compact and light car. Its four-cylinder engine was oversquare ($102 \cdot 8 \times 74 \cdot 9$ mm), which permitted the use of exceptionally large valves (which proved fragile, as they were highly stressed at maximum rpm). Initial output of this engine had been around 250 bhp at 9000 rpm. The chassis of the BRM was a space frame of small-diameter tubing; suspension was by wishbones and oleo-pneumatic struts at the front, by de Dion, transverse leaf spring and shock absorbers at the rear – an arrangement which was to prove far from satisfactory, and was eventually substantially revised. Normal Lockheed or Dunlop disc brakes were used at the front, and a single disc on the transmission at the rear. The car was very light (approximately 1300 lb), and when it was 'right' was unquestionably very fast – maximum speeds achieved by the fastest car of each marque over a timed tenth of a mile at Silverstone during the 1956 British Grand Prix were: BRM, $137 \cdot 40$ mph; Vanwall, $136 \cdot 88$ mph; Lancia-Ferrari, $134 \cdot 83$ mph; Maserati 250F, $133 \cdot 83$ mph. But some-

how BRM misfortunes seemed to be carried over from the V-16 to their 2·5 litre car.

Gordini concentrated on his eight-cylinder cars, which were never fast enough to be competitive, although they did become reasonably reliable.

Surprisingly, another French car appeared, bearing a name evocative of long-past glories – Bugatti. Built at the behest of Roland Bugatti, this T251 owed nothing to Molsheim tradition; on the contrary, in conception it was ahead of its time! As the Bugatti company had long since ceased building automobiles, Colombo was retained to design this GP car. He placed the engine transversely behind the driver, in a space frame, with flank fuel tanks, and in effect used de Dion suspension front and rear, with locating radius rods, shock absorbers and disc or drum brakes.

The five-speed gearbox and final drive were in unit with the engine. In this Colombo followed his Alfa practice, making up his eight of two blocks of four cylinders, with power take-off and ancillary drives from a central gear train. A power output of 275 bhp at 9000 rpm was claimed for this $75 \times 68 \cdot 8$ mm engine. Circumstances were against this last Bugatti. The story of inadequate resources is familiar, and in this case only too sadly true. Although the first of the two cars built was completed late in 1955, several fundamental faults, in road holding for example, were not ironed out by the time the T251 appeared for its race debut six months later. In the light of what was to come, it was most unfortunate that this almost prophetic car was abandoned, doubly unfortunate in that a decade later a French government was to invest considerable sums in restoring the racing blue of France to glory. . . .

British science, as represented in the Vanwall, and Italo-French ingenuity, in the Bugatti, were poorly rewarded in 1956, when the straightforward traditional know-how of Ferrari and Maserati again reigned supreme. The Ferrari team had an invaluable asset in Fangio. After a few races his effective number two was a British driver, Peter Collins, who shot to stardom; although he had started the season almost as team reserve driver, he soon overshadowed the only Italian in the team, Castellotti. Collins' great friend, Mike Hawthorn, was to spend the year almost in the wilderness, with BRM and Vanwall. The third of a trio of British drivers who on ability were the only challengers for Fangio's crown, Stirling Moss, led the Maserati team.

The season opened in Argentina, where for almost half its distance, the Grand Prix was led by Argentine newcomer Carlos Menditeguy; when he spun off Musso took over for Ferrari, then Moss for Maserati until his engine failed, letting Behra into the lead. Fangio had twice spun his own car, to all intents and purposes a pure Lancia D50 at that stage in

The semi-streamlined eight-cylinder Gordini, neat in appearance but ineffectual in racing.

the year. He took over Musso's car, to pass Behra and win at 79·34 mph from the French driver and Hawthorn, who was driving the BRM-owned and substantially modified Maserati 250F.

In the European early-season events, Ferrari contested only the Syracuse Grand Prix (gaining a 1-2-3, Fangio-Musso-Collins) and the Silverstone International Trophy, while in England Moss made hay, after a successful New Zealand outing, where he won the Grand Prix at Ardmore in his 250F. He drove this to win at Aintree, Goodwood and Crystal Palace, but for the International Trophy was persuaded to drive the new Vanwall. Initially, Hawthorn led this race in a BRM, and set a new lap record; when he retired, Moss moved into the lead, drew steadily away from Fangio, and kept the Vanwall in front to win at 100·47 mph – an average higher than the old lap record speed.

In a nominally sports car race at the same meeting, Roy Salvadori drove a single-seater Cooper powered by a 1·5 litre Coventry Climax engine, built in anticipation of a new Formula 2 which was to come into effect in the following year. In this rear-engined car he won quite clearly at 95·13 mph from Colin Chapman in a Lotus-Climax. At the time, nobody saw any Grand Prix significance in these couplings of Cooper-Climax and Lotus-Climax. . . .

The first European race in the Championship was the Monaco Grand Prix, where Moss led from flag to flag to gain his first Continental Grand Prix victory. The drama of this race centred on the Ferrari team, however, and on Fangio. At least during the first half he was uncharacteristically flustered, battering his car against straw bales, kerbs and a wall before retiring it and taking over Collins', to place it second at the end of the 100-lap race. Moss' winning speed was 64·94 mph.

Despite a damp circuit, the next Grand Prix was won at almost twice that speed. The Belgian race at Spa opened with a duel between Fangio and Moss, and ended with a victory for Peter Collins (at 118·43 mph) from temporary Ferrari team mate Paul Frère, Moss, who had taken over Perdisa's Maserati after his own shed a wheel, and the Vanwall driven by Schell.

Vanwall potential was again demonstrated in the French Grand Prix. In practice at Rheims three Ferrari drivers, two Vanwall drivers and three Maserati drivers, in that order, improved on the lap record which had stood to Mercedes since 1954. Hawthorn joined the Vanwall team, and Colin Chapman took the place of Trintignant, released to drive the Bugatti T251 in its only race. Chapman's driving talents were considerable, although he is nowadays seldom recalled as a racing driver, and this event should have seen his Grand Prix debut. However, during practice he collided with Hawthorn, and only the latter's car could

Gioacchino Colombo's extremely original Bugatti T251, with Pierre Marco at the wheel. This car had an eight-cylinder engine mounted transversely behind its cockpit, and in this respect was well ahead of its time.

be repaired for the race. Ferraris monopolized the front row of the grid, private Maseratis and French cars the back three rows, the Bugatti slower than two of the eight-cylinder Gordinis.

In the early stages of the race, Ferraris held the first five places, while Schell over-revved his Vanwall engine and was the first to retire. However, Hawthorn, who was tired after racing in the preceding 12-hour sports car event, was called in to hand over his car. Schell worked this back towards the leaders, set a new lap record, at half-distance had the green car among the Ferraris, and fought through to second place. Then the Vanwall fell back, with its throttle linkage awry (this was a curiously familiar detail failing in this car, for far too long). A broken fuel pipe cost Fangio the lead, and he eventually finished fourth, while Collins went through to win his second successive Championship victory, at 122·21 mph, from Castellotti and Maserati driver Behra.

British hopes raised by Schell's performance were dashed at Silverstone, when Fangio's 1956 luck changed and he won the British Grand Prix at 98·65 mph, by a clear lap from the Ferrari shared by Collins and de Portago, and another lap ahead of Behra. The best-placed British car was fourth, Fairman's Con-

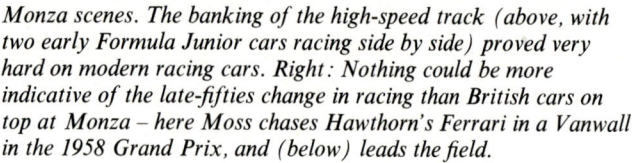

Monza scenes. The banking of the high-speed track (above, with two early Formula Junior cars racing side by side) proved very hard on modern racing cars. Right: Nothing could be more indicative of the late-fifties change in racing than British cars on top at Monza – here Moss chases Hawthorn's Ferrari in a Vanwall in the 1958 Grand Prix, and (below) leads the field.

naught. The BRMs were very fast, and initially ran first and second, but retired, as did the Vanwalls.

On the twisting 14·2 miles of the Nürburgring, Fangio was the absolute master, winning the German Grand Prix at 85·57 mph by almost a minute from Moss, who in turn was nearly five minutes ahead of Behra. Fangio lapped at 87·74 mph, at last breaking the lap record set by Lang in the 1939 Eifelrennen with a 3 litre supercharged Mercedes-Benz.

The last Championship event of the year, at Monza, was much less certain. Once again the full circuit was used, including the notorious banked track, which caused trouble for most teams during practice and the race. The battering which chassis and, particularly, suspension components received because of its irregularities was accentuated by the high *g* loadings. In practice tyres failed, de Dion tubes cracked, shock absorbers and steering arms broke.

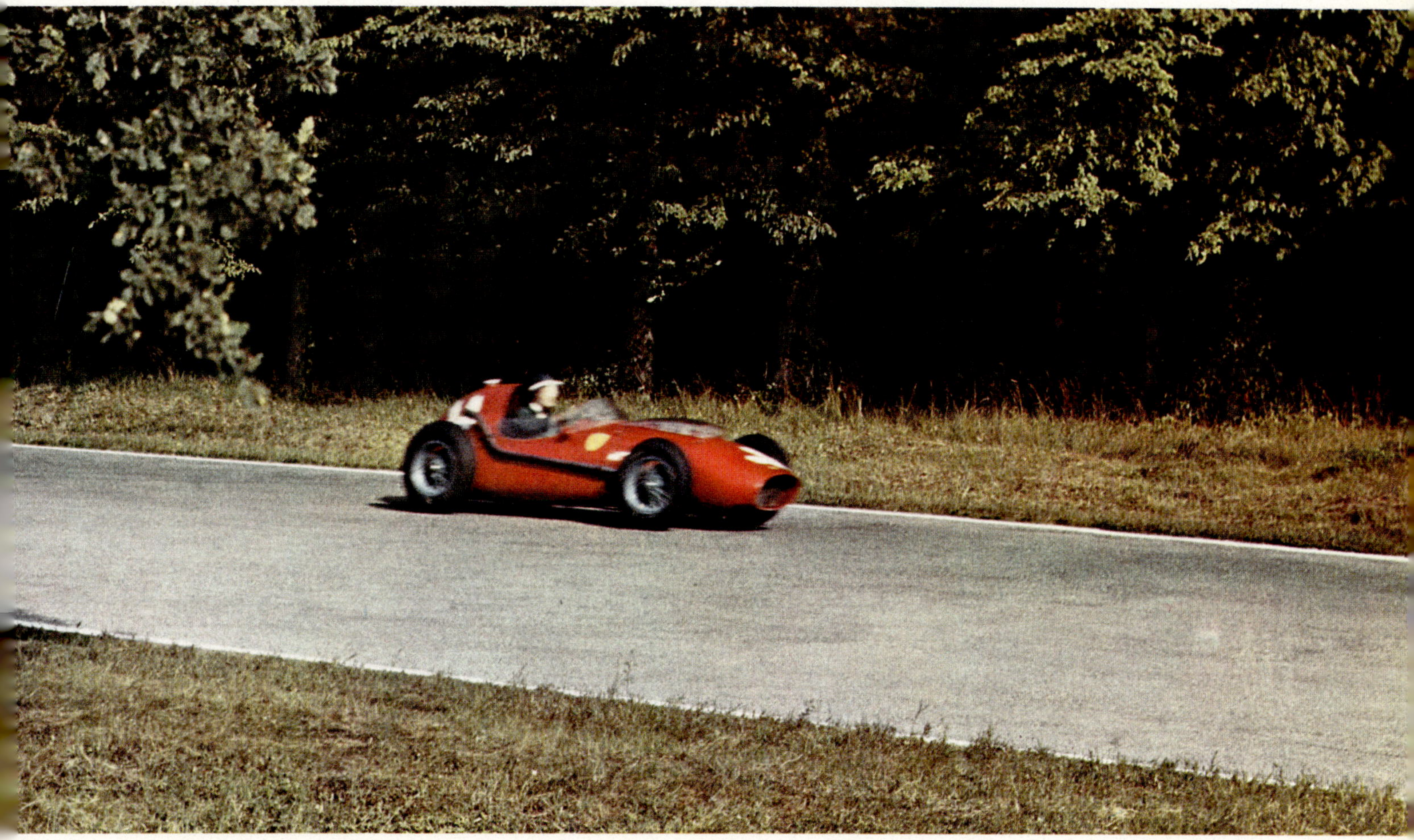

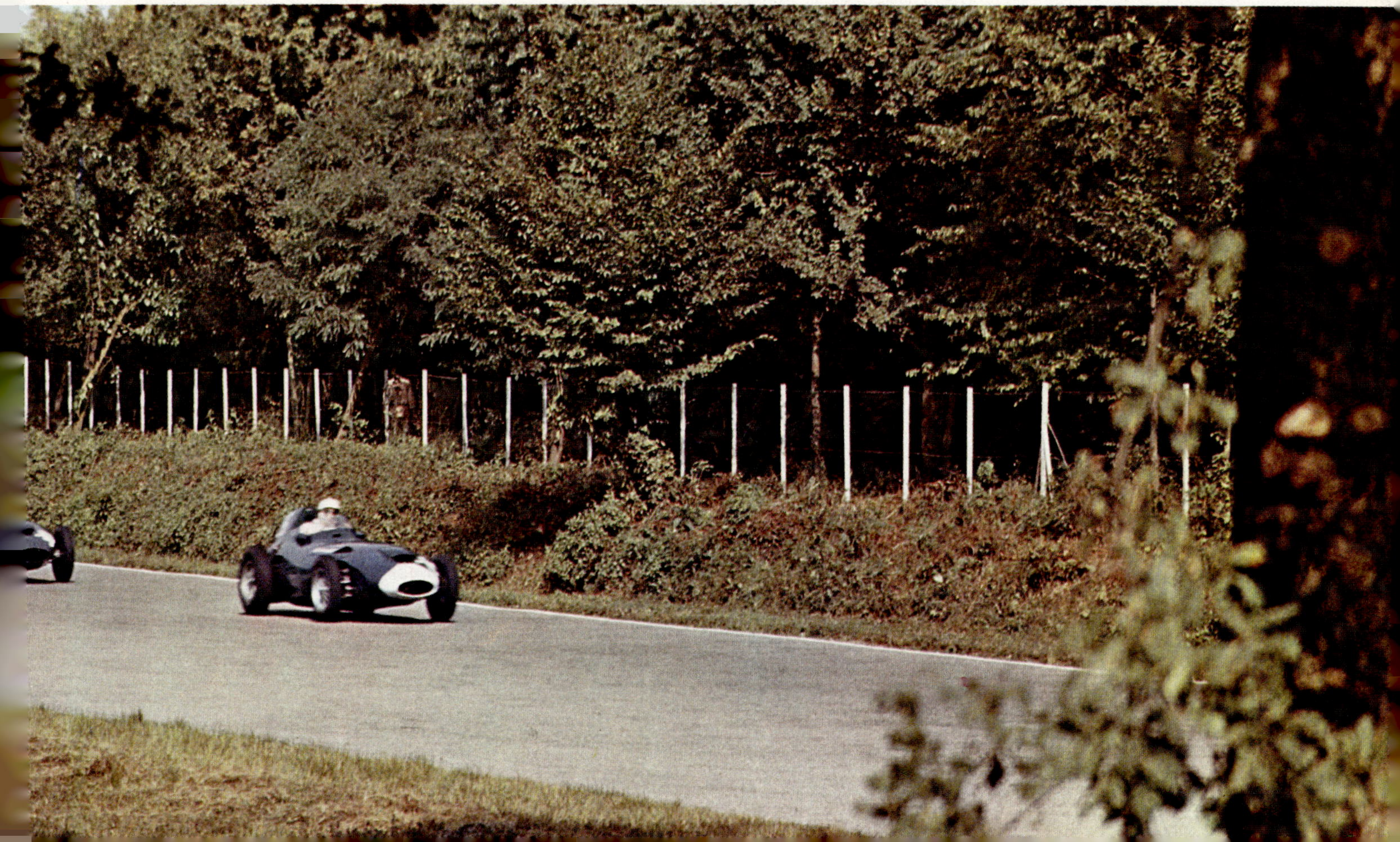

Once again the front row of a grid was the property of Scuderia Ferrari, while Behra and Moss with new and revised Maseratis shared the second row with a Vanwall, driven on this occasion by Taruffi. Further back were three Connaughts, surprising entries for this very fast race.

Determined to shine in front of their home crowd, Castellotti and Musso shot into the lead as the flag fell; three laps later both were in the pits with treads stripped from tyres. Fangio, Moss and Schell then fought out the lead, until a steering arm failed on the Ferrari, and an oil pipe on the Vanwall. Other retirements left Moss pursued by Musso (racing as hard as ever, but destined to have another frightening moment), Collins and Flockhart – the Connaughts may have lacked speed, but they were proving to have the stamina which was almost as important.

Fangio sat on the pit counter, watching his chances of taking a fourth World Championship slip away with every lap that Moss led, until Collins, well-placed in the Championship himself, voluntarily brought in and handed over his relatively heathly Ferrari.

Fangio began a grim chase, of Moss' now off-tune Maserati and Musso's Ferrari. The Maserati actually ran out of fuel with five laps to go, and as Moss coasted towards the pits it was helpfully nudged on by Maserati driver Piotti. Musso inherited a brief lead, then a steering arm failed, and he survived a lurid high-speed skid to sit out the rest of the race. His Maserati refuelled, Moss got away from the pits again in the lead, and went on to win at 129·7 mph, by 5·7 seconds from Fangio. Fangio's second place points were sufficient to clinch the Championship (from Moss and Collins). The Connaughts driven by Flockhart and Fairman were third and fifth, the Maseratis driven by Godia and Piotti fourth and sixth.

This was a climactic ending to the season, and as it turned out, to Italian predominance, although this was hardly apparent as the next year opened. However, a sign of changing times was that Moss, who could have the pick of teams, now had sufficient confidence in the Vanwall as a car with which he could win the World Championship to join the team.

Fangio left Ferrari, with relief, and returned to Maserati, for what was to be the last season in front line racing for driver and team. The 250F was still Maserati's principal car, in lightweight form for leading drivers. In terms of sheer bhp, the six-cylinder engine was becoming outclassed, but on all but the fastest circuits there was compensation in the handling qualities of the car. A replacement engine was in preparation, and was raced, although never developed to full raceworthiness during the year. This was a 60 degree V-12 (68·5 × 56 mm), in which problems of broadening the usable rev range were not wholly overcome. It was also dogged by carburation troubles. By

Opposite: Luigi Musso with the raucous V-12 Maserati 250F at Monaco in 1957 and (below) Archie Scott-Brown racing a Connaught at Silverstone. Above: Hawthorn in a Dino 246 Ferrari and, below, one of its predecessors, a hybrid with a Lancia V-8 in a Super Squalo chassis.

the end of the season the engine was producing about 310 bhp at 10000 rpm; then a decade was to pass before a Maserati V-12 was raced effectively in the Grands Prix. In 1957 it was installed in adapted 250F chassis.

Ferrari's V-8 cars were further removed from their Lancia origins, while the engine had reached the end of its useful development life (producing a maximum of 280 bhp at 8500 rpm). The Lancia lines were completely lost as the pannier tanks disappeared; basic-

ally, the suspension was modified to incorporate coil springs, although variations were tried during the year. The team received an early-season setback when Eugenio Castellotti was killed in a Modena test accident, and ended the year without a single *grande épreuve* victory. However, by that time, the Scuderia had a promising new "pure" Ferrari under development, and showing race promise.

This was based on their 1·5 litre V-6 Formula 2 car, which in fact was heavy for that class. By the last race of 1957 its engine had been enlarged to 2417 cc, and proven on the petrol which was to become the obligatory fuel in 1958, when the car was to be campaigned as the Dino 246 Grand Prix car.

The Vanwall and the BRM were refined, the former to confirm its 1956 promise, the latter at least towards eventual raceworthiness. The principal change on the Vanwall was the substitution of coil springs for the transverse leaf in the rear suspension, while troubles in the throttle system were largely ironed out.

The 280 bhp reliably produced by the Vanwall four at 7500 rpm was equalled, but at a higher engine speed, by the BRM unit. But the Bourne team was still dogged by bogies, some of which were no longer real in 1957 (reputations proved more difficult to eradicate than some physical problems). On the advice of Colin Chapman, the suspension of the car was radically altered, and the oleo-pneumatic struts at the front and transverse leaf springs at the rear were discarded, in favour of coil springs.

Connaught reworked their engines again, to give an inadequate 255 bhp, but otherwise proposed to campaign their B-types little changed – resources were almost exhausted. One car was rebodied with a high-tailed 'tooth paste tube' body, in an experiment which proved inconclusive. A C-type derivative was stillborn, and a rear-engined Connaught under construction was abandoned when the team was wound up before the end of the season.

This was but one of several attempts to revive the rear-engined layout for Grand Prix cars during the post-war period, for the principle was known and proven. The revival came about, not by any conscious application of theory by an established Grand Prix constructor, but rather by an accident of evolution by the least pretentious of all racing car manufacturers.

At the suggestion of the Coopers, père et fils, and R. R. C. Walker, Coventry Climax produced a 1·9 litre (86·4 × 86·8 mm) version of their 1·5 litre twin

Bright twilight. A Dino Ferrari, with which the Scuderia fought a long front-engined holding action, being pushed to the grid at Monza. In the background the road and high-speed circuits go their separate ways, and it was the use of the latter in 1960 which made for a last victory for a front-engined GP car.

ohc engine, which gave some 175 bhp and of course slotted into the simple, light and agile Cooper T41 Formula 2 car. In the 1957 Monaco Grand Prix, Jack Brabham raced the first Cooper-Climax Grand Prix car (ironically, at about this time Coventry Climax abandoned work on their FPE Formula 1 V-8, as it was felt that the 260 bhp it developed in bench trials would be inadequate for racing!).

As Cooper began to emerge as a force, another constructor who had worked on a similar lightness and simplicity basis, Amédée Gordini, gave up.

In the Argentine Grand Prix, Ferrari ran 1956 cars, and the Maserati team dominated the race, Fangio winning at 80·47 mph, from Behra, Menditeguy and Schell. Back in Europe, however, Collins and Musso headed Moss in the Syracuse GP, after the Vanwall had lost time at the pits. Then the Italian and British

teams went their separate, national, ways until the Monaco Grand Prix. Here Moss crashed at the chicane on the fourth lap, and Collins and Hawthorn were put out of the race in a chain reaction. This left Fangio to lead to the end of the 105-lap race, to win at 64·75 mph, while Brooks similarly held second place. Remarkably, Brabham had the little Cooper in fifth place at half-distance, and with two laps to go he was third! But a fuel pump failure meant that the Australian pushed across the line, to be classified sixth.

Fangio was the master in the French GP at Rouen, winning at 100·02 mph from the Ferrari team, Musso, Collins and Hawthorn. Then Vanwall promise became reality, at Aintree, where in the British GP Tony Vandervell's patience was at last rewarded. Moss shot away into the lead, stopped with an ignition fault, and took over the second Vanwall from Tony Brooks, who

was suffering the after effects of a Le Mans accident. Moss worked the car back up to third place then, in a long overdue change, fortune favoured the British team – the engine of race leader Behra's Maserati blew up, and second man Hawthorn punctured a tyre on the debris of the Maserati engine. So Moss and Brooks shared the triumph of the first all-British win in a World Championship Grand Prix, at 86·80 mph, from the Ferraris driven by Musso and Hawthorn.

The Nürburgring is a very different circuit to the flat and smooth Aintree, and the suspension of the Vanwalls proved hopelessly at variance with its bumps. So once again a Championship race was between Ferrari and Maserati, or rather Ferrari and Fangio, for he drove a fantastic race for the Trident. Knowing that rear tyres would have to be changed during the race, the Maserati team started Fangio with half-full tanks, and for the last time in Grand Prix history this ploy came off. Fangio duly led at his pit stop, but this took so long that Hawthorn and Collins passed into an apparently safe lead, and their pit signalled them to maintain their pace. Soon, however, they were being urged on, for Fangio put in fastest lap after fastest lap, and with the last he took the lead, and the race. His average speed for the 312 miles was 88·79 mph, faster than the 1956 lap record, and he cut that by 24 seconds.

Because there were so few Championship races in 1957, the Pescara GP was elevated to this status. This was the first time two Championship races had been run in one country and, incidentally, this race was the last for GP cars on the long-established Adriatic coast circuit. Vanwall suspension was now adequate, and although Musso initially led in the only Lancia-Ferrari present (Enzo Ferrari was indulging one of his periodic threats to give up racing), Moss soon took a green car into the lead, to win at 95·52 mph and by over three minutes from Fangio.

Despite this, Italian enthusiasts were staggered to see three Vanwalls qualify for the first three places on the grid for the Italian Grand Prix, ahead of Fangio in a 250F and Behra in the 12-cylinder Maserati. These were the only Italian cars to challenge the Vanwalls in the race, but only for a quarter of its distance; after that Moss drew steadily away, to win at 120·77 mph from Fangio.

That was the last Championship race of the season, which saw Fangio gain his fifth world title, from Moss and Musso. Ferrari had failed to win a single major race, an outcome in large part due to their cars – the Lancia-Ferraris were abandoned after the Italian GP – but also in part to a lack of cohesion in the team. Mechanical work at Maranello was now concentrated on the little V-6 car, which was run in the Modena GP in 1·8 litre form (Musso and Collins placing them second and fourth), and for the last race of the season,

Opposite: a Vanwall, driven by Stirling Moss, and a BRM, driven by Jean Behra. Above: in this 1958 quartet at Monza, Ferrari drivers Hill and Hawthorn are fighting off the Vanwalls driven by Moss and Brooks.

the Moroccan GP, appeared with a 2417 cc (85 × 71 mm) engine. This '246' V-6 was designed from the outset to run on petrol, obligatory fuel for the Grands Prix from 1958, and was to appear in two alternative forms, with one or two overhead camshafts to each block, the former giving better low-speed torque, the latter greater power. The car was thoroughly orthodox, with a tubular space frame, ifs and de Dion rear end (later replaced with a swing axle layout) and was to become the last successful front-engined GP car.

That Casablanca event also saw BRM venturing out of England for a major race for the first time since the French GP, the team being embarrassed as much by a lack of top-flight drivers as by mechanical disabilities. The 2·5 litre BRM had been driven to win secondary events, at Caen and Silverstone, and the team was at last beginning to climb from the depths.

Although Maserati had gained the major Grand Prix honours in 1957, the Moroccan Grand Prix was the last race for a full Maserati team, for the company was in a parlous financial state, largely as a result of catastrophic sports-racing car activities. Fittingly, therefore, Jean Behra drove a Maserati to victory in Morocco, at 112·64 mph from the Vanwall driven by Stuart Lewis-Evans and the BRM driven by Maurice Trintignant.

Maserati retired, and so from full-time racing did one of the greatest of all drivers, Juan Manuel Fangio. Grand Prix racing was about to enter a new phase, Ferrari versus British teams.

Decisive Revolution

In extending the life of the 2·5 litre Formula to 1960, the CSI also responded to pressure from fuel companies in banning the use of 'exotic' fuels and making obligatory 'commercial petrol', which was eventually defined as 100–130 octane aviation fuel. This was a major embarrassment to those teams whose engines had not been designed to run on petrol, BRM and Vanwall, and dealt a severe blow to independents who hoped to keep the Maserati 250F in the front line of racing. At the same time the minimum distance was reduced from 500 to 300 kilometres (or 2 hours).

This changed the outward face of racing, in that fuel stops were no longer required, and as tyres wore better, pit stops – save to retire or drop hopelessly down running orders – became increasingly rare (the Dunlop R5 came into almost universal use, especially when Englebert withdrew at the end of 1958). The short race distances, coupled with the better consumption of petrol-burning engines, also meant that less fuel had to be carried, and designers had fewer problems in producing a car which remained 'balanced' for the duration of a race, and so in turn the 'design revolution' of the late fifties was abetted by the rules.

The Ferrari Dino 246 was the most powerful engine used in 1958, producing some 280 bhp at 8500 rpm. During the season work on the car was aimed at ironing out handling problems, but towards its end another shortcoming was recognized, and both Dunlop and Girling disc brakes were tried in place of drum brakes. Maserati completed two lightweight 250F3s, but the 250F quickly became obsolescent.

The Vanwall four was extensively reworked to burn petrol efficiently; whereas this engine had produced up to 290 bhp in 1957, its maximum power output in

The Monza 'Races of the Two Worlds' were contested by gaudy American roadsters and a few local cars (the unmistakable shape of a Ferrari is coming into the pits to join a pair of track cars on the right).

221

1958 was 262 bhp at 7500 rpm. BRM had greater problems, particularly with their large valves, which suffered ill the loss of the cooling properties of alcohol, and at the beginning of 1958 the power produced by the engine of the Type 25 was no more than 250 bhp, at 8000 rpm. The car itself was modified, its former stressed skin cockpit section being abandoned in favour of a full tubular space frame, and the front suspension was revised to complement the Chapman-inspired set-up at the rear.

The Cooper was still growing up, and arguably was not to become a 'full' Grand Prix car until 1959 (although in 1958 it went well enough with a 2·2 litre version of the Coventry Climax FPF engine to win two Championship races, the ever-present reactionary element in racing remained reluctant to admit that it was any more than a freak!). The Coopers built in 1958 were no longer simply adapted F2 models, having *inter alia* wider bodies, sturdier gearboxes and the disc brakes which were still only optional on the F2 cars. The 2·2 litre engine had excellent torque characteristics, but produced only some 195 bhp, in-adequate on paper and in fact on fast circuits. But the cars were light, frontal area was low, handling excel-lent and they were fully exploited by drivers, who seemed to have unusual confidence in these unassum-ing little devices.

New to the Grand Prix ranks in 1958 was the marque Lotus, with the 16, which like the Cooper was derived from a Formula 2 car. Its enlarged, 1·96 or 2·2 litre, Coventry Climax engine was, however, installed ahead of the driver, tilted at various angles to cut down frontal area (in the most extreme case, at 61 degrees, which led to carburation and induction problems). Drive was taken from this to a combined gearbox and final drive unit. The light tubular space frame carried coil spring and wishbone link front suspension and Chapman strut-type irs. The very clean bodies inevitably attracted a 'mini-Vanwall' nickname, while the cockpit was very cramped by the standards of the time, although in fact it foreshadowed forthcoming normal practice.

Stirling Moss opened the season by winning the Argentine Grand Prix in R. R. C. Walker's 1·96 litre Cooper-Climax, a last-minute entry. Moss drove a clever tactical race, and rival teams were misled into thinking that he would stop for a tyre change (as in the extreme heat, and on an abrasive circuit, their cars had to). But in fact pit team and driver judged the race to a nicety, and the first of the Ferraris (Musso's) was beaten by 2·7 seconds; Hawthorn placed another Dino 246 third and Fangio a Maserati fourth. Two weeks later, he gained an easy victory in the *formule libre* Buenos Aires GP, his last in a Grand Prix car.

Meanwhile during the southern hemisphere sum-mer, the New Zealand series was run. The principal event, the New Zealand Grand Prix, was won by Brabham in a 1·96 litre Cooper, from Ross Jensen, then regarded as the most promising local driver, in a Maserati 250F. At Invercargill a month later Jensen won, from another New Zealander, one Bruce McLaren, and Brabham (both driving Coopers).

This year Ferrari had an excellent run in the European preliminaries, Hawthorn winning at Good-wood (from Brabham and Salvadori in Coopers), Collins at Silverstone (from Salvadori in a Cooper, Gregory in a Maserati, and Behra in a BRM), and Musso at Syracuse (from Bonnier and Godia in Maseratis), where Maria Teresa de Filippis started her career as the only woman driver in latter-day Grand Prix racing, and placed her Maserati fifth. Moss headed a Cooper 1-2-3-4-5-6 in the F1/F2 Aintree 200!

Monaco produced surprises – as it so often does! First, a grid dominated by British cars, with a Vanwall, a BRM and a Cooper on the front row, two Coopers on the second, and two Vanwalls on the third with the first of the Ferraris. In the opening stages Behra led in a BRM, then Hawthorn in a Ferrari, Moss in a Van-wall, Hawthorn again. But before half-distance these favoured runners had retired, and Trintignant led in the dark blue Walker Cooper which Moss had driven in Argentina. And the little Frenchman stayed in front, to gain the first *grande épreuve* victory for a rear-engined car since 1939, at 67·98 mph from the Ferraris of Musso and Collins, Brabham's Cooper, Schell's BRM and Allison's Lotus (Team Lotus made their debut here, and so did Graham Hill in one of their cars, which he had well placed when it lost a wheel).

Matters returned more nearly to normal in the Dutch Grand Prix, which was run for the first time since 1955, where Moss won in a Vanwall (at 93·95 mph compared with Fangio's 89·65 mph in 1955), from Schell and Behra in BRMs, Salvadori's Cooper and Hawthorn in the best of the poorly-handling Ferraris. A Vanwall, this time driven by Tony Brooks, won the Belgian GP at 129·93 mph (in 1 hour 37 minutes, making this the shortest *grande épreuve* run to that time). Allison's Lotus was fourth, but came much closer to winning than the results suggest, for it was running strongly at the end, whereas Brooks' Vanwall had a failing gearbox, second man Hawthorn coasted past the flag with a piston blown in the engine of his Ferrari, while third man Lewis-Evans crawled across with a broken front wishbone link on his Vanwall!

The French Grand Prix saw nostalgia, tragedy and the return to form of Ferrari. At Rheims Fangio raced for the last time, and placed a lightweight Maserati fourth, considerably not lapped by race-winner Hawthorn (whose last GP victory this was to be). Luigi Musso crashed and was fatally injured in the long right hand swerve leading away from the pits, which was safely 'on' at full throttle for only a few drivers; Musso was the last ranking Italian driver, and years were to pass before new Italians came forward to take his place. Hawthorn's average was 125·46 mph, and he won comfortably from Moss, von Trips and Fangio.

Ferrari won at Silverstone, too, when Collins led Hawthorn past the flag, at 102·05 mph, ahead of Salvadori's Cooper. The Vanwall team was ready for the Nürburgring in 1956 – it was BRM's turn to discover and suffer the suspension problems involved at the 'Ring – and Tony Brooks won the German GP for Vandervell's team at 90·35 mph. Tragedy again struck the Ferrari team, when Peter Collins was fatally injured as he was thrown from his car. Coopers were second and third, von Trips' Ferrari fourth, and in fifth place came the first finisher in the concurrent Formula 2 race, Bruce McLaren, making an auspicious *grande épreuve* debut.

The Portuguese Grand Prix, at Oporto, was a Championship race for the first time, and for Hawthorn provided a much debated point which was to prove decisive in the Championship. Moss won, Hawthorn finished second after a late spin and restart, and put in the fastest lap, which until 1960 was worth a Championship point. Over the tram lines and cobbles of the Oporto circuit Moss averaged 105·03 mph.

The Italian Grand Prix saw Ferrari field the 256 variant of the V-6, which had an increased stroke to give a capacity of 2451 cc, and an American newcomer to the Grands Prix, Phil Hill. He actually led the race in the early stages, then Hawthorn and Moss

duelled for the lead; Moss' retirement apparently left Ferraris in command, but tyre stops cost them the race, and let Brooks through to win in a Vanwall (at 121·21 mph). Hawthorn and Phil Hill placed Ferraris second and third, and were followed by two more Americans, Carroll Shelby and Masten Gregory, who shared a Maserati 250F.

The World Championship hinged on the Moroccan Grand Prix, which for the only time ranked as a Championship event. Moss did all that he could, in winning and setting the fastest lap; Hawthorn did all that he had to, in finishing second, to take the Championship by a single point. The newly-instituted Constructors' Championship, however, went quite clearly to Vanwall. In a black season, this race was overshadowed by another fatal accident, to fast-rising driver Stuart Lewis Evans, whose Vanwall crashed and caught fire. Before the year was out, World Champion Mike Hawthorn was to die in a road accident, after he had announced his retirement from racing.

So the new season opened without a World Champion driver, and without the team which had won the Constructors' Championship, for ill-health forced Tony Vandervell to retire from full Grand Prix participation.

In 1959 the Ferrari was disc-braked, and had an engine producing 295 bhp at 9000 rpm (but lacking in torque lower down the range), with road-holding qualities better on fast than on slow circuits. BRM

The early F1 Coopers inspired their drivers with confidence – as is evident in this photograph of Moss attacking a Silverstone corner.

were at work on a rear-engined car, which was to appear before the end of the season, but for most of the year campaigned their front-engined machines, little changed. Colin Chapman had altered the Lotus 16 to accommodate a full 2·5 litre Coventry Climax engine, but this car was to have a less successful season than in 1958. Maserati 250Fs lingered, in independent drivers' hands and depressingly far down results lists.

A newcomer to the front-engined ranks was the Aston Martin DBR4/250, classically handsome even to its Borrani wire wheels. It was derived from the DBR1/300 sports cars, which meant that in 1958 it was big and heavy; its six-cylinder (83 × 76·8 mm, 2492 cc) engine had a power output approaching 280 bhp at 8250 rpm, and its road manners were impeccable. But it appeared on the circuits two or three years too late. . . .

The Cooper was now indisputably a Grand Prix car, and in 1959 was to win five of the eight Championship races. It remained simple, functional and adaptable. The Coventry Climax engine had been enlarged to 94 × 89·9 mm (2495 cc), and with a new cylinder head which appeared towards the end of 1959, gave 239 bhp at 6750 rpm. Like the car, it was simple and compact, and with suitable gearing propelled the Cooper at a straight-line speed little short of those achieved by Grand Prix cars of purer pedigree – and the Cooper could outmanoeuvre all of them. Moreover, the Cooper team had the services of Jack Brabham, who brought to the GP circus the art of chassis tuning, hitherto too widely ignored. (This in fact was the first season when a Cooper works team as such set out to campaign the whole Championship

The 1959 Monaco GP saw Brabham (above, leading Moss) win his first Championship race, and the 1960 race saw a grid almost entirely made up of rear-engined cars (below). The GP Aston Martin (opposite, driven by Salvadori in the Portugese GP) was born years too late.

series, an enterprise which was to be astonishingly successful and – by the grand standards of Grand Prix racing – extraordinarily economical).

The simple Cooper chassis were always tempting to 'improvers', and in Formula 1 independent Cooper-BRM, Cooper-Maserati and Cooper-Ferrari variants duly appeared. None of these achieved the success of the Cooper-Climax, although Walker's substitution of a Colotti five-speed gearbox for the normal Cooper Citroen-based four-speed box was effective.

This year the Argentine series lapsed, and European participation in the New Zealand races was not yet numerically strong (the two principal events, the New Zealand GP and the Lady Wigram Trophy, saw victories for Moss in a Cooper and Flockhart in a BRM; in both Brabham and McLaren were second and third in Coopers). The European preliminaries were reduced in number, to British events. At Goodwood the full-size Coventry Climax engines were raced for the first time, and powered the Coopers of Moss and Brabham to first and second places ahead of a pair of BRMs. Ferraris driven by Behra and Brooks took the Aintree 200, on reliability rather than speed, as the principal Coopers and BRMs retired. In the Silverstone International Trophy the Aston Martin made an apparently promising debut, Salvadori placing one second behind Brabham's winning Cooper (102·73 mph) and equalling the lap record;

Flockhart was third in a BRM, Phil Hill fourth in a Ferrari and Jack Fairman fifth in a Maserati-engined Cooper.

Seven of the 16 starters in the Monaco GP were rear-engined, and four of them were classified among the six finishers, first (Brabham, 66·74 mph), third (Trintignant), fifth and sixth (McLaren and Salvadori). The other two places were taken by Ferraris (Brooks and Phil Hill). There was more variety at Zandvoort for the Dutch GP, and a result unique in the Championship races of the formula. The hard-fought race was led by Brabham and Moss in Coopers, and Jo Bonnier in a BRM, and at the end the Swedish driver gained BRM's first major race victory, at 93·56 mph from Brabham and Gregory in Coopers. The Aston Martins were outclassed in practice, and did not last long in the race; Innes Ireland placed a Lotus fourth, the best placing for the marque in the season, while Behra and Phil Hill were fifth and sixth in Ferraris.

Ferrari power told in the next two races the team contested. In heat so extreme that the road surface was melting and breaking up, Brooks led the French GP at Rheims from start to finish in a Ferrari, while behind him the field was thinned as much by the physical distress of drivers as by mechanical derangements. Moss briefly took second place, and broke the lap record, in an independently-entered BRM, before

Above: outstanding Cooper drivers at the end of the seven-year formula were Brabham (left) and Moss (right). Newcomers to the rear-engined ranks in 1960 were BRM, with the T25-based P48 (here driven by Gurney) and Lotus, with the 18 (driven by Ireland). A lone lightweight Vanwall (opposite, Brooks on the Rheims grid) made no impression on racing, nor did the American Scarab (below, driven by its creator, Lance Reventlow).

retiring, so Phil Hill was runner-up in another Ferrari, followed by Brabham in a Cooper.

Apart from the Centro-Sud Cooper-Maseratis and a 250F, the British GP at Aintree was a British affair, for Ferrari labour disputes kept the Italian team away (their principal driver, Tony Brooks, was lent a

Vanwall, which did not last long in the race). Jack Brabham led throughout, to win from Moss and McLaren, in a final order which read, Cooper, BRM, Cooper, BRM, Cooper, Aston Martin, Cooper.

Ferrari returned for the German Grand Prix, an out-of-character two-part race run for politico-economic reasons on the Avus track, two parallel stretches of motorway, linked by a 55 mph 180 degree corner at one extremity and the steeply banked and bumpy North Curve of the pre-war track at the other. Predictably the Ferraris were fastest, although in both parts they were surprisingly challenged by Coopers, and on aggregate scored a clear 1-2-3 victory, Tony Brooks at 146·71 mph heading the team's two Americans, Dan Gurney and Phil Hill.

Almost as predictably, a Cooper won the Portuguese GP on the Monsanto circuit outside Lisbon. This was Walker's car driven by Moss. On paper Monza should have reversed this result; in fact, the Italian GP was won by Moss in Walker's Cooper, at 123·38 mph. The race turned on tyre wear, and Walker team strategy. The Ferraris had to stop to change tyres, and it was expected that the Coopers would. But Moss let the Ferrari drivers set the pace, and ran through non-stop, to win from Phil Hill (Ferrari), Jack Brabham and three more Ferraris. More than any other race result, this showed how 'right' the Cooper layout was, a fact already tacitly acknowledged by BRM, who ran their own first rear-engined car in practice for the Italian race.

The first US Grand Prix, on the Sebring airfield circuit, rounded off the season, and settled the Championship. A thin field, which included a Kurtis midget, started, and seven cars finished. Moss' Championship chances evaporated as his gearbox failed after six laps; Brabham ran out of fuel while leading within half a mile of the finish, and pushed his car across the line to be classified fourth. His Cooper team mate Bruce McLaren took the chequered flag, becoming the youngest driver ever to win a Grand Prix. Trintignant was second, and set the fastest lap in his Cooper when it had a broken rear wishbone (a remarkable feature of these Coopers was that they could still be raced with maladies which in other cars would have meant retirement), while Brooks was third.

Jack Brabham took the World Championship, from Brooks and Moss, and Cooper took the Constructors' Championship.

The racing world now had to face the rear-engined reality, the quiet revolution which was wholly accomplished in 1959. That German race at Avus was to prove to be the last full Grand Prix to be won by a front-engined car, the French race the last true road race GP to fall to a front-engined car (in 1960 the Italians were to arrange their Grand Prix to obtain a similar result, but as the British teams stayed away, this race was quite unrepresentative).

The 1960 Cooper T53 was a substantial, yet lithe, machine, in which the most notable change was in the suspension, where Jack Brabham had at last persuaded the Coopers to throw away their transverse springs in favour of coils 'all round'. BRM built their first, and far from handsome, rear-engined cars around components from their conventional machines and, perforce, Ferrari started to work in the same direction, using a Dino 246 V-6 in their first rear-engined car (but as far as the season's racing was concerned concentrating on the outmoded Dino 246).

The most interesting convert was Colin Chapman, who probably held out against his own better theoretical judgments in 1959 – all round, quite a lot of pride had to be swallowed in following the example of the Cooper crudities. But if he followed at all, it was only in the basic example, for Chapman is a true innovator, and in execution he pursued his own original lines, which were soon to be copied by others. The Lotus 18 was a light car, which lacked the streamlining of its front-engined predecessor, but made up for any loss there in frontal area. Within the multitubular space

Monza scenes in the early 1960s, most taken at the 1960 GP when Ferrari gained a hollow victory (in the lower centre shot, a GP Ferrari is 'towing' an F2 Ferrari to a class victory while a Cooper makes for the bankings). Perhaps Fangio, Conotti and Spotorno are discussing the changing times, which led, for example, to Bandini (top, centre) turning to a British constructor (Lotus) for a competitive car?

Rear-engined cars soon began to appear refined–this Lotus driven by Moss is far removed from the early Coopers. Below: Bonnier's BRM leads the 1960 Monaco field. Airfield races were at the other racing extreme, but still rear-engined cars were on top (below, right, Cooper leads Ferrari at Silverstone).

frame the driver reclined, not yet to the semi-prone position which was to come, but no longer classically upright. Suspension was by wishbones and coil springs/dampers at the front, while at the rear Chap-man used a lower wishbone to the hub carrier, with an articulated fixed-length drive shaft in effect acting as an upper wishbone, in conjunction with parallel radius rods and coil springs/dampers. The suspension geometry was such that the roll centre was very low.

A lone lightweight Vanwall flitted across the racing scene, and so did a new front-engined Grand Prix car, the last to be built on conventional lines. Lance Reventlow's Scarab was conventionally very correct,

beautifully constructed, and outwardly self-contradictory in that while a very low bonnet line was achieved by laying the fuel-injected four-cylinder engine on its side, the driver sat upright in a very roomy cockpit. The car was heavy and under-powered (230 bhp was claimed for the engine, compared with the 245 bhp given by the Coventry Climax four in 1960). After a few attempts to qualify, and one start, the disillusioned Scarab team returned to the USA.

The Argentine Grand Prix enjoyed a one-year revival in 1960, and fell to McLaren in a 1959 Cooper, at 82·77 mph from the Ferrari driven by Allison. In New Zealand Brabham took the Grand Prix and the Lady Wigram Trophy, from McLaren and David Piper in a front-engined Lotus.

The important non-Championship races in England fell to Innes Ireland driving a Lotus 18, from Moss and Bristow in Coopers at Goodwood, from Brabham and Graham Hill in a BRM at Silverstone. For the main season, Rob Walker and Stirling Moss turned to Lotus, and with his 18 Moss took pole position at Monaco. Here, the fastest 16 drivers in practice qualified for the race grid, and to do so all had to lap in under the fastest lap time achieved in the 1959 race. The three Ferraris were the only front-engined cars on the grid, as they were to be almost everywhere in 1960, and eventually they were the last front-engined cars to run in Championship GPs.

Bonnier initially led the race in a BRM, Moss passed, Bonnier repassed as Moss stopped for a loose plug lead to be attached, then to all intents and purposes the BRM retired, leaving Moss to win at 67·46 mph from McLaren and Phil Hill in a Ferrari.

In the Dutch Grand Prix Jack Brabham began a run of five victories, finishing ahead of Ireland, Graham Hill and Moss, who had been delayed when a kerbstone thrown up by another car damaged one of his Lotus' wheels. Among those who retired was a new driver, making his Grand Prix debut in a Team Lotus car: Jim Clark.

At Spa Moss crashed in practice when a stub axle failed; together with Alan Stacey's fatal race crash, this stirred up an outcry about Lotus frailties, which has recurred at intervals ever since. Although at times seemingly well-founded, this generally derives from an inability to equate strength with anything but outward and visible weight and massiveness (in a similar vein, the Italian Press has been given to harrying Ferrari when Italian drivers have been killed in his cars). During this tragic Belgian meeting, Cooper driver Chris Bristow was also killed, apparently crashing after striking a bird while at high speed. Brabham won the race at 133·62 mph, and he headed a Cooper 1-2-3, with McLaren and Gendebien second and third. A fifth place gave Clark his first Championship points.

This year the Cooper was clearly the fastest car at Rheims, and once the three Ferraris had retired, all with final drive failures, Coopers took the first four places (Brabham, at 131·97 mph, Gendebien, McLaren and Taylor), followed by Team Lotus' three Scottish drivers, Clark, Flockhart and Ireland.

Graham Hill in a BRM provided the challenge to Brabham in the British Grand Prix, in a stirring drive which started after the rest of the field had left the

Phil Hill on his way to victory in the 1960 Italian GP.

starting grid. He stalled his engine as the flag fell, but in 55 laps climbed through to lead the race. With four laps to go, a slight error cost him six places. So Brabham won again, averaging 108·69 mph over 225 Silverstone miles. He was followed past the flag by another driver new to Grand Prix racing in 1960, John Surtees, and by his Lotus team mate Ireland.

Effectively, there was only one more mainstream Grand Prix in Europe in 1960, for the German race was downgraded to Formula 2 in order to produce a German victory, and the Italians took the only course which might lead to an Italian victory, by running their Grand Prix on the Monza road and high-speed track. The British teams refused to have anything to do with this, so Ferrari duly gained a hollow 1-2-3, from a scratch field of second-line cars. Between the two races, the Portuguese Grand Prix was run at Oporto, led for most of its distance by Surtees, who retired (Brabham won from McLaren and Clark).

One Championship Grand Prix remained under the 2·5 litre formula, the American event, run at Riverside before a small crowd (in the following year this race was to find a permanent and appreciative home at Watkins Glen). Here Moss won, at 99·00 m.p.h. from Ireland, McLaren, Brabham and Bonnier.

The Championships were of course Brabham's and Cooper's before this race was run. McLaren and Moss were runners-up in the Drivers' Championship, Lotus and Ferrari in the Constructors' Championship.

This wound up a most successful formula, which had seen vast changes come over racing. The mechanical changes have been recalled, and were spreading to other classes, to sports cars and even to the Indianapolis home of arch-conservatism. Of the less tangible changes, perhaps the most significant was in attitudes; throughout the sport there was an increase in professionalism, and this formula was perhaps the last under which an amateur or playboy driver might expect to achieve anything in motor racing's premier class. The last great drivers whose overall approach to the sport was semi-professional were Mike Hawthorn and Peter Collins. For better or for worse, there was to be little room for drivers who were not professionals in the new Grand Prix racing to come.

To the sorrow of many, the era of the 'kit Grand Prix car' had almost come about in 1960, for small constructors who could never have undertaken Grand Prix programmes in earlier years were able to do so, because of the availability of 'off the peg' Grand Prix engines. As the decade ended, the only pure constructors still active were Ferrari and BRM.

THE REAR-ENGINED PERIOD

Third Level Racing

The first Formula 3 never achieved wide popularity on the Continent, and during the second half of the fifties began to stagnate even in Britain; as it inevitably went into decline a replacement class was obviously needed. If nothing else, half-litre racing had pointed the value of *ab initio* single seaters, so while some countries turned towards small sports cars a new class was devised in Italy, on a national basis. This was inspired by a simple single-seater which Morini and Filippi had exhibited in 1956, as the prototype of a batch which they proposed to build for one-make races. However, the author (Johnny Lurani) saw wider possibilities: a national racing class, which came into being in Italy in 1958, and an international class. This was proposed to a CSI meeting in January 1958, and by the Autumn of that year it had been agreed, to come into effect in 1959 with international status, as Formula Junior.

From that point it has evolved steadily, being superseded by a Formula 3, which naturally and logically arose from it in 1964, and which was in turn revised for 1971. In effect there has thus been a continuing formula at this level, and in many ways it has been the most successful single-seater class in the history of racing. Save for a few 'senior' drivers, most of the men in Grand Prix teams at the end of the decade had served a term of apprenticeship in Formula Junior or Formula 3, among them World Champions Jim Clark, John Surtees, Denis Hulme, Jackie Stewart and Jochen Rindt. As an end in itself, racing at this level has almost invariably been close and hard, with enormous spectator appeal.

Perhaps on the debit side, Formula Junior soon became a very professional class, although in part this

Italian constructors naturally dominated the first season of Junior racing, but their cars – these Stanguellini are typical – were obsolete in conception, and in performance were soon to be made obsolete almost overnight.

reflected a general rise in racing standards – additional single-seater classes have been slotted in at a lower level to fulfil at least part of the original Formula Junior purpose. Since the first Junior seasons it has not been a breeding ground for technical innovation, constructors preferring to refine or hand down ideas proved in other classes. With chassis and running gear becoming increasingly similar, drivers looked to their engines to give them advantages, and the engine tuners developed their proficiency in wringing power from production-based units to extraordinary lengths.

Formula Junior was largely built around its engine regulations. These stipulated the use of power units (at least, cylinder block and head) from production cars homologated by the CSI, the annual production rate requirement to qualify being 1000 units. Over-head camshaft engines were specifically barred. Two capacity limits were laid down, 1100 cc (coupled with a minimum car weight of 400 kg. 882 lb) and 1000 cc (car weight, 360 kg, 793 lb). Cylinder bore could be altered to achieve these capacities, but not stroke. The gearbox also had to originate from an homologated touring model, although no restrictions were placed on the actual gears, in principle brakes and fuel systems had to be the same as those on the production models from which engines were taken (e.g., drum or disc brakes), and self starters were obligatory.

These, then, were the basic ingredients of a formula which was to be outstandingly successful. Italian constructors naturally had the advantage of a head start as Formula Junior spread through the Continent in its first international year. Generally, their cars followed

the classic front-engined pattern, exemplified in the early pace-setting Stanguellini. This was built around Fiat components, with an offset cockpit allowing the correspondingly offset drive line to be taken alongside it, a simple tubular chassis, with light alloy bodywork and a live beam axle at the rear. Borrani wire wheels completed the illusion of a real racer, but in his whole conception of a racing car for the sixties Vittorio Stanguellini had been looking backwards. He was not alone in this – Conrero, Dagrada, Massimino and Poggi in their PM-Poggi, Osca, Taraschi and Volpini were among the better-known Italian constructors who followed the time-proved conception. Branca, de Sanctis, de Tomaso and Faccioli on the other hand were more alive to reality, and mounted their engines at the rear, although most of them were to have short lives as constructors.

When Maserati gave up single-seaters, even Italian private teams turned to Britain for cars. This Cooper was run by Mimmo Dei's Scuderia Centro Sud, and driven by Bandini (above) among others.

For power units most of them turned – almost by reflex – to the robust Fiat 1100 cc (68 × 75 mm) ohv four. With twin Weber carburetters, this would give at least 75 bhp at 6500 rpm, and of course tuners working on it had a wealth of experience to draw on. Only a few Italians ignored it. Angelo Dagrada achieved some success with the Lancia V-4, while the short-lived Intermeccanica initially used a linered-down Peugeot engine.

Enthusiasm for Junior racing spread rapidly through the Continent in 1959. Initially at least, greater interest was shown in France and, particularly, Germany, than in Britain, where motor sport generally was healthier. The tendency was to concentrate on extracting power from engines, at the expense of chassis and suspension development, and French interest soon waned when it became apparent that French engines, Renault,

Simca, Peugeot, could not be made competitive in international events. Results with the Monomill derivatives which were the earliest French cars to appear were no more encouraging, and apart from 'one-offs' efforts lapsed until the French racing revival got under way.

Early German work on their native two-stroke engines – DKW in the West, and its Wartburg equivalent in the East – seemed promising in the first Junior phase. In 980 cc (76 × 74 mm) form 80 bhp was obtained from selected units, chosen above all for their accurately-cast ports, at fairly modest engine speeds. The leading tuners were Alfred Hartmann, who claimed 80 bhp at 5600 rpm, and Gerhard Mitter, whose 1097 cc DKW engines produced 85 bhp at 5500 rpm. Much higher outputs were claimed, but not borne out in car performances.

For a while Hartmann and Mitter were also the leading German car constructors, both building front-engined cars with rather odd lines. Their counterpart in East Germany, Heinz Melkus, claimed a mere 70 bhp from his AWE-Wartburg engines, but in the handful of cars he built he at least mounted them behind the cockpit, and in 1960 must have gained considerable satisfaction from a Melkus victory in an international event at Hockenheim.

The two-stroke had a relatively short life in this class, where one of the last cars to use it was a Saab, interesting as the only Junior to be built by a leading company. This had a brief career, on Scandinavian circuits.

In the first British Junior to appear, the front-engined Elva, a Mitter-tuned DKW engine was the specified alternative to the more usual BMC power unit. During the year, the virtues of Formula Junior were recognized in Britain, and at the end of the year three significant British Juniors were first raced.

Two of these, Cooper and Lola, were directly descended from their constructors' existing racing and sports-racing cars; the third was the Lotus 18, new in every respect, and the end-product of sophisticated design philosophy uninhibited by traditions. Eric Broadley's Lola was probably the cleanest and neatest of all front-engined Juniors, and for a while these cars were able to hold their own against the new rear-engined generation – a school which Broadley was to join in little over a year – not least because their fully-independent suspension made for good road-holding. The Cooper T51 was in effect a scaled-down version of that company's Championship-winning Formula 1 and 2 cars, although it never quite fulfilled that implication of promise.

The Lotus became the Junior to beat. It was the first rear-engined car built by Colin Chapman, and had uncompromisingly square lines, relying on low frontal area rather than streamlining for drag reduc-

237

tion. Following Lotus practice, the 18 had a very rigid space frame, weighing only 60 lb, with completely detachable glass fibre bodywork. Suspension was of course independent all round, by unequal-length wishbones, coil spring/damper units and anti-roll bar at the front, single lower wishbones, coil springs/dampers and radius rods at the rear. Drum brakes were used front and rear. A Cosworth-tuned Ford 105E engine was virtually standard on the Lotus 18, driving through a Renault gearbox (later to be replaced by a modified Volkswagen box).

The association of Cosworth and Ford was to have

an enormous impact on motor racing in the sixties. Cosworth Engineering had been formed by Keith Duckworth and Mike Costin, hence Cosworth. Ford had introduced their new Anglia in 1959, with the 105E engine, which in production form was rated at 39 bhp at 5000 rpm. This 992 cc unit had an over-

One of the few British front-engined Juniors was the Gemini (left, driven by Geoff Duke), while one of the few modestly successful rear-engined Italian Juniors was the Wainer (right, driven by Manfredini). Pace-setters once the formula was international were Cooper (opposite, driven by John Love) and Lotus (below, driven by Jim Clark).

square bore-stroke ratio, eight-port head and excellent 'breathing'. Apart from the assumed disadvantage of a three-bearing crankshaft, it obviously offered scope – and a challenge – to tuners; in the long run, it proved to have greater development potential than any other small production engine.

The 1960 Cosworth-modified 105E featured high-lift camshafts; special main and big-end bearings, pistons and connecting rods; modified cylinder heads and inlet and exhaust manifolds; solid rocker shafts and two twin-choke Weber carburetters. Components such as pistons, crankshaft and flywheel were accurately balanced, and the firing order was revised. The result was a racing engine which produced 85 bhp at 7500 rpm – and led in the long run to a Cosworth-Ford engine which dominated Grand Prix racing.

In its first season, the tuned 105E appeared to be on a par with Fiat-based engines and the only other British power units to feature in Formula Junior, modified BMC A series engines. These became almost standard in Cooper Juniors. An orthodox long-stroke four, which had been in existence for several years, this BMC engine was normally bored out to 994 cc for Junior use. In its basic cylinder head design it had less development potential than the 105E, but in 1960 comparable power was extracted from it, 75–80 bhp at 7500 rpm.

These British cars and engines opened a new chapter in Junior racing. Of the 19 major races in 1960, Lotus won 13, Cooper 4 and Osca 2. In the Lottery GP at Monza in June, Colin Davis scored the last important victory for a front-engined Junior, driving an Osca-Fiat. During the remaining years of the formula, Italian constructors struggled to catch up, but although Stanguellini, Volpini, Dagrada and others turned to rear-engined designs, and de Sanctis and Wainer fought an effective rearguard action, the gap which had suddenly opened was too great to close. French and German constructors just gave up,

and the initial American effort, which in 1960 had included the small-series production front-engined BMC and rear-engined Dolphin, soon faded away. British cars, and soon Ford-based engines, became the only competitive equipment, to which even leading Italians were forced to turn.

The form of these British new-wave cars was first seen in a Goodwood duel between Jim Clark (Lotus) and John Surtees (Cooper) at Easter, and at Monaco a little later in 1960 the Italians were to fully discover what the British had made of their junior class for amateurs. Italians cars had dominated the first Monaco Junior race, in 1959; a year later they were routed before it started – the fastest Italian car qualified for a place on the fourth row of the grid, and the best final placing was 10th. In 1959 Michael May had set the class lap record at 61·45 mph, in 1960 Clark raised it to 65·75 mph (in 1963 Frank Gardner set the Monaco Junior record at 70·68 mph – faster than the 1959 Grand Prix lap record!).

During the next three seasons the Junior class became increasingly sophisticated, and at least in its upper echelons, increasingly professional. Cosworth introduced a bored-out 1100 cc version of their Junior engine in 1961, and other tuners began to extract competitive power from the 105E. Outputs reached 100 bhp in 1961, and in the following year 100 bhp per litre was achieved.

Lotus produced the 20 successor to the 18 in 1961, as smooth and streamlined as the 18 had been 'square'. Lola turned to rear engine mounting, as did other British challengers such as Alexis and Gemini. In the T56 Junior, Cooper threw away their transverse-leaf rear suspension, having already been persuaded by Jack Brabham with their 'senior' cars that coil springs and wishbones were more elegant and efficient. And at Goodwood in high summer, Gavin Youl gained an encouraging second place in the first race outing of a new car, an MRD. This was soon to wear its true

Some of the cars of the Formula 3 which succeeded Formula Junior. Above: a Branca; left: a Matra MS1; below: a Brabham. Opposite: top a BWA and a Brabham; centre: a Lotus and a Wainer; bottom: a de Sanctis.

Motta
Motta
62

MAGNETI MARELLI
45

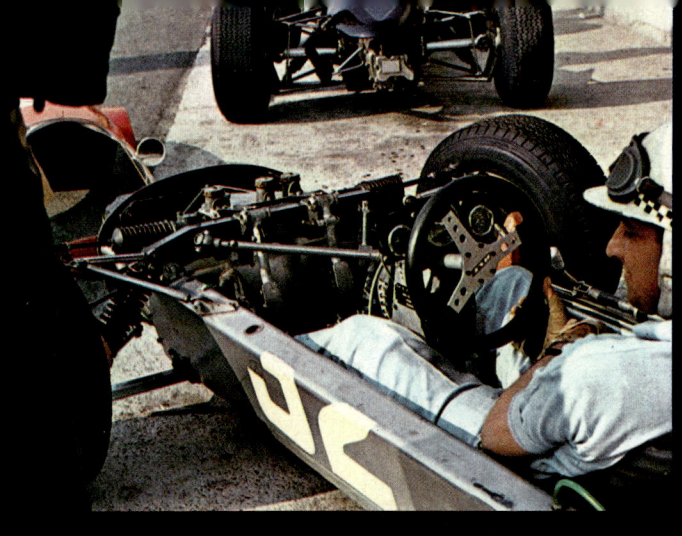

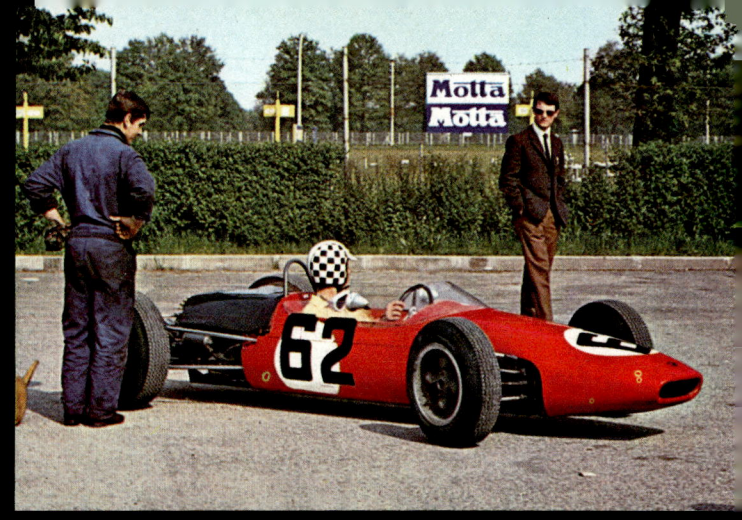

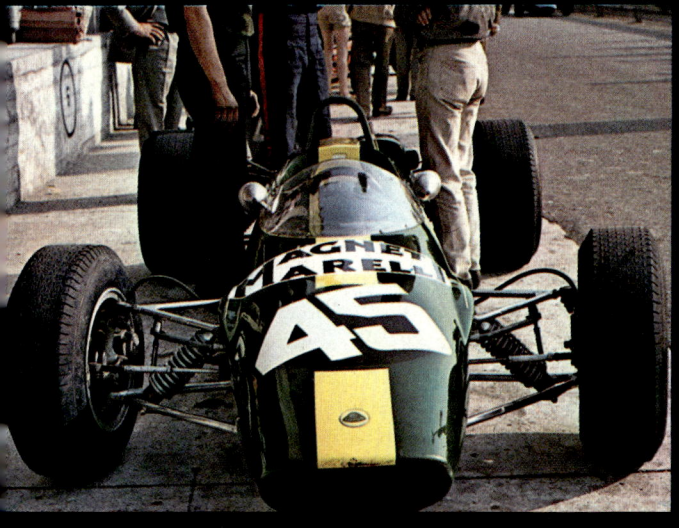

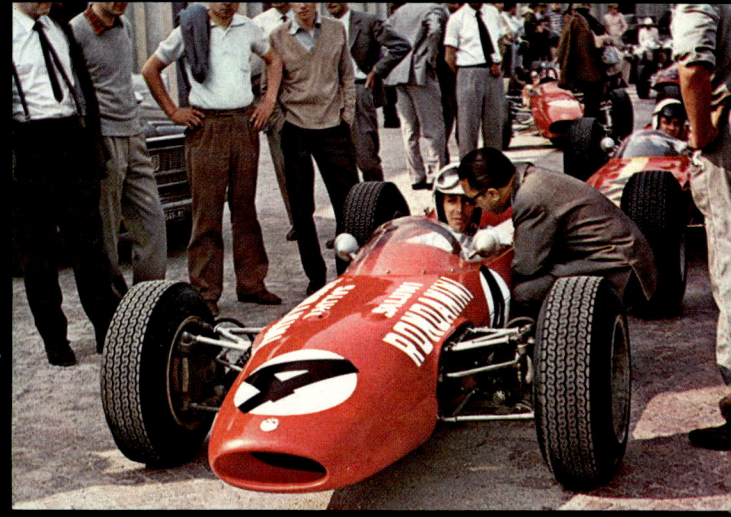

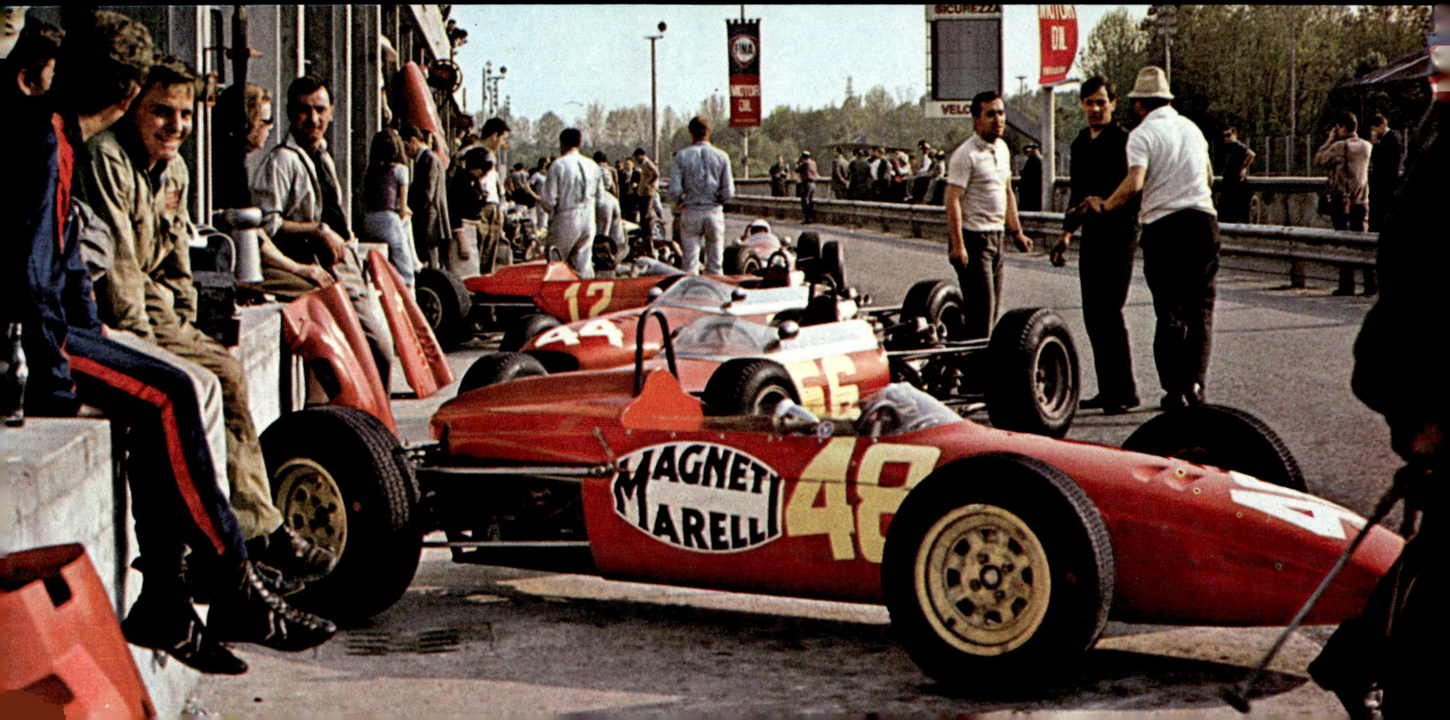
FINA
MOTOR OIL
12
44
56
MAGNETI MARELLI
48

colours, as the first-born of the new marque Brabham.

The later Juniors closely followed contemporary Grand Prix car lines, and this by then far-from-junior class saw semi-prone driving positions, monocoque chassis, inboard suspension units, wide-rim wheels and disc brakes. The very substantial world market was monopolized by British manufacturers – firms like Lotus were able to think in terms of a three-figure annual production – and to sustain this race-proving was essential to refining designs and as publicity.

In top-class racing quasi-works teams, such as the Ron Harris Lotuses, Ken Tyrrell's Coopers or the Midland Racing Partnership Lolas, ruled the circuits. While this was far removed in spirit from the intentions of the formula's founders, it was a natural reflection of trends in a booming sport. At lower levels it did fulfil its original purpose, and more, for it became the most widespread single-seater class in racing history, throughout the Western world and even into Russia. But by 1962 thoughts were inevitably turning to restricting performance and costs, and for 1964 a new Formula 3 was devised to replace Formula Junior.

In the major races of the last Junior year the names most often at the top of results lists were Peter Arundell and Mike Spence (Lotus), Denis Hulme and Frank Gardner (Brabham), Richard Attwood and David Hobbs (Lola). Where the works teams were not present, independents got a look in, for example Gerhard Mitter, still perservering with a DKW engine in a Lotus, 'Geki' in Italy with a Ford-engined de Sanctis and Jochen Rindt, making his first single-seater appearances in a Cooper.

Some 250 major Formula Junior races were run during its international span. A hundred of these were won by Lotus, 58 by Cooper, 20 by Stanguellini, 17 by Brabham and 12 by Lola, the rest being divided among a dozen makes.

The new Formula 3 picked up where Formula Junior left off. Its principle limiting rule was applied to engines, where a throttling flange with a maximum diameter of 36 mm had to be interposed between carburetter and inlet manifold. Minimum car weight was 420 kg (924 lb), engine bore and stroke could be altered, valve gear actuation was free, only four forward speeds were permitted in gearboxes. The hoped-for results were not achieved, because engine development continued and careful study of gas flow largely overcame the 36 mm flange restriction – towards the end of the six-year life of this formula, outputs of 115 bhp were achieved consistently, as much as 130 bhp in some units. These were of course also bhp/litre figures, and in this light quite remarkable for production-based engines – although the basically Ford units modified by Felday, Lucas, Holbay, Novamotor or Tecno revving at 10000 rpm sounded far removed from their still-humble production origins! Cosworth, incidentally, had abandoned their development work for this category, to concentrate on their F1 and F2 engines.

Under this formula progress in chassis design was in refinement rather than in revolution. Over its whole span, Brabhams were consistently in the forefront, and generally considered the best cars for independent drivers. Cooper made an excellent start, before disappearing altogether. Lotus lapsed, falling completely out of favour in the middle years, but coming back strongly with their 59 in the last two years. Matras appeared, to herald strongly a French resurgence in single-seater racing, until their basic MS5 design was ruled out by a minor change in the regulations, requiring bag fuel tanks which could not be fitted into the monocoque. In the second half of the period a new Italian manufacturer, Tecno, emerged from the kart-building offshoot of an industrial machinery firm rather than from a background of race car building. Alexis, Birel, Chevron, Bellasi, de Tomaso, de Sanctis, March, Martini, Pygmee and Titan were among other constructors who built cars to the formula at one stage or another through its life.

One very real technical novelty, which came and went, was the use of the Daf Variomatic transmission. This was the first use of an automatic transmission in single-seater racing cars, but it proved successful only in conditions ideal for it.

Initially, manufacturers were less involved in actual

Formula Junior provided an ideal single-seater finishing school, for drivers such as Andrea de Adamich (opposite in a Lola) and Frank Gardner (above, in a Brabham).

racing in this class, and the Ford domination of small-capacity engine racing received a one-year setback. The Ken Tyrrell team, running BMC-powered Coopers, signed a new Scottish driver for 1964, Jackie Stewart. He scored 11 runaway victories in 13 starts, before moving on with Tyrrell to higher classes.

This effectively left the formula to Ford-based engines. Alpine tried to break in with Renault power units in their Brabham-inspired chassis, and odd East German races were won by unknowns with Wartburg engines behind them. By a curious twist, in the last year of the formula the most potent Ford-based engines were produced in Italian tuning shops, by Novamotor and Tecno. During the period, Hewland

gearboxes came to be used almost exclusively.

Inevitably, quasi-works teams reappeared, although in Formula 3 the leading independent drivers were able to race with them on level terms. The first year was Stewart's, and leading drivers of the next phase included Jean-Pierre Beltoise, Piers Courage, Jacky Ickx, Chris Irwin, Jean-Pierre Jaussaud, Roy Pike, Johnny Servoz-Gavin and Jonathan Williams. The peak season was probably 1969, when drivers of the calibre of Reine Wisell, Ronnie Peterson and Emerson Fittipaldi showed the brilliance that was soon to take them out of the class.

Racing was generally close, and often of a high standard. But slip-streaming was inevitable with such closely-matched cars, and in the last year of the formula this was coupled with some questionable race tactics, as 'career' drivers raced for the victories which they felt essential if they were to gain promotion.

Once again a 'performance-limiting' revised formula was introduced, for the 1971 season. This also relied upon restricting the supply of the one free element an engine needs to function – air. This time the regulations required a 20 mm 'hole' placed *outside* the induction system, which itself had to be boxed in a completely air-tight container. The engine capacity limit was raised, to 1600 cc. Early races showed that the limitation was too severe, so in the summer of 1971 it was eased, and a 21·5 diameter restrictor permitted. Engines could thus rev more freely (and became a little noisier) and race speeds returned to the level reached in the last year of the preceding Formula 3.

Races were fiercely contested by very large fields, particularly those in the generously-endowed Shell championship. This was won by Australian David Walker, driving a works Lotus 69 – the combination to beat in 1971. Numerically, Ford-based engines remained dominant, the most successful being prepared by Novamotor; the only other basic engines to be really successful were the Renault units used in works Alpines, which were the first single-seaters from this French company to be really competitive at an international level. On the starting grids, however, Brabham, Lotus and March cars were most numerous, while other marques represented included Chevron, Ensign, Martini, de Sanctis, Branca and Tecno. Some of these were models carried over from the previous Formula 3 and some, notably the Brabham BT35, March 713 and Chevron B18, were utility chassis, which with appropriate power units served for other classes, such as Formula B.

The effective up-grading of racing's third-level single-seater categories made room for other classes to fulfil the 'cadet' role once envisaged for Formula Junior. Some of these were purely national, the Italian 850 class and Formule France, for example.

Two cars of the lesser classes which found wide international acceptance, F Ford (a Lotus, opposite top) and F Vee (left). Centre left: the Italian 850 cc class – this is a de Sanctis – had only a very limited appeal. Tecno F3 cars (bottom left) spearheaded an Italian revival at this level. Below: representative cars of the 1600 cc F3 at Crystal Palace, left to right, a March 713, a Lotus 69 and a Brabham BT35.

Two others found international acceptance, Formula Vee, for cars built around Volkswagen components, and Formula Ford, which gained wide popularity remarkably quickly. In all their characteristics, FF cars closely resembled the more powerful single-seaters conforming to CSI international formulae, and as well as being *ab initio* machines were therefore stepping stones for ambitious drivers – this in turn leading once again to increasingly 'professional' attitudes.

Formula 2 Episodes

The first post-war second-level single seater class naturally lapsed when it became the Grand Prix formula, and another Formula 2 did not come into force until 1957, for cars with 1·5 litre engines, running on commercial fuel. This was to enjoy considerable success, and in turn become the Grand Prix formula. Before that happened, it was to be the instrument by which significant new names were introduced into top-class racing, notably Coventry Climax, Cooper and Porsche.

Coventry Climax had a long history of engine building, and between the wars had supplied the power units for several small-run production cars, including some with sporting pretensions. In 1937 the company built its first fire pump, and in 1950 built the prototype of another, the 1022 cc ohc five main bearing FW. This was necessarily flexible and responsive, and proved an ideal basis for a high-performance competition engine, for which purpose it was first used, bored out to 1097 cc, in a Le Mans Kieft in 1954. In the following year it was more widely used, and when the forthcoming Formula 2 was announced in 1956 was bored out again to 1460 cc (FWB), and raced in F2 prototypes. By the time the Formula officially came into effect, the FPF twin ohc derivative was available, and through four seasons it became the mainstay of the formula. An oversquare unit (81·2 × 71·7 mm, 1475 cc), it was developed to produce 145 bhp at 7500 rpm for the last year of the formula.

Cooper were quick off the mark, built an F2 prototype in a matter of weeks, and raced it in the 'trial' F2 race at the 1956 British GP meeting, where it won handsomely. This T41 stemmed directly from the F3 Coopers, with a simple tubular frame, transverse leaf and wishbone suspension and Cooper cast magnesium alloy wheels. To accept the FPF in 1957, the car was lengthened and widened, and once over engine and transmission teething troubles was very successful.

The 1958 car was lower and again wider, and had

Above: Brabham leading Lewis-Evans, both in 1·5 litre F2 Coopers, at Brands Hatch in 1958. Below: Behra driving the first Porsche single-seater, an adapted RSK sports car. The 1 litre Formula saw the re-emergence of French single-seaters (right, two Matras, driven by Schlesser and Scarfiotti, among a bunch at Brands Hatch in 1966).

coil spring front suspension. In 1959, the Climax-engined cars were joined on the circuits by a pair with twin ohc Borgward engines, developing 160 bhp at 8 500 rpm, which also enjoyed some success.

For the last three years of the formula, a Constructors' Championship was arranged; Cooper won it in each season, in 1960 sharing it with Porsche, when of course the Surbiton firm also completed its second double, taking the F1 championship as well (moreover, the F2 Coopers were usually raced by independents). In 1958 Coopers won 10 of the 13 major races, while in 1959 they enjoyed a virtual monopoly of success (the only other leading places fell to Ferrari, a second at Syracuse; Porsche, second and third at Rheims, third at Zeltweg; and Lotus, second at Zeltweg, third at Brands Hatch).

Although during the first three years of the formula there were recurrent fears that it might become another Cooper one-make class, as had F3, there were other manufacturers in the field and Coopers were defeated on occasion, which meant that the class

246

remained healthy. Cooper's principal British opponent was Lotus, whose first single-seater was the F2 16, from which the first GP Lotus was later derived. It suffered prolonged teething troubles, particularly in the transmission and rear suspension, and seldom finished a race in its first year. Progress towards competitive raceworthiness was slow, although the cars were occasionally well-placed (Allison was second in the 1957 Gold Cup, and at the end of the 16's career, Graham Hill placed one second between Brabham's Cooper-Climax and Moss' Cooper-Borgward at Brands Hatch). At the end of 1959 Lotus abandoned it in favour of the F2 version of the rear-engined 18.

Two other front-engined British cars, the Lister and the Laystall, made no impression on the circuits.

Ferrari entered this class with a thoroughly conventional 'scaled-down GP car' which, as already related, became the GP car which carried the Scuderia through its 1958-60 rearguard action. For Formula 2 its V-6 engine (70 × 64·5 mm, 1490 cc), gave 170 bhp at 9000 rpm in its first season, some 20 bhp more towards the end of the formula. This Ferrari was therefore by a generous margin the most powerful car of the formula; it was also far and away the heaviest. It made a promising debut at Naples, traditionally an early-season test race, and Trintignant brought it successfully through its real baptism of fire, narrowly triumphing over a horde of Coopers at Rheims. Thereafter, it was raced only spasmodically, for the Scuderia was as ever heavily committed to racing in other classes. It was substantially revised and lightened in 1960, and then superseded by a rear-engined

car (which in turn was a useful prototype for the 1961 GP car). This won first time out on Porsche's home circuit, Solitude, was towed to a class victory in the inconsequential Italian GP, and was then beaten by Bonnier in a Porsche on Ferrari's home circuit, Modena.

Other Italian F2 cars, Oscas and a de Tomaso, made little impact, French constructors showed virtually no interest (and none beyond the project stage), but under this formula Germany, represented by Porsche, re-entered single-seater racing.

The German company had built up a formidable competition record with their small sports cars, powered by air-cooled twin ohc flat four engines, and one of these, the RSK, was the basis of the first F2 Porsches. The first to race were in fact sports cars, and handicapped by their heavy bodies (with one of these Edgar Barth won the F2 section of the 1957 German GP). From these was evolved the first central-cockpit single-seater, still with wheel-enveloping bodywork. This was obviously suited to the fast Rheims circuit, and here Behra drove the first one to victory in 1958, at 116·43 mph – faster than Fangio in a GP Mercedes in 1954.

In 1959 a proper single-seater F2 Porsche appeared, and during the last two seasons of the formula these cars were driven by several prominent drivers, Graham Hill, Surtees, Bonnier, Gurney and von Trips among them. Their successes persuaded the AvD to run the 1960 German GP as an F2 race, over the little-used Nürburgring South Circuit, and Porsches duly triumphed in a miserable, rain-soaked race (Porsche

drivers Bonnier and von Trips were first and second, Brabham third in a Cooper).

At the end of the season Cooper and Porsche shared the F2 Constructors' Championship. Although some of the cars lingered on as Grand Prix machines, the 1·5 litre Formula 2 naturally expired as the 1·5 litre Grand Prix formula came into force in 1961.

The need for a second-level single-seater formula where up-and-coming drivers could race with, and presumably learn from, the established stars did not lapse however, and in 1964 a new Formula 2 came into force. This admitted engines of up to 1000 cc, with not more than four cylinders, and stipulated a minimum car weight of 420 kg (925 lb).

This formula was sometimes denigrated as of little or no consequence, as save in two very important respects, it was mechanically a British monopoly. But it amply fulfilled its driver purpose, most startlingly perhaps at the Crystal Palace in 1964 when Jochen Rindt shot to prominence by defeating the established Grand Prix aces, while other drivers such as Jackie Stewart took an important step up through racing in it.

By and large constructors produced cars in direct line of succession from their Formula Junior cars, and during the first period of the formula these were invariably powered by the Cosworth SCA engine. This tended to result in closely similar performances, and on fast circuits the least desirable form of close racing, for top drivers had little opportunity to use their skill to break clear of slip-streaming bunches (on the credit side, it also led to close racing between top drivers on circuits with more drivers' problems).

Brabhams were generally dominant in the first year, but in 1965 honours were more evenly spread: of the 14 principal races Brabham won five, Lotus five, Lola three and Alexis one; the most successful drivers were the Grand Prix aces, Clark gaining all of Lotus' victories, Hulme, Brabham, Hill and Rindt gaining Brabham's, Amon, Attwood and Surtees Lola's.

Towards the end of that year, however, a significant new coupling appeared on the entry lists – Brabham-

Honda. Jack Brabham arranged the exclusive use of the twin-ohc Honda engine for his team, and thus gained a significant power advantage of some 20 bhp over his Cosworth-engined rivals (the 150 bhp produced by the Honda engine was at that time the highest specific output achieved by a normally aspirated petrol-fuelled racing engine). Of 15 major F2 races in 1966, the Brabham team won 12 (Brabham 10, Hulme 2), did not contest two and were beaten once, by Rindt at Brands Hatch in the closing race of the formula. The three races not won by the Brabham team fell to Cosworth-engined Brabhams, so the whole season smacked of monopoly.

In fact, other teams' efforts to get on terms meant that the season was exciting, while interest and significance was added by the return of French cars to front-line racing, in Formula 2. While Brabhams took nine of the second places, and Lotus two, four went to a new marque, Matra. Moreover, from the beginning of the season, and in the first Matra second placing (at Barcelona), there was an important coupling of names with Matra, Ken Tyrrell and Jackie Stewart. Tyrrell persuaded Stewart to try this then little-known French car, and from that point this brilliant manager/driver pair were on the way towards a World Championship, to setting the seal on the French racing renaissance that had begun with the first Formula 3 Matra in 1965, and towards founding a new marque. The high point for Matra came in 1967, however, when three French drivers dominated the Formula 2 section of the German Grand Prix, Jean-Pierre Beltoise winning this at 80·06 mph.

Overall, the 1000 cc Formula 2 belonged to Brabham, and to Ford-based engines, which powered the winning cars in 35 of the 48 principal races. With the coming of the 3-litre Grand Prix formula, the gap from 100 cc became too great, and consequently a new Formula 2 was devised.

Indianapolis and Monza

After an outburst of originality immediately before and after the second world war, US oval track racing – which to the world at large generally means Indianapolis – fell into a complacent technical rut, under the carried-over pre-war regulations (4·5 litre unsupercharged engines, 3 litre supercharged engines), and from 1957 regulations imposing limits of 4·2 and 2·8 litres (255 and 171 cu in). In the late forties front wheel drive cars won the 500, and for a long time some teams tried to persuade the screaming supercharged Novi eights to hold together for 500 miles, occasionally succeeding in getting one to the chequered flag, but never ahead of the field (the third achieved by Duke Nalon in 1948 was the best-ever for the superb but temperamental Novi in its Indianapolis career).

Generally, however, the tight introspective world of the USAC revolved around the Meyer-Drake

Offenshauser-engined roadster throughout the 1950s. Development was painfully slow, as these devices were regarded as ends in themselves. The outside world of road racing was largely ignored, and by the technological standards of road racing, the roadster was anachronistic at the end of the decade. But this was symptomatic of the condition the USAC and Indianapolis Establishment apparently preferred. The 500 was OK as it was, progress was anathema to the rituals of May in Indiana, stagnation was an ideal situation.

The front wheel drive Blue Crown Specials won three times in the late 1940s, driven by Mauri Rose in

A 1951 Bellanger Special, a typical USAC 'roadster' racing car, with front mounted Offenhauser engine and rigid suspension front and rear.

1947 and 1948, Bill Holland in 1949. When the 1950 race was cut short by rain at 136 laps, the leader was Johnny Parsons in a conventional Offenhauser-powered Kurtis Kraft roadster (a 'Wynn Friction Proof Special').

Disguised with sponsors' names, machines of this type came to monopolize the race. They conformed to a standard pattern of a strong tubular chassis frame, rigid axles front and rear (without differentials), front-mounted Offy engine, usually angled from the vertical in chassis, and sometimes installed horizontally, and offset to load the left-hand side (the constant radius turns of the tracks encouraged a biased weight distribution). Cockpits were usually offset to the right, with transmissions running alongside. Brake efficiency was not considered of great importance, although discs of a type were in general use on US tracks before they were in Europe (as were self-sealing tanks), and two-speed gearboxes were generally considered quite adequate, for rolling starts were the rule.

The twin-ohc Meyer-Drake Offenhauser engine reigned supreme, increasingly in fuel-injected form. Apart from the Novi, the only variety in power units came in occasional stock-based, Chrysler or Studebaker, V-8s. The high power outputs claimed for these, up to 370 bhp, somehow never materialized on the tracks. . . .

Indianapolis qualifying speeds gently rose, through the ritualistic periods in May which were to amuse and aggravate the Europeans who were to invade the track in the sixties, and who apart from the prize fund were to regard the 500 as just another motor race. There was a corresponding increase in race speeds: Bill Holland was the first winner to average over 120 mph (121·33 mph) in 1949, while the 130 mph mark was passed by Bill Vukovitch in 1954 (130·84 mph). Incidentally, not until 1952 did the Indianapolis winner's speed exceed that of Farina with a 1·5 litre Alfa Romeo in the 1940 Tripoli GP (or indeed, Varzi's speed in the 1933 Avusrennen).

In 1952 a Cummins diesel took pole position, at 138 mph, and four Ferraris were entered. Ascari qualified one of these, at 134·3 mph, and worked it up to sixth place after an hour's racing, when he spun to retirement as the left rear wheel collapsed (apart from the Novis, credited with 600 bhp, this Ferrari was the most powerful car in the race, with some 380 bhp compared with the 360 bhp of the Meyer-Drake fours; however, it lacked the low-range torque of the Offy, and thus lost on acceleration out of corners).

Vukovitch crashed when leading this race with a few miles to go, so that it fell to Troy Ruttmann,

driving an Agajanian Special (a name which was to become important to Europeans a decade later!). Vukovitch won in 1953, in a race run in torrid heat – one driver who collapsed in the pits with heat exhaustion later died in hospital – and slowed by accidents. He won again in 1954, when the race was unusually free of trouble, but was killed in a multiple pile-up with cars which he was lapping when leading the 1955 race. The last race under the 4·5/3 litre regulations fell to Pat Flaherty at 128·49 mph, by the narrow margin of 21·5 seconds from Sam Hanks, whose car had reputedly already run in ten 500s!

In spite of the smaller engines, the race speed went up again in 1957, when Hanks won at 135·60 mph in one of George Salih's light and low-built roadsters (a Belond Exhaust Special). That year some of the roadsters were brought to Europe, to Monza, where Indianapolis cars had occasionally performed well in the distant past.

The 1957 Monza 500 Miles, however, was planned to exploit the banked high-speed track which had been completed at the autodrome in 1955. Ten of the leading American track drivers were invited to compete, and did so; their European counterparts declined, so that the only opposition to the American cars came, apparently incongruously, from a trio of Ecurie Ecosse D-type Jaguars. The fastest qualifying speed was 177·05 mph, by Tony Bettenhausen in a Novi, but true to form this car did not last long in the first part of the three-part race (an arrangement dictated by the bumpy Monza bankings, sensibly as transpired, for there were many breakages to be repaired between each part). Three Indianapolis cars survived the three parts, to take the first three places on aggregate, Jimmy Bryan winning at 166·06 mph; the dark blue Jaguars filled the next three places.

The 1958 Indianapolis 500 was marred by a tremendous accident on the first lap. This involved 17 cars, of which eight were to all intents and purposes destroyed, and cost the life of Pat O'Connor. The restarted race was won by Bryan at 133·79 mph, in a Belond AP Special, a Salih-designed car with its Offenhauser engine installed horizontally.

This car headed the US entry for the second Monza 500, which in 1958 was contested by some leading Europeans with specially prepared cars, notably a 4·2 litre V-8 Eldorado-Maserati for Moss and two Ferraris for Musso, Hawthorn and Phil Hill to share, a 4·1 litre V-12 and a 3 litre V-6. With the big Ferrari, and a considerable dash of personal bravery, Musso was the fastest qualifier at 174·2 mph, and he led the first part of the race for some time. At the end of the day, however, the American cars triumphed again, Jim Rathmann winning in Joe Zink's Watson-built Leader Card Special at 166·72 mph, which made the 1958 Monza 500 the fastest race ever run at that time

American track cars have always been colourful, but for decades changed little in outward appearance – or mechanical make-up. The Cummins (centre left) proclaims its unusual power unit; below it is the Dean Van Lines Special which Jimmy Bryan drove to victory in the 1958 Indianapolis 500.

(Lang's 'record' 162·61 mph in the 1937 Avusrennen at last being 'beaten'). However, despite the unquestioned immediate appeal of these roadsters on the high-speed track, the Monza event was never run again.

At Indianapolis in 1959 all the cars which qualified to start were powered by Meyer-Drake Offenhauser engines, and as at Monza in 1958 the winning chassis was an A. J. Watson Leader Card Special, this time driven by Roger Ward (at 135·86 mph).

Later that year, Ward drove a Midget in the US Grand Prix, an odd exercise in itself, but the point to which the Indianapolis revolution of the 1960s can be specifically traced back. For Ward became friendly with the Cooper team, and an outcome of this was that after the 1960 US Grand Prix, a Cooper was driven in trials at Indianapolis by Jack Brabham. He lapped at around 145 mph, which in itself was not startling – Rathmann's winning average in 1960 was 138·77 mph. But it was achieved with a 2·5 litre engine, and the little green car was fast enough through and out of the turns to lead a few people to think, and to produce Kleenex sponsorship for a Cooper entry in the 1961 race.

For this Coopers built a slightly offset car, with a specially developed 2·7 litre version of the Coventry Climax FPF. This of course meant that the car was sadly underpowered, and although Brabham's ninth place was thus all the more creditable, the Indianapolis Establishment did not, or would not, read any significance into it. A. J. Foyt won that race, at 139·13 mph.

Roger Ward took a roadster to victory again in 1962, topping 140 mph over the 200 laps for the first time (140·29 mph). This year Mickey Thompson essayed rear-engined entries, but his tuned stock Buick V-8s did not produce adequate power, while the cars handled oddly on 12 inch diameter wheels, with wide flat tyres (which in themselves were strangely prophetic).

Watching that race was Colin Chapman, at Indianapolis as a guest of Dan Gurney, who drove one of the Thompson curiosities (into retirement after 92 laps), and one or two senior Ford personnel. The 500 would never be the same again. . . .

The 1.5 Litre Years

In the Autumn of 1958 the International Sporting Commission met in London to determine a new Formula 1, to come into effect in 1961. As so often in the history of motor racing, the governing body was anxious about rising speeds, and concerned above all to restrain them. So once again a secondary formula, a voiturette class or the post-war equivalent, Formula 2, became the Grand Prix Formula.

Engine capacity was limited to 1·5 litres (with an academic minimum of 1·3 litres), superchargers were not permitted, and the minimum dry weight of cars was set at 500 kg, which before the formula came into force was reduced to 450 kg (992 lb). Self-starters became obligatory, as did their use in races, and replenishment with oil once a race had started was forbidden. This was a considerable contribution to racing safety, for it meant that teams would make every effort to ensure oil-tight engines and gearboxes, and thus at least incidental spillage on circuits would be avoided. Safety considerations were also apparent in other directions, for example in the dual braking systems and roll-over bars (metal hoops rising higher than the drivers' heads to support the weight of an inverted car) which were required.

When it was announced at the Royal Automobile Club, this formula was greeted with derision, particularly from British racing interests, hardly in keeping with the sedate surroundings. A boycott was proposed and, encouraged by the knowledge that the CSI decision had been far from unanimous, a powerful lobby demanded its abolition and the simple continuation of the 2·5 litre formula.

The CSI refused to retract, and in 1960 confirmed the formula. At the same time lip service was paid to the protests and a parallel Intercontinental Formula was instituted. To all intents and purposes, the object of this was to extend the life of the 2·5 litre class, for it admitted single-seaters with engines of between 2 and 3 litres. It was to prove a complete fiasco, and the net result of the tumult and shouting from the British point of view was the loss of valuable development time. The 2·5 litre racing class survived healthily only in Australia and New Zealand, and lasted through the sixties in the Tasman Series.

Continental constructors, which to all immediate intents and purposes meant Ferrari, gave some support to the protesting faction, but got on with the job of developing new machinery for the formula. The German firm of Porsche entered Grand Prix racing, but initially only with updated 1960 Formula 2 cars. Having broken step, British constructors were caught on the wrong foot – numerically, British entries were strong, but while constructors waited for 1·5 litre V-8 engines to be built they had to make do with Coventry Climax FPF fours, some in uprated Mk 2 form but none good for more than about 150 bhp.

The Ferrari appeared to have much in common with its F2 predecessor, but was in fact a new car. Its tubular chassis, based on four large-diameter tubes, was straightforward, as was the wishbone suspension fore and aft. Two engines were used during 1961, the 65 degree V-6 Dino 156 and a new 120 degree V-6. Both were twin overhead camshaft units, and had common dimensions, 73 × 58·8 mm (1476 cc). The earlier engine had a claimed output of some 180 bhp at 9000 rpm, while the 120 degree unit produced 190 bhp at 9500 rpm. This was a better-balanced engine and its characteristics were well-suited to high-speed circuits, while the wider vee helped to lower the car's centre of gravity.

The Italian-domiciled Argentinian Alessandro de Tomaso flirted with Grand Prix racing, building a Massimino-designed car for four-cylinder Osca or Alfa Romeo engines, and later in the formula built his own eight-cylinder engine.

The first Formula 1 Porsche was a carefully-designed interim car, to serve while a flat 8 engine was prepared. Its 'boxer' four-cylinder twin-ohc engine had been developed via Formula 2 from a sports car unit, and was of course air-cooled, though to little advantage. Unusual features were an all-synchromesh gearbox, and until the middle of the season drum brakes.

Coopers had advanced little in basic design or appearance, and bore an additional handicap in their weight. Most, including of course the works T55s, were Climax-powered, but odd cars appeared with Maserati and Alfa Romeo engines.

Even BRM used the Climax engine in interim cars, the only time that 'bought-out' power units have been employed in a Bourne single-seater. Secondary British

In 1961 only Stirling Moss in Rob Walker's Lotus 18 (left) was able to beat the Ferraris (right, Baghetti in the French GP). The situation in 1962 was very different, as shown by the German GP grid, with a Porsche, two BRMs and a Lola leading away.

cars which appeared briefly and unimpressively in the Grand Prix arena included the Maserati-engined Emerysons.

Outstanding among the Climax-engined cars was the Lotus 21. Clearly ahead of the field in chassis and suspension design, the 21 had an outstandingly sleek body, and its frontal area was reduced by lowering the driver into a semi-reclining position. Front suspension coil springs and dampers were aboard, out of the airstream, while at the rear deep hub carriers were used with transverse links.

The first representative race of 1961, the first where a Ferrari ran, was the Syracuse Grand Prix. A single

Two representative cars of the 1·5 litre Formula, a Ferrari (above, Surtees coming out of the Monaco tunnel) and a Brabham (right, driven by Brabham), and the least conventional car of the early sixties, the four-wheel drive Ferguson (below, driven by Graham Hill). Preceding pages: Siffert in a 1966 Cooper.

Ferrari was entered for Grand Prix novitiate Giancarlo Baghetti, and the combination proved good enough to head clearly full German and British teams.

The Championship season opened at Monaco, where the better handling qualities of the British cars were almost sufficient to offset the Ferrari power advantage of some 20–30 bhp. Stirling Moss in Rob

Walker's updated Lotus 18 made up for the deficit in a tremendous virtuoso drive, winning by 3·6 seconds from Ferrari driver Richie Ginther. Both lapped only one-tenth of a second outside the record, so at least on a slow and twisting circuit the effects of the CSI efforts to restrict speeds were already doubtful.

At Zandvoort for the Dutch Grand Prix all the team Ferraris had 120 degree engines for the first time; these gained the first three places, on the starting grid, and in the race finished first, second and fifth, split by the Lotus 21 driven by Clark and the 18 driven by Moss. This race was unique in World Championship history, as no drivers made pit stops and all 15 cars which started ran through to be classified. On the very fast Spa circuit in Belgium the Ferraris predictably outclassed the rest of the field, and ran through to team orders to achieve a 1-2-3-4 victory. Phil Hill's winning speed was 128·15 mph, the third-fastest ever achieved on this circuit.

The French Grand Prix on the similarly fast Rheims circuit should have seen a similar result. The Ferraris again dominated practice, but in the race the three works cars fell out and Baghetti was left to uphold Ferrari honour in the nominally independent 65 degree car. In the closing laps he battled like a seasoned veteran with Porsche drivers Gurney and Bonnier, and beat the American across the line by a tenth of a second to save the day for Ferrari. Curiously, having in his first Formula 1 season won two secondary races, the Syracuse and Naples Grands Prix, and now a Championship race – the first Italian driver since Alberto Ascari to do so – Giancarlo Baghetti

faded and never again featured among the front runners in a major race.

Their Rheims lapse behind them, the Ferrari team took the first three places in the British Grand Prix at Aintree. Of no little interest in this race was the Ferguson P99, a development one-off for the Ferguson four-wheel drive system. Its Coventry Climax engine was mounted in front of the cockpit and drove through a Colotti five-speed gearbox. The power split between front and rear wheels was equal, which proved a far from ideal arrangement as drivers were unable to use the throttle as a steering aid. Although ruled out of the race results because of a minor infringement, it made a great impression. This was confirmed later in the non-Championship Gold Cup race at Oulton Park, where Stirling Moss showed that it could out-corner every other car. Its win in this event stands as the only one for a four-wheel drive car in a Formula 1 race, and perhaps in part because of it, too much was expected of the next generation of four-wheel drive cars. One other minor distinction belongs to the Ferguson P99 – it was the last front-engined car to appear in Grand Prix racing.

The first Coventry Climax V-8 was rushed through for the next Grand Prix, at the Nürburgring. This was a conventional 90 degree twin-ohc V-8, 63 × 60 mm (1494 cc), which initially produced 170 bhp. It first appeared in a too-hastily adapted Cooper driven by Jack Brabham, who was second-fastest in practice and led the field away from the start. Then he was caught out on a damp patch of track, for the Cooper had come to the line with 'wet' tyres on the front wheels

259

and 'dry' tyres at the rear, and retired into the Nürburgring trees. The race became a duel between Moss and the Ferrari team, the former choosing to ignore Dunlop technicians' warning about the high wear rate of the then-new high-hysteresis tyres on the mainly dry circuit. He exploited their cornering powers to the utmost, until rain came in the closing

Lorenzo Bandini in action in Ferraris on very different circuits. Above and below, in 1965, driving the eight-cylinder 1·5 litre car through the Karussel at Nürburgring, and leading the Italian GP field into the Parabolica at Monza. Opposite: at Monaco's station hairpin with the 1966 2·4 litre 'stand-in' car which he placed second in the race; a similar Ferrari had an outstanding career in Tasman racing.

phase and handicapped the pursuing Ferraris. Moss' winning speed was 92·34 mph, while in one of the Ferraris Phil Hill set a new Nürburgring lap record of 94·89 mph.

A second V-8 was seen in practice for the Italian Grand Prix. This was the BRM engine, again a 90 degree unit but considerably more over-square than the Climax V-8, with bore and stroke of 68·5 × 50·8 mm giving a capacity of 1498 cc. Whereas the Climax engine at this stage had four Weber twin-choke carburetters, the BRM engine had a Lucas fuel injection system. It was not raced at Monza, where Brabham's Cooper was the only V-8 car to start.

This Italian GP was marred by tragedy, when Clark and von Trips collided in the braking area for the Parabolica curve at Monza. The Ferrari left the track, and 14 spectators and Wolfgang von Trips were killed. The accident caused an enormous outcry, and Clark was harried by the Press for a long time, although no blame attached to either driver. Phil Hill won the race, in the sole Ferrari to survive, to win the World Championship for himself and the Manufacturers' Championship for Ferrari, whose cars had started in seven Championship races, gaining five victories, five second placings and four third places.

The Italian team therefore ignored the last race of the season, the American Grand Prix, where Innes Ireland gained the first Championship race victory for Team Lotus. In America V-8-engined cars, a Cooper and a BRM, had been fastest in practice, and obviously a winter's development work would make them wholly competitive. Meanwhile, there was a palace revolution at Modena, when Chiti, Bizzarini and several other technicians left Ferrari *en masse* – a loss which was to be keenly felt in 1962. The door was wide open for the British comeback. . . .

The two new British V-8 engines powered a formidable group of cars in 1962. New teams joined the established British trio of BRM, Cooper and Lotus, notably the Bowmaker-sponsored Lolas and, later in the season, Jack Brabham's own Brabham team.

At the beginning of the season the Coventry Climax engine was producing some 187 bhp at 8500 rpm, the BRM V-8 190 bhp at 10,500 rpm with fuel injection, or 183 bhp at 9750 rpm with carburetters, the form in which it was sold to private owners. In terms of power output there was little to choose between these two engines, the 65 degree V-6 which Ferrari raced in 1962 and the Porsche flat-eight which was to appear during the year. In 1961, British chassis design in part compensated for a power handicap; in 1962, with rough equality in power between the leading teams, it was to give the British a decisive advantage.

Cooper, it was true, had not made the same advances as Lotus and BRM, and in fact were to gain their only victories of the 1·5 litre formula in the first half of the

season. Their car was lighter than the 1961 model, and had a six-speed gearbox. BRM had a well-mannered, dependable car which was to take the Championship, and which initially was distinguished by eight individual exhaust stacks. The Lola was a conventional space frame car, which had road-holding deficiencies throughout the season. Jack Brabham's early-season experience with a Lotus 24 give him a yardstick in this respect, and although his first Tauranac-designed space frame BT3 Grand Prix car was technically unexciting it was to prove thoroughly competent.

Lotus started the season with their 24, a new space-frame Grand Prix car designed for the Coventry Climax V-8, rather than a developed Formula 2 car modified to accept it. Then for the first Championship race, Chapman introduced the monocoque 25, which was to start a design chain reaction.

The Lotus brought back to Grand Prix racing the monocoque structure with which Gabriel Voisin had briefly flirted in the mid-1920s, and with all the advantages of later aircraft experience to draw on. The hull was made of stressed aluminium sheet, transversely braced by steel bulkheads and cross-members. This was an inherently rigid structure, resistant to twisting, and light – it weighed only 70 lb compared with the 82 lb of the basic frame of the Lotus 24. The frontal area of the 25 was minimal, with the driver in an even more pronounced semi-prone position, in a tight-fitting cockpit with a tiny steering wheel. Drivers took a little time to become accustomed to this new fashion in cockpits, but until it became universal the march which Chapman had stolen on his rivals was all too obvious to the eye as grids formed up.

After a season with four-cylinder engines, Porsche produced their eight-cylinder car. The multi-tubular chassis was new, and suspension members were inboard (although the drag reduction thus achieved must in large part have been offset by the shoulders of

Porsche's number one driver, Dan Gurney, standing proud of the cockpit screen!). Porsche disc brakes and a Porsche six-speed gearbox were used. The cylinder banks of the engine were opposed, each having twin overhead camshafts and ducting to extract maximum benefit from the flow from a fan mounted horizontally above the engine, for as in all Porsches this was air-cooled. Cylinder dimensions were 66 × 54·6 mm (1498 cc), and the claimed power output was 185 bhp at 8500 rpm.

There was early-season talk of a Ferrari with a transverse air-cooled engine built in collaboration with Gilera, but in the metal the Italian team had only mildly revised versions of their 1961 car to defend their Championship – and on the grids it looked curiously old-fashioned. The V-6 engine had new four-valve cylinder heads, giving an increase in power, although this did not reach the claimed 200 bhp at 10,000 rpm. It was transmitted through a six-speed gear-box.

During the year the first 12-cylinder engine for this formula was built by Maserati, but never developed or installed in a car. In an echo of Colombo's Bugatti T251, and in anticipation of a later Honda, Alfieri's engine was designed to be installed transversely, and in unit with the transmission.

Early in the year Stirling Moss' racing career ended when he crashed in a Lotus-Climax at Goodwood, for reasons which have yet to be explained.

The opening Championship race of the season was the Dutch Grand Prix, which could be described as the first definitive 1·5 litre race as none of the principal contenders was a car carried over from a previous

The combination of Jim Clark and the Lotus 25 (below) and the Coventry Climax V-8 engine (opposite) set the Grand Prix pace for three years of the 1·5 litre Formula.

formula. Pole position was gained by John Surtees (Lola), with Graham Hill's BRM and Jim Clark's Lotus 25 alongside it. Surtees' fastest practice lap was 1 min 32·5 sec; the fastest Ferrari driver was reigning World Champion Phil Hill, whose best lap was completed in 1 min 35·0 sec. In the race, Graham Hill gained his first Championship victory, ahead of a Lotus driven by Taylor and Hill's Ferrari.

A multiple accident at the start of the Monaco Grand Prix eliminated three cars, and only five were still running at the end of the 100-lap race. Bruce McLaren headed these, to gain for Cooper their only Championship victory of the formula, while Phil Hill and Lorenzo Bandini placed their Ferraris second and third (a more realistic impression of Ferrari potential would have been based on their fourth-row grid positions). Clark lowered the circuit record to 1 min 35·5 sec (73·67 mph) before retiring, when the engine of his Lotus 25 wilted.

The Spa lap record was still out of reach of a 1·5 litre car, but Clark got within four seconds of it in winning the Belgian Grand Prix. Then the British teams raced in a non-Championship at Rheims, only a week before the French Grand Prix at Rouen, which of course hardly left adequate time for overhauls and preparation. In practice at Rouen, 14 of the 17 starters improved on Musso's 1957 Grand Prix lap record. Ferrari was absent because of industrial strife in Italy, but the Porsche team returned after a brief withdrawl for intensive modification and development work, and Dan Gurney won the race for the German team, by a clear lap from Maggs' Cooper and a collection of sick British cars – a BRM, with Ginther controlling his throttle by hand, McLaren's Cooper, with a cracked main chassis member, and Surtees'

Lola, which was stuck in third gear.

The first four Championship races of 1962 had been won by cars of four different makes. The fifth, the British Grand Prix, was completely dominated by Jim Clark in a Lotus 25. The sixth, the German event, held much promise – Porsche were racing on their home ground, Ferrari produced a lighter smaller car built on 'British' lines around well-tried mechanical components, while the Formula 1 Brabham appeared for its first race. Altogether, there were cars of nine makes on the grid, including Keith Greene's BRM V-8-engined Gilby and an ENB-Maserati, which was a 1961 Emeryson revamped by the Belgian team. Interest centred on the front row, for Gurney had gained pole position in a Porsche, and had Hill, Clark and Surtees alongside him; all four had improved on the lap record in practice.

Although run in a downpour, the *Grosser Preis* was enthralling, as from the second lap Graham Hill drove one of his finest races to hold off determined attacks by Surtees and Gurney – at the end 4·4 seconds separated first and third. Jim Clark was fourth, after a drive which is too often overlooked, because he was 'only' fourth (he neglected to switch on his pumps at the start, and got away well behind the rest of the field).

Outstanding Scots. Right: Jim Clark in a Lotus 33 at Brands Hatch, and, above, Jackie Stewart in a BRM.

McLaren's Cooper was fifth, and Rodriguez' Ferrari sixth – six different makes in the first six!

Unusually, Ferrari produced no novelties at Monza, where a new de Tomaso with a flat-eight engine designed by Massimino fleetingly appeared on the Grand Prix stage – it was undeveloped when brought to practice and did not qualify to start. On this fast circuit the first two cars on the grid, a Lotus and a BRM, had equalled the lap record – the race-slowing intentions of the CSI had not held good for long. In the Italian Grand Prix first and second places were taken by BRMs – at last the shame of their 1951 Monza fiasco was erased.

Jim Clark won the American Grand Prix in a Lotus 25 ahead of Graham Hill, both of whom therefore went to South Africa for the final race of the season with a chance of taking the Championship. A lost crankcase bolt, and consequently lost engine oil, cost Clark the race when he was in the lead. Graham Hill won, to become World Champion, while BRM gained the Constructors' Championship – success after 12 years of often frustrating endeavour.

Outwardly, there were changes for 1963. The quasi-works Lola team was wound up, with only one victory, in a secondary event at Mallory Park, to its credit; the cars were taken over by Reg Parnell. John Surtees joined Ferrari, whose cars were refined versions of the one-off lightweight raced in 1962, still with the 120 degree V-6 engine (which with Bosch fuel injection had a power output approaching 200 bhp). BRM produced a new semi-monocoque car, and had to put a disproportionate effort into attempting to make it raceworthy. The Lotus 25 was changed only in detail, in mid-season appearing with the single-plane crankshaft Coventry Climax V-8 and a Hewland gearbox.

Front-line Coventry Climax engines were fitted with a Lucas fuel-injection system, tried at the end of 1962, and in this form produced 190 bhp at 9000 rpm. Porsche retired, but the gap was apparently filled by a new Italian works team, ATS. The British Racing Partnership was formed out of the UDT-Laystall team, and produced the BRM-engined BRP monocoque on Lotus lines. The American-backed Scirocco also used BRM engines, in a chassis with Emeryson origins.

Of the newcomers, ATS was on paper the most promising. Automobili Turismo e Sport had been formed by a powerful triumvirate, Brilli, Patino and Volpi. The technical staff was headed by Carlo Chiti, and the works drivers were Phil Hill and Giancarlo Baghetti. The car at least had a distinctive shape, covering an undistinguished space frame. Its twin-ohc light alloy 90 degree V-8 (66 × 54·6 mm, 1494 cc) gave 190 bhp at 10,500 rpm, and drove through a Colotti six-speed gearbox. The racing history of the ATS was little short of pathetic. . . .

This was in any case Jim Clark's season. He won seven of the ten championship races, finished second once and third once.

Other constructors were still working to catch up with the sophisticated Lotus 25, which by 1963 was fully developed. Their cars were tending to become more uniform in appearance, as well as in make-up. While wheel diameters got smaller, tyres grew ever wider and played an increasingly important role. Of necessity, driving became more precise, in part because of tyre characteristics, in part because there was no surplus power in the 1·5 litre engines for a driver to use in certain circumstances to get himself out of trouble. Car 'tuning' for circuits, an art to which little attention had been paid less than a decade earlier, became standard practice in this increasingly sophisticated Grand Prix class.

The 1963 season opened with several secondary races, of which Team Lotus won those they entered. They did not, however, win the opening Championship race, the 21st Monaco Grand Prix. Jim Clark, almost 'as usual', built up a substantial lead, but with 20 laps to go relaxed his gear changing with the result that the box selected both second and fourth gears. Graham Hill went through to win at 72·42 mph in a 1962 BRM ahead of his team mate Richie Ginther, while on the last lap John Surtees set the lap record at 74·45 mph as he tried to take third place from Bruce McLaren.

Clark led the next four races, the Belgian, Dutch, French and British Grands Prix, from start to finish, aided at Rheims by a generous ration of good fortune (he built up a good lead in the early stages, then his engine refused to pull at high rpm and his pursuers gained, only to be thwarted as rain slowed the race and offset his handicap).

Generally his closest challengers were Hill and Surtees, while the marque Brabham was beginning to make an impression. The green and gold cars were usually among the fastest in practice, Dan Gurney placed a Brabham second in the Dutch Grand Prix and at the end of July, Jack Brabham drove his own Brabham to win the non-Championship Solitude Grand Prix. Just over a month later, in the first Austrian Grand Prix on the bumpy and primitive Zeltweg circuit, as other top rank drivers fell out, he won by no less than five laps from Tony Settember's Scirocco!

Before that, however, another stirring German Grand Prix had been run at the Nürburgring, Surtees duelling with Clark until a faulty plug slowed the Scot, when Surtees pulled away to score his first Championship victory for Ferrari. His race speed was 95·82 mph, faster than the previous lap record!

Although a new Ferrari V-8 had been tested, it was not run in the Italian Grand Prix, although a new Ferrari car was. Small and sleek, this was a semi-monocoque on Lotus lines, with reinforcing tubes, as an interim measure powered by the 120 degree V-6. With it Surtees gained pole position, lapping over a second faster than the driver alongside him on the grid, Graham Hill. The relative merits of the other Italian GP car, the ATS, were only too sadly illustrated, for Phil Hill was fourteenth fastest (his best practice took 9·5 seconds longer than Surtees' 1 min 37·3 sec), while Baghetti just qualified the other ATS. Graham Hill led the race, and Surtees led it, but Clark won it, from Ginther's BRM and McLaren's Cooper.

BRMs were first and second in the American Grand Prix at Watkins Glen, followed by Clark, already World Champion elect because of his unapproachable points score in European races. The last two races, in Mexico and South Africa, fell to him by generous margins, from the Brabhams of Brabham and Gurney respectively. The Constructors' Championship clearly went to Lotus, with BRM and Brabham as runners-up.

To keep ahead, Lotus refined their design in 1964, sufficiently to justify redesigning it Type 33, although

Graham Hill in a BRM, followed by Dan Gurney in a Brabham and John Surtees in a Ferrari, in the 1964 British Grand Prix at Brands Hatch.

throughout the first half of the season the team campaigned 25Bs. Following their then-normal practice, Lotus made their not-quite-current models available to private teams, and in 1964 Reg Parnell's team raced 25s. BRM turned to a proper stressed-skin monocoque, while in the T69 and T73 Cooper used sheet metal to increase the rigidity of their tubular chassis. Brabham remained faithful to the apparently outmoded space frame.

Ferrari produced their V-8, using it to carry some chassis loadings, although main reliance was on square tubes linking the monocoque and a sub frame carrying the suspension at the rear. The new engine was initially 64 × 57·8 mm (1487 cc) and fitted with carburetters, in which form it produced 200 bhp at 10,700 rpm; later a 'flat' crankshaft was adopted, giving dimensions of 67 × 52·8 mm, and in this form, with fuel injection, the engine was developed to produce some 215 bhp at 11,000 rpm. At this time the short-stroke (72·4 × 45·5 mm, 1496 cc) Coventry Climax V-8 produced some 195 bhp at 9500 rpm, while the BRM V-8 had been developed to give over 200 bhp at 11,000 rpm.

Most cars now ran with 13-in diameter wheels, fitted with Dunlop R6 tyres, and tyres increasingly influenced the finer points of suspension design. The 'tyre war' was soon to open, although until the very last race of the 1·5 litre Formula the British company was to have a monopoly in race successes.

The pre-season warm-up races were notable for the speed of the Ferraris at Syracuse, where in a V-6 car Bandini set a new lap record at 108·02 mph, and a near dead-heat at Silverstone between Brabham and Hill,

the Australian winning by a wheel. In the first Championship race, at Monaco, Hill won by a clear lap from Richie Ginther, in the process nudging the lap record up again, to 74·92 mph, while under pressure from Jim Clark. The reigning champion drove a remarkable race, for when his rear anti-roll bar worked loose he 'simply' adapted to the changed handling of his Lotus 25B, and speeded up to keep ahead of the field, until he made an inevitable pit stop. Clark won an unremarkable Dutch Grand Prix, and then a most remarkable Belgian Grand Prix. Having made a pit stop for water he was back in fourth place as the race neared its end. But, instead of racing past the pits into the last lap, race leader Dan Gurney stopped for fuel; there was none at his pit, so he restarted in the spluttering Brabham, to stop on the circuit. Graham Hill inherited the lead, but not for the full distance of the last lap, as a pump in the BRM failed to transfer fuel from a supplementary tank. This appeared to leave Bruce McLaren with victory in his grasp – but with perhaps two miles to go to the finish, the engine of his Cooper cut out and he coasted to within sight of the flag. At this stage Clark accelerated out of the last corner, past the Cooper and the chequered flag and on, to run out of fuel on his cooling-down lap!

At Rouen in the French Grand Prix Dan Gurney gained the first Championship race for the marque Brabham, with Jack himself third behind Hill. Gurney's race speed (108·73 mph) exceeded that of the previous lap record, which Brabham reduced by 5·5 seconds (speed: 111·37 mph). Hill pursued Clark unavailingly throughout the British Grand Prix at Brands Hatch, finishing less than three seconds behind, and well ahead of Surtees. During practice for this race, BRM produced a four-wheel drive car, using the Ferguson system; heavy and under-developed, its lap times were not competitive, and the team abided by their immediate intention not to race it – in fact they never did race it, but perhaps learned sufficient lessons from it, as BRM was one of the few constructors not to essay a four-wheel drive car five years later.

There was more technical interest at the Nürburgring for the next Championship round, for here the first Honda Grand Prix car made its unauspicious debut. Interest centred on the rear of this challenge from Japan, where as expected Honda had made use of their motorcycle experience in an engine with twelve cylinders, which at this first appearance were fed by twelve miniscule motorcycle-type carburetters. A 60-degree unit (55 × 52·5 mm) it had four valves per cylinder, with of course two overhead camshafts to each bank. It reputedly revved to 13,000 rpm and gave its theoretical peak power of 225 bhp at 12,500 rpm, although at Nürburgring the reality seemed a little more modest.

This engine was mounted tranversely in a tubular frame, which also carried the suspension and six-speed gearbox, behind the rear bulkhead of the monocoque of the RA-270. Save for the rear suspension, which incorporated inboard coil springs linked by struts to the top wishbones, the rest of the car was conventional, although hardly pleasing in appearance, or convincing in workmanship. Its driver was Ronnie Bucknum, whose task was in effect to race-test towards raceworthiness. At the Nürburgring there were problems with the outboard disc brakes, engine cooling and carburation, which meant that it seldom ran on twelve cylinders (for the next race the dozen carburetters were replaced by fuel injection). The Europeans, braced for an onslaught of Honda motorcycle proportions, were almost relieved to see an oil catch tank contrived from a tin can! Bucknum's best practice lap was completed in 9 min 34·3 sec, compared with the 8 min 38·4 sec of pole position driver John Surtees, and he spun out of the race.

Surtees won his second successive German GP for Ferrari at 96·56 mph, gaining the first victory for the eight-cylinder car, from Graham Hill (BRM), Bandini's V-6 Ferrari, Siffert's Brabham and three BRMs.

The Austrian Grand Prix achieved Championship status, and was won by Bandini in a V-6 Ferrari after the faster cars had fallen out, most with suspension or transmission failures on the bumpy Zeltweg concrete. Ginther finished second in a BRM, and private owner Bob Anderson brought his blue Brabham-Climax

through to a well-deserved third place.

At Monza Ferrari produced a 12-cylinder engine but ran it only in one practice session. This was an extremely compact flat-12 (56 × 50·4 mm), married to a chassis and suspension closely similar to that of the V-8 car. BRM introduced a revised version of their V-8, with exhausts in the vee instead of at the sides, which made for neat installation. An ATS, substantially remodelled as the Francis-ATS by the one-time mechanic to Stirling Moss was also entered; with Lucas fuel injection its engine produced perhaps 200 bhp at 11,000 rpm.

This time Graham Hill was on pole position, and he stayed there as the flag fell, with the BRM's clutch seized in the 'out' position. Perhaps surprisingly, Gurney was next to him in a Brabham, outwardly by no means the cleanest car for the fast autodrome track; he traded the lead with Surtees for two-thirds of the race, until his battery wilted. Surtees was third on the front row, in a V-8 Ferrari, and he won the race by over a minute from McLaren's Cooper, with Bandini third in another V-8 Ferrari. Moreover, Surtees set a new Monza lap record at 135·90 mph.

As Graham Hill won the American Grand Prix from John Surtees, the final round of the Championship became decisive – in Mexico, Clark, Hill or Surtees could win. The outcome was not settled until the last lap of the race. Hill fell out of the running early after a collision with Bandini, and a consequent pit stop; Clark led from the start, but within a few laps of the end an oil pipe split. Despite this he led into the last lap, but failed to complete it. With two laps to go Surtees, in a V-8 Ferrari, was fourth behind Bandini, in a flat-12 Ferrari, who slowed to let him through – Surtees needed to finish second to gain enough points to take the Championship, and he did. Almost incidentally, Dan Gurney won the race. . . .

The 1965 Championship opened on New Year's Day, in a South African Grand Prix dominated from the start of practice to the chequered flag by Jim Clark, driving a slightly revised Lotus 33. Surtees and Hill, faithful to Ferrari and BRM for the last year of the formula, were second and third, while in sixth place was a newcomer to Grand Prix racing, Jackie Stewart in a BRM.

Inevitably there was a lull before the European season, and the introduction of such technical novelties as there were in the last year of a formula. Coventry Climax introduced a four-valve version of their FWMV engine, which produced around 215 bhp at 10,500 rpm; Ferrari used their well-tried V-8 and the

Drivers' briefing before the 1966 Italian Grand Prix. Ginther, Hulme, Spence and Bonnier can be seen facing the camera, Clark and Brabham are on the right, Rindt (red scarf) and Arundell (red helmet) in the foreground.

The Honda team (Bucknum and Ginther) preparing for the 1965 French GP.

flat-12, which had a claimed output of 220 bhp at 12,000 rpm; BRM were satisfied with their revised V-8; Honda claimed no less than 230 bhp (at 11,000 rpm) at the drive shafts for their V-12, as much as 240 bhp at the flywheel; this was installed in a generally cleaned-up car, which was revised in detail and designated RA-272.

So much for the engines raced. Built, tested but never raced (and it was not needed to maintain the firm's superiority) was the Coventry Climax FWMW flat 16 (54·1 × 40·64 mm). Factors leading to the choice of 16 cylinders in this unit were the greater piston speed and area made possible (in the latter case 56·6 sq in, compared with the 45 sq in of the eight-cylinder engine); the theoretical bhp calculated on a piston area basis was 250, although only 220 bhp was claimed.

As the flat 16 was revealed, Coventry Climax chairman Leonard Lee announced that his company would withdraw from racing at the end of 1965 – an enormous blow to British constructors, who had come to rely on 'bought-out' Climax engines (in fact, the company was to put some effort into a gap-filling engine for the first year of the next formula). The Coventry company was involved in Grand Prix racing for less than ten years, but in that time their engines powered more Formula 1 winners than any other manufacturer's in the history of racing, 96 between 1958 and 1966.

The opening races accurately showed the form of the coming season, Clark winning at Goodwood and Syracuse, while at Silverstone Stewart beat Surtees by three seconds. Team Lotus ignored the Monaco Grand Prix, preferring to concentrate on Indianapolis (where Clark won). Hill drove his customary brilliant Principality race, scoring a third consecutive victory,

in spite of stopping in the chicane escape road, and pushing to restart. Ferraris were second (Bandini) and fourth (Surtees), split by Jackie Stewart, who had spun away the race lead at one stage.

Clark scored his fourth consecutive Belgian GP victory at Spa, the first of five which were to gain him the Championship before the end of the European season. Stewart was second in the Belgian event, where Richie Ginther gained the first Championship point for Honda finishing sixth. In the French GP, run for the first time on the sinuous Clermont Ferrand circuit, Clark again won from Stewart; at Silverstone he won from Hill, this time by a narrow margin as he nursed an engine with low oil pressure and Hill set a new record on his last lap (114·29 mph); at Zandvoort, Stewart followed Clark over the line. Jim Clark clinched his Championship in the German GP, and he lapped the Nürburgring at over 100 mph (101·22 mph) for the first time in its history. The Italian GP saw a characteristically close group race, primarily between the BRMs of Stewart and Hill, which finished in that order, and Clark's Lotus, which retired with a dozen laps to go. In this last 1·5 litre race on a fast circuit, he set the record at 135·43 mph.

Graham Hill won the American GP, for the third year in succession, and the 1·5 litre formula ended in Mexico with a surprise result. Richie Ginther swept through from the second row of the grid at the start, and led the race to the end, to score the first Grand Prix victory for Honda, and the first for Goodyear. Bucknum placed the other Honda fifth, and second man Dan Gurney also used Goodyears on his Brabham.

So the 1·5 litre formula ended on a note of change. This was appropriate, and above all singled it out from preceding post-war formulae. During its span, chassis design progressed by enormous strides, which in particular meant that road holding improved to a degree unimagined when the formula was announced. In terms of power for capacity, its engines had been the most powerful unsupercharged units in the history of racing. Only the eights had been wholly developed, the twelves had not been fully exploited and the most advanced of all 1·5 litre engines, the Climax flat 16, was not even used in racing. Around virtually any given road circuit, certainly where direct comparisons were possible, the 1·5 litre cars were the fastest Grand Prix cars of all time.

The slump to mediocrity feared when the formula was announced had not come to pass, the cars had not become miserably uniform roller skates, and all drivers had not been dragged down to the same level. The formula died on its feet, and ironically its passing was most lamented in Britain, for British constructors were as unprepared for its successor as they had been in 1961.

The Revolution reaches the Tracks

Three important visitors to the 1962 Indianapolis 500, Colin Chapman and Dan Gurney from the world of road racing, and Don Frey from the Ford Motor Company, went their separate ways after the race, Chapman and Gurney to Monaco, Frey to Detroit. But all three had similar thoughts. The first two schemed a car, the Ford man initiated modest work on a racing V-8; within weeks, the two thus-far independent sides came together, and agreed to work together. After the 1962 US Grand Prix another Formula 1 car ran round the Indianapolis track on test, Clark lapping at 143 mph in a 1·5 litre Lotus 25 and, like Brabham two years earlier, getting through corners remarkably quickly.

Early in 1963, the Lotus-Ford project became a firm commitment, Lotus built a prototype car, to which Ford contributed substantially in cash and with their first engines, pushrod ohv V-8s. In early tests with the first Lotus 29, Gurney lapped the Brickyard at 150·5 mph. In May the race cars were ready; these followed the 25 in basic conception, but unlike the prototype had offset suspension. Clark and Gurney qualified them for the second and fourth rows for the start, at 149·75 mph and 149·02 mph compared with Parnelli Jones' pole speed of 151·15 mph. Significantly, Clark and Gurney achieved these speeds with engines giving some 370 bhp, compared with the 430 bhp of the 26 Offenhauser engines present, and the claimed 700 bhp of the three supercharged Novis in the race. However, the Lotus was light, and the Ford engine ran on pump fuel, so these cars had a much better fuel consumption, and were expected to run the 500 miles with only one fuel stop.

The two little British cars looked wildly out of place at Indianapolis, for apart from their spindly appearance, they were green, a colour regarded with horror by the track-racing circus. But where it mattered, in performance, the Lotus-Ford was adequate. In the early stages, Clark and Gurney ran behind the leaders, but moved ahead as the roadsters made their first fuel stops. Clark led from lap 67 to lap 95, when he was called in for a tyre inspection and fuel. Jones led from this point, making his fuel stops when the yellow caution flags enforced slower running after incidents (during these periods, Clark lost more time than the experienced oval track drivers, as he did not thoroughly appreciate the interpretation of the rules).

In the final stages, Clark closed on Jones, but was deterred from actually challenging for the lead by the oil which the roadster was generously laying on the track. Despite specific and dire warnings that any car losing oil would be called in, the race officials simply lacked the courage to black flag a car which was in the lead, and moreover belonged to J. C. Agajanian, one of the most powerful figures in the Indianapolis Establishment.

So Parnelli Jones won, at 143·14 mph and by 33·8 seconds from Jim Clark. But many regarded Clark,

Foyt in a traditional Indianapolis roadster, the last to win the 500, in 1964, and (below) Jim Clark carving past another of that outmoded breed during his winning 1965 drive in a Lotus 38.

Lotus and Ford as the moral winners, and their point was proved when Clark drove a Lotus-Ford to a clear victory in the Milwaukee 200 ten weeks later. From this point the heavy, flashy, front-engined Indianapolis roadster was doomed, although the species did not become extinct overnight – indeed, A. J. Foyt drove a Sheraton-Thompson roadster to win the 500 in 1964. Among the 33 starters were 13 rear-engined cars, including the first three after qualifying, Clark's Lotus 34 (158·83 mph), Marshman in a Lotus 29 and Ward in a car built by the renowned roadster constructor A. J. Watson. These had new Ford ohv V-8s, unlike the 1963 engine pure racing units, while six rear-engined cars (including a Brabham) had Offenshauser engines. Among the front-engined cars was a four-wheel drive Ferguson-Novi.

Clark led from the start, until the race was stopped by a multiple accident, in which veteran Eddie Sachs and rookie Dave McDonald died. Soon after the restart, the Lotus cars were out of the race, Marshman after losing oil when a drain plug was ripped out as he left the track to avoid another car, Clark and Gurney with tyre troubles. Foyt won, in a Watson roadster, from Ward in a rear-engined Watson car.

As in 1963, the Lotus was proved at Milwaukee, where Parnelli Jones gained a flag-to-flag victory in one of the Indianapolis 34s, running, ironically, as an Agajanian entry.

The result which had been inevitable since 1963 was achieved in 1965, when Jim Clark won in a Lotus, the first foreign combination to take the 500 since 1916, when Italian expatriate Dario Resta won in a Peugeot. In this race there were 17 cars with Ford engines behind their cockpits, 10 with rear-mounted Offenhausers. Louis Meyer was now taking over responsibility for the Ford V-8s, which on methanol fuel were producing up to 500 bhp.

Foyt took the pole position at 161·23 mph, from Clark in a Lotus 38 and Gurney. Foyt put up the only challenge to Clark, and once he retired with transmission failure, the Scot won almost as he pleased. He led for 190 of the 200 laps, aided by the outstanding Lotus pit work, in the hands of the Woods brothers (at Clark's first fuel stop, for 50 gallons, the Lotus was at a standstill for just under 20 seconds). In spite of new regulations, introduced after fires in the 1964 race, which restricted the fuel capacity of cars to 75 gallons, imposed a minimum of two pit stops, and required gravity refuelling, Clark averaged over 150 mph (150·686 mph) for the first time in the history of the race. Parnelli Jones was second, 118 seconds behind, and Mario Andretti third, in his first big-time race, driving a Brawner-Ford (in effect, a copy of a Brabham).

In 1965, too, most of the major oval-track championship events, eight of 13, went to Ford-powered

cars. So inevitably these were numerically dominant in the 50th 500, in 1966. The Offenhauser, which in 1965 had not powered the winning car for the first time in 19 races, was nevertheless showing remarkable evergreen qualities, and appeared in new turbocharged and supercharged 2·8 litre forms (these developed up to 600 bhp, compared with the 450 bhp of the 'standard' Offy, and the 520 bhp of the Ford V-8s). Once again a multiple collision – only yards after the start – meant that a 500 was stopped and restarted. When it was properly under way, Lloyd Ruby appeared to take command in an Eagle (Dan Gurney's new marque), but he was black-flagged for losing oil, and another newcomer from the Grand Prix world, Jackie Stewart, took over the lead in a Lola.

A failed oil pump side-lined Stewart on the 191st lap, and Graham Hill came through to win in another Lola, ahead of a surprised Clark, who had been misled by a lap-scoring error in the Lotus pit, and finished thinking he had won. McElreath was third in a Brabham Ford.

By 1967 the track racing fraternity had become accustomed to rear-engined cars, the European Grand Prix stars were by no means so prominent, although Gurney was second-fastest qualifier in one of his Eagles, and the Offenhauser revival was progressing. But into this scene of hardly-digested novelty, Andy Granatelli introduced a new STP Oil Treatment Special, the Paxton turbine engined car. This had a Pratt and Whitney helicopter turbine, for this new role delivering some 550 bhp, mounted to the left of the cockpit, and driving all four wheels through a Ferguson transmission. And unlike the turbine cars entered in 1962 and 1966, this one worked.

Parnelli Jones led in the turbine from the start, for 18 laps. Then it rained, and the race was stopped. When it was restarted on the following day, the STP car ran away from the field, apart from a short spell when Jones spun to avoid another car and Gurney took the lead. It appeared set to win clearly, but with three laps to go a bearing failed in the transmission, so that the device was classified only sixth. Foyt won again, at 151·208 mph in a Lotus 38-based Coyote-Ford, from Unser's Lola-Ford. The only GP driver to finish was Hulme, fourth in an Eagle.

The aftermath was a hasty amendment to the regulations, intended to cut the turbine down to size by reducing the permitted area of the annulus, or engine air intake, a blazing row between Granatelli and the USAC, and more turbine cars in 1968. Shelby withdrew his during practice, but three STP cars started. These were Lotus 56 'wedge-bodied' rear-engined machines, and in a repeat of the 1967 situation, one of these led into the last ten laps, then failed (Lotus' unused spare car was later to appear in Formula 1 guise). In 1968 Bobby Unser won the 500

*Mario Andretti in the outwardly cumbersome Ford-engined Hawk
which he drove to victory in the 1969 500, and (below) taking the
lead at the start of the race.*

Wedge noses, and overall aerodynamic efficiency, are very evident on these two significant cars, neither of which actually won the 500, for which they were primarily intended. Left: Peter Revson in the 1971 Offenhauser-engined McLaren M16. Right: Graham Hill in the Pratt and Whitney gas turbine powered Lotus 56, which also had four-wheel drive on Ferguson principles.

in an Eagle, powered by a turbocharged 171 cu in Offy, at 152·88 mph. Dan Gurney was second in an Eagle with a stock block Ford V-8 (newly provided for in the rules, stock block power units were admitted with a maximum capacity of 305 cu in, 5 litres), while Hulme was again fourth, in an Eagle with an unsupercharged Ford racing engine of 255 cu in (4·2 litres).

The regulations dealt even more harshly with turbines in 1969, and effectively stifled further development in that direction, just as four wheel drive was to be put down after that year's race. Of the four wheel drive cars which appeared for the 1969 race, the STP Lotus 64s showed enormous potential, but were withdrawn after a practice accident resulting from a hub casting failure; three Lola T150s and a Lotus 56 rebuilt with an Offenhauser engine qualified to start, two of the Lolas on rows one and two. In the line-up, 30 of the cars had turbocharged Ford or Offenhauser 2·8 litre engines, while there were two Repco-engined Brabham BT25s and Gurney's stock-block Ford-engined Eagle.

At the end of 500 miles, Mario Andretti won for Granatelli in a Hawk-Ford, at 156·87 mph, while Bobby Unser placed one of the four-wheel drive Lolas second and Gurney was third. Jack Brabham completed only 58 laps, but Peter Revson brought the second Brabham into sixth place (so to the varied machinery which has finished the 500 over the years was added an Australian engine).

The rear-engined car with Ford or Offenhauser turbocharged engine was the Indianapolis norm in 1970, when all the front-row drivers qualified at over 170 mph, with Al Unser taking pole in a Colt-Ford at 170·22 mph. He won the race, too, at 155·75 mph from Mark Donohue in a Lola T153 and Dan Gurney in an Eagle, the first Offenhauser-engined car to finish.

Within the now-accepted pattern, new standards were set by the McLaren M16 in 1971, although as had so often been the case in the past, the pace-setting car failed to win the race, then confirmed its Indianapolis promise in a lesser track event within weeks (at Pocono). The McLaren was light, neat and aerodynamically efficient, and the three entered were on the first two rows after qualifying, with Peter Revson on pole with a four-lap average of 178·69 mph. Mark Donohue led for a quarter of the race, until the gearbox of his M16 failed, and at the end Al Unser won again, the first driver to do so in consecutive years since 1953–54, in a car which was a replica of his 1970 Colt-Ford. Revson was 23 seconds down in his M16, and A. J. Foyt placed a Coyote-Ford third.

During the decade since rear engines came to Indianapolis as a real force, many of the old Brickyard traditions had been eroded, the outward face of the race radically altered, and a repetitive chain sequence of innovate, imitate, set up. Restriction by regulation at the end of the 1960s limited originality again, but detail refinement saw to it that speeds continued to increase in the Memorial Day classic. This became but one of three major 500-mile USAC races in 1971, the other two being run at the new Pocono and Ontario tracks, which basically are more sophisticated than the Brickyard. However, although they may be of theoretically equal ranking, these races are unlikely to displace the Indianapolis 500 as the pre-eminent track race.

The Return of Power

At the end of 1963 the CSI surprisingly reversed their usual post-war policy of restraining Grand Prix performance potential by progressively limiting engine sizes, and proposed a 3 litre formula to come into effect in 1966. This time there was no dissent, for although the 1·5 litre cars had proved to be remarkably fast around any given circuit, a 'return to power' was welcomed.

Broadly, an upper capacity limit for unsupercharged engines of 3 litres was laid down, perhaps in the hope that the USAC might adopt it. Provision was also made for 1·5 litre supercharged engines, but the obligation to use pump fuels meant that this alternative was academic – 'exotic' fuels are essential if a supercharged engine is to give similar power to a normally aspirated unit of twice the capacity. Rotary engines were also allowed for, although none appeared in practice, as were gas turbines, and eventually a turbine-powered Grand Prix car did appear. The minimum weight of cars was initially set at 500 kg.

During the life of the formula it was to be altered in detail several times, once in great haste, when the aerodynamic aids unforeseen when the rules were drawn up were abruptly restricted following a series of incidents and accidents. A fundamental mechanical restriction was applied when the formula was at mid-term, when the number of engine cylinders was limited to twelve. Under this formula the pace of tyre development was of increasing importance. Tyres grew wider and wider, to a stage where the cross section of a racing tyre was near-square. Hand in hand, tyre compounds kept pace with the increasing power of engines through their qualities of adhesion, although drivers were to find that when pressed to the limits of their lateral adhesion they could 'break away' alarmingly suddenly. These tyres required changes in suspension geometry, as variations in camber could not be tolerated and ideally suspension movements were confined to the vertical plane.

Aerodynamics were to be used as a positive aid to road-holding and to putting power onto the road in the late 1960s, in this succeeding to such an extent that when the four-wheel drive which the pundits insisted would be essential to make effective use of the 400 bhp expected of engines was essayed it proved to give no worthwhile advantages.

Away from the technical aspects, and in common with other sports, commercial pressures increased, and an age of gaudy sponsorship which Grand Prix followers would hitherto have thought appropriate to US track racing came to the traditional road circuits. Some of these circuits were to fall into disuse, too, or be radically altered as a new safety-conscious wave swept through racing.

Thus in many respects the 3 litre formula saw more changes in the face of racing than any other. But in its opening season racing proceeded much as before, with the familiar drivers in cars usually painted in traditional colours, racing over the customary circuits at speeds not much higher than those achieved by 1·5 litre machines.

Before the formula even came into effect, most British constructors received an enormous setback: early in 1965 Coventry Climax announced their intention to withdraw from racing, at the end of the 1·5 litre formula that year. Apart from a pair of special 2 litre V-8s prepared as stand-in engines for Jim Clark, this decision was carried through, and the constructors who had relied upon Climax power had to look elsewhere. But work began on a new British V-8, which was to dominate the Grands Prix. . . .

One thing appeared abundantly clear before the first season of the new formula opened, that as in 1961

Simplicity pays dividends – Jack Brabham in his Repco-Brabham BT20, which he drove to win the 1966 Championships (above). Power personified – but with obvious bulk, complexity and weight: the first 3 litre Honda (right).

Ferraris were favourites, being prepared when other teams were not. After being left behind in chassis design by the enormous strides forward in 1962, the Scuderia had almost got back onto terms in this aspect during the remaining three seasons of 1·5 litre racing. Now Ferrari were well-placed to exploit their enormous resources of experience with V-12 engines, and as always had the capability to produce race-worthy new power units very quickly.

In fact the 312 engine was hardly new, being a 60 degree V-12 derived from the twin ohc (per bank) 3·3 litre sports car unit, appropriately reduced in capacity to 2978 cc (77 × 53·5 mm), and in 1966 producing some 330 bhp. This was mounted in a workmanlike semi-monocoque, semi-space frame chassis. A similar car, in fact a 1965 chassis, was powered by the 2·4 litre six-cylinder engine, an up-dated 265 bhp version of the unit used in the last years of the 2·5 litre formula. This was one of the few 1966 machines to be near the 500 kg minimum weight limit. Thus Ferrari appeared well-equipped for all types of circuits.

However, on the first day of January 1966 another 3-litre car led the South African Grand Prix for most of its distance, a Brabham of very modest specifica-

tion. Less than a year earlier, it had seemed unlikely that Brabham would be able to contest the 3-litre Grands Prix, but he fell back on his association with the Australian Repco engineering firm, which had already set in train plans to build a simple lightweight V-8 replacement for the ageing Coventry Climax FPF engines which were the backbone of Tasman racing. Designed by Phil Irving and Ron Hallam, this was based on the light alloy Oldsmobile F85 block, and there were no problems in stretching it to serve as a 3 litre GP engine. A single ohc V-8 (88·9 × 60·3 mm), it produced only 300 bhp, at 8000 rpm, by the middle of 1966; but it was light and simple, with excellent torque characteristics and no great thirst for fuel.

This Repco engine was installed in two Tauranac chassis, BT19 and BT20, both closely similar (the former had in fact been built for the never-raced Coventry Climax 16 cylinder engine, the latter was the definitive 1966 car). These had space frames evolved from that of the original GP Brabham, and thus tried and known even if lacking in sophistication, and rigidity. The suspension was equally straightforward, with twin wishbones, coil springs and anti-roll bar at the front, lower wishbones and upper links, radius rods, coil springs and unit-roll bar at the rear.

If the Brabham was an object lesson in simplicity and lightness, the T81 monocoque with which Cooper briefly returned to the Grand Prix forefront was notable for its bulk and excess weight, at least until a Honda set new overweight standards late in 1966. Cooper's search for an engine had taken them to Maserati, through a group association with the British concessionaires for the Italian company, and to the V-12 which had its origins in the engine raced in the Grands Prix of 1957. This was of course appropriately increased in capacity (to 75·2 × 56 mm, 2998 cc), and appeared considerably less cluttered with ancillaries than in its earlier life. Nothing, however, could disguise its size and weight, to offset its 315 bhp (at 9500 rpm).

BRM produced an equally massive and considerably more complex engine halfway through the season, an H-16. In effect, this comprised two opposed piston eights (in fundamentals substantially derived from the successful V-8), mounted one above the other and driving through connected crankshafts to a six-speed gearbox. On the bench, this engine developed 400 bhp early in its life; on the circuits it was to be a constant source of problems. Behind the rear bulkhead of the

BRM P83 the H-16 served a load-bearing function, carrying the rear suspension, as it did in the Lotus 43. In the early-season races, and for some time alongside the H16, BRM raced their earlier cars, with the V-8 enlarged to 2 litres, to give 260 bhp at 11,500 rpm.

Team Lotus, the pace-setting team of the preceding formula, was in a curious position, and in 1966 was forced to use either the special 2 litre Coventry Climax V-8s, or the bulky BRM H-16 (in the 43) while a new power unit was prepared for them.

Two more leading drivers emerged as Grand Prix constructors in 1966, Bruce McLaren and Dan Gurney. Robin Herd's extremely clever McLaren M2B had a novel stressed skin hull formed in Mallite, a 'sandwich' material of two layers of aluminium bonded to balsa wood. This made for an extremely rigid structure, and it was of little account that this was also bulky, for it was thus matched to the power units which sadly let down the project. These were a

Among challengers to Brabham (opposite, top, driven by Hulme) in the first 3 litre years were Cooper, with a bulky Maserati engine (above) and McLaren, initially with a modified version of the Ford Indianapolis V-8 (left).

279

*Above: Richie Ginther testing the Honda RA 273. Right: The
'36-valve' Ferrari which Ludovico Scarfiotti drove to win the 1966
Italian Grand Prix. Below: BRM P83s, with the H-16 engine, in
front of the Monaco pits, with a 2 litre BRM on the left.*

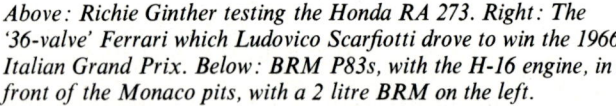

destroked version of the Ford 'Indianapolis' V-8, which produced a great deal of noise, but only just over 300 bhp with outstanding unreliability, and a Seremissima V-8, which produced less power, but did so slightly more reliably, and with a lot less noise.

The AAR Eagle was nominally American, although the initials were to be more accurately rendered Anglo-American. Dan Gurney was the moving force behind this project, and Len Terry's monocoque design was perhaps the most handsome car to race on the GP circuits in 1966, well proportioned despite its size (which was due in part to the intention to use the same hull in a USAC track car). For most of the season it was powered by the Coventry Climax 2·7 litre 'four', while the Weslake-designed 60 degree V-12 for which it was designed was completed.

This did not appear until the last Championship race in Europe, where the 3 litre Honda also made its debut. This was an excessively heavy machine, weighing in at nearly 750 kg. Its raucous V-12 was unquestionably powerful, probably producing more honest bhp than any other 1966 GP engine, but that weight was a great handicap.

After coming within an ace of winning in South Africa in his BT19, Jack Brabham did win the Silverstone International Trophy, in no uncertain fashion at 116·06 mph from Surtees' V-12 Ferrari and Bonnier's Cooper. Two weeks earlier, Surtees had driven the V-12 Ferrari to win the Syracuse Grand Prix, from his team mate Lorenzo Bandini in the smaller V-6 Ferrari.

This car proved well-suited to the Monaco circuit for the first Championship race of the new formula, but despite their apparent capacity handicap the V-8 BRMs were even better machines on the day, and of course the British team had the upper hand in driving talent. This proved to be a race of attrition, and only four cars were racing as it ended, Stewart's BRM (77·29 mph), Bandini's V-6 Ferrari, Hill's BRM and Bondurant's BRM.

The Belgian Grand Prix provided the result generally expected, a victory for a 3 litre V-12 Ferrari. This was driven by John Surtees and he finished 42·1 seconds ahead of Rindt, who drove a gallant race in a Cooper. It was not, however, a result from which any conclusions could be drawn, as unexpected rain swept across the circuit during the first lap, and the inevitable spins, gyrations and accidents eliminated half the field.

It also proved to be Surtees' last race for Ferrari, for he tired of political machinations and after an odd episode at Le Mans quit the team. Through this the Scuderia almost certainly lost one, possibly two, World Championships, while Surtees suffered further frustrations, and eventually a new marque was born. So the French Grand Prix saw Surtees in a Cooper-Maserati cockpit.

Above: Jo Siffert accelerating a Cooper-Maserati out of the Gasworks hairpin at Monaco. Below: Dan Gurney in his handsome Grand Prix Eagle, and (bottom) its Weslake designed V-12.

It also saw the first race start for a BRM H-16 engine, ironically in a Lotus, not a BRM. Bandini pulled out a handsome lead in a Ferrari, but lost it when his throttle cable failed, and so Jack Brabham gained the first-ever *grande épreuve* victory for a driver in a car bearing his own name. His speed at Rheims was 136·90 mph, making this with one freak exception the fastest *grande épreuve* ever run, and he was followed by Parkes (Ferrari), Hulme (Brabham), Rindt and Gurney, gaining a Championship point in his Eagle.

No Ferraris appeared at Brands Hatch for the British Grand Prix, and Brabham led from flag to flag (at 95·49 mph); he was followed by Hulme, and the Brabham pair lapped the third driver, Graham Hill. In Holland Brabham won again, after a valiant challenge by Jim Clark in a Lotus 33, who was poorly rewarded with a third place behind Hill after a pit stop. Brabham's fourth consecutive victory came at the Nürburgring, at 86·64 mph from Surtees and Rindt in Cooper-Maseratis, and Hill and Stewart in 2 litre BRMs. As in Holland, Ferrari achieved only sixth place – the pre-season favourite was not living up to expectations, and Brabham was scoring by the positive virtues of lightness and simplicity rather than by the defaults of other teams.

Brabham won only one other race in 1966, the non-Championship Oulton Park Gold Cup, but he quite clearly won the Championship – a quite remarkable achievement with resources so modest as to appear inadequate. He did not finish in the Italian Grand Prix at Monza, where as so often new machinery appeared, and where the speed promise of the 3 litre formula was at last fulfilled – 16 of the 20 cars on the grid bettered the lap record in practice.

Among them was the Honda, seventh fastest in the hands of Richie Ginther, an Eagle at last fitted with its V-12, which was plagued with fuel and electrical system problems throughout the meeting, Ferraris with revised 36-valve engines for which 385 bhp was claimed, and which took the first two places on the grid, and the Lotus 43 with which Clark was third-fastest qualifier. Here, too, Dunlop's fortunes reached their nadir, for only one car wore tyres made by the company which had equipped all but one winner in the previous formula.

In the first half of the race the lead changed hands between Ferrari, Brabham, Honda and Cooper drivers, but throughout the second half was firmly held by Ludovico Scarfiotti, who became the first Italian to win the race since 1952. His speed was 135·48 mph, an improvement of 5 mph on the record speed set in 1965.

The American Grand Prix result came as a surprise, for few people ever expected a BRM H-16 to run untroubled through a race. Those in the BRM team cars at Watkins Glen did not, but Clark's in a Lotus did, and he won at 114·94 mph from Rindt, Surtees and Siffert in Cooper-Maseratis. In the Mexican Grand Prix, Surtees snatched victory from Brabham and Hulme, and thus became runner-up in the Championship.

The 1966 season had been one of mixed fortunes, although with a clear cut result, which was generally attributed to personal achievement and a dash of opportuneness. It hardly seemed likely that the straightforward Brabham approach could pay off again in 1967 – only some 330 bhp was claimed for the Repco engine, whereas most other power units were developed through the winter to give around 400 bhp.

The Repco engine was refined in detail, to lose most traces of its Oldsmobile origins, and was installed in the BT24, which was as unremarkable in sophistication as its forerunners. BRM persevered with the H-16, the while working on a V-12 which had been initiated as a sports car engine and was to make its Grand Prix debut in the McLaren M5 late in the year (Bruce spent most of the season waiting for it, and in the early events raced an M4B F2 car modified to accept a 2 litre BRM V-8).

Power seemed to reside with three V-12s. Ferrari started the season with the 36-valve unit and finished it with a 48-valve V-12, in common with Eagle and Honda. Ferrari used the 1966 car initially, and a new lighter model from mid-season – the singular was often appropriate to Ferrari race entries, as for much of the season the Scuderia was reduced to running a pair of cars for one driver, Chris Amon (Lorenzo Bandini was killed in an accident at Monaco, Michael Parkes was injured at Spa, while Scarfiotti left the team).

The Gurney-Weslake Eagle engine produced 415 bhp at 10,000 rpm, and few of Gurney's misfortunes could be attributed to it. The Honda V-12 produced power – at least 400 bhp at 11,000 rpm – but still not enough to compensate for the weight of the car; under pressure from John Surtees, who drove the Japanese car in 1967, a new Lola-influenced car was built during the summer. The Cooper and the Maser-

ati engine were revised, but apart from a lucky win in the year's opening race, the combination was never competitive or reliable.

On paper, 1967 should have been a V-12 year, but in fact in the championship races teams using V-12s won three races of eleven. Four fell to Repco-engined cars, four to cars with a new V-8 which had 'Ford' cast into its rocker covers. . . .

That power unit did not appear until June, however, and until then the Grands Prix seemed to be settling down after the first almost tentative 3-litre season. Most of the principal drivers retired during the South African GP at Kyalami, so that local driver John Love worked his way through to the lead in an old Cooper-Climax, only to have to stop for fuel with seven laps to go, and finish second behind the Cooper-Maserati driven by Pedro Rodriguez. This, incidentally, was the last Grand Prix victory for a Cooper.

Before the European season opened, Scottish drivers contested the Tasman races to good effect, Clark winning four races in a Lotus Climax and Stewart two in a BRM, leaving only one to a native-born driver, Jack Brabham. In the European preliminaries honours were well-distributed. Gurney drove his Eagle to victory over Bandini's Ferrari and Siffert's Cooper in the Brands Hatch Race of Champions; Brabham and Hulme placed their Brabhams first and second in the Oulton Park Spring Cup, ahead of Surtees' Honda; Parkes took the Silverstone International Trophy in a Ferrari, ahead of Brabham and Siffert, and finished the Syracuse GP in a dead heat with his team mate Scarfiotti.

Ferrari's season-long troubles began at Monaco, where Bandini died in a ghastly accident. Amon placed the other red car third – the first of four such placings he was to achieve in 1967, the best of the year for Ferrari. Hulme won that race, at 75.89 mph and by a clear lap from the 2-litre BRM V-8-engined Lotus driven by Hill.

Before the Dutch GP, Ford unveiled the Cosworth DFV engine, which was the second stage of a £100,000 commission to Keith Duckworth, and although that sum was by no means the sum of Ford's involvement, in isolation or total context it must have represented one of the best buys ever in motor racing. Duckworth's DFV (Double Four Valve) was a compact, neat and essentially straightforward 90 degree V-8 (85.74 × 64.77 mm). Intended from the outset to be a load-bearing member, it was short, although not particularly narrow (that dimension was less important), and its ancillaries were designed onto it rather than hung around it as afterthoughts. It immediately met Duckworth's self-imposed target of 400 bhp, and later in 1967 was rated at 410 bhp at 9000 rpm.

The DFV originated from Colin Chapman's approach to Harley Copp and Walter Hayes of Ford

John Surtees in the Honda RA300 with which he won the 1967 Italian Grand Prix. Opposite: Andrea de Adamich testing a Ferrari at the end of the same year.

after Coventry Climax had announced their withdrawal, and was initially specifically intended for a Lotus. This car was the 49, in which designer Maurice Phillippe made no radical departures. It was a straightforward monocoque, in which the hull ended at the rear bulkhead; the engine was attached to this at four points, while the rear suspension was attached to the rear of the engine through triangulated frames.

Team Lotus raced their 49s first in the Dutch Grand Prix, where Hill was fastest in practice, and led the race for ten laps before retiring. Brabham took over the lead for only five laps, and he was then passed by Clark, who led to the flag to give the Lotus-Ford a triumphant debut.

For the rest of the season, Team Lotus enjoyed mixed fortunes – the DFV suffered very few teething troubles, the Lotus rather too many. But there was little doubt that the Lotus-Ford set a new standard.

In the Belgian Grand Prix cars with multi-cylinder engines took the first five places. As such a result was not to be repeated in the following seasons, it is worth recording: Gurney (Eagle V-12), 145·99 mph; Stewart (BRM H-16); Amon (Ferrari V-12); Rindt (Cooper-Maserati V-12); Spence (BRM H-16). Once Clark had lost his early lead at a pit stop, Stewart took over and got an H-16 BRM as near to winning a race as one was ever to come. But Stewart had gearchange problems, and gave way to Gurney, who thus became the first American in a car which was at least nominally American to win a European Grand Prix since Murphy in 1921.

Financial and political pressures took the French GP to a silly little circuit 'round the car parks' at Le Mans, where Brabham and Hulme scored a Brabham 1-2. At Silverstone Clark and Hill dominated the British GP, until a screw worked loose in the rear suspension of Hill's Lotus, which left Clark to win at 117·64 mph from Hulme and Amon. Both Lotus failed again at Nürburgring, and so, heart-breakingly, did Gurney's Eagle when he was leading comfortably on the 13th of 15 laps. This left Hulme and Brabham to score another 1-2. It appeared even more likely that Brabham simplicity was going to take the Championships again when Brabham and Hulme took the first two places in a rain-soaked Canadian Grand Prix at Mosport (when their strongest challenge came from McLaren, giving the BRM V-12 its first race).

Two weeks later the Grand Prix circus was back in Europe, at Monza for an intensely dramatic Italian Grand Prix. For this, Ferrari produced their 48-valve 312, but even at Monza only one car (the only ranking Italian driver, Scarfiotti, drove an Eagle, while the up and coming de Adamich was in a Cooper and Baghetti in a Lotus-Ford). Honda and John Surtees produced their Lola-inspired, British-built, Honda. In the race the superiority of the Lotus-Ford was clearly demonstrated, Clark leading until a tyre punctured and he lost a lap while a wheel was changed. Then Hill built up a lead of nearly a lap, but his engine died. Clark actually pulled back that whole lap to regain the lead in a stupendous virtuoso drive, only to be thwarted when the Lotus fuel pumps failed to pick up the last two gallons in the tanks. As he coasted towards the finish, Brabham and Surtees repassed him, Surtees snatching the lead at the exit from the last corner, to win by half a length, at 140·51 mph.

The Lotus 49s gained a 1-2 in the American Grand Prix, and in so doing provided Ford of America with sufficient publicity to amply justify at one blow the Ford of Britain 'investment' in Grand Prix racing! For their victory, Team Lotus were greatly indebted to good fortune, for Hill drove most of the race with

The complex BRM H-16 engine, which contrasts markedly with the neat and smooth appearance of the Lotus 25B of the previous formula (opposite top). Below: Chris Amon in a '48 valve' 1969 Ferrari. Opposite, centre: one of the last of the true private owner-drivers in Grand Prix racing, Bob Anderson in his Climax-engined Brabham. Bottom: Bruce McLaren in the 2 litre BRM V-8-engined McLaren M4B.

an inoperative clutch, faulty gear selector and sundry lesser problems, to finish second, and Clark covered the last two laps with a broken suspension mounting and the attached rear wheel at an odd angle.

Clark won the Mexican Grand Prix, his fourth of the year, but finished only third in the Championship; Brabham was second at Mexico City, and was Championship runner-up; Hulme finished third, and took the Championship.

In the late autumn, the Spanish Grand Prix was revived on the artificial, barrier-enclosed Jarama circuit, which satisfied few people yet in a changing climate of opinion about safety and spectator facilities seemed to point to the race circuits of the future. The race, incidentally, gave Clark and Hill a walkover 1-2.

Meanwhile, in the summer of 1967 a decision had been taken which was to determine the outcome of most Grands Prix for the next few seasons. Ford agreed that Cosworth should make the DFV available to other Grand Prix teams.

Cosworth Domination

In the opening race of 1968, in South Africa, it seemed that no more than logical progress would be made in the third year of the 3 litre formula. But 1968 was to be a year of change, of tragedies and triumphs, and of almost complete Ford domination, through Cosworth in Formula 1, and reflected in most other racing classes.

At Kyalami most teams presented little-changed machinery – the Brabham, Cooper, Eagle, Honda, Lotus and McLaren cars were all more or less as they had been at the end of 1967, while Ferrari returned in force with a three-car team. Only BRM of the established marques had a new car, a monocoque designed by Len Terry and powered by the V-12 engine, for which 390 bhp was claimed. There were also two Matras on the grid, an F2 car entered by the French company, and an interim Matra MS9 entered by Matra International.

This in fact was Ken Tyrrell's team, and the MS9 was a 1967 F2 car modified to accept a Cosworth DFV, the first to be installed in anything but a Lotus. The largely British Matra International team, using MS10 and MS80 Matras, was to be mainly responsible for reviving French Grand Prix glories. . . .

Jim Clark was on pole position of the Kyalami grid, Hill and Stewart in the MS9 sharing the front row with him. As an indication of things to come, Stewart led the first lap, and held second place for the next 26; he retired when his engine failed, and Clark and Hill won clearly for Team Lotus, from Rindt, having his first race in the Brabham team. This was Clark's 25th World Championship race victory, so that he surpassed Fangio's record. It was also his last.

Jim Clark never raced again in a Formula 1 car, although with a Lotus 49T he won the 1968 Tasman Championship, scoring four victories to the two achieved in the series by Amon in a Ferrari and the single races which fell to McLaren in a BRM and Courage in a McLaren. Jim Clark's last victory came

in the Australian Grand Prix at Sandown Park, when he narrowly beat Amon. He did not race in Britain again, for in April 1968 he died in an accident which has never been satisfactorily explained, driving a Formula 2 Lotus 48 at Hockenheim.

For the only two preliminary races run in 1968, the McLaren team also had DFV engines, and used them

A new name came into Grand Prix racing in 1967 – Ford, cast into the rocker covers of Duckworth's brilliant DFV engine (above). It was first mounted in the Lotus 49 (below).

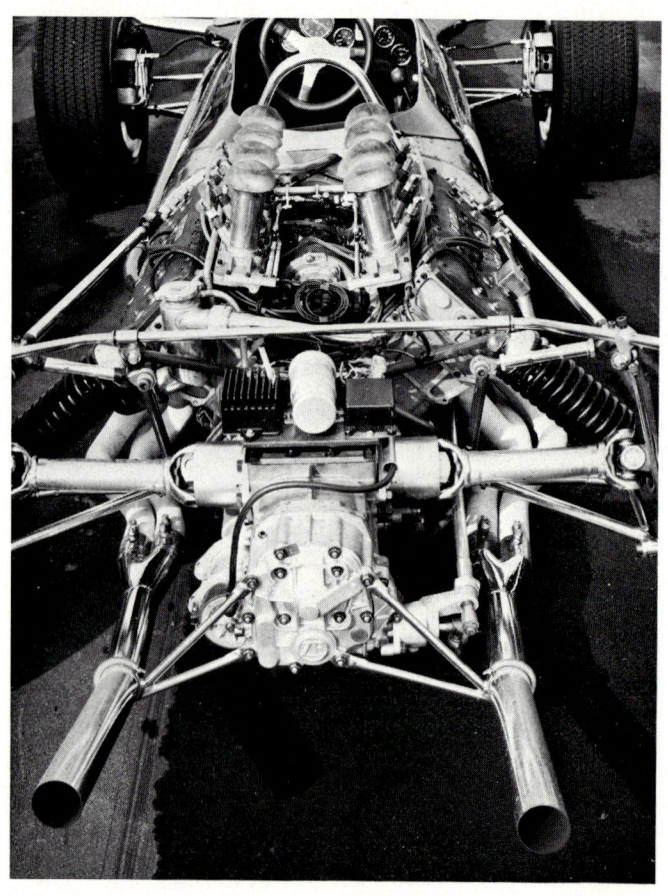

to good effect to win both at Brands Hatch (McLaren) and Silverstone (Hulme). In the Race of Champions, the full colours of an 'outside' sponsor were carried on a Grand Prix car for the first time, on the revised Lotus 49 driven by Graham Hill, now entered by Gold Leaf Team Lotus.

This team arrived for the Spanish GP with only one driver, and very subdued, for Mike Spence had been killed while testing a Lotus at Indianapolis. The further revised 'wedge-tail' 49, which unwittingly foreshadowed imminent aerodynamic developments, was therefore not raced, and Hill used his earlier 49. The Honda entry was a refined version of the mid-1967 car, weighing nearly 1300 lb – still well over the limit – but now with a claimed 430 bhp to propel it. The Brabham team had one new Repco 860 twin ohc engine, which reputedly produced 375 bhp, but blew up in practice, thus accurately indicating the dismal Brabham season that was to come.

The BRMs were V-12-engined P126s, for the H-16 had been firmly set aside. The Cooper T86B also used the BRM V-12, for which 400 bhp at 10,000 rpm was now rather optimistically claimed. Jackie Stewart was not entered, for a minor injury sustained in an F2 race

Jim Clark on his way to a first-time-out victory for the Lotus 49, in the Dutch Grand Prix, closely followed by Denny Hulme in a Brabham.

kept him out of racing for a short, and as it transpired possibly vital, period; Beltoise therefore joined Tyrrell's team for this race, while waiting for the Matra Sports Matra V-12 to be readied.

Rodriguez led, Beltoise led, Amon led, and all three retired, which left Hill to fend off Hulme and gain a timely victory for Team Lotus. Redman and Scarfiotti brought Cooper-BRMs into rather flattering third and fourth places.

Hill went on to gain his fourth victory in the Monaco GP, in the wedge-tail Lotus 49B, at 77·82 mph from Attwood in a BRM and two plodding Coopers (Bianchi and Scarfiotti) which were two laps down. Here the V-12 Matra MS11 made its shrieking debut, racing for 12 laps before Beltoise ran out of road. This car was the end-product of French Government benevolence, or more accurately a massive cash 'loan' towards the end of demonstrating French technology on the circuits of the world. It was a straightforward monocoque, and its engine an untidy V-12, which produced a great deal of noise and, perhaps, 400 bhp at 10,000 rpm.

An aerodynamic trend which was to gallop ahead of itself started at Spa – wings. The Ferraris and Brabhams appeared with small fixed aerodynamic devices over their gearboxes. These attempts to gain aerodynamic downthrust were not new in principal, or

Grand Prix stars of the late 1960s (opposite, from left to right and top to bottom): Graham Hill, Chris Amon, Jackie Ickx, Jack Brabham with Ron Tauranac, Bruce McLaren, Mario Andretti with

Colin Chapman. Above and below: Brands Hatch scenes in 1966, Rindt and Ligier in Cooper-Maseratis, and Brabham taking the flag.

application – May had experimented with a wing on a Porsche, Chaparrals had raced with them, and Bruce McLaren had tried one on his M2A test single-seater in 1965 (for the 1968 Belgian GP his team used simpler tail spoilers). The race was surprisingly won by McLaren, too, at the end unbeknown to its driver, Bruce McLaren! Amon led initially – as was to happen often during the season – Surtees took over, Hulme led a lap, Stewart led until the penultimate lap, when he had to stop for fuel. So McLaren, expecting to finish second, won at 147·14 mph, from Rodriguez' BRM. Bruce thus became the second driver to win a World Championship race in a car bearing its driver's name.

The Dutch GP saw the first major race victory for a French car since Behra's in a Gordini at Rheims in 1952. At Zandvoort, in a rain-soaked race, this was scored by Stewart in a Cosworth-powered MS10, at 84·66 mph from Jean-Pierre Beltoise in a V-12 Matra (which turned out to be the best performance for that car for some time to come).

The French GP saw the only break in the Ford-

Left: Jim Clark, here followed by Stewart in the first F1 Matra, in the 1968 South African GP. Above: 'biplane' aerofoils on Rob Walker's Lotus 49, driven at Brands Hatch by Jo Siffert.

Cosworth domination in the season. The Ferrari team gambled that the roads would remain wet throughout the race, and started one car with 'wet' tyres, while the other teams fitted 'dry' or 'intermediate' tyres (the differences being in compounds as well as treads). It stayed wet, so Belgian Jackie Ickx was able to score a welcome victory for Ferrari (at 100·45 mph), ahead of Surtees' Honda, Stewart's Matra and Elford's Cooper.

This race was tragic. Honda insisted their new RA302 be raced, to back up a French sales campaign and despite Surtees' protests that it was not raceworthy. This distinctly novel car had an air-cooled 120 degree V-8 engine, suspended from a 'beam' member extending from the main hull, to which the gearbox and rear suspension were also mounted. The cockpit was further forward than in contemporary single-seaters, and the RA302 was hung about with air intakes and coolers – all in all, not a handsome device. Jo Schlesser, inexperienced in this class, was nominated to drive it, and on the third race lap he lost control in a fast curve and crashed against a bank. The wreck burned fiercely, and Schlesser had no hope of escape.

This Rouen meeting also saw the first potentially serious accident attributable to 'wings'. Colin Chapman had turned to these devices after the Dutch GP, and characteristically had done so more thoroughly than other teams. Lotus aerofoils were large, and mounted directly to the rear suspension – there is, after all, little point in applying downthrust to a complete chassis, as Ferrari, Brabham and McLaren were doing. The downthrust of the Lotus 'wings' was calculated to be 400 lb at 150 mph, at some small cost in drag. An unforeseen side effect seemed to be exposed when Lotus driver Jackie Oliver crashed in French

Cooper's last Grand Prix car used the BRM V-12 engine (above), while Matra's first 'all Matra' GP car was this MS11, which made its debut at Monaco in the hands of Jean-Pierre Beltoise.

GP practice, apparently when the airstream over his 'wing' was disturbed as he trailed another car.

Nevertheless, Lotus persevered with their large wings, and all the 49Bs in the British GP carried them. All three 49Bs led the race, too, but the works cars fell out, leaving Jo Siffert to win in Rob Walker's private 49B (at 104·83 mph). Amon and Ickx placed Ferraris second and third.

The German GP was run at Nürburgring in atrocious conditions of rain and fog, and won very clearly by the combination of Stewart, the Matra-Ford and Dunlop rain tyres. Graham Hill in second place was over four minutes behind the Scot. The Italian GP fell to Hulme, who for this high-speed event chose to race his McLaren without 'wings' and their drag (his race speed was 145·41 mph). He took the lead before the half-distance, and only five other drivers completed the race (in a season notable for mechanical unreliability); the only close 'Monza-type' battle in the closing stages was between Servoz-Gavin (Matra-Ford) and Ickx (Ferrari) who finished second and third.

The Canadian GP occupied a more logical place in the calendar, and was run at the picturesque Mont Tremblant circuit, where Hulme and McLaren achieved a McLaren 1-2 ahead of Rodriguez' BRM. Stewart then gained a clear victory in the American GP, from Graham Hill, and therefore the World Championship title was open as the circus moved on to the last race of the year.

In that Mexican GP, Hill, Stewart and Hulme, contenders for the title, for a while occupied the first three places. However, Hulme and Stewart both ran into trouble, leaving Hill to win the race for Lotus and a second World Championship for himself.

In 1969 many technical novelties appeared, but these were not proven through race successes – the outstanding cars at the end of the year were those which had been developed logically through slow evolution. The Ford-Cosworth DFV dominated the season, and powered every race-winning car; the Ferrari and BRM V-12s proved neither competitive nor reliable.

Other possible challengers disappeared. Honda retired from racing, as perforce did Cooper when they were unable to obtain backing for a further season, and Eagle, as Dan Gurney decided to concentrate on American racing. Matra recognized that their V-12 could not be made competitive in its original form, and left Tyrrell to uphold their honour with Matra-Fords. Brabham despaired of the twin ohc Repco engine, and turned to the DFV to power his revised BT26A, the last space-frame car in GP racing. BRM concentrated on a 48-valve version of their V-12, in P138 and from mid-season P139 chassis. The reports of many-cylindered Ferrari engines in unusual formats ('W' was generally suggested) were never con-

*Above: Denny Hulme (McLaren) leading Jackie Ickx (Brabham)
in the 1969 Mexican Grand Prix. Below: the Brabham team, with
Jack leading his Belgian number two, Ickx.*

firmed in metal at race circuits, and although by the autumn Ferrari had a new flat-12 on test, the team relied on the V-12 throughout the racing season.

Cosworth users were Lotus, with the 49B serving another term while a four-wheel drive successor was built, Brabham, McLaren with the M7A and M7C, and Matra with the MS80. For the best DFV engines, 430 bhp at 10,000 rpm was claimed; the Ferrari V-12 had a similar output, while the new BRM V-12 was rather hopefully reported to produce 450 bhp at 10,500 rpm.

The South African GP saw Stewart lead from start to finish, when he headed Hill and Hulme. The Scot then took the Matra to another victory ahead of Hill in the Race of Champions, then Brabham won a saturated International Trophy from Rindt in a Lotus 49B. Thus far in Formula 1 races, Lotus had achieved three second places (their Tasman record was little better in 1969, for Rindt and Hill gained two victories and four second placings in 14 starts, while the championship went to Ferrari driver Chris Amon). For the Spanish GP at Barcelona's Montjuich circuit, the size of the Lotus rear aerofoils was increased, so that they gave an effective downthrust of up to 600 lb. This proved too much for the structures, and their col-

The 1968 British Grand Prix field moving up from the dummy grid to the start, with three Lotus 49s and Amon's Ferrari at the front. Below: Hulme in the Cosworth-engined McLaren M7A in 1969.

293

294

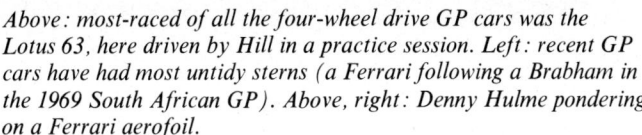

Above: most-raced of all the four-wheel drive GP cars was the Lotus 63, here driven by Hill in a practice session. Left: recent GP cars have had most untidy sterns (a Ferrari following a Brabham in the 1969 South African GP). Above, right: Denny Hulme pondering on a Ferrari aerofoil.

lapses led to Hill and Rindt crashing dramatically, and to the CSI first banning aerofoils, then severely restricting their size and height. Amon looked set to win that race, until his Ferrari engine failed, leaving Stewart to win from McLaren.

At Monaco Graham Hill won for the fifth time, a quite remarkable achievement in the race which every driver wants to win above all others. Piers Courage was a solid second in the independent entrant Frank Williams' Brabham BT26, followed by Lotus 49Bs driven by Siffert and Attwood.

At Zandvoort attention was distracted from the wing controversy by a pair of four-wheel drive cars, the Lotus 63 and the Matra MS84. The Lotus was the more sophisticated of these, and intended as a replacement for the 49B in the front line, whereas the French car was strictly experimental, and run very much as a

second string by Tyrrell's team. Both had DFV engines mounted back to front behind the cockpits, with central gearbox/differential units. Although in their initial public appearance these cars were disappointing, there seemed every reason to assume that they would be developed to raceworthiness, when at some cost in weight, mechanical complication and power loss in transmission, they would have greatly increased powers of traction and, particularly, cornering.

Neither car was raced in the Dutch GP, when Stewart scored another convincing victory, this time from Siffert (Lotus) and Amon (Ferrari) at 111·04 mph. Stewart then won the French GP on the sinuous Clermont-Ferrand circuit, when to the delight of the French crowd his team mate Beltoise followed him past the chequered flag in second place.

A Lotus 63 started in that race, although it did not race very far, and the British GP field included no fewer than four cars with four-wheel drive, two Lotus 63s, the Matra and the McLaren M9A. Completed, but not ready to be raced, was the Cosworth four-wheel drive car (which at one stage might even have been the Ford GP car). Designed by Robin Herd, this

A Lotus 49C, driven by Jochen Rindt.

A BRM P153, photographed at the Bourne works.

A Brabham BT33, driven by Jack Brabham.

A McLaren M14A, driven by Bruce McLaren.

A Ferrari 312B1, driven by Jackie Ickx.

A March 701, driven by Jo Siffert.

was theoretically the most advanced of the four types, but it was never raced, although spasmodic development work continued on it for some time (in 1971 it became part of the Wheatcroft collection, ironically in company with a Cisitalia 360). Advances in suspension and tyre design meant that available power could be effectively put on the road through two wheels; four wheel drive led to excess weight and complication, and power loss in transmission.

That British GP marked the point where disillusionment with four-wheel drive really set in; two of the cars finished, the Matra and a Lotus, in 9th and 10th places remote from the long Stewart-Rindt duel for the lead, and Stewart's eventual 127.25 mph victory over Ickx and McLaren. The best showing for a four-wheel drive car during the year was Rindt's second place in a Lotus 63 in the minor Oulton Park Gold Cup, the best in a Championship event Servoz-Gavin's sixth in the MS84 in the Canadian GP. Then four-wheel drive was forgotten until 1971.

In the German Grand Prix Stewart, the man to beat in 1969, was fairly and squarely beaten by Ickx in a Brabham, but the Scot bounced back to take the Italian GP from Rindt, Beltoise and McLaren in a stirring finish, when 0.19 seconds covered the four cars! Stewart's speed was 146.96 mph. Once again only a single Ferrari started in the Italian GP, driven by Rodriguez, as Amon was thoroughly disillusioned with the V-12 and the new flat 12 had so far suffered only test failures.

The Brabham team scored a first and second, Ickx and Brabham, in the Canadian Grand Prix, and then in the American race Jochen Rindt at last gained the Grand Prix victory which had eluded him for so long. Courage was second, and John Surtees achieved a reasonable result for BRM, in a season troubled by mechanical problems and personnel upheavals in the team, placing a P139 third.

Jackie Stewart had the World Championship sewn up well before the Mexican Grand Prix, where he could finish only fourth behind Hulme's McLaren and Ickx' and Brabham's Brabhams, in a race influenced and decided even more than most by tyre commitments. Stewart's success was shared with the Tyrrell team and Matra, a partnership which was to be split up as the season ended.

The rate of change in the Grand Prix world accelerated during the opening seasons of the 1970s, although it was not as so often in the past forced by changed regulations, but stemmed from tangible developments, and new attitudes and approaches to the sport. There was an influx of new drivers, and as the pendulum swung there were suddenly fewer British drivers in Grand Prix racing than for many years. There was an increasing pre-occupation with circuit safety, although often there was little unanimity of opinion on this score. The truth was to be found in a wide band of variables between two unrealistic extremes, that the true Grand Prix test was on classic road circuits and that extreme measures

to make these 'safe' would destroy their character, or that the future of racing was in clinical artificial circuits, almost 'stadium' road circuits.

Costs continued to soar, in part because Grand Prix drivers sought parity of income with the stars of some other sports, where although the degrees of skill required of players might be no less, the risks were minimal. Some of the traditional Grand Prix supporters withdrew in the face of rising costs, others reduced their racing budgets, so the search for 'outside' sponsors became ever more important to teams. This led to some apparently strange alliances, between Yardley and **BRM** for example, which in practice proved successful for both parties. Only Ferrari and Matra remained faithful to the honoured national racing colours of the past.

This search for cash also led to an outburst of 'rent-a-drive' arrangements, whereby drivers who could either sponsor themselves or arrange sponsorship independently, became members of Grand Prix teams, often only transient members (it was seldom realized that in fact this sort of arrangement is almost as old as Grand Prix racing, although it had never happened on such a scale in earlier periods).

Jackie Stewart in a Matra MS80 – the combination to beat in 1969 (opposite, followed by Hill and Hulme in the Dutch GP). The Lotus 72 (right) was the radical new shape on the circuits in 1970, while the de Tomaso (below, in South Africa) made only spasmodic appearances.

Apart from this outward change, apparent mechanical variety returned, after years when it was a constant complaint that all Grand Prix cars looked alike. The first new constructor to arrive on the Grand Prix scene in 1970, March, did so with considerable ballyhoo. The company had been formed only a few months earlier, and immediately launched a programme which appeared to be over-ambitious, including cars for all the international single-seater formulae and CanAm sports racing machines. Essentially, therefore, the first Herd-designed March GP car, the 701, was straightforward, and almost inevitably Cosworth-DFV-powered. Apart from the STP-backed works team, it was used by independent equipes, among which Tyrrell's was the most prominent. Matra was by this time a subsidiary of Chrysler, through its Simca associations, and it was therefore unthinkable that they should continue to use the DFV engine, with its prominent Ford associations; in the 1970 MS120, Matra raced their own V-12, much modified, and full of sound and fury which still signified insufficient power. Reigning champion Jackie Stewart chose to remain faithful to Tyrrell and Ford, and because of existing sponsorship arrangements Tyrrell initially had no alternative but to turn to March. Later in the season, however, it became clear that Tyrrell regarded the 701 as only a stop gap.

Other new names appeared on the circuits during the year. Team Surtees produced their slim, angular, DFV-powered TS7 by mid-season, and until it was ready raced a modified McLaren M7 – at last John Surtees was his own master. Alessandro de Tomaso produced another of his occasional Grand Prix cars, to the designs of Gianpaolo dall'Ara, and with DFV power. This 505 made more appearances than earlier racing de Tomasos, as its race entrant and manager was the energetic Frank Williams. He had run a Brabham in 1969, and made encouraging progress with the de Tomaso, until his driver, Piers Courage, was killed in an accident.

The rather humble DFV-engined Bellasi was also

Matra returned to the Grand Prix circuits 'in their own name' with the MS120 (left), which seldom appeared a potential winner. Once teething troubles were overcome, however, the Lotus 72 (above) won Championships for Lotus and Rindt.

raced a few times in 1970 and 1971 by Silvio Moser.

A name with a long and honourable history re-appeared on the Grand Prix lists, Alfa Romeo. This came about almost by proxy, for Alfa provided a modified version of their sports car V-8 to be raced in McLaren chassis, by the McLaren team. This was not a successful partnership, for modifications to reduce the height of the V-8 also reduced its power, while the driver nominated by Alfa Romeo, Andrea de Adamich, failed to come wholly to terms with the rather inflexible McLaren M14 chassis.

Of the established Grand Prix teams, Lotus produced the most radically new car, the 72. In this Chapman and Phillippe achieved a new shape, which gave excellent penetration (the nose was clean of radiator intakes, for these were mounted alongside the cockpit, this positioning also saving some weight and complication in plumbing to the DFV engine), and minimal unsprung weight (the 72 was the first GP car for years to have front as well as rear brakes inboard). A form of variable rate suspension was incorporated, through the use of torsion bars. Inevitably, Lotus had teething troubles with this car, although these paled beside those suffered by the only private entrant to race a 72 in the Grands Prix, Rob Walker. Once the 72 was raceworthy, Gold Leaf Team Lotus enjoyed a run of success with it; until it was ready, the old 49s were raced, in a slightly revised form, designated 49C.

Slowly through 1970, the Ferrari 312B was brought to raceworthiness, to the point where it became the

car to beat, and Ferrari seemed set to end the reign of the Cosworth DFV. In this car the flat 12 engine (74·0 × 52·8 mm) was hung from a beam extension of the stressed skin chassis. The rest of the car was straightforward, and the combination of good handling qualities and the power of the engine (as much as 460 bhp at 11,500 rpm was claimed for it at the end of the season, compared with the 430 bhp at 10,000 rpm of a representative DFV) made the 321B a formidable contender.

In their startling new Yardley colours, BRM also began to emerge from a long dark tunnel in 1970, and save for Ickx' fortuitous 1968 French GP victory, their P153 became the first car to defeat a Cosworth powered machine in a classic race since 1967. Tony Southgate's P153 was a low bulbous monocoque, powered by a much-revised version of the 48-valve BRM V-12, which was the second most powerful engine in GP racing in 1970, producing up to 435 bhp at 11,000 rpm.

In the BT33, Ron Tauranac produced the first monocoque F1 Brabham, and for most of the year this sound car was one of the fastest around any given circuit. Brabham's season started on a high note, when Jack won the first Championship race, then declined through a series of disappointments, and ended with Jack Brabham retiring from racing. MacLaren Racing introduced the similarly conventional M14, and enjoyed a similarly promising start to the season. However, after the third Cham-

By 1971 all Grand Prix cars no longer looked alike, although most of them were powered by the Cosworth DFV. Opposite, top to bottom: the March 711, in which Herd attempted to gain an aerodynamic advantage (driven by Ronnie Peterson); the Tyrrell, which overwhelmingly took the Championships (here driven by Francois Cevert); the Brabham BT34 (driven by Graham Hill). Below: the Surtees TS9 (driven by John Surtees).

pionship race, Bruce McLaren was killed while testing a CanAm car at Goodwood, and for the rest of the year his GP team did not fully recover from this blow, for apart from the personal loss, Bruce's design and development talents had been absolutely invaluable.

The ever-youthful Jack Brabham scored his last Championship victory in the South African GP, at 111·70 mph, and cars of four other makes filled the next five places – McLaren (Hulme), March (Stewart), Matra (Beltoise) and Lotus (Miles), while after a serious American GP accident in 1969 Graham Hill made a brave return to racing and placed Walker's aged Lotus 49 sixth. Eleven cars of 25 starters were racing at the Kyalami finish, but in the Spanish GP at Jarama the ratio of retirements returned to the depressing 1969 norm – five cars were classified. Jackie Stewart took this race for the upstart marque, March, while Andretti and Servoz-Gavin placed other March 701s third and fifth (the other places were filled by McLaren and Hill). Sandwiching the Spanish race, the only early-season non-championship events in Europe also fell to March drivers, Stewart at Brands Hatch and Amon at Silverstone.

At Monaco an unusually high percentage of the starters – 50 per cent – were still racing at the finish. Jack Brabham lost this race on the last corner of the last lap, when he left his braking too late, and his relentless pursuer through the closing stages, Jochen Rindt, scored a last classic win for the Lotus 49. Jack extricated his BT33 from the straw bales, and crossed the line second. Rindt's average speed was 81·84 mph, and he cut nearly two seconds (in 85) from the lap record, to leave it at 84·56 mph.

A new chapter appeared to open at Spa, where the Cosworth-engined majority were roundly defeated by Pedro Rodriguez in a V-12 BRM, thus giving the

Bourne team their first *grande épreuve* victory since 1966. His speed was 149·94 mph, despite a chicane contrived in the fast Malmédy sector in response to the contemporary safety clamour. Amon was second in a March, Beltoise and GP novitiate Ignazio Giunti third and fourth in Matra and Ferrari – three 12 cylinder cars in the first four. For a spell, however, any conclusion which might have been drawn from this were proved hopelessly wrong by Jochen Rindt and the Lotus 72. Once the car was raceworthy, Rindt at last achieved the results his ability had for some time warranted. In a Dutch GP overshadowed by Piers Courage's fatal accident in a de Tomaso, he won clearly from Stewart and a pair of Ferrari drivers, Ickx and another newcomer, the Swiss Gianclaudio Regazzoni, who after a tempestuous career in lesser classes was suddenly to blossom as a top-flight driver.

Rindt scored again in the French GP at Clermont-Ferrand, and by the grace of another Brabham miscalculation, in the British GP at Brands Hatch. Here Jack lost the race when leading with two corners to go, as he ran out of fuel; this time he coasted into second place behind the Austrian.

At the Nürburgring authorities failed to satisfy drivers' safety requirements, the German GP was run at the characterless Hockenheim circuit, where Rindt won again, after a close slip-streaming race with Ickx. Hulme was third and another newcomer fourth, Brazilian Emerson Fittipaldi in the Lotus 49 which he had driven in his GP debut at Brands Hatch.

In 1970 the Austrian Grand Prix was revived, on the splendid new Osterreichring circuit, and improbably after the years of Cosworth superiority it was dominated by cars with 12-cylinder engines – of the first seven cars, only the Brabham driven into third place by the German Rolf Stommelen had a V-8.

Here Ferrari promise was at last fulfilled, as Ickx and Regazzoni finished first and second, while Stommelen was followed by two BRMs, a Matra and a Ferrari.

The Oulton Park Gold Cup was notable on two counts: John Surtees drove a Surtees TS7 to win, from Rindt, and Stewart raced a Tyrrell for the first time, setting a lap record before retiring. Ken Tyrrell disclaimed ambition when his car was announced to a surprised racing world, appropriately in a Ford show-room, explaining that he had become a constructor only reluctantly. The Tyrrell was the first car designed by Derek Gardner, and showed meticulousness rather than shattering originality, and in its lines was strongly reminiscent of the Matra MS80. In its first half season it achieved little in terms of race results, but the team made enormous progress towards the pace-setting raceworthiness which was to richly reward Tyrrell and Stewart in 1971.

Practice for the Italian GP was overshadowed by Rindt's fatal accident in a Lotus 72, which led to a great deal of acrimony, to Lotus' withdrawal from the race and to the team's non-appearance in Italy in 1971. The largely partisan crowd forgot this, however, as Regazzoni made a well-judged break from a slip-streaming group of drivers to win at 147·07 mph in a Ferrari. Then Ickx and Regazzoni went on to score a Ferrari 1-2 in the Canadian GP, and repeated this finishing order in the Mexican GP. Between these two races, Rodriguez easily led the American GP once Stewart had retired the very fast Tyrrell. But with seven laps to go the Mexican had to stop for fuel, and he finished a disappointed second behind Fittipaldi, whose win secured the constructors' championship for

Lotus, and the drivers' championship for Jochen Rindt, who thus became motor racing's first posthumous Champion.

From these races in the second half of 1970 it appeared that the tide really had turned in favour of 12-cylinder engines, and there was nothing to contradict this in the early 1971 races, when Ferraris were obviously favourites after their late-1970 revival. Mauro Foghieri refined the 312B, as the 312B2, with a distinctly wedge-shaped body, a revised flat-12 engine with an effective rev range to well over 12,000 rpm, and a substantially different rear suspension. This had its dampers mounted inboard, and horizontally, a system which at first appeared to function well; soon, however, it became suspect and for the rest of the season it was difficult to resolve how great a part it played in Ferrari's problems, and how important were vibrations generated by tyres (the fashionable problem in 1971, although by no means new).

The BRM P160 was a refined version of the P153, and during the year two further improved versions of the V-12 were evolved for it, with revised heads, and shorter stroke. Matra technicians continued their search for power, which after an encouraging first 1971 race, still proved elusive.

The new McLaren, M19, was chiefly notable for its suspension, where designer Ralph Bellamy incor-

The make-up of formula cars followed a set pattern through the sixties, simply scaled up or down according to class – opposite, two Formula 3 cars, a Lotus and an Alpine; above: Formula 2 cars, Brabhams following a Tecno; below: Formula 1, an early 3 litre Ferrari.

porated a link mechanism to achieve a progressive rate of springing, so that towards the extremities of suspension travel movement was more limited than in the normal 'mid-height' attitude. Curiously, this car showed real potential only at each end of the season.

Expediency had ruled that Robin Herd's first GP March was thoroughly conventional; its successor, the 711, was a radically different car. It followed the Lotus 72 (and sports car precedents) in having side-mounted radiators and inboard brakes front and rear (although after early season incidents, March reverted to normal front brakes). The monocoque body of the 711 bore a resemblance to only one earlier formula car, the F2 Protos, which was more than coincidental as Protos designer Frank Costin was a party to the March. In this, aerodynamic efficiency was to make up for the power deficiency which it was assumed that teams using the Cosworth DFV would suffer in 1971; in practice, March had considerable problems before efficiency was achieved, and the 711 seldom wore all of its smooth all-enclosing bodywork in the first half of the year. This year, too, March ran Alfa-engined cars, in an effort which was more co-ordinated but little more successful than the McLaren-Alfa arrangement in 1970.

The Tyrrell, fast but unreliable in 1970, was

changed only in detail, while Team Surtees introduced an improved version of the TS7, designated TS9. In 1971 a two-, and sometimes three-car Surtees team was raced (under the blue and white banners of Brooke Bond Oxo, who transferred their sponsorship to Team Surtees as Rob Walker gave up running his own GP car and lent the support of his experience to Surtees). Rob Walker's driver in 1970, Graham Hill, joined the Brabham team, now controlled by Ron Tauranac, while Jack Brabham himself maintained his interest from a distance. Tauranac built just one Formula 1 car for 1971, the BT34. In most respects this was a conventional DFV-powered car, but in the hull Tauranac went to great lengths to safeguard the driver in the event of an accident, and at the front he mounted two separate radiators, outrigged on the nose aerofoil (which was thus of generous proportions) and exhausting air over the front suspension members.

Lotus only changed details on the 72, but after a year of intense speculation, produced the first gas turbine-engined Grand Prix car at the Race of Champions (several years after turbine cars had appeared in sports car racing). This was the 56B, which had been envisaged in 1968 when the Lotus 56 was built for Indianapolis. It had a Pratt and Whitney STN6/76 engine, suitably modified from its Indianapolis form to meet the 3-litre regulations. This drove through all four wheels, so this form of drive incidentally returned to road circuits for a season almost by accident. The outward shape was that of the original 56, although during the year its flanks swelled to incorporate tanks to give it Grand Prix range. The 56B required new driving techniques, particularly in the combined use of brake and accelerator pedals, for the car had to be slowed while the turbine speed was kept near the optimum, as it picked up relatively slowly. In part because it was heavy and needlessly complex, it made little impact during its one year of Grand Prix life.

Once again a season opened with Grand Prix cars racing in Argentina, contesting a rather thinly-supported non-Championship race with F5000 cars. Amon was the outright winner of the two-part event, after a rather forceful drive in a Matra MS120. In the first Championship event, a minor failure cost Hulme the South African GP when he was leading with only four laps to go; the race fell to Andretti's Ferrari 312B1, from Stewart, Ickx in another Ferrari, and Wisell's Lotus 72.

Top: BRM scored a welcome victory in 1970 when Pedro Rodriguez, here leading Amon, won the Belgian GP. The gas turbine at last appeared in a Grand Prix in 1971, when Lotus experimentally raced the 56B (here driven by Emerson Fittipaldi in its Brands Hatch debut). Right: the modern Grand Prix car – this is a Ferrari 312B2, driven by Clay Regazzoni – is a compact yet surprisingly large piece of machinery.

The first race in Europe, the Brands Hatch Race of Champions, apparently confirmed Ferrari superiority, for Regazzoni won in a 312B2 Ferrari from Stewart in a Tyrrell. The Lotus 56B made its debut here, unimpressively, and retired after 33 of 50 laps. Only a week later another non-Championship race was run, at Ontario in California, and here Andretti again won for Ferrari, from Stewart and Hulme. Then at Oulton Park Rodriguez won the Rothmans Trophy in a BRM, from Gethin in a McLaren and Stewart. So far all the signs had continued to point to 12-cylinder superiority . . .

But in Barcelona's Monjuich Park the pendulum swung in favour of the Cosworth DFV, although in the Spanish GP only hesitantly and because of the brilliance of Jackie Stewart. He gained the first victory for the marque Tyrrell, by a narrow margin from Ickx' Ferrari after a race-long duel.

Hill's victory in the Silverstone International Trophy meant little, save that it was his first Formula 1 win since 1969 and Brabham's only Formula 1 win of 1971. On this fast circuit considerable attention was focused on the Lotus 56B, and it appeared significant that Fittipaldi drove it into a strong third place in the second part of the race (having retired during the first part).

Stewart crashed at Silverstone, but scored a convincing victory in the next Championship race, at Monaco. Here Ronnie Peterson gained second place in a March 711, the first of several excellent drives which were to make him Championship runner-up at the end of the season and confirm the scintillating ability he showed in Formula 2, where he became the 'natural' successor to Jochen Rindt. (In the next F1 race, a non-Championship event dedicated to Rindt at Hockenheim, Peterson was again second, to Ickx' Ferrari).

Safety took priority over Spa, and there was no Belgian Grand Prix on this fast and demanding circuit (or any other) in 1971. Weather and tyre choice were in combination disproportionate factors in determining the Dutch GP, where teams using Firestone tyres enjoyed an extraordinary advantage, and where Ickx and Rodriguez fought out the lead, the Ferrari driver beating the BRM driver by 10 seconds. To Ferrari supporters, and most of Italy, the result of the French GP on the new, and very artificial, Paul Ricard circuit at Castellet seemed equally unrealistic, for Stewart and Cevert scored a 1-2 for Tyrrell, with such apparent ease that there was a flurry of excitement, centred on ludicrous allegations of illegal engines or fuels!

However, this result was only confirmed by the

brief British Grand Prix (the race was run in just over an hour and a half, in common with several others in 1971). Stewart won again, at 130·48 mph from Peterson and Fittipaldi. The first six cars had Cosworth engines, which seemed to set the clock back a year or two! Stewart then took less than an hour and a half to win the German GP, at 114·4 mph over a Nürburgring modified in the interests of safety. Here he was again followed by his young French team mate François Cevert, the pair clearly heading the Ferraris of Regazzoni and Andretti.

The results list of the Austrian Grand Prix looked surprisingly different from others of the year. Jo Siffert drove a commanding race to lead from flag to flag in a BRM P160, Fittipaldi was second in a Lotus 72, and Tim Schenken, an Australian member of the new generation of drivers, was third in a Brabham BT33. This was Jo Siffert's last victory, for at the end of the season he died when his BRM crashed in a non-Championship race at Brands Hatch (this was also the first fatal accident in a BRM in the marque's 21-year history).

None of the established Grand Prix stars featured in the desperate last-lap jostle which as so often in the past decided the Italian Grand Prix. Winner in 1971, by the nose of his BRM, was Peter Gethin, at 150·75 mph. Less than a fifth of a second covered runners-up Peterson (March), Cevert (Tyrrell) and Hailwood (Surtees). Before this race was run, Jackie Stewart had gained his second World Championship, and Cevert's third place clinched the constructors' championship for Tyrrell, a marque which was just over a year old.

In a Canadian Grand Prix cut short in vile conditions of rain and mist, Jackie Stewart rubbed in his superiority by winning, and Ronnie Peterson his growing stature by at times leading the Scot, and finishing second. McLaren fortunes revived at Mosport, where established American driver Mark Donohue placed an M19A third, in his first-ever Grand Prix drive, and Denny Hulme finished fourth.

As the Mexican Grand Prix was cancelled, not so much because of inept crowd control in 1970 (as had once seemed probable), but because Mexico's greatest driver Pedro Rodriguez had been killed in an insignificant event, the American GP became the last Championship race of 1971. As if to rub in the 1971 superiority of the highly professional Tyrrell team, this fell to their number two driver, François Cevert. Siffert was second in a BRM, the marque which had taken the place of Ferrari as the season's closest challenger to the Cosworth engined cars; Peterson placed a March 711 third. This order conveniently sums up the Grand Prix 'order of merit' at the end of 1971, with Cosworth engined cars on top for the fourth year, but with the Grands Prix in a vibrantly healthy state.

Jackie Stewart in the March 701 which he drove in the first half of the 1970 season, before turning to the new Tyrrell.

Second Level Racing

Among the proliferating racing car classes in the late 1960s, Formula 2 retained its position as the principal secondary formula, although it was ignored in North America and in Britain faced a rival for spectators', promoters' and entrants' attentions in Formula 5000, the American Formula A adapted to local requirements.

In step with the increase in Grand Prix engine capacity to 3 litres, the size of engines for the 1967–71 Formula 2 was increased, to 1300–1600 cc. The number of cylinders was limited to a maximum of six, and engines had to be based on the block of production units, and in the case of Ferrari this led to an extraordinary situation: Fiat undertook to build a series of sports cars around a detuned version of the Ferrari Dino engine, in order that the type could be homologated, and then used as the basis of an F2 racing engine. Thus a 'production' engine was based on a pure racing unit, and in turn a racing engine based upon it!

On paper, therefore, this Ferrari V-6, in a sound straightforward Ferrari chassis, should have dominated Formula 2 racing. In fact, it was really successful only in the 1969 Argentine Temporada, which re-introduced top-level European racing to South America after a lapse of several years (and two exploratory F3 seasons). Pedigree, it seemed, counted for no more in Formula 2 than in contemporary Grands Prix.

The 235 bhp claimed for the race-bred Ferrari V-6, at 11,000 rpm, was soon matched at considerably lower engine speeds by the power output of the Ford-based Cosworth four-cylinder engine.

This FVA was based on the Cortina 116E block, and was in effect the first step towards the DFV

Top: two outstandingly successful Formula 2 cars, a Brabham and a Matra. Right: the Ferrari Dino, promising on paper, but seldom a winner on the circuits.

J.P. BELTOISE
EQUIPE MATRA ELF
10
DUNLOP
MATRA F2

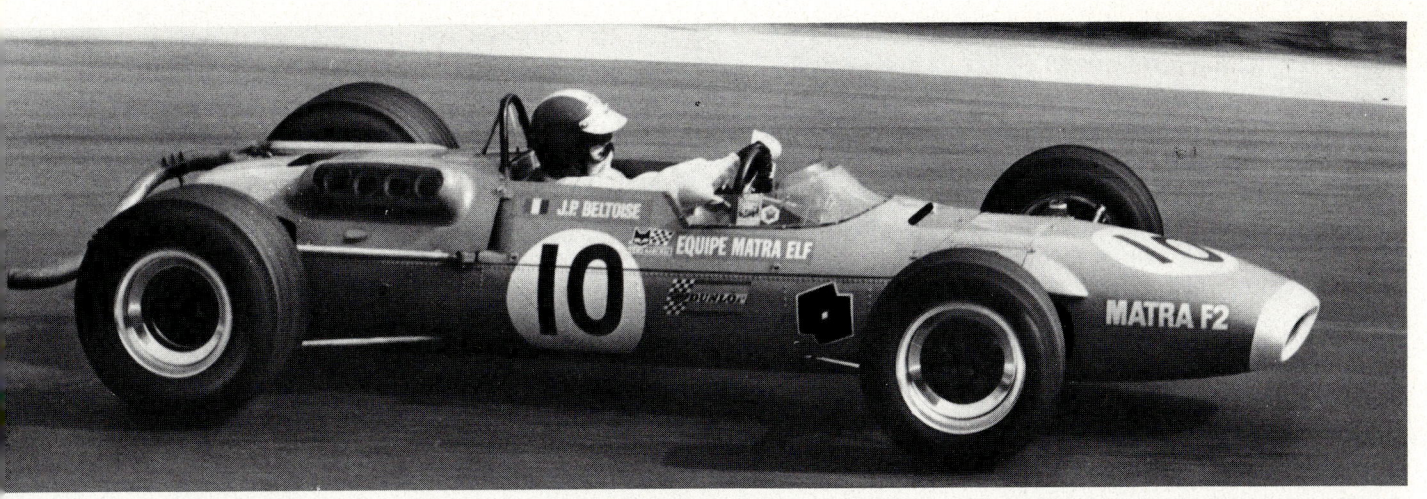

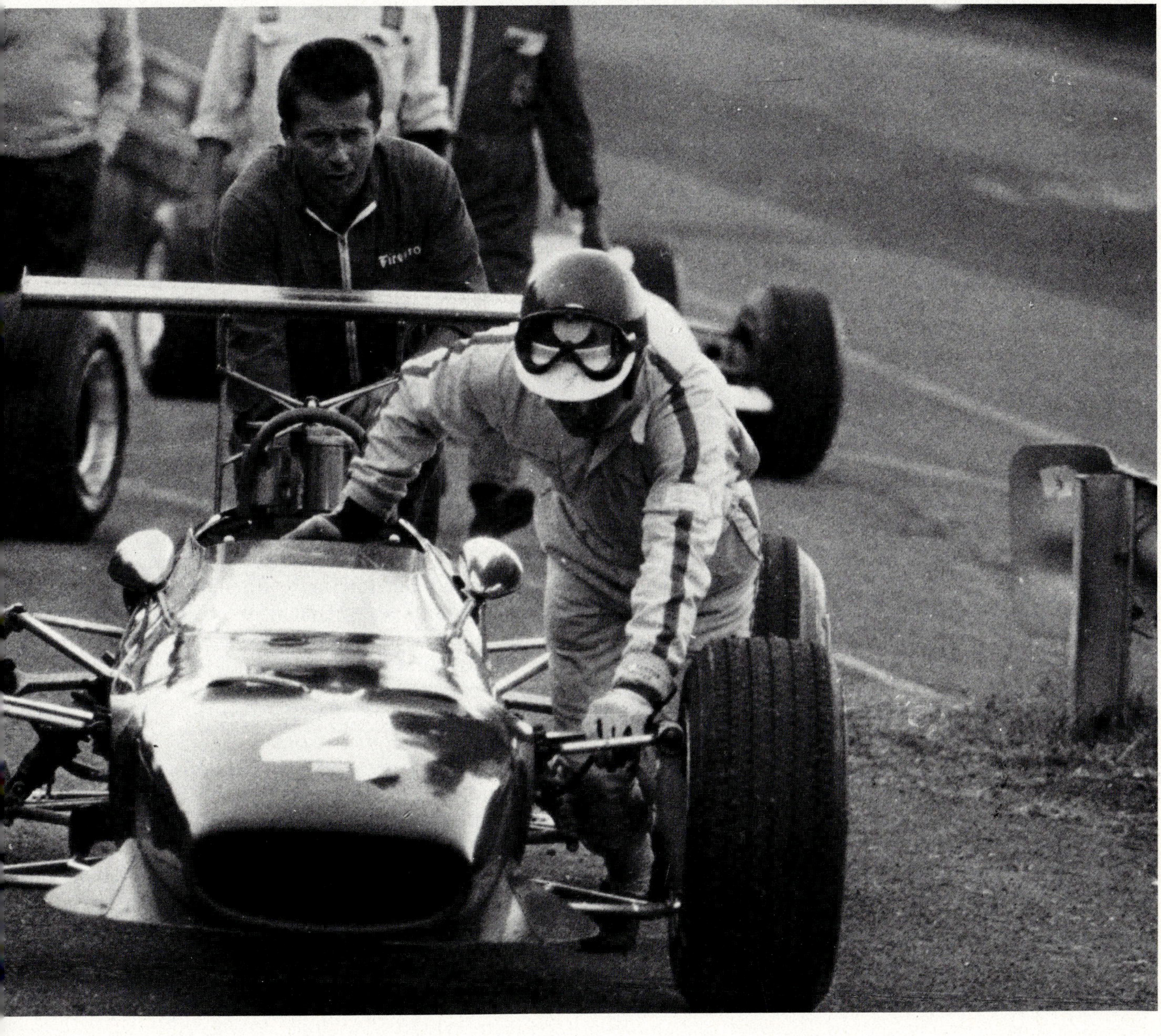

Grand Prix engine – almost a working design study. It was a four-cylinder, four inclined valves per cyclinder, twin ohc unit, which first ran on test early in 1966, almost immediately exceeded the 200 bhp output target, and was fully raceworthy before the formula came into effect at the beginning of 1967. It became the dominant, at times universal, engine of the formula.

Although several engines were essayed, for example an Alfa Romeo Guilia-based 'four', which was never really developed, and an experimental Mitsubishi unit which was never actually raced in Formula 2, the only other power units to challenge the Ferrari six and Cosworth four were built by BMW.

The German company entered single-seater motor racing under this formula, using their own engines in their own cars (whereas the Cosworth units were of course simply supplied to other constructors). In both respects, BMW got off to false starts. Their first four-cylinder F2 engines, designed by Apfelbeck, were notable for their ingenious valvegear, which on paper promised to be unusually efficient. The four very large valves were disposed radially to ensure a perfectly hemispherical roof to each combustion chamber, this making for an ideal and generous gas flow. However, in practice the complexity of the valvegear meant that paper promise was not fulfilled, and BMW reverted to conventional four-valve engines. These were mounted in a series of BMW chassis, initially British-designed and some built by the Dornier aircraft company, and the team experienced considerable teething problems with these as well as their engines.

Eventually, in 1970, BMW enjoyed a successful season, winning six of the 20 F2 races, and the company then withdrew from racing. Ferrari had already given up this class, after gaining two victories in Europe at the end of 1968 and taking the Argentine series early in the following year (an odd F2 Ferrari thereafter made spasmodic appearances in private hands).

In general, constructors using the Cosworth FVA dominated the field, notably Brabham, Lotus and March, French Matras and Italian Tecnos. Less successful marques included Chevron, Lola, McLaren, Merlyn and Protos, the latter building cars with a very original stressed hull built of wood, to the designs of Costin, Pygmée and de Tomaso.

Apart from the Protos, designers followed the general trend in parallel with Formula 1 and 3, with Brabham remaining faithful to space frames in face of the otherwise universal monocoques.

During four years, Jochen Rindt was the driver to beat in Formula 2, although he was never eligible for the European Championship. 'Graded drivers' – those who had achieved a measure of success defined by World Championship points or their performances in sports car classics – were debarred from this F2 championship, although up to six were permitted to run in an F2 race. This ensured that the European Championship did not become the property of established aces, and that up and coming drivers could race with their 'seniors', a system which worked out well in practice.

In the early years of the formula, honours were divided between Brabham, Lotus and Matra. The French company dropped out, coincidentally as the relatively new Italian marque Tecno became a force, and in the last year of the formula March became a prominent marque, with their 712. The 1600 cc Formula 2 never became stale; despite a uniformity of power plants and close similarities between most of the cars, it provided some sparkling racing, brought real international life to circuits such as Thruxton, and was even the instrument whereby international motor racing was introduced to one South American country, Colombia.

Halfway through its term there were suggestions that Formula 2 might be supplanted by a new class, Formula 5000, at least in Britain. This class was born as Formula A in the USA (where in 1971 it took on the title adopted for the European version, Formula 5000), for single-seater cars powered by production-based engines of up to 5 litres (in North America 3-litre pure racing engines have also been eligible, and hence some redundant Grand Prix cars have raced in this class).

Invariably, the larger engines used have been American V-8s – even the Rover V-8 used by odd contenders has American origins – and in this respect it has been a curiously alien class in Europe, where racing engines are by no means scarce. These American V-8s had an inherent drawback, in that they are relatively cumbersome, and this led to no small problems in achieving balanced cars on accepted European lines, and when race-tuned many F5000 engines proved outstandingly unreliable. Chevrolet units have dominated the class, where Ford engines have made little impression; the best gave over 400 bhp in the first F5000 season, and power outputs thereafter roughly kept pace with those achieved in Formula 1.

Several British constructors welcomed the introduction of this class of racing into Britain, and to odd Continental circuits, for it provided a means whereby the cars which they exported in some numbers could be race-tested within short distances of factories (F5000 racing spread to South Africa and to Australia and New Zealand, where the Tasman Series rules were revised to admit these cars). The leading manufacturers have been McLaren, Lola, and John Surtees' company, whose first car was the F5000 TS5; other constructors who have dabbled in the class, including

Lotus, have achieved little success. Four-wheel drive appeared in F5000 in 1969, just anticipating its short-lived vogue in Formula 1; this Hepworth experiment was inconclusive in circuit racing, although very successful in hill-climbs.

Formula 5000 failed to live up to its promise during its first three British seasons, close races being the exceptions, processional events punctuated by retirements the rule. Performances within the class varied widely, between the works or quasi-works drivers, and the amateurs who made up fields with outclassed cars. When the top drivers have enjoyed reliability, their individual performances with these sometimes ill-handling cars have been impressive, and the infrequent close races have been spectacular. Peter Gethin, in quasi-works McLarens, dominated the first two seasons, while the more open 1971 season was generally between Frank Gardner (Lola) and Mike Hailwood (Surtees), first and second in the championship, while David Hobbs gained the corresponding American championship with an older McLaren.

Formula 5000 and front-line Grand Prix cars were matched in some races, notably the Silverstone International Trophies and Oulton Park Gold Cups, and in the Questor Grand Prix at the new Ontario Motor Speedway in California in 1971. In these the 5-litre machines were outrun by 3-litre Formula 1 cars, so part of the promise of power equating with circuit speed proved illusory. Throughout its first three years Formula 5000 remained an uncertain quantity, although it did provide 'big-engined' single-seater racing as a substitute for the big sports-racing car events which for a time vanished from the European circuits.

The first F5000 Championships fell to Peter Gethin in McLarens (above), and to Frank Gardner (below, in a Lola T300, leading Hailwood at Oulton Park).

Lower down the scale Formula B racing flourished in America, around cars with a performance potential roughly between those of Formula 3 and Formula 2. This class was also 'imported' into Britain, as 'Formula Atlantic', in 1971, at a time when it appeared that the 1600 cc Formula 3 might have an uncertain future. Formula Atlantic admitted cars with engines of a similar capacity, and in practice Ford-based units were invariably used; chassis, by such constructors as Brabham, Chevron and Palliser, were virtually identical with those used in other classes. Once the inlet restrictor limit on 1600 cc Formula 3 engines was eased in the summer of 1971, the performance differential between the two classes became negligible – a matter of one second on the short Brands Hatch circuit – and so the appeal of Formula Atlantic as anything but a 'poor man's Formula 2' or an alternative to the intensely competitive Formula 3 became limited.

Index

Brabham *continued*
    BT34, 304, 306
    BT35, 245
Bragg, C., 53
Branca FJ car, 240
Brandon, E., 180
Brands Hatch, 182
Brauchitsch, M., 120
Brilli Peri, Count G., 88
Bristow, C., 231
British Grand Prix, 1926, 97; 1927, 100;
    1948, 165; 1949, 165; 1950, 170;
    1951, 175; 1952, 193; 1953, 195;
    1954, 220; 1955, 208; 1956, 211;
    1957, 219; 1958, 223; 1959, 226;
    1960, 231; 1961, 259; 1962, 264;
    1963, 266; 1964, 268; 1965, 270;
    1966, 282; 1967, 284; 1968, 291;
    1969, 295; 1970, 304; 1971, 309
Brivio, A., 103
BRM, acquired by Owen Organization,
    178
    Type 15 V–16, 167, 169 *et seq*
        Mk II, 178; last race, 208
    Type 25, 202, 208, 210, 222
    P48, 226
    P56, 262 *et seq*
    P61, 266
    P261, 267 *et seq*; 2 litre version, 281
    P83, 279 *et seq*
    P126, 286 *et seq*
    P138, 291
    P139, 291 *et seq*
    P153, 303
    P160, 305 *et seq*
    Climax-engined car, 255
    four-wheel drive car, 268
    V–8 engine, 262 *et seq*
    V–12 engine, 282
    H–16 engine, 279
Brooklands, 42, 43, 94, 97, 98, 100, 139,
    156
Brooks, C.A.S., 208, 219
BRP GP car, 266
Bruce-Brown, D., 38, 39, 51
Buenos Aires Grand Prix, 1954, 201;
    1958, 222
Bugatti, E., 23, 62, 96
    acquires Millers, 104
Bugatti, R., 23
Bugatti, 1911, 39
    'Black Bess', 59
    T13, 64, 91
    T22, 71, 91, 100
    T30, 68, 74, 78
    T35, 68, 82, 84, 92
    T35B, 97, 103
    T37, 89, 97, 139
    T39, 96
    T51, 108, 115
    T53, 110
    T54, 109
    T59, 116, 119
    1938 *monoplace*, 128, 150
    T251, 210, 211
Buick Bug, 40
Burman, B., 55

BWA FJ car, 241

Campari, G., 63, 64, 66, 83, 86, 87, 106,
    107
Canadian Grand Prix, 1967, 284;
    1968, 291; 1969, 298; 1970, 304;
    1971, 309
Cappa, G.C., 69, 99
Caracciola, R., 95, 109, 110, 120, 126,
    136, 156
Castellotti, E., 216
Cavalli, 69, 71
Ceirano CS4, 95
Cevert, F., 309
Chadwick, L.S., 71
Chadwick, 1908 supercharged, 37
Chapman, C., 210, 216, 236
Chassagne, J., 65, 67
Chevrolet, G., 63, 65
Chevrolet, L., 63
Chiribiri voiturette, 92
Chiron, L., 101, 104, 109, 112, 115, 120,
    161, 166
Christie front-wheel drive cars,
    1905, 26
    1907 GP car, 33
Circuit des Ardennes, *see* Ardennes
    Circuit
Cisitalia, formation, 155, 160
    1100 cc, 164, 182, 183
    T360, 160, 165
City to city races, 19
Clark, J., 231, 271 *et seq*, 282 *et seq*
CMN, 63
Cobb, J., 146
Collins, P., 210 *et seq*, 223
Colombo, G., 143, 191, 210
Colt Indianapolis car, 275
Commission Sportive International, 9
Connaught Type A, 190, 192, 195
    Type B, 199, 207
    Type C, 216
    Type D, 210
    rear-engined project, 216
Cook, H., 140
Cooper, C., 180
Cooper, J., 180
Cooper 500 cc cars, 155, 179
    et seq; 998 cc JAP-engined, 187
    T20, 192
    T23, 195
    T41, 211, 218, 222, 224
    Indianapolis car, 253
    T51, 236, 239
    T53, 226, 228 *et seq*
    T55, 255
    T56, 239
    T69, 267
    T73, 267
    T81, 256, 279 *et seq*
    T86B, 287
    retire from racing, 291
Cooper-Alta, 195
Coppa Acerbo, 1932, 110; 1934,120;
    1935, 123; 1936, 123; 1937, 126;

Coppa Acerbo *continued*
    1938, 134
Coppa Ciano, 1930, 106; 1932, 110;
    1938, 134, 143
Coppa Florio, 1904, 22; 1907, 34;
    1908, 37
Cornelian, 1915 Indianapolis, 60
Cosworth FJ engine, 238
    DFV, 16, 283 *et seq*
    FVA, 310 *et seq*
    SCA, 248
    Grand Prix car, 298
Coupe de *l'Auto*, 46 *et seq*
Courage, P., 299
Coventry Climax FPE engine, 218
    FPF, 222, 224, 225, 246, 253
    FMWV, 218, 259 *et seq*, 276
    FWMW flat–16, 270
    withdraw from F1 racing, 270
Coyote Indianapolis car, 272
Cremona Circuit, 1924, 77
Crystal Palace, 156
CTA-Arsenal, 155, 158, 160, 163
Cummins Indianapolis car, 251
Cyclecars, 90, 91
Czaikowski, Count S, 115
Czechoslovak Grand Prix, 1930, 106;
    1931, 109; 1932, 112; 1933, 115;
    1934, 122; 1937, 127; 1949, 166

Daf Variomatic transmission, 243
Davis, F., 138
Dawson, J., 45
DB Formula 1 car, 1955, 207
Delage, 1913 GP, 54
    1914 GP, 56 *et seq*
    1914 Indianapolis, 59
    1923 GP, 74
    1925 GP, 84, 86, 87, 91
    1926 GP, 97
    1927 GP, 93, 96, 99 *et seq*; in
        voiturette racing, 140
    V–12, 94
Delahaye, 1938 GP, 129
Diatto, 1922, 70
    1925 GP, 88
    20S, 95
Diatto Clement, 33
Divo, A., 75
DKW-based FJ engines, 236
Donington Park, 156
    Grand Prix, 1937, 127; 1938, 134
Dreyfus, R., 106, 133
Duckworth, K., 283
Duesenberg, 60
    1919 Indianapolis, 62
    1921 GP, 63, 66, 77
    1924 supercharged, 77
    1926–29 engines, 102
    Ferrari, 114
Duray, A., 30
Duray, L., 104
Dusio, P., 160, 183
Dutch Grand Prix, 1952, 193; 1953, 195;
    1955, 208; 1958, 222; 1959, 225;

318

Acknowledgements

The majority of the illustrations in this book were collected by the Italian publisher, l'Editrice dell'
Automobile; the publishers of the English-language edition are indebted for additional photographs to:
Associated Press, British Petroleum Company, Daimler Benz, Ford of Britain, Gulf Oil Company,
David Hodges collection, *Motor*, Nigel Snowdon, United Press International, and Yardley of London.